ANTITRUST
IN THEORY
AND PRACTICE

Russell G. Warren
Dean of Richmond College and
Associate Professor of Economics
University of Richmond
Virginia

ANTITRUST IN THEORY AND PRACTICE

Russell G. Warren
Dean of Richmond College and
Associate Professor of Economics
University of Richmond
Virginia

I.S.B. N. NO. 0-88244-076-4
Library of Congress Catalog No. 74-20369

To My Mother and Father

EDITORS' PREFACE

The approach of this text is to emphasize the interface between the legal and economic aspects of national antitrust policy and regulation. The author, Dean Russell Warren significantly contributes to a better and wider understanding of the complex subject of antitrust by consistently treating each topic in an interdisciplinary manner. Now more than ever is such understanding desirable. Current national problems of inflation, unemployment, energy shortages and others have been linked to antitrust activity by some observers in a causative relationship. Some critics characterize current regulatory policies as unnecessary contributors to these social and economic problems and conclude that enforcement must be relaxed. Others attribute the malaise to a failure to have vigorously enforced our antitrust laws, and they propose far reaching regulatory legislation. Regulation is an evolutionary process that produces both positive and negative results. The important fact is that we know far too little about the effects of public regulation on the industries involved and on the economy as a whole. Yet, too often the relevant economic concepts are not considered or are used in ways that represent only a distorted shadow of their original meanings. It would be naive to expect to find definitive answers to the troublesome questions concerning firm and industry performance much less the appropriate economic structure of the economy at this stage of our knowledge. However, an important step in this process is a more effective integration of legal and economic view points.

In *Antitrust in Theory and Practice* Dean Russell Warren contributes to the legal and economic interface of regulatory policy. His materials are liberally cross referenced, and economic and legal dimensions are interwoven in a purposeful, revealing fabric. The materials are organized and presented in such a manner that they are at the same time sufficiently sophisticated for the economics student and comprehensible to those in other fields. As a result of its interdisciplinary subject matter and approach, *Antitrust in Theory and Practice* is included in both the Grid Economics Series and the Grid Series in Law.

Robert J. Gaston (Economics)
The University of Tennessee

Thomas W. Dunfee (Law)
University of Pennsylvania

PREFACE AND ACKNOWLEDGMENTS

The contents of this book reflect the view that of all the interfaces between government and business, antitrust is one of the most relevant to students of economics and business. Furthermore, an analysis of antitrust problems provides an excellent vehicle to demonstrate the application of microeconomic theory to real-life decisions. For these reasons, I chose to concentrate entirely on antitrust when I first taught government regulation of business. Although I have continually reappraised this decision, I have not found sufficient justification to change it.

My first students had a tremendous workload. I wanted them to become familiar with that part of microeconomics which was relevant to antitrust and with the important articles on most of the business practices which fall under the provisions of the antitrust laws. I also wanted them to have more than a superficial understanding of both the economics and law presented in the major antitrust cases. This necessitated their spending considerable time in the law library as well as reading numerous books and periodicals on economics. In addition they also engaged in active class discussion because I wanted them to realize that many of the questions raised in antitrust economics do not have clear-cut answers.

In general, the students were enthusiastic, and I believe the classes were successful. Nonetheless, I realized that there was a need for a book such as this to shorten the students' research time while still satisfying the following teaching objectives. First, I wanted the book to make a clear distinction between Sherman Act and Clayton Act litigation. Second, I wanted it to contain enough microeconomics to pave the way to an understanding of antitrust issues. However, because the students' time is limited, I did not want to include that part of microeconomics which has limited application. Third, I wanted it to present the important antitrust cases in sufficient detail so that the students would be able to appraise the decisions of the courts and the Federal Trade Commission. Where applicable, I also wanted it to survey analyses of cases by leading economists and lawyers. Fourth, I did not want the book to present antitrust issues in "black and white" terms. Students are capable of understanding that most issues of public policy do not have clear-cut answers. Moreover, since education is the process of learning to think, I did not want to thwart that process. Finally, and most important, I wanted to present the economics of each of the various business practices which fell under the provisions of the Sherman and Clayton Acts. I hope that I have achieved these objectives by writing this book and that it will be helpful to teachers with similar objectives.

The manner in which I have written the book to some degree reflects my desire to simplify the learning process for the student. For example, I believe that it is important to present the economics and the law of a specific business practice together, rather than presenting the economics of all business practices in one section of the book and the law in another section. Even the best students have a difficult problem piecing together the law and economics if they are scattered throughout a book. Of course, because the economics of some business practices is similar, there is some repetition. When this occurs, I attempt to minimize it by cross referencing the material and I have found that reinforcement is an important part of the learning process. I have also separated business practices prosecuted under the provisions of the Sherman Act from those prosecuted under Clayton Act provisions so that the student will be able to distinguish between the two. Yet, because some practices can be prosecuted under the provisions of both acts, the distinction is somewhat artificial. The teacher who finds this troublesome could first cover the introductory chapters (I-IV). He then could cover *Chapter V* on the Sherman Act and *Chapter X* on the Clayton Act, after which he could return to *Chapter VI* to study the various business practices.

The book is designed for students in economics or business. Although a principles course in economics would aid the student reading this text, it is not absolutely necessary. Therefore, I hope that it will be used by law students. I firmly believe that the greatest single problem in antitrust is that lawyers and economists have failed to understand one another.

Only through the active participation and encouragement of many individuals could this manuscript be completed. Because all of the individuals have been friends of long standing it is with much pleasure that I acknowledge their role. Lit Maxwell served as librarian throughout the time required to complete the project. He processed numerous interlibrary loans and kept me abreast of new articles and books in antitrust economics. Louise English edited and typed the manuscript. My student assistant, Jim Landrigan, enthusiastically performed both research and typing chores. Paul Reinarman, my research assistant during the summer of 1971, provided material which was invaluable to the completion of the project. My secretary, Mrs. Amelia Fernandez, processed numerous requests for permission to quote from other authors. I also gratefully acknowledge the financial assistance provided by the University of Richmond and the two grants provided by the Shell Oil Foundation.

Four individuals made particularly generous contributions to the manuscript. Dean W. David Robbins provided administrative support and reduced many teaching chores so that I could have time to write. Additionally, because he originated and guided my career, I owe him a debt which I will never be able to repay. Dr. Clarence R. Jung and Dr. William R. Hart provided extensive suggestions as well as constant interest and encouragement. Finally, Michael D. Pratt helped collect the numerous articles and law cases used to check the accuracy of the manuscript, played the role of student in reading it, offered suggestions which had a significant effect in making the content correct and readable, and had the impossible job of keeping my work organized. Although technically he was my research assistant, his total dedication to, and enthusiasm for the project was always that of a partner and understanding friend.

I hope that all who helped with the manuscript will feel some pride of accomplishment and will realize how much I appreciate their effort. Of course, any errors that appear are my responsibility.

Russell G. Warren   June 28, 1974
                                 University of Richmond, Virginia

TABLE OF CONTENTS

THE CHOICE OF POLICY TO COMBAT MONOPOLY POWER

SECTION I

When business is uncontrolled, monopolistic firms develop which exercise their power to the detriment of consumers and competitors alike. The majority of U.S. citizens believe that business has to somehow be controlled to thwart monopolies. The United States chose to do this by enacting antitrust legislation. Yet there are a number of alternative policies which could be used to accomplish the same objective. We consider the alternatives in this section.

THE ALTERNATIVES
TO LAISSEZ FAIRE

A number of actions have been suggested to reduce the anticompetitive elements in a capitalistic economy. They include the elimination of special privileges granted to business by government, government regulation of business, government ownership of business, the use of "countervailing power" and the use of antitrust laws. Each action is analyzed in this chapter.

INTRODUCTION

In the 18th century, when economics was in its infancy, most economists endorsed a laissez faire economy. They thought that the best economy was one with the least government involvement. This attitude was understandable. Most of Europe had experienced the oppressive mercantilist era which was inundated with government control. Individuals were unhappy with this system, and there is substantial evidence that the economy itself was none too effective. With this historical background in mind, Adam Smith contended that the economy was self-regulating through the operation of an "invisible hand." The invisible hand was, of course, the concept that individuals working toward their own self-interest would maximize the welfare of others.

The simple fact of the matter is that unregulated capitalism does not work perfectly well. When a modified form of laissez faire was tried in this country, it had many faults including the existence of monopolistic elements. When left to their own self-interests some businesses found that they could increase their welfare by colluding with competitors, driving competitors out of business with "unfair" practices, and earning monopolistic profits at the expense of the consumer. Such practices occurred throughout most of the 19th century in the United States. Specific instances will be seen in Chapter V where we discuss the development of the Sherman Act and analyze antitrust cases heard in the latter part of the 19th century.

Accompanying the development of monopoly power was the growing opinion that something had to be done to curb monopoly power and its anticompetitive effects. In other words, the concept of laissez faire somehow had to be modified. Altogether the body of literature making up the criticism of laissez faire has suggested five general modifications:

A. The Government should stop granting special privileges to business;

B The Government should regulate business;

C. The Government should take over the ownership and operation of business;

D. "Countervailing power" should be allowed to develop;

E. Antitrust laws should be passed.

The reader already knows which alternatives were chosen. While a few businesses are regulated, the great majority are placed under the antitrust laws. But because the choice was made so long ago, many people forget that these alternatives still exist. Antitrust does not have to be the policy of the land. More important, it is not necessarily the best policy. Even though this book is about antitrust, it is well to begin by considering the nature of the alternatives. It is important to note that the following analysis is not designed to select the best alternative. Literally hundreds of thousands of pages have been written in the pursuit of the optimum policy and the answer is nowhere in sight.

ELIMINATION OF TARIFFS AND OTHER GOVERNMENT PRIVILEGES

One partial solution to the monopoly problem has been suggested by individuals who believe that some monopoly power is government induced. They argue that if the government would simply stop granting special privileges to some businesses, competition would be increased. "Special privileges" have included tax concessions such as the depletion allowance, patent rights, government "bail outs" given to the railroads and the aircraft industry, tariffs, laws which limit price competition and government procurement methods. We will concentrate on the tariff issue.

Strong competition automatically prohibits the development of monopoly power and the exercise of that power. Competition can come from foreign as well as domestic sources. Yet tariffs can effectively give domestic firms the ability to acquire monopoly power by cutting off foreign competition. If, for example, steel, sugar, beef, textiles, appliances and electronic equipment were allowed to enter this country freely, corresponding American industries would feel greater competitive pressure and perhaps experience a reduction in their monopoly power.

The argument that the elimination of tariffs will increase competition is a sound one which should be accepted to some degree as a means to control monopoly power in the United States. Of course, foreign trade alone will not ensure that all U.S. industries will be competitive. Moreover there are some valid reasons for tariffs which should be considered before the country engages in a wholesale elimination of them. Nevertheless, the policymaker should be certain that valid reasons do exist for protectionism. Many tariffs exist merely to protect businesses. These result not only in the creation of monopoly power but, additionally, in the need for yet more tariffs to protect the growing inefficiency which may result from protectionism.

PUBLIC REGULATION

Another alternative method of controlling monopoly power is to leave the ownership of business in private hands but to establish various public commissions to oversee the operations of each company. The commissions could control prices, entry into the market, the accounting systems and other reporting systems of business, acquisitions by one firm of other firms, and product quality. Such an approach has one very desirable result: public regulation would make it almost impossible for a firm to exercise monopoly power unless the regulatory commission was negligent or inefficient.

Regulation of this type is not hypothetical. It is used in the United States to control the operation of many businesses which produce products judged to be very important to the national interest. Railroads, television stations, privately-owned roads and bridges, and airlines are only a few of the activities regulated in the national interest. Regulation is also used to control natural monopolies. These are companies that experience such great cost reductions when their output increases that it is not practical to allow a large number of competitors.[1] The various telephone companies, electric companies, and natural gas companies are representative of this group. Because of the cost reductions, it is desirable to grant a monopoly to these companies. But they are regulated so that they do not exercise their monopoly power.

It is conceivable that all business could be regulated in a similar manner. The Supreme Court has already determined that it is constitutional to do so. In *Nebbia* v. *New York* the Court held that legislature may impose any form of regulation on any industry provided that the reason is not capricious or discriminatory.[2] Not only could business be regulated in this manner; the regulation would probably be successful in curbing the exercise of monopoly power. Yet there are several reasons explaining why most businesses are not regulated. First, a large amount of manpower and skill would be absorbed by the regulatory commissions. Regulation would be tantamount to attaching a "super board" of managers to each company. It is doubtful whether the country has the manpower, much less the expertise, to establish boards on such a large scale. Second, our citizens prefer as little government intervention as possible in the operation of business. Politically speaking, a large increase in the number of regulated companies would not be popular. Third, there is extensive evidence that the U.S. experience with regulation has not been an overwhelming success. Con Edison, for example, has a serious problem financing its future capital needs, and the Interstate Commerce Commission did not anticipate the bankruptcy of Penn Central. The Civil Aeronautics Board did not develop a general policy to reconcile airline routes and schedules with the development of technology in airplane production. The Federal Power Commisssion contributed to the shortage of natural gas through price control regulation. At the same time there is evidence that some regulated enterprises make excess profits at the expense of the consumer and the environment.

The causes of such problems are numerous. Economists have not provided regulators with adequate analytical tools for sound regulation, and even if such tools existed, the regulator must have an extensive knowledge of the operations of a company before he can make a proper decision. Appointments to regulatory bodies are often a means for a politician to repay a political debt. This can result in the appointment of incompetent individuals. Finally, some regulators have become more concerned with the interests of the regulated than the interests of the general public. Others are so dedicated to the public that they forget that a regulated industry must earn a normal return on its investment.

Finally, it is doubtful that so extensive a remedy is needed to eliminate anticompetitive practices. By and large, competition itself regulates most businesses fairly well, and it is costless to the government. It is only in exceptional cases that government needs to intervene. The treatment of these exceptional cases by establishing regulatory boards for each company is analogous to driving carpet tacks with a sledge hammer.

GOVERNMENT OWNERSHIP OF BUSINESS

The most severe policy to remedy the imperfections of capitalism is to turn the ownership of all business over to the government. This approach approximates the policy adopted by the Soviet Union and Communist China. There is a massive body of literature on this policy which was initiated well before Karl Marx' work. Numerous benefits have been suggested to defend government ownership, and at least an equal number of detrimental effects have been presented by the defenders of private enterprise. Theoretically, the approach will work if government-owned businesses act in the citizens' best interest and if the individuals working with the day-to-day operations of business have a strong enough incentive to perform a good job.

But the issue is not whether the system will work theoretically. It is whether it will function in practice, and whether citizens can place enough faith in their government to hand over the means of production. Citizens of this country have not been willing to do this, and unless their attitude changes drastically, there will be little ownership of business in the future. Therefore, although government ownership of all business presents an alternative means of curbing monopoly power, it is not an acceptable alternative in this country. It is not, however, an alternative that should be shoved out of the policy-maker's mind simply because words with moral overtones like "communism" and "socialism" are thrown against it in argumentation. An understanding of this alternative requires at least as much study as that required for an understanding of capitalism.

COUNTERVAILING POWER

When a firm has monopoly power, most solutions to eradicate the power are directed toward changing the firm's practices or the structure of the industry in which it operates. J. Kenneth Galbraith's solution is unique in that it does not look to the firm or the industry for a solution. Instead, Galbraith believes that power from a buyer or seller outside of the industry will neutralize power within an industry. Specifically, he believes that if a firm has monopoly power in the sale of a product, "countervailing power" will develop on the buying side to combat the monopoly power. Likewise, if a firm has monopsony power in purchasing products, countervailing power will develop on the selling side.

The fact that a seller enjoys a measure of monopoly power, and is reaping a measure of monopoly return as a result, means that there is an inducement to those firms from whom he buys or those to whom he sells to develop the power with which they can defend themselves against exploitation. It means also that there is a reward to them, in the form of a share of the gains of their opponents' market power, if they are able to do so. In this way the existence of market power creates an incentive to the organization of another position of power that neutralizes it.[3]

Galbraith thought that the development of labor unions was an example of a countervailing force which developed to combat the monopsony power of large corporations. He also contended that large retail chains developed to combat the monopoly power of producers and processers of food products.

Galbraith did not deny that normal competition within an industry plays a role in limiting the monopoly power of any one firm, but he implied that countervailing power played a more important role. He also believed that countervailing power is self-generating and that, with a few exceptions, the market operation will solve its own problems. In spite of these observations, Galbraith did not argue against government intervention in the market place. Where countervailing power is not effective he would support a government attack on monopoly power.[4] However, he offered an important word of warning about the government's attack on monopoly power. The government should not eliminate countervailing power without eliminating the original monopoly power. This, he contended, had been done in numerous instances of antitrust enforcement.

The antitrust laws have been indiscriminately invoked against firms that have succeeded in building countervailing power, while holders of original market power, against whom the countervailing power was developed, have gone unchallenged. Such action has placed the authority of the law on the side of positions of monopoly power and against the interests of the public at large. The effects have been damaging to the economy and also the prestige of the antitrust laws.[5]

If countervailing power worked perfectly well there would be no need for antitrust laws, and there are probably some markets in the U.S. economy in which it does work. However, the theory has some serious limitations which prohibit its being the major policy in the treatment of monopoly. These problems will be considered here because even a brief evaluation of its limitations will suggest that countervailing power is not a feasible way of treating monopoly problems. Perhaps the greatest problem is that even if countervailing power does develop, there is no assurance that the consumer will benefit from it. For example, suppose that food processers have monopoly power and, to nullify that power, countervailing power develops among food retailers. Is there any assurance that consumers will receive food at relatively low prices? While there is a possibility, there is certainly no assurance: The only way to ensure that they benefit would be for them to develop countervailing power of their own. The recent consumer protection movement represents a beginning in that direction, but consumers' power is still weak to non-existent. A second problem is that even if countervailing power develops, its evolution may take time. During this period a firm with monopoly power can exercise that power to the detriment of his suppliers and customers alike. If the period of time is small we can afford to wait for countervailing power. But if it is long, very few people are willing to wait and would prefer some other policy. It would have done little good to tell the workers of the 1800s that by the 1930s there would be strong national unions to combat large employers.

Gailbraith, himself, noted that economic conditions can upset the development of countervailing power as well as the delicate balance between two already-existing combative powers. Suppose that "A' is a seller of products and that he has significant monopoly power. "B" represents some buyers. If the economy is in an inflationary period such that there is a shortage of products, "A" is in an enviable position. He has a number of buyers from which to choose, and it is no time for "B" to be developing or exercising power. On the other hand, if the economy is in a deflationary period such that "A" has an excess supply of goods, "B" is in an excellent position to develop and exercise countervailing power.

The final problem with countervailing power is that it does not appear to have developed in any significant degree in the United States economy. Of course, Galbraith did warn us of the danger of using this argument against his theory. Yet several critics of his thesis have served up numerous instances in which countervailing power has not played an important role in inhibiting the exercise of monopoly power.[6] Although Galbraith might dismiss these instances as exceptions to the rule, it is fair to say that most economists are unwilling to rely on countervailing power as a major force to control monopoly. As George Stigler wrote during the Christmas season of 1954:

I want to close with an apology for the consistently negative attitude I have felt compelled to take with respect to Galbraith's theory. One would like to speak well of so urbane and witty a presentation. Especially at this season one would like to avoid expressing doubts that a mysterious, benevolent being will crawl down each and every chimney and leave a large income as well as directions to the nearest cut-rate outlet. Yet even at this season Galbraith cannot persuade us that we should turn our economic problems over to Santa.[7]

SUMMARY

Our government has chosen to curb monopoly power and monopoly practices by passing antitrust laws. This policy is supplemented by government regulation of natural monopolies and of industries which are very important to the natural interest. This book is concerned with the various antitrust laws and the anticompetitive practices outlawed by these laws. Yet it is extremely important that as we get involved in the study of antitrust we do not forget that there are alternative policies which could be adopted to either supplement the laws or completely replace them. These alternatives should always be in the back of the policymaker's mind.

NOTES TO CHAPTER I

[1]Natural monopolies are discussed in more detail in *Chapter III.*
[2]291 U.S. 502 (1934).
[3]John Kenneth Galbraith, *American Capitalism: The Concept of Countervailing Power,* Revised ed. (Cambridge, Mass.: Houghton Mifflin Company, 1956), pp. 111-112.
[4]*Ibid.,* p. 138.
[5]*Ibid.,* p. 141.
[6]See, for example, Walter Adams, "Competition, Monopoly and Countervailing Power," *Quarterly Journal of Economics,* LXVII (1953), 469—492, and George J. Stigler, "The Economist Plays with Blocs," *American Economic Review,* XLIV (1954), 7-14.
[7]*Ibid.,* p. 14.

THE NATURE
AND DESIRABILITY
OF COMPETITION

SECTION II

The major objective of the antitrust laws is to preserve competition. The purpose of this section is to probe the meaning of that objective. In Chapter II *we consider the meaning of competition, and in* Chapter III *the advantages and disadvantages of having a competitive economy are presented. These concepts will be used throughout the remainder of this book to analyze specific business practices with regard to their effect on consumer welfare.*

THE GENERAL NATURE OF COMPETITION

Throughout this book we will discuss the concept of competition. The purpose of this chapter is to clarify the general and technical meaning of the concept so that we avoid confusion later. Additionally, we will provide a standard to determine whether a firm and an industry are truly competitive.

INTRODUCTION

The primary objective of the antitrust laws is to make the United States economy competitive. Consequently, before studying antitrust in any detail it is important for the reader to have a good grasp of the meaning of competition. This might seem like a simple objective. Not a day passes but that most of us either use the word or think of the concept. Yet it is because of the word's familiarity to all of us that it is important to discuss it in some detail. It has come to mean many different things to people. Different meanings lead to a breakdown of communication between economists, and between lawyers and economists.

Hundreds of books and thousands of articles have probed, analyzed, and summarized competition. The material presented here is limited to a discussion of:

A. Competition as the primary objective of antitrust policy;
B. A general definition of competition;
C. Economists' models of competition;
D. The concept of monopoly power;
E. The concept of workable competition.

THE PRIMARY OBJECTIVE OF ANTITRUST

Before discussing the meaning of competition it is important to understand that the primary purpose of the antitrust laws is to promote competition.[1] The Sherman Act of 1890 prohibits practices which are anticompetitive. Both the Clayton and the Federal Trade Commission Acts of 1914 specifically state that their objective is the promotion of strong competition between business firms. In *United States* v. *South-Eastern Underwriters Association*, the Supreme Court stated that " . . . the purpose [of the antitrust laws] was . . . to make of ours, so far as Congress could under our dual system, a competitive business economy."[2] And the Attorney General's National Committee to Study the Antitrust Laws stated on the first page of its 1955 study that the primary goal of the antitrust statutes is to preserve competition.[3]

The fact that antitrust laws are designed to promote competition raises some important questions. What type of competition does antitrust policy preserve? What degree of competition should be promoted? What happens when the objective of competition comes in conflict with other objectives of the antitrust laws? Should strong competition be an objective of antitrust? Such questions have no simple answer. Even those who have spent a lifetime studying antitrust still wrestle with them.

A GENERAL DEFINITION
OF COMPETITION

All of us have experienced competition in one form or another and we know that in its simplest sense, it is rivalry. Rivalry can be defined as two or more persons willing and able to engage in a contest to determine a winner. For rivalry to exist, the number of possible winners must be something less than the number of contestants. A winner may be thought of as someone who can improve his situation relative to what it was before he first entered the competition. Depending on the game played, a winner may improve his monetary, psychological, or sociological position. Thus a competitor need not place first to be considered a winner.

Naturally, the definition given is applicable to many varied activities—activities including baseball, war, academic grades and the election of the president of the United States. However, this book is not about those types of competition. It is about competition among firms selling products. For economic competition to exist at all, two requirements must be met. First, there must be two or more firms selling a similar product. Just how similar the products must be is a difficult question that will be discussed in Chapter XIII. Second, the firms engaged in competition must want to compete. If instead, they collude or admit defeat, the game does not get off the ground.

Additional requirements have to be met in order to have competition of any significant degree. First, there must be a fairly large number of sellers so that they act independently of one another. Second, there should be relatively free entry into a market so that potential competitors can exert pressure on existing ones if they make "excess profits." Third, no one firm should have a significant cost advantage over its competitors that cannot be overcome with time and effort. If one firm has a permanent cost advantage, competition will not last long. Fourth, these should be a relatively large number of buyers so that purchasers cannot exercise monopsony power. Fifth, buyers should not collude with one another; nor should sellers collude among themselves. Finally, both buyers and sellers should have knowledge about the market place. Imperfect knowledge impedes rational decisions.

Throughout the literature on antitrust, many forms of competition are encountered. Two of the most important classifications are: price and nonprice competition, and hard and soft competition. It is important to understand their meaning.

PRICE AND NONPRICE COMPETITION

Firms use many tools to engage in competition, one of which is to attract customers by offering a favorable price. Such competition is especially prevalent when firms sell products for which the consumer has no strong brand attachment. Perhaps the best example of this existed in the days when gasoline stations had price wars. Economists talk frequently about price competition because price phenomena are easy to quantify. However, much of the competition between firms is nonprice competition which is characterized by little deviation in prices between competing firms but strong differentiation (real or imaginary) in quality, service, product packaging, advertising and other product dimensions. In some industries, nonprice competition is the only form of competition. For example, most morticians consider price competition to be a violation of business ethics, and for this reason, they rely almost solely on nonprice competition.

HARD AND SOFT COMPETITION

Consider, for a moment, a heavyweight fight between two contenders for the crown. Suppose that the rules have been modified such that the fighters have the choice of either knocking out their opponent or killing him. A knock-out only insures that the winner wins this title. The loser has a chance for a return bout. On the other hand, death of the opponent guarantees the winner that he will never have to do battle with this opponent again. The knock-out approach is analogous to "soft competition" and the death approach to "hard competition." In business terms, soft competition threatens firms' profit levels but not their lives. Hard competition threatens both.

Which form of competition is more desirable? The answer depends on the degree to which hard competition benefits consumers and the number of competitors in an industry. Most consumers benefit from hard competition in the short run. However, in the long run, firms may be driven out of business, and the remaining firms may be able to make excess profits at the expense of consumers. When should hard competition be allowed? If there is a large number of competitors in an industry such that hard competition can never reduce their numbers significantly, it might be an acceptable means of competition. If, on the other hand, there are only a few competitors such that the elimination of a few firms can reduce competition significantly, the consumer might be harmed in the long run.

Alternately, hard competition, like most warfare, might eventually result in a "cease fire." In the market place this means that firms will no longer compete but, instead, charge the same prices, offer the same services, etc. This can also harm the consumer by denying him the benefits of competition. It is clear that hard competition should not always be endorsed by public policy. As we shall see, many of our antitrust decisions are designed to promote soft competition.

ECONOMISTS' MODEL OF COMPETITION

Over the past sixty or seventy years, economists have developed models describing four degrees of competition: pure competition, monopolistic competition, oligopoly, and pure monopoly. These classifications fill the spectrum from the least amount of competition imaginable (pure monopoly) to the greatest degree of competition imaginable (pure competition). Knowledge of these models will further our understanding of competition and provide a framework for analyzing competitive practices.

PURE COMPETITION

Pure competition is the most competitive market imaginable. It is characterized by a large enough number of sellers and a large enough number of buyers so that neither one buyer nor one seller affects the price of the product. Both buyers and sellers are called "price takers" because they accept a price which is determined by the interaction of industry demand and supply. In the long run, new firms can enter a purely competitive industry. Therefore firms operating in this market know that if they make excess profits in the short run, new entrants will drive their prices down and eliminate their excess profits. Firms in a purely competitive industry offer an identical product and since consumers have no brand attachment, they shop only for the lowest price.

At this point, the reader may be trying to think of an industry in the United States that fits this description. He should end his search. Pure competition is an invention of the economist which in reality does not exist. Even the agricultural sector of our economy, while exhibiting some of the characteristics of pure competition, falls short of being purely competitive. Yet even though it does not describe existing markets, the concept provides an analytical tool to demonstrate the advantages of competition to society.

Figure I shows a simple graphical model of a representative firm operating in a purely competitive industry in the short run. The

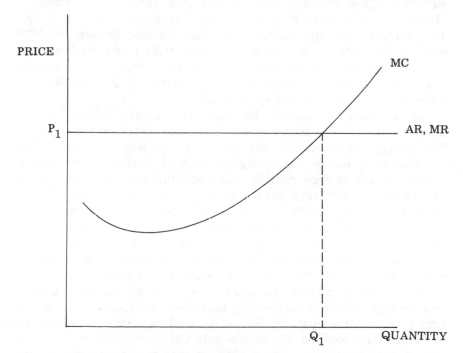

THE PURELY COMPETITIVE FIRM IN THE SHORT RUN
FIGURE I

curve labeled AR is the firm's average revenue curve (demand curve).[4] It shows the average income (not including an allowance for cost) from the sale of various units of production. MR is the firm's marginal revenue curve which shows the additional revenue gained from the sale of each incremental unit of the product. The same curve is labeled both AR and MR because the two are equal for a competitive firm. The industry price is the price the firm will charge (P_1). This explains why purely competitive firms are called "price takers."

MC represents the marginal cost curve which shows the cost of producing incremental units of the product. The fact that the curve is upward sloping indicates that each additional unit costs more than the preceding unit. Economists believe that in the short run, only some factors of production such as labor can be varied to increase output. Others, like land, can only be varied in the long run. Increasing costs exist because the firm eventually gets too many variable factors relative to the fixed factors; the factors get out of optimum proportion and cause increasing cost.

It pays the firm to produce the output level where marginal cost equals marginal revenue. That occurs at quantity Q_1 in *Figure I*. Marginal revenue exceeds marginal cost for quantities less than Q_1. This implies that the addition to total revenue (shown by MR) exceeds the addition to total cost (shown by MC), and the firm gains by producing all units less than Q_1. However, marginal cost is greater than marginal revenue for quantities greater than Q_1, and the firm loses on the production and sale of these units.

Up to this point nothing has been said about profit or loss. To discuss this, we need to consider the average cost curve which shows the average cost incurred by the firm at varying levels of output. This includes both the average marginal cost of production (more frequently called average variable cost) and the average fixed cost of production. Fixed cost does not vary with the level of output. Insurance paid by the firm, contractural rental fees, and the salaries of top management must be paid whether the firm produces a large quantity of output or nothing at all. Average cost is shown in *Figure II* and labeled AC. Following the tradition of economists, it includes a "normal return" on the owner's investment and effort.

The level of profit can be determined by comparing average cost and average revenue. Remember that the optimum output of the firm is Q_1. At that quantity the average cost and average revenue can be located by looking up to the relevant curves and over to the vertical axis. If average revenue is above average cost, the firm makes an excess profit. This means that it is making a return exceeding the

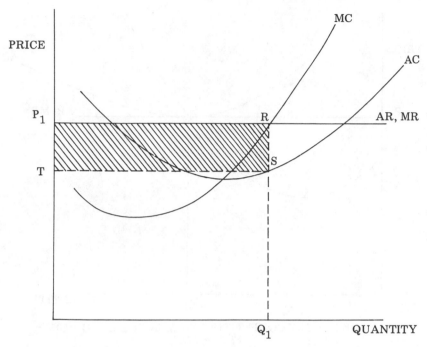

THE PURELY COMPETITIVE FIRM IN THE SHORT RUN
FIGURE II

normal return on the owner's investment. In *Figure II*, average profit is the distance RS and total profit is the area $RSTP_1$.

The purely competitive firm may make either an excess profit or a loss in the short run. In the long run, however, it will receive only a normal return. Graphically, this means that its average cost curve will be tangent to the average revenue curve at the quantity produced. To understand this, remember that one of the characteristics of pure competition is that free entry and exit of firms takes place in the long run. If, in the short run, firms in the industry experience a loss, then, in the long run, some of them will leave the industry. This will decrease industry supply, raise industry price, and raise the firm's average revenue curve (which represents industry price). This process will continue until the firms just earn a normal return. At that point firms will stop their movement from the industry. Conversely, if firms in the industry are making an excess profit in the short run, new firms will enter the industry, increase industry supply, reduce industry price, and move the firm's average revenue curve down until it is tangent to the average cost curve. The long run equilibrium of the firm is shown in *Figure III*.

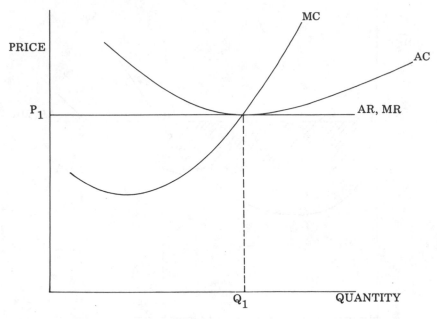

THE PURELY COMPETITIVE FIRM IN THE LONG RUN
FIGURE III

One final observation should be made concerning the purely competitive firm. Notice in *Figure III* that the firm's average cost curve is at its lowest point in equilibrium. This means that it is producing the product at the lowest average cost possible. This phenomenon occurs because of the strong competition that purely competitive firms face. If they produce the product at any output other than the lowest cost quantity, they will lose money in the long run.

PURE MONOPOLY

Pure monopoly appears at the opposite end of the competitive spectrum. It is characterized by a single seller of a product for which there are no close substitutes. Therefore, if the consumer wants the product he must buy from the monopolist. Even in the long run the monopolist is isolated from the threat of competition.

It is difficult but not impossible to point to a real world example of pure monopoly. Public utilities usually do not face competition as we saw in Chapter I, but these firms are controlled by government agencies so they do not exhibit the behaviorial characteristics of a pure monopoly. If products are defined narrowly then a few nonregulated companies have pure monopolies. The Polaroid camera which develops its own film is without a competitor, although the consumer who is willing to have his film developed by a processor considers it in competition with other cameras. For those few who must have a Cadillac and not a Lincoln or Imperial, the Cadillac Division of General Motors has a pure monopoly. Probably the most significant reason for the few pure monopolies is that our antitrust laws have successfully inhibited their development. Even though pure monopolies rarely exist in this country, an analysis of the firm operating under such conditions is important to the understanding of competition. Some firms act in a manner very similar to that of a monopoly, and therefore, a knowledge of the purely monopolistic firm will give insight into the actions of some existing firms in the United States economy.

Figure IV graphically demonstrates some of the characteristics of

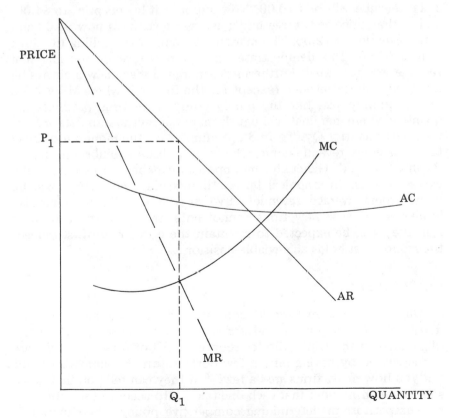

THE PURELY MONOPOLISTIC FIRM
FIGURE IV

pure monopoly. MC represents marginal cost, which resembles the cost curve of the purely competitive firm. AR shows the average revenue or demand curve of the firm. Its downward slope looks quite different from the average revenue curve of the purely competitive firm. It is sloped this way because of the law of diminishing utility. The law states that each additional unit of a product yields less satisfaction to the consumer than prior units, and therefore consumers will purchase additional units of the product only at a lower price. Since there is only one firm in this industry, the industry demand curve and the firm's demand curve are identical.

MR is the marginal revenue curve of the monopolist. It differs from the marginal revenue curve of the purely competitive firm in two ways. It is no longer equal to average revenue, and it slopes downward. An example should make both points clear. Suppose a pure monopolist can sell two units of its product at $5.00 a unit. Total revenue will be $10.00. Now suppose it lowers price to $4.00, and at that price sells three units; average revenue is now $4.00 and total revenue is $12.00. The marginal revenue from selling the third unit is $2.00. This demonstrates that average revenue and marginal revenue are not equal. Furthermore, marginal revenue will always be less than average revenue (except for the first unit where MR = AR).

The monopolist, like the purely competitive firm, produces the quantity where marginal cost equals marginal revenue. In *Figure IV* it produces quantity Q_1. To find optimum price, the monopolist looks to the average revenue curve. The monopolist's equilibrium price is P_1 in *Figure IV*. Generally, monopolists can be expected to make excess profits. In graphical terms, their average cost curve will be below their average revenue curve at the equilibrium quantity. Moreover, because new firms cannot enter the industry in the long run, they can be expected to maintain these excess profits. Indeed, the monopolist holds an enviable position.

OLIGOPOLY

Oligopoly is a real world concept. The automobile, cigarette, detergent, and appliance industries are only a few of the many oligopolies in the United States economy. All of these industries are characterized by having only a few competitors. Economists cannot tell you how many firms are "a few" but they can tell you that it is a small enough number that each one takes into account the actions of his competitors in determining competitive policy. The situation is analogous to a poker game between a few friends. In planning his strategy, each player naturally considers the cards he is holding.

However, to be successful, he must also consider the personality, knowledge, willingness to take risks, and other characteristics of his opponents. Based on these factors each player determines his policy vis à vis his opponents.

Most oligopolistic firms produce products which have a high fixed cost. Additionally, their consumers generally have a strong brand attachment which is difficult to overcome by a new producer. These characteristics effectively limit entry into the oligopolistic industry. The oligopolistic industry may sell either differentiated or undifferentiated products. Steel companies, for example, sell almost identical products. Automobile producers sell a fairly differentiated product, yet they too are in an oligopolistic industry. Sometimes one can find an oligopolistic industry in which firms sell identical commodities. However, because of the different nature of advertising, credit services, product service, product image, etc., it can be said that they sell a differentiated product.

It is extremely difficult to derive a model representing the oligopolistic firm because the actions of the firm depend on the actions and reactions of its competitors. Moreover, for every set of competitors there is a different set of actions and reactions, and for this reason there is no such thing as a typical model of oligopoly. Given the differences in the way firms play the "oligopolistic game" any one of four conduct patterns may exist in an industry. (1) The firms may overtly collude in their activities so that in reality they do not compete. (2) They may collude tacitly. This case is only distinguished from the first one by absence of a formal agreement between oligopolies to follow certain patterns of behavior. Nevertheless, by observing each other's actions a form of collusion develops. (3) Firms may engage in open competitive warfare in the form of strong price competition, advertising, etc. (4) Firms may follow a "live and let live" policy where through attack and counter attack, they maintain their competitive position but do not try to increase it. This approach generally develops out of a fear that playing the competitive game may cause sleeping competitors to awake and vie for a larger share of the market. Professor Bain has aptly called this behavioral pattern a "stalemate."[5]

Economists have struggled with the problem of deriving an oligopolistic model for over a hundred years with no significant results. Probably the easiest model of oligopoly to derive is that describing duopoly: A market structure in which there are two sellers of a product. Yet even in this limiting case of oligopoly the outcome still depends on the assumptions made about the actions and reactions of the two firms, and there is no one set of assumptions that can be made which matches real world conditions. The "theory of games" is the newest analytical approach to the study of oligopoly. The models developed using this approach are sophisticated, elaborate, and "neat" to analyze, but they need more developmental work if they are ever to be applicable to either the understanding of competitive processes or the formulation of antitrust policy.

Despite the problems accompanying the analysis of oligopolies, the most popular model (although not necessarily the most accurate) will be discussed to give the reader an idea of the complexities involved in the derivation of an oligopoly model. Paul Sweezy devised what is popularly called the "kinked demand curve model" of oligopoly.[6] He began his analysis by presenting two demand curves; one labeled DD', and the other labeled dd'.[7] These are shown in *Figure V*. dd' shows the various quantities of goods a firm can sell at different prices, assuming that the firm's competitors keep their price constant at P_1. DD' shows various quantities the firm can sell assuming that competitors always charge the same price it charges. The dd' curve is drawn to the left of the DD' curve at prices higher than P_1 to indicate that a firm sells less when it charges a price higher than that charged by its competitors as compared to a situation where they raise their prices to meet its price. Conversely, the dd' curve is drawn to the right of the DD' curve at prices lower than P_1 to indicate that a firm sells more when it charges a price lower than that charged by its competitors as compared to a situation where they lower their prices to meet its price.

From this bit of analysis, Sweezy devised a demand curve for the oligopolistic firm. He constructed his model to describe the market conditions encountered by a price follower. In other words, some other firm in the industry sets the price of his product at P_1, and the remaining firms (the price followers) set their prices at the same level. He assumed that if a firm other than the price leader raises price, no one will follow. The firm with the higher price moves along the dd' demand curve at prices above P_1. However, if a firm other than the price leader lowers price, all firms follow. Therefore at prices below P_1, the firm moves along the DD' curve. The resulting demand curve for the price follower is shown in *Figure VI*. Since the price follower can rarely gain by raising or lowering price, the Sweezy model shows the tendency of oligopolistic firms to set price at the level determined by the price leader and leave it there until the price leader changes the price.

The implication of the model is that prices tend to be rigid in the oligopolistic industry. Several industry studies have supported this conclusion, and in Chapter VI we will see that rigid prices have

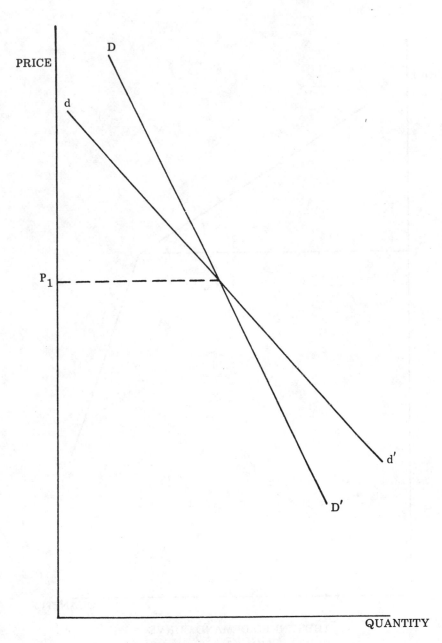

THE DD′ AND dd′ DEMAND CURVES
FIGURE V

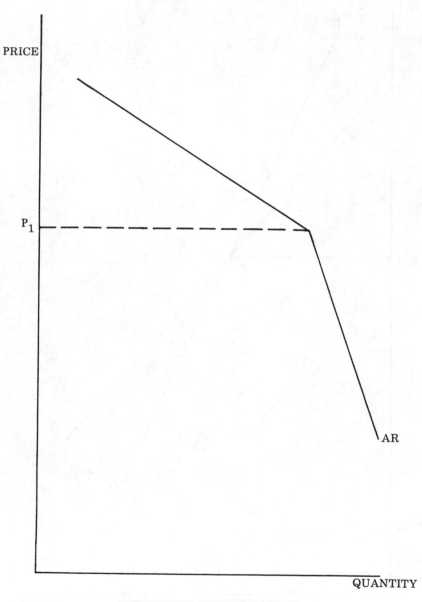

THE KINKED DEMAND CURVE
FIGURE VI

occasionally been attacked by antitrust authorities. However, there has been some argument about the existence of a kinked demand curve for the oligopolistic firm.[8] The model is based on the assumption that consumers are sensitive to price changes of individual firms in an industry. That is, they will move readily from firm A to firm B if B charges a lower price. If that is true, a kinked demand curve exists. However, to the extent that consumers have a strong brand attachment to one firm, the dd' curve tends to coincide with the DD' curve, and a kinked demand curve does not exist. In short, when firms in an oligopolistic industry sell differentiated products, the kinked demand curve concept is suspect, and there is evidence that a large number of oligopolistic firms sell differentiated products.

Essentially, the reader now knows most of the important information about the kinked demand curve. Yet oligopolies, like other forms of competition, have marginal revenue curves, marginal cost curves and average cost curves. These, along with the kinked demand curve, are shown in *Figure VII*. The marginal cost and average cost curves are just like those encountered in the study of pure monopoly

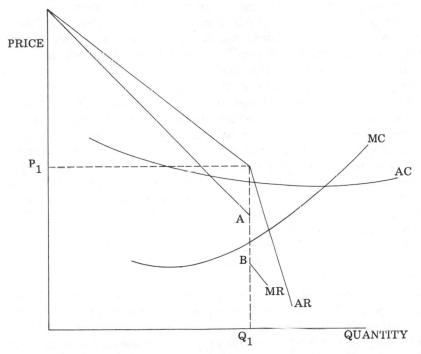

THE KINKED DEMAND CURVE MODEL OF OLIGOPOLY
FIGURE VII

and pure competition. However, the marginal revenue curve has a unique shape. The top part of the MR curve is marginal to the dd' curve. The bottom part of the MR curve is marginal to the DD' curve. At quantity Q_1 (corresponding to P_1) the marginal revenue curve is discontinuous. This is shown from point A to point B in *Figure VII*. If the marginal cost curve crosses this discontinuity, the firm will be in equilibrium.

MONOPOLISTIC COMPETITION

A monopolistically competitive industry is characterized by a large number of sellers supplying slightly differentiated products. There is usually some brand attachment on the part of consumers which gives the seller some control over the price. In the long run, there is relatively easy freedom of entry which exposes the monopolistically competitive firm making excess profits to the threat of new competition. Measured in terms of sheer number, the majority of businesses in the United States are monopolistically competitive. Service stations, drugstores, and grocery stores represent only a few examples of firms which engage in monopolistic competition.

The model of monopolistic competition was devised by Edward Chamberlain.[9] In the short run it looks like the model of pure monopoly. But there are significant differences between the model of monopolistic competition and the model of pure monopoly, the most important one being that the monopolistically competitive firm has rivals. This means that the firms have to divide industry demand among themselves with the exact division of that demand depending on the firms' ability to compete. This implies that the demand curve of a monopolistically competitive firm is less than industry demand. The demand curve (AR) is shown in *Figure VIII* with the marginal revenue curve corresponding to it (MR). The monopolistically competitive firm has a marginal cost schedule, which, like all others, is subject to diminishing returns in the short run. Equilibrium for the firm is at the quantity where marginal cost equals marginal revenue. In *Figure VIII*, the firm produces quantity Q_1 and charges price P_1.

In the short run the monopolistically competitive firm may either earn an excess profit or incur a loss. Thus its average cost curve may be either below or above the average revenue curve at the equilibrium quantity. In *Figure VIII* it is shown below the average revenue curve, indicating that the firm is making an excess profit. Because of the free entry and exit of competitors the monopolistically competitive firm will just make a normal return in the long run. To understand this, assume that in the short run the firm is making an excess profit.

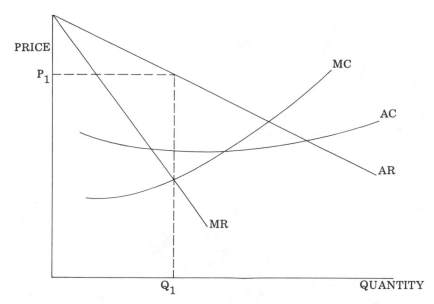

THE MONOPOLISTICALLY COMPETITIVE FIRM IN THE SHORT RUN
FIGURE VIII

This profit induces potential competitors to enter the market, and when this occurs the industry demand will be divided among more competing firms. As a result, each individual firm's demand curve will shift downward. Firms will continue to enter the industry, and individual demand curves will shift downward until competing firms are just making a normal return on their investment. Then there will no longer be an incentive for new firms to enter the industry. The long run equilibrium position is shown in *Figure IX*. The reader will notice that the average cost curve is tangent to the average revenue curve at the quantity produced by the firm. This means that the firm is neither making an excess profit nor a loss.

If the monopolistically competitive firm incurs a loss in the short run, some firms will leave the industry. Their exit will shift the demand curve of each remaining firm upward. The process will continue until average cost curve is just tangent to average revenue curve at the quantity produced. At that point there will no longer be an incentive for firms to leave.

This model, like the one for pure competition, demonstrates the importance of free entry. When potential firms are able to enter the market they constantly pressure the existing firms to satisfy the consumers' needs. Free entry will make the monopolistically competitive firm more responsive to consumer needs than the oligopolistic firm.

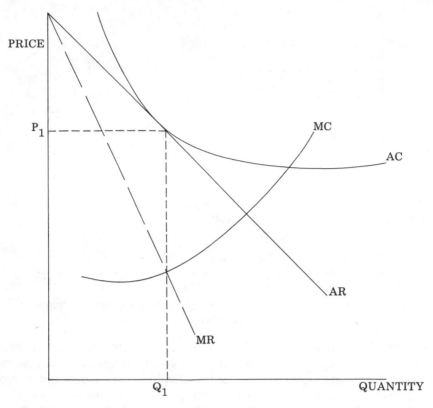

THE MONOPOLISTICALLY COMPETITIVE FIRM IN THE LONG RUN
FIGURE IX

A NOTE ON ECONOMISTS' MODELS

As noted earlier, the models that have been presented are helpful in understanding the competitive practices which come under the antitrust laws and in formulating antitrust policy. However, before going further, we should understand that they have serious limitations which prevent them from being the sole analytical tool for antitrust. These limitations are:

1. The models do not describe perfectly every industry in our economy. They only approximate the market conditions in which firms operate.
2. The models emphasize price competition. Although they can be modified to express nonprice competition, such modifications are limited.
3. The models emphasize structural characteristics of firms. They

are not dynamic and hence slight performance aspects of competition.

4. The models are presented in a language which is unfamiliar to some lawyers and judges. If they are to be truly helpful to those in the legal profession, they should be expressed in plain English, not in graphical or mathematical terms.

THE CONCEPT OF MONOPOLY POWER

The term "monopoly power" (sometimes referred to as "market power") will be used throughout much of this book. Therefore it is important to understand its meaning. Kaysen and Turner have effectively defined the term by saying that, "A firm possesses market power when it can behave persistently in a manner different from the behavior that a competitive market would enforce on a firm facing otherwise similar cost and demand conditions."[10] The degree of monopoly power that a firm has depends on the structure of the industry in which the firm operates. For example, if a firm is a pure monopoly, then it has a great deal of monopoly power. If it is oligopolistic, the firm has significant monopoly power, but not as much as the pure monopolist. It probably cannot charge as high a price as the pure monopolist because it does face some degree of competition. However, it almost certainly could charge more than the pure competitor because of the lack of entry of new competitors, the fact that it may collude with its fellow oligopolists, and the fact that its consumers probably have some brand attachment to its product. Because the performance of firms can affect or overcome the structure of the market in which they compete, performance is also a variable that must be considered in analyzing monopoly power.[11] It is also important to note that even if a firm has monopoly power, that power is not necessarily exercised.

Theoretically, the degree of monopoly power that a firm has can be measured by the difference between marginal cost and price at the equilibrium quantity produced. We have already seen that in a purely competitive industry marginal cost equals price in equilibrium. No monopoly power exists in this market. On the other hand, the pure monopolist's ability to affect market price brings about a significant divergence between marginal cost and price in equilibrium. These two market structures represent the two polar cases of competition. In between them, firms display varying degrees of monopoly power.

Economists realize that it is almost impossible to measure this power precisely. Therefore, they have devised various indices which indirectly measure it. Their methodology is both interesting and sound. Still, the courts have generally rejected most of the measures, and the data required to compute the indices is difficult to collect. Therefore, the indices have little applicability to antitrust. Four of the indices are discussed in the appendix to this chapter.

THE CONCEPT OF WORKABLE COMPETITION

Economists point to pure competition as the ideal market structure. Yet, all economists know that a world composed of purely competitive firms is a "never never land." Furthermore, the model of pure competition is not very helpful to lawyers and judges in appraising the degree of competition in an industry. In fact, the U.S. Attorney General's National Committee to Study the Antitrust Laws went so far as to say, "Nor should the courts be expected to be able to utilize pure and perfect competition in adjudging any given market situation."[12]

It is desirable to have an alternative standard to follow in answering the question, "Is industry A or firm X competitive?" The concept of workable competition is designed to answer the question by providing conditions which should be satisfied for a firm to be competitive. "Competitive," as it is used here, has a unique meaning. It does not mean purely competitive but instead, some degree of competition which is reasonably attainable and which can be expected to satisfy the needs of the consumer reasonably well. Of course, this definition is vague. What does "reasonably attainable" mean? Obviously it means a different thing to the socialist than the proponent of free enterprise. To what degree are the consumers' needs satisfied if they are satisfied "reasonably well"? The answers to these questions require many subjective value judgments.

The concept of workable competition is based on the fact that pure competition is not attainable. It also is based on the recognition that pure monopoly is not desirable and does not have to be tolerated in our economy. Workable competition falls *somewhere* between these two extremes, but just where it falls is the source of confusion. For this reason, Richard Low has stated: "The concept of workable competition, like many a human being, was born in glory, raised in triumph, and, subsequently, widely considered a failure. Considerable skepticism exists as to whether it can even be defined."[13] Despite the problems of definition, workable competition deserves careful study. Like it or not, our economy is neither purely competitive nor purely monopolistic. We live with a competitive structure somewhere between the two extremes, and we analyze the competitive structure of firms in antitrust to determine if they are workably competitive, not purely competitive. Antitrust remedies to change the structure and behavior of a firm do not make the firm purely competitive, only more competitive. The definition of workable competition is really symptomatic of the major problem of antitrust: how to satisfy the needs of the consumer while at the same time offering an attainable policy. The concept of workable competition renders some insight into the problems of analyzing a real world competitive situation. Furthermore, its study will suggest some criteria that can be used to analyze business practices and determine appropriate antitrust policy. Several aspects of workable competition are being used by our courts to judge cases.

Workable competition was originated by J. M. Clark. Many other economists as well as some lawyers have struggled with the concept. The comments by Corwin Edwards, Jesse Markham, and the Attorney General's National Committee are considered here in addition to Clark's contributions.

THE CLARK APPROACH

Professor Clark established two "formal" requirements and several "informal" ones which he believed should be satisfied for an industry to be workably competitive.[14] The formal and informal requirements are not independent of one another. An industry usually must meet the formal requirements in order to meet most of the informal ones and vice versa. Clark's requirements deal mostly with industry structure; they do not analyze the actual performance of an industry. Naturally, structure may be used to predict performance, but the correlation is not a perfect one.

The Formal Requirements

1. "Single-firm demand functions [must be] more elastic than those of groups of industries—that is, those that include the products of competitors."[15]

This implies that by lowering its price or offering some other inducement, a firm would be able to take customers away from its competitors. A firm with a demand schedule of the same elasticity as the industry demand schedule could, by lowering price, only attract customers who did not already buy in the industry. In other words, it would bring new customers into the industry—not raid the customers of competitors. Obviously, a firm would have more incentive to reduce price if it could expect two sources of new customers, one from outside the industry and another from its competitors. Furthermore, this analysis should not be limited to only price reductions (although Clark had a strong attachment to price competition). It applies to all inducements a firm can offer to gain new customers. Generally speaking, the greater the deviation of elasticity of demand between the firm and the industry, the stronger will be the firm's incentive to offer these inducements.

> 2. "A substantial number of firms small enough relative to the whole market in which they compete, to have strong competitive incentives (though there is no need for atomistic smallness) and economically strong enough to make their competitive pressure count."[16]

For competition to be viable, Clark believed that firms should be of an optimal size. On one hand, each firm's supply should be small enough relative to industry demand to permit a large number of competitors in an industry. Given this large number, the firms would act independently of one another and forestall either overt or tacit collusion. On the other hand, firms should be large enough to have the financial resources necessary for research and development.

The Informal Requirements[17]

1. Consumer Competence.

The consumer must be aware of and be able to evaluate differences in price, quality, service, and other product dimensions. Otherwise, it is ineffective for firms to offer diversified products and relatively low prices. For example, it is not beneficial for a detergent company to charge a lower price per ounce than its competitors if consumers are unable to detect the number of ounces in a box of detergent.

2. Firms must attempt to protect their competitive position.

Clark believed that in order to have effective competition, firms have to be constantly on the defensive. That is, they must combat competitive attacks on their market position. For example, suppose that firm A offers the consumer a lower price, a better product, or somehow improves the product package offered. To have effective competition, firm B must wish to improve its product package to combat A's strategy. In this way, the consumer will be ensured of strong competition between A and B. If firm B does not have a combative strategy, firm A may win the battle, and consumers may be left with few competitors from which to purchase their product.

Furthermore, combative strategy ensures the consumer that firms are constantly attempting to find new ways to meet his demands. This informal requirement follows logically from the first formal requirement. The greater the divergence between industry elasticity of demand and firms' elasticity of demand, the greater will be the tendency to engage in competitive attacks and counter attacks or as Clark put it "a series of initiatory moves and defensive responses."

3. Willingness of firms to
initiate competitive
attacks.

For defensive competition to exist, there must be offensive competition. Some firm must initiate the battle with the expectation that it can improve its standing in the industry. According to Clark, rival firms' expected responses to offensive competition are the major variable determining the nature and degree of offensive competition. If the initiating firm expects no response from competitors, it could achieve significant gains from offensive competition and would have a strong inducement to engage in it. If on the other hand, it expected immediate and identical responses from competing firms such that any gains are neutralized, the firm probably would not engage in offensive competition. Obviously, the response of most competitors to offensive competition lies somewhere between these extremes. The important point is that some firms must think they can gain by engaging in offensive competition. These firms are innovators in the industry and prod their competitors to engage in defensive competition. The attack and counter attack can improve consumer welfare.

4. Support of the antitrust laws
and the basic morals of trade.

Businesses can make gains in two ways. They could offer products to consumers which are better than those of their competitors. In this way they play the competitive game by the rules, and the most efficient firms win. Alternatively, they could cheat by taking unfair advantage of their competitors or by somehow fooling the consuming public. By this method, long run gains are rare, but firms can frequently make short run gains. Clark's fourth condition simply requires that competitors play the game fairly.

THE EDWARDS APPROACH

Professor Corwin Edwards has presented the most comprehensive set of conditions for workable competition of any author. His conditions, like those of Clark, deal mostly with structure and are designed to provide "freedom of choice" for both the buyer and seller. This provides both parties with available alternatives. In Edwards' words, his conditions are:

1. There must be an appreciable number of sources of supply and an appreciable number of potential customers for substantially the same product or service. Suppliers and customers do not need to be so numerous that each trader is entirely without individual influence, but their number must be great enough that persons on the other side of the market may readily turn away from any particular trader and may find a variety of other alternatives.
2. No trader must be so powerful as to be able to coerce his rivals, nor so large that the remaining traders lack the capacity to take over at least a substantial portion of his trade.
3. Traders must be responsive to incentives of profit and loss; that is, they must not be so large, so diversified, so devoted to political rather than commercial purposes, so subsidized, or otherwise so unconcerned with results in a particular market that their policies are not affected by ordinary commercial incentives arising out of the market.
4. Matters of commercial policy must be decided by each trader separately without agreement with his rivals.
5. New traders must have an opportunity to enter the market without handicap other than that which is automatically created by the fact that others are already well established there.
6. Access by traders on one side of the market to those on the other side of the market must be unimpaired except by obstacles not deliberately introduced, such as distance or ignorance of available alternatives.
7. There must be no substantial preferential status within the market for any important trader or group of traders on the basis of law, politics, or commercial alliances.[18]

Clark and Edwards are very similar in their approach to workable competition. However, Edwards took a more specific approach in formulating his criteria. He maintained that workable competition required a large number of buyers and sellers, relatively equal power among competitors, the existence of the profit motive as the major objective of business, no collusion, free entry, and no artificial barriers on either side of the market which forestall the existence of strong competition.

THE MARKHAM APPROACH

Professor Markham observed that the criteria established by Clark and Edwards have one serious limitation. They are basically structural and, hence, neglect the dynamic forces in an industry. In other words, they are designed to determine by their structure if firms in an industry are workably competitive at one point in time. Markham contended that whether or not workable competition exists can only be determined by performance and structure over time. For example, an industry with a small number of firms today may have a large number of firms in ten years. If the seeds exist for the development of a large number of competitors, should the industry be declared unworkable? Should government attempt to change its structure when with the passage of time the problem will correct itself? The answer to these questions is probably "no," although many people would disagree because the answer depends on what is the appropriate time horizon for antitrust policy. The point here is that determining if an industry is workably competitive requires more than a static analysis. Markham contended that the introduction of dynamic concepts to the determination of workability would modify the usefulness of structural criteria. As he put it, "If changes in the structural characteristics of an industry over time are to be admitted to the concept, a stated set of conditions is not only inapplicable to all industries at once but also loses its applicability to the same industry at different stages of development."[19]

Markham also suggested that appropriate criteria for determining workable competition should weigh an industry's competitive performance as well as its structure against the desirability of having government make remedial changes in the structure. In lieu of a list of requirements he suggested that "An industry may be judged to be workably competitive when, after the structural characteristics of its market and the dynamic forces that shaped them have been thoroughly examined, there is no clearly indicated change that can be effected through public policy measures that would result in greater social gains than social losses."[20] Under Markham's rule an industry first would be analyzed in terms of its performance and its structural characteristics. Then, even if the industry is not competitive, the analyst would ask if government could make a change which would bring gains to society greater than the costs of making the change.

This approach has several advantages over those of Clark and Edwards. First, it analyzes performance. Second, it incorporates the cost of public policy into the determination of the industry's workability by asking if it is practical to change the structure of the industry. Third, it does not apply the same structural standards to each industry at every point in time. The Markham approach does have a serious fault. It leaves open the choice of both structural and performance characteristics to the analyst, and obviously the choice of criteria will vary from person to person. Thus it is important to settle on some criteria which are acceptable to the majority of individuals involved in the determination of antitrust policy.

THE ATTORNEY GENERAL'S APPROACH

S. Chesterfield Oppenheim, a law professor and authority on antitrust laws, hoped that the concept of workable competition would be used by the courts to formulate better antitrust policy for oligopolies. He petitioned Congress to adopt the concept, and he played an important role in the formation of the Attorney General's National Committee to Study the Antitrust Laws. He hoped that one of the recommendations of that committee would be the adoption of the concept of workable competition for antitrust litigation. The committee, however, concluded that workable competition "does not provide a standard of legality under any of the antitrust laws," and specifically rejected the concept.[21]

There are two major reasons for the rejection of the concept. First, as we have already observed, the concept of workable competition is vague and would provide an indefinite standard for the courts to follow. According to the committee,

> ... the "doctrine" of workable competition is only a rough and ready judgment by some economists, each for himself, that a particular industry is performing reasonably well—presumably relative to alternative industrial arrangements which are practically attainable. There is no objective criteria of workable competition, and such criteria as are proffered are at best intuitively reasonable modifications of the rigorous and abstract criteria of perfect competition.[22]

Second, the use of workable competition might condone specific restraints which would be outlawed by many in both the legal and economic professions. Putting it another way, opponents of workable competition fear that its application by the courts might result in the condoning of specific anticompetitive practices when the overall performance of the industry is "acceptable." Dirlam and Kahn suggested some consequences of the adoption of workable competition.

> If "efficiency," "progressiveness," and "usefulness for national defense" are to acquit a company or industry, the government should presumably condone most instances of cartelization or monopolization in the fields of electronics, chemicals, petroleum, and chain store distribution, regardless of whether the specific restraints had anything to do with good over-all performance.[23]

Does this mean that the concept is dead? The answer is "no." Even the committee recognized that it "provides the courts with the tools of analysis in making the functional inquiry into problems of competition and monopoly."[24]

SUMMARY

In this chapter the meaning of the term "competition" has been clarified. During the study we learned that the term is not an easy one to define. Yet, because the major objective of the antitrust laws is to promote competition, it is essential to derive some acceptable meaning. We defined competition in a general way and noted some essential requirements for its existence. We also saw that economists have developed models which describe competition under various market structures. Finally, we analyzed the concept of workable competition and concluded that although it is not fully accepted by the courts, it does give some criteria to use in determining whether sufficient competition exists in an industry. Perhaps the most important thing introduced in this chapter is the realization that there is not one acceptable definition of competition. This implies that although the antitrust laws are designed to promote competition, there is dissent concerning what competition is, what types of competition should be promoted, and how much competition there should be. This, as the reader can imagine, causes many problems in antitrust law enforcement.

NOTES TO CHAPTER II

[1]It is also important to realize that the protection of competition is not the only objective of antitrust. Non-economic objectives are discussed in *Chapter IV*.

[2]322 U.S. 533, 599 (1944).

[3]U.S. Attorney General's National Committee to Study the Antitrust Laws, *Report* (Washington: Government Printing Office, 1955), p. 1.

[4]The reader who has not encountered graphical models of competition before may find it helpful to refer to a basic text in economics. See, for example, Paul A. Samuelson, *Economics*, 8th ed. (New York: McGraw-Hill Book Company, 1970), pp. 407-483.

[5]Joe S. Bain, *Industrial Organization* (New York: John Wiley and Sons, Inc., 1968), p. 29.

[6]Paul M. Sweezy, "Demand under Conditions of Oligopoly," *Journal of Political Economy*, XLVII (August 1939), 568-573.

[7]The curves were originated by Edward Chamberlain, *The Theory of Monopolistic Competition*, 8th ed. (Cambridge: Harvard University Press, 1962), pp. 74-100.

[8]See, for example, George Stigler, "The Kinky Oligopoly Demand Curve and Rigid Prices," *Journal of Political Economy*, LV (October 1947), 432-449.

[9]Chamberlain, pp. 130-176.

[10]Carl Kaysen and Donald F. Turner, *Antitrust Policy, An Economic and Legal Analysis* (Cambridge, Mass.: Harvard University Press, 1959), p. 75.

[11]"By performance economists mean the effectiveness or efficiency with which, from the economic point of view, a firm or industry acquits itself. Is it dynamic or lethargic? Is it quick to introduce new methods and improve its products? What is the course of its prices? What is the rate of profit? Is 'progress' its 'most important product'?" George W. Stocking, *Workable Competition and Antitrust Policy* (Nashville: Vanderbilt University Press, 1961), p. 125.

[12]U.S. Attorney General's National Committee to Study the Antitrust Laws, p. 338.

[13]Richard E. Low, *Modern Economic Organization* (Homewood, Ill.: Richard D. Irwin, Inc., 1970), p. 43.

[14]J. M. Clark, *Competition as a Dynamic Process* (Washington, D.C.: The Brookings Institution, 1961).

[15]*Ibid.*, p. 480.

[16]*Ibid.*, p. 481.

[17]*Ibid.*, pp. 466-479.

[18]Corwin Edwards, *Maintaining Competition* (New York: McGraw-Hill, 1949), pp. 9-10.

[19]Jesse W. Markham, "An Alternative Approach to the Concept of Workable Competition," *American Economic Review*, XL (June 1950), 361.

[20]Markham, p. 361.

[21]U.S. Attorney General's National Committee to Study the Antitrust Laws, p. 316.

[22]Markham, p. 339.

[23]Joel B. Dirlam and Alfred E. Kahn, *Fair Competition: The Law and Economics of Antitrust Policy* (Ithaca, New York: Cornell University Press, 1954), p. 41.

[24]U.S. Attorney General's National Committee to Study the Antitrust Laws, p. 316.

APPENDIX TO CHAPTER II
THE MEASUREMENT OF MONOPOLY POWER

Many individuals have derived measures of the concept of monopoly power that was discussed earlier. In this appendix the contributions of Professors Lerner, Bain, Rothschild, Morgan and Papandreou will be considered. While their measures have limited application to antitrust matters, their methodology is interesting. Moreover, an analysis of their contributions gives the reader an appreciation for the tremendous problems encountered in estimating the amount of monopoly power possessed by a firm.

THE LERNER INDEX

Professor Abba Lerner expressed the degree of monopoly power possessed by a firm as:

$$\frac{\text{Price--Marginal Cost}[1]}{\text{Price}}$$

Because price is used in the denominator as a reference number, the index permits comparison of monopoly power between different firms and industries. The reader familiar with microeconomics will also recognize that when the firm is in equilibrium, the Lerner index is the inverse of the equation for price elasticity of demand. Price elasticity can be computed by the equation:

$$\frac{\text{Price}}{\text{Price--Marginal Revenue}}$$

but in equilibrium, marginal cost and marginal revenue are equal. Because Lerner thought that equilibrium was rare, he warned against substituting the inverse of the elasticity equation for his index.

Lerner suggested that the degree of monopoly power in an industry could be computed by averaging the degree of monopoly power possessed by all of its members. Likewise, although the index is designed to compute the degree of monopoly power at one point in time, successive indices can be averaged to compute monopoly power over time.[2] In a world of costless information, the index would be extremely useful. However, in reality it is sometimes very difficult to compute marginal cost or elasticity of demand. This is the major reason explaining why the index has limited application.

THE BAIN INDEX

Professor Joe Bain suggested measuring the degree of monopoly power by the difference between price and average cost.[3] Naturally,

Bain recognized that his approach would not yield the same answer as would the difference between price and marginal cost, and, therefore, he said that his approach would only serve as an indicator of a probable discrepancy between price and marginal cost.

Bain's analysis is demonstrated in *Figure X*. The firm has a degree of monopoly power indicated by the divergence between price and marginal cost (XZ) at the equilibrium quantity. Bain suggested that since marginal cost is sometimes difficult to measure, the difference between average cost and price at equilibrium (XY) could serve as an indicator of monopoly power. In other words, Bain contended that if excess profits exist, monopoly power also will exist.

To compute excess profit, Bain first expressed the rate of return on a firm's investment in any one year as:

$$i = \frac{R-C-D}{V}$$

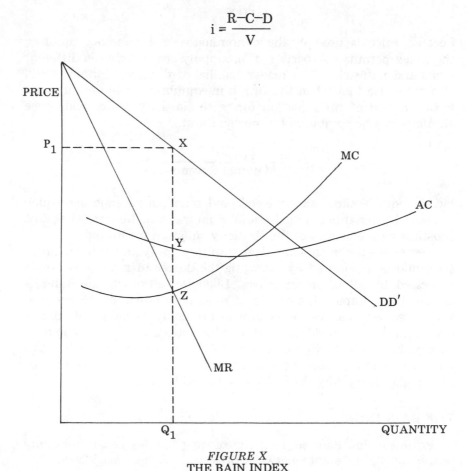

FIGURE X
THE BAIN INDEX

where

i   is the rate of return.

R   is annual revenue.

C   is the annual current cost of earning yearly revenue. It includes such costs as wages, plant maintenance, insurance costs, raw materials cost and promotion costs.

D   is the annual depreciation. It is largely made up of costs incurred in prior years for capital investment which is used up in the production of this year's output.

V   is the value of owners' investment for the year.[4]

Since the numerator of the index is net revenue and the denominator is investment, the numerical result is a rate of return.

If, in the long run, a firm operates in a purely competitive market, it would not make excess profits but only a normal return. According to Bain, a normal return on investment can be considered as the best annual interest rate that can be earned in the capital market. Therefore, if the firm earns only a normal return, the "i" in the above equation will equal the annual interest rate. Keeping this in mind, a transposition of the above equation and a definition of "i" as the best annual interest rate in the capital market will yield:

$$R-C-D-i\,(V) = O$$

when the firm makes a normal return on investment. If, on the other hand, net revenue exceeds the return investors would have received from the capital market then the firm earns excess profits and:

$$R-C-D-i\,(V) > O$$

Therefore, Bain's index of monopoly power is measured by the extent to which

$$R-C-D-i\,(V)$$

exceeds zero. Bain was careful to note that only when the index indicates monopoly profits over a series of years can one suspect that the firm had monopoly power. Furthermore, he recognized that his approach was not a substitute for qualitative analysis of a firm. He only conceived of the index as a supplement.

It is important to consider the fundamental relationship upon which the index is based: the relationship between excess profits and monopoly power. Is it always valid to expect that a firm earning excess profits over time possesses monopoly power? Conversely, is it valid to claim that a firm which does not earn excess profits is void of such power? The answer to both questions is "no." A firm possessing monopoly power may not exhibit excess profits if it is inefficient. Likewise, a firm may exhibit excess profits because of efficiency, not monopoly power. This observation is not meant to imply that the Bain index is worthless. Used with qualitative analysis, it can be a helpful guide to the determination of monopoly power.

THE ROTHSCHILD INDEX

K. W. Rothschild used the DD' and dd' demand curves encountered earlier in this chapter to compute an index of monopoly power.[5] The reader will remember that both of the demand curves represent the demand for a firm's products, but the DD' curve assumes that all of the firm's competitors follow its pricing policy while the dd' curve assumes that the firm charges a different price than that charged by its competitors. The two curves are reconstructed in *Figure XI*. Rothschild reasoned that if the firm is a pure monopoly, its dd' curve would be identical to its DD' curve. Alternatively, if the firm is a pure competitor, its dd' curve would be a horizontal line originating at the price charged by its competitors, P_1. Based on this observation he thought that the degree of divergence between the DD' and dd' curves would be a good measure of monopoly power. The degree of divergence is measured by comparing the slope of the dd' curve to the slope of the DD' curve. The degree of monopoly power possessed by the firm in *Figure XI* would be slope A divided by slope B. If the firm is purely competitive the index would equal O because the slope of dd' would be O. Likewise, if the firm is a pure monopoly the index would equal 1 because the slope of DD' and the slope of dd' would be identical. The degree to which the index approaches 1 expresses the degree of monopoly power possessed by a firm.

Rothschild's index is perfectly logical because it measures the degree to which a firm is able to raise its price above that of its competitors and maintain its sales. If the firm possesses significant monopoly power, it will be able to raise its price without experiencing a significant reduction in output. Alternatively, if it has little

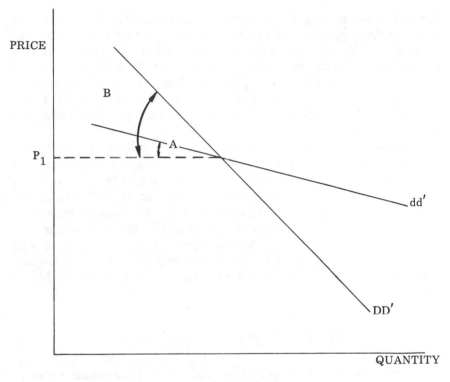

FIGURE XI
THE ROTHSCHILD INDEX

monopoly power it will experience relatively large losses in sales when it attempts to raise price.

The major problem with the index is that it is extremely difficult to calculate the DD′ and dd′ curves and hence difficult to compute the index. Rothschild was aware of the practical limitations of his index.

> If in our theoretical work we feel a need for some measurement, we should forge a tool which will best suit our theoretical need and should not allow ourselves to be side-tracked by the consideration of any statistical material just because it is easily available.[6]

THE MORGAN AND PAPANDREOU INDICES

Theodore Morgan suggested that the degree of monopoly power possessed by a firm could be measured by a "coefficient of insulation."[7] It is computed by a modification of the cross elasticity of demand equation, and it measures the degree to which a firm is able to maintain sales when its competitors reduce their price. Although the actual computation will not be presented here the concept is very similar to measuring the extent to which dd′ deviates from DD′ at prices below P_1 in *Figure XI*. When the firm has significant monopoly power it will lose relatively few sales when its competitors sell at a lower price. When it has little or no monopoly power, its sales will drop significantly.

Professor Papandreou suggested that in addition to using the Morgan index, it was also important to calculate a "coefficient of penetration."[8] This is a measure of the ability of a firm "to cut into the volume of another firm's sales by reducing price."[9] This index includes a measure not only of a firm's ability to raid its competitors by lowering price, but also its ability to satisfy the new demand by virtue of its available supply. Where a firm has the ability to raid its competitors and supply the new customers, it has more monopoly power than if it could get the new customers but is not able to supply them.

NOTES TO CHAPTER II APPENDIX

[1] A. P. Lerner, "The Concept of Monopoly and the Measurement of Monopoly Power," *Review of Economic Studies*, I (1934), 169.

[2] *Ibid.*, p. 171.

[3] Joe S. Bain, "The Profit Rate as a Measure of Monopoly Power," *Quarterly Journal of Economics*, LV (February, 1941), 273.

[4] Joe S. Bain, *Industrial Organization* (New York: John Wiley and Sons, Inc., 1968), pp. 388, 390.

[5] K. W. Rothschild, "The Degree of Monopoly," *Economica*, IX (1942), 24-39.

[6] *Ibid.*, p. 30.

[7] Theodore Morgan, "A Measure of Monopoly in Selling," *Quarterly Journal of Economics*, LX (May, 1946), 461-463.

[8] Andreas G. Papandreou, "Market Structure and Monopoly Power," *American Economic Review*, XXXIX (1949), 883-897.

[9] *Ibid.*, p. 890.

THE ADVANTAGES AND DISADVANTAGES OF COMPETITION

CHAPTER III

Almost everyone agrees that competition is a good thing but the reasons why are difficult to articulate. In this chapter we will identify these reasons. Additionally we will learn that competition is not always desirable.

INTRODUCTION

Why should competition be a major objective of antitrust policy? If you asked an individual on the street, he might tell you that he does not like the existence of power in any form and therefore prefers competition to monopoly. Another person might tell you that he expects consumers to benefit where competition exists and be hurt where it does not exist. He might even point to some industry where competition is weak and attempt to show you the resulting harm to consumers. Certainly this would be the response if the person you interviewed were Ralph Nader. We all have some opinion of why competition is preferable to monopoly, but most of our ideas are cloudy because the term "competition" has moral overtones.

THE ADVANTAGES OF COMPETITION

There are two distinct approaches which can be used to demonstrate the advantages of competition. In the first, equilibrium conditions of firms engaged in pure competition and pure monopoly can be contrasted to demonstrate the effect of monopoly on economic welfare. This approach emphasizes the fact that consumers are harmed when monopoly power exists and implies that economic resources are misallocated. The second approach introduces conditions necessary for society to reach the optimum degree of economic welfare and then shows why only pure competition satisfies all of these conditions. While it demonstrates that monopoly power harms consumers, it more clearly demonstrates that this power causes a misallocation of resources.

CONTRAST OF EQUILIBRIUM CONDITIONS

In the last chapter we saw that pure competition and pure monopoly are at opposite ends of the competitive spectrum. One represents the most competitive situation imaginable, and the other represents the least competitive situation. By comparing the two we can uncover some adverse effects resulting from monopoly elements in our economy. Furthermore, even though we are comparing two market structures that do not exist, the conclusions reached will be valid for any comparison of a more competitive situation to a less competitive one—for example monopolistic competition versus oligopoly.

Assume that an industry can be transformed overnight from pure competition to pure monopoly. The equilibrium conditions for pure competition will be observed first. Then the industry will be transformed into a monopoly, and those equilibrium conditions will be observed. Remember that throughout this analysis *industry* equilibrium is being analyzed.

The industry average revenue or demand curve is shown in *Figure I* (AR). There is no reason to expect the curve to change when the market structure is altered; therefore it will remain the same for both pure competition and pure monopoly. A marginal cost curve for the industry is also shown in *Figure I* (MC). This is derived by horizontally summing the marginal cost curves of the individual firms in the industry. Since each purely competitive firm produces up to the point where marginal cost equals average revenue, the industry equilibrium exists where industry marginal cost equals industry average revenue. The quantity produced in pure competition will be Q_c, and the price charged would be P_c.

Now suppose that all of these purely competitive firms merge into a pure monopoly. The merger will create a new equilibrium price and quantity because the pure monopoly is large enough to have control over the price it charges. To sell more it must lower its price, and this implies that marginal revenue is less than average revenue. Marginal revenue (MR) is shown in *Figure I*. The monopolist produces the quantity where marginal cost (unchanged from the purely competitive situation) equals marginal revenue. It produces quantity Q_m and charges price P_m.

Comparing the equilibrium conditions of the purely competitive industry with those of the monopolistic industry, we find that the monopoly produces less of the product and charges a higher price. Is this bad? The answer is yes, because monopoly reduces society's welfare as compared to what it might have been if pure competition

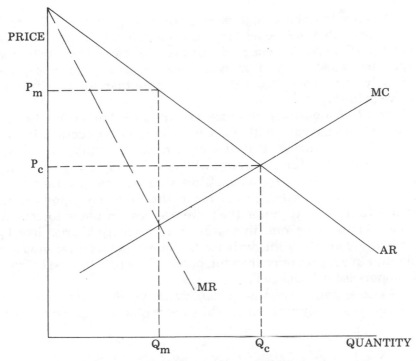

CONTRAST OF EQUILIBRIUM CONDITIONS BETWEEN
PURE COMPETITION AND PURE MONOPOLY
FIGURE I

existed. To understand this, assume that the only cost to society of
producing this product is that experienced by the firm. This being
the case, the marginal cost curve shows the cost to society of
producing additional units of the product. The average revenue
curve, on the other hand, shows the value to society of having the
product. (It indicates what each unit is worth to society by showing
how much individuals are willing to pay for the product.) To maximize society's welfare the product should be produced up to the
point where its value just equals its cost. The purely competitive
industry does this, but the pure monopoly produces less than the
optimum quantity. Therefore, the welfare of society can be increased
by moving from pure monopoly toward pure competition.[1]

The reader might ask if there are any exceptions to this conclusion. The conclusion is always correct if the marginal cost curve for
the monopoly is identical to that for the purely competitive firm,
but this condition is not always true. Suppose that the monopolist
experiences higher marginal costs of production. Then he would

produce even less and charge even more than is shown in *Figure I*. But suppose that by being large the monopolist is able to take advantage of decreasing marginal and average costs of production as output increases. Then if marginal cost goes down enough, the monopoly may charge less and produce more than the purely competitive industry.

Figure II demonstrates this case. On the graph the monopolist has decreasing average costs with a larger quantity of production. In fact he is still experiencing it at the equilibrium quantity, Q_m. Each purely competitive firm, however, will produce only a small quantity like Q_c. Thus the purely competitive firm will be operating on a higher part of the average cost curve than the pure monopolist. Because firms have to cover their average cost in order to stay in business in the long run, they will have to charge a price like P_c shown in *Figure II*. In this instance the purely competitive situation will result in a higher price than the purely monopolistic case because the monopolist will charge P_m.

This exception occurs when a *natural monopoly* exists. A firm has a natural monopoly when it exhibits decreasing average costs up to

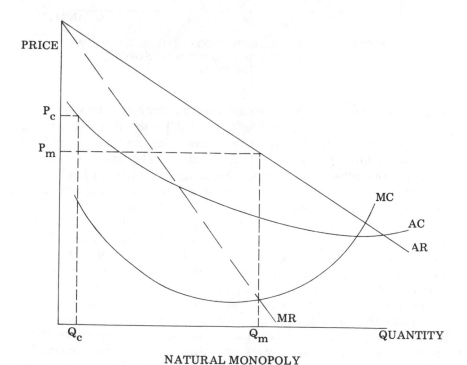

NATURAL MONOPOLY
FIGURE II

the quantity produced for the entire market. These are prevalent in the U.S. economy, but they are generally regulated industries like telephones, electricity, and water. Therefore, although natural monopolies represent an exception to the rule established earlier, most are already regulated and do not usually come under antitrust litigation. The great majority of businesses analyzed in antitrust cases fall under the normal categories of increasing cost, constant cost, or decreasing cost industries where costs do not decrease enough to make the firm a natural monopoly.

Monopolies cause reductions in economic welfare in other ways besides charging higher prices and restricting output. Because the monopolist produces less than the socially optimum quantity, it hires fewer factors of production. The problem here is that the monopolistic industry may be the most efficient place for factors of production to work. Yet, if output is restricted, the factors will have to be employed elsewhere, causing a reduction in the overall productivity of the economy.

Additionally, the monopolist probably will not produce where average total cost is at its lowest point. The reader will remember from the last chapter that in the long run, the purely competitive firm produces where average total cost is at its lowest point. This implies that the firm utilizes the optimum-sized plant in the most efficient manner such that if it produces either more or less, its average cost would rise. The monopolist, because of the absence of competitive pressures, may produce anywhere on the average cost curve depending on the demand for his product. This means that he may waste resources which could be used to make the economy more productive.

We have seen that the pure monopolist can place society in an undesirable position. There is, then, a sound basis for being against monopolies. Furthermore, the reader should remember that the conclusions shown here are applicable to any comparison of a less competitive situation with a more competitive situation.

PARETIAN OPTIMALITY AND PURE COMPETITION

The second approach demonstrating the advantages of competition centers on the idea that in order to have economic efficiency several conditions must be satisfied. Only pure competition will satisfy all the conditions. Economic efficiency is defined as a situation where no individual in society can be made better off materially without making another individual worse off. To achieve economic efficiency members of society must make adjustments which improve the welfare of one or more of its members without harming another member. When all such adjustments have been made, the economy is termed "efficient" in the economic sense.

Beyond this point further adjustments will harm one segment of society and benefit another segment. Since the utility functions of different individuals or groups of individuals are unknown, it is impossible to say whether the net effect on society of further adjustments is good or bad without making value judgments. The economist does not consider such adjustments within the scope of economic policy.[2]

Vilfredo Pareto introduced the concept of economic efficiency which has come to be called Paretian Optimality. The conditions for Paretian Optimality are:

1. The marginal rate of substitution between any two commodities must be the same for any two customers.
2. The marginal rate of technical substitution between any two inputs must be the same for any pair of producers.
3. The marginal rate of substitution between any two commodities must be the same as the marginal rate of transformation between these two commodities for any producer.

Each of these will be considered in turn.

The first condition requires that consumers hold a combination of various commodities such that they no longer have an inducement to trade with other consumers. For example, suppose Frank values product x twice as much as product y. Suppose, on the other hand, that Alfred thinks that x's and y's have the same value. Welfare could be increased by Frank giving y's to Alfred in exchange for x's. The trading should continue until the two consumers place the same value on the two products. Another way of stating this is to say that in equilibrium their marginal rates of substitution (MRS) are equal where marginal rate of substitution means the value of one good in terms of another.

The situation is shown graphically in *Figure III* with the aid of an Edgeworth Box Diagram. Suppose Frank and Alfred each has a set of indifference curves for coats and oranges.[3] Frank's indifference curves start at the origin Y. Curves shown moving away from Y indicate higher levels of utility. Coats are shown on the vertical axis and oranges on the horizontal axis. The slope of an indifference curve at any point is the marginal rate of substitution of oranges for coats. Alfred's indifference curves start at the origin Z. Curves further away from Z indicate higher levels of satisfaction. The slope

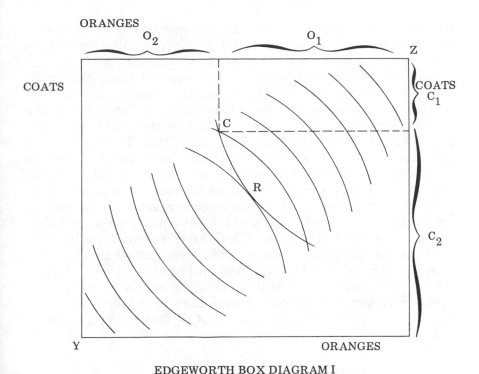

ORANGES

EDGEWORTH BOX DIAGRAM I
FIGURE III

of Alfred's indifference curves at any point also indicates the marginal rate of substitution of oranges for coats. The dimensions of the box show the available quantities of coats and oranges to be divided between both consumers.

Suppose the two consumers are located at point C on the graph. At this point Frank buys O_2 of oranges and C_2 of coats and Alfred buys O_1 of oranges and C_1 of coats. Have the two consumers fulfilled the first condition for Paretian Optimality? The answer is "no." Since the slopes of the two indifference curves are not equal, the marginal rates of substitution of the two consumers are not equal, and it will pay them to trade.

Consider a movement to point R. This would require that Frank give up some coats for more oranges and Alfred give up some oranges for more coats. Frank stayed on the same indifference curve when moving to R, meaning he neither gained nor lost from the transaction. Alfred, on the other hand, did gain by moving to a higher indifference curve. At point R the slopes of Frank's and Alfred's indifference curves are equal so their marginal rates of substitution are equal. The two consumers have maximized their welfare as evidenced by the fact that the marginal rate of substitution between coats and oranges is the same for our two consumers.

Pure competition insures that consumers will satisfy this condition. The purely competitive firm charges the same price to every consumer. Each consumer will maximize his welfare by buying a combination of two goods where his indifference curve is just tangent to his budget constraint.[4] This means that the slope of each individual's indifference curve is equal to the slope of the budget constraint. If each individual pays the same price for the goods, the slopes of their indifference curves must therefore be equal in equilibrium. Since the slope of all indifference curves will be the same in equilibrium, their marginal rates of substitution will be equal. This is shown in *Figure IV*. The slope of line AB represents the ratio of the prices of the two goods. Since the indifference curves are tangent to it at point R, both individuals have an incentive to move to that point. It is important to note that market structures other than pure competition may well permit the same thing. The only requirement necessary to satisfy this condition is that all consumers pay identical prices for a product.

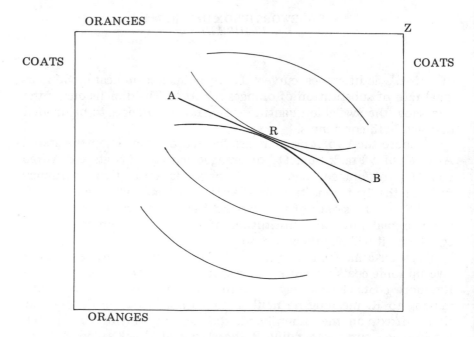

EDGEWORTH BOX DIAGRAM II
FIGURE IV

The second condition for Paretian Optimality is that the marginal rate of technical substitution between any two factors of production must be the same for any two producers purchasing the factors. This condition emphasizes production instead of consumption, but is similar to the first condition. Producers buy factors of production instead of final products. The value of a factor to them is its marginal product; i.e., the additional output of a final product resulting from the use of the factor. The marginal rate of technical substitution describes the quantity of one factor of production that can be exchanged for another while holding output of the final product constant. Suppose Firm A knows that in the production of its product three workers have the same output as one acre of land. On the other hand, suppose that Firm B knows that in the production of its product one worker has the same output as one acre of land. B is indifferent to workers and land, but A prefers land because it is more productive in the manufacturing of its product. Clearly it would pay Firm A to exchange workers for land until the marginal rates of technical substitution between the two firms are equal.

For a graphical approach, mentally substitute two factors of production for the two products in *Figure III*. An indifference curve for factors of production is called an isoquant and its slope is the marginal rate of technical substitution. When the isoquants for the two firms are just tangent, the second Paretian Optimality condition is satisfied. This condition will again be satisfied under conditions of pure competition since factor prices are the same for all producers. The marginal rate of technical substitution will be the same for all producers, and this will insure that factors of production are used in the most productive manner. Pure competition may not be necessary to satisfy this condition.

The third condition for Paretian Optimality requires that the marginal rate of substitution between any two commodities be the same as the marginal rate of transformation between these two commodities for any given producer.

A product transformation curve shows various combinations of two goods that can be produced, assuming full employment, optimum use of resources and a given state of technology. Its slope shows the amount of one good that has to be given up in order to produce an additional unit of the other good. This is called the marginal rate of transformation (MRT).

A product transformation curve (AB), and a series of indifference curves for one individual (I_1, I_2) are shown in *Figure V*. The optimum level of production is at point T because this allows the individual to reach the highest indifference curve possible. At point T

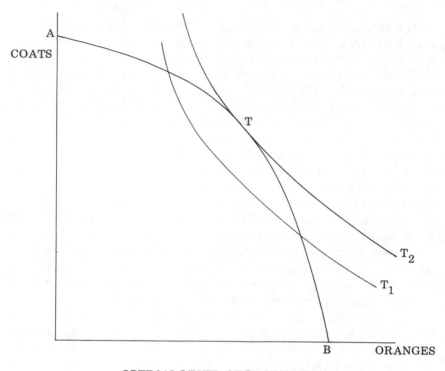

OPTIMAL LEVEL OF PRODUCTION
FIGURE V

the indifference curve is just tangent to the product transformation curve making the marginal rate of substitution equal to the marginal rate of transformation. This is just a fancy way of saying that society is producing a certain quantity of various products such that the consumer's demands are met in the best way possible. It is not difficult to extend this analysis to two or more consumers when you realize that because of the first Paretian Optimality condition, all consumers in equilibrium have the same marginal rate of substitution for any two products.

The following analysis shows how only in pure competition will this condition be met. Once again, the marginal rate of transformation shows how much of one good must be given up in order to produce a unit of another good. It also shows the marginal cost of one good divided by the marginal cost of the other good. To see this assume that the marginal cost of producing coats is $5.00 and the marginal cost of producing oranges is $2.50. To produce an additional unit of C would cost $5.00. In terms of O, however, it would cost 2 O's (2 × $2.50). Hence the marginal rate of transformation between C and O is 2:1 which is equal to the ratio of their marginal costs: \$5.00:\$2.50. Thus the marginal rate of transformation of C for O is equal to $\dfrac{MC_C}{MC_O}$.

Remember from the last chapter that in equilibrium, the purely competetive firm produces where marginal cost equals price (average revenue). We therefore know that $\dfrac{MC_C}{MC_O} = \dfrac{P_C}{P_O}$. We also know that the consumer will choose an equilibrium position such that the marginal rate of substitution for goods C and O will be equal to $\dfrac{P_C}{P_O}$ so only pure competition will insure that:

$$\text{MRT of C for O} = \frac{MC_C}{MC_O} = \frac{P_C}{P_O} = \text{MRS of C for O}$$

meaning that in equilibrium the marginal rate of substitution between any two commodities is the same as the marginal rate of transformation between these two commodities for any producer. Pure competition is the only market structure which can bring about the third Paretian Optimality condition because it is the only market structure where price equals marginal cost in equilibrium.

When monopoly elements forestall the attainment of Paretian Optimality they cause misallocation of factors of production and final products. This results in overall inefficiency in the economy, and it is for this reason that economists dislike monopolies.

Two reservations should be made about our analysis of the Paretian Optimality conditions. First, if one of the three conditions cannot be satisfied in any market, it is not necessarily advantageous to satisfy the other two conditions. Second, Paretian Optimality analysis is subject to the assumption that no external economies or diseconomies exist. Both of these reservations will be explained in turn.

The "theory of second best" states that "It is not true that a situation in which more, but not all, of the optimum conditions are fulfilled is necessarily, or is even likely to be, superior to a situation in which fewer are fulfilled."[5] A simple example will clarify this idea. Suppose that all firms in an economy have monopoly power such that they produce an output where marginal cost is less than price. If we alter one of those firms by having it produce where marginal cost equals price, we probably will reduce rather than increase economic efficiency. The change will result in a redistribution of resources to the altered firm. If increasing costs exist, this can allocate too many resources to that firm and too few to the remaining ones such that overall efficiency is decreased. The implication of the theory of second best is that piecemeal adjustments in the economy are not always beneficial to society. Yet because it is impossible to evaluate the overall performance of the economy at one time, we have the alternative of making piecemeal adjustments or no adjustments at all. Given that choice the government and most economists have decided to make adjustments through our antitrust laws, but the reader should be warned that theoretically we are on dangerous ground when doing this.

A favorable external economy is a favorable effect on one or more persons or firms arising from the actions of other persons or firms. An unfavorable external economy is the same thing except that it involves an unfavorable effect. For Paretian Optimality conditions to hold—even under pure competition—external economics must not exist. The optimality conditions are based on the assumption that the cost curves and demand curves of a firm reflect the total cost and benefit to society of producing a product. Yet when favorable or unfavorable economies exist, they do not. For instance, a factory emits black smoke from its plant. The smoke gets on the clothes of local residents and causes the clothes to darken. Clearly one of the costs of production is the discomfort the residents receive. Yet this is not included in the costs of production of the firm. In this case society's costs differ from the individual firm's costs. Imagine another case—this one involving demand. Person A buys a new Rolls Royce and parks it in front of his house. The presence of the car makes the neighborhood look prestigeous and improves the welfare of A's neighbors by increasing property values. Clearly the satisfaction that the neighbors receive from A's car is not reflected in A's demand curve for the car. Hence the demand curve does not reflect the total satisfaction that society gets from the automobile. Only when no externalities exist can Paretian Optimality be achieved because only then do the cost and demand curves reflect society's cost and benefit.

COMPETITION AND ECONOMIC FREEDOM

Most economists value competition because it provides for an efficient use of resources. Yet some economists and many lawyers value it for quite a different reason. In their opinion competition promotes democracy in the marketplace. One of the characteristics of strong competition is relatively free entry of new firms into an industry. This competition allows individuals who want to engage in a certain business to do so provided they have the "know how" and the financial resources required. Monopolies, on the other hand, restrict entry and curb the opportunity of the individual wanting to engage in business. Thomas C. Clark is a leading proponent of the preservation of competition to maintain democracy in the marketplace. This former Associate Justice of the Supreme Court has said that, "The philosophy of the antitrust laws is that the freedom of every person to carry on the business of his choice is the nature of a personal liberty as much as a property right . . . the enactment of the antitrust and trade regulation laws is the answer of Congress to this problem."[6]

Very few people would deny the desirability of allowing individuals the right to compete. However, this objective might come in conflict with the preservation of economic efficiency. Should we, in the name of democracy, allow a firm to continue to produce even if it is inefficient? To do so will maintain democracy in the marketplace, but the consumer suffers by paying higher prices to support the inefficient firm. The answer involves a value judgment, but we will consider it as we study the decisions of the courts.

THE ADVANTAGES OF COMPETITION—
A SUMMARY

Competitive pressure places the firm in a position where it has to be responsive to the needs of consumers. If it is not responsive, the consumer can always turn to an alternative source for a product. Hence, competition forces the businessman to offer his product at a relatively low price or to offer some other important inducement to the consumer. Moreover, competitive pressure forces the businessman to seek an efficient method of producing his product. By offering both low price and efficient production the businessman promotes the efficient allocation of resources and permits us to get the most out of our economy. Finally, competition helps to insure that democracy exists in the marketplace—both for the producer and the consumer. Alternatively, the absence of competition implies that the consumer will not get as much for his dollars and that there is less reason to expect resources to be allocated efficiently.

THE DISADVANTAGES OF COMPETITION

Not all individuals support the conclusions of Paretian Optimality analysis, and not all believe that the existing monopoly power in the

United States should be reduced. Those that have explored the advantages of monopoly offer some cogent arguments for their side which deserve consideration.[7] The leading arguments in support of a significant degree of monopoly power are:

1. Firms with monopoly power provide invention and innovation to aid in the development of our economy.
2. Large firms experience economies of scale, and
3. The cost of eliminating or reducing monopoly exceeds the benefits received from dissolution of firms.

Before going further, the first two arguments should be clarified. Their proponents do not argue for monopoly power *per se*. In the great majority of cases they argue for bigness, and although bigness need not imply monopoly power, it frequently does. The point is that when proponents of large firms defend the benefits arising from them, they generally recognize that monopoly power can accompany bigness. However, they contend that the advantages of bigness will more than offset any disadvantages resulting from monopoly power.

ADVANTAGES OF INVENTION AND INNOVATION

Both J. Kenneth Galbraith and the late Joseph Schumpeter have argued that most of the innovation and invention in this country has arisen from the actions of large firms. They have further argued that if the size of these firms is reduced (to reduce monopoly power), the invention and innovation will be retarded. Explaining his argument, Schumpeter said,

> As soon as we go into details and inquire into the individual items in which progress was most conspicuous, the trail leads not to the doors of those firms that work under conditions of comparatively free competition but precisely to the doors of the large concerns—which, as in the case of agricultural machinery, also accounts for much of the progress in the competitive sector—a shocking suspicion draws upon us that big business may have had more to do with creating that standard of life than with keeping it down.[8]

Galbraith projected the same opinion when he said that

> ... a benign Providence who, so far, has loved us for our worries, has made the modern industry of a few large firms an almost perfect instrument for inducing technical change. It is admirably equipped for financing technical

change. Its organization provides strong incentives for undertaking development and for putting it into use. The competition of the competitive model, by contrast, almost completely precludes technical development.[9]

Schumpeter and Galbraith base their thesis on two major arguments. (1) Monopoly power may allow a firm to earn excess profits which can be used for invention and innovation. (2) Monopoly power allows a firm a greater return on new technological development. This, in turn, can provide incentive to offer invention and innovation.

Admittedly, many large corporations have developed significant inventions. And most likely those firms making monopoly profits are better able to afford research and development. Additionally, the argument that monopoly power promotes innovation would seem, at least at face value, to have some validity. To understand this argument, remember that the pure monopolist will have no one in his industry copying his invention. Therefore he will receive all of the profits arising from it. Even an oligopolistic industry with few firms has a great incentive to innovate because even though the invention will be copied by competitors, it will still be shared by relatively few firms. On the other hand, the competitive firm will have its invention copied by many competitors, and because there are so many of them the returns will be small for each competitor.[10]

None of these arguments, however, implies that the small firm engaged in fierce competition does not have an incentive to innovate and invent. There is generally a time lag between the time one firm puts an invention on the market and the time when its competitors copy it. During that lag the competitor can make profits, and the longer this time period the stronger his incentive to invent and innovate. Additionally, some inventions are subject to patent law which will extend the inventor's return on his discovery. Competitors have other incentives to invent. The lazy firm which does not come up with new ideas while its competitors do, can lose profits. Pride in the firm can also act as a tremendous stimulus of invention. The point is that there is no reason to suspect that small firms will not come up with new inventions and innovations.

Empirical evidence is the best source to turn to for an answer to the question, "is bigness required for invention and innovation?" We will see that the results of studies are somewhat conflicting, and thus we will not get a clear-cut answer. Frederic Scherer studied over three hundred of the largest firms in the United States and found that as the size of a firm increased, the *percentage* of its income going into research and development decreased.[11] Whereas Scherer

emphasized the input end of the question, Edwin Mansfield emphasized the output side and determined that as a firm grows larger its
inventive output decreases.[12] Jewkes, Sawers, and Stillerman found
that in absolute terms the number of inventions coming from large
corporations did not seem significant. In their study of the sixty
most important inventions, it was concluded that more than one half
came from independent inventors, less than one half came from
corporations and of that half, a significant amount was done by small
corporations.[13]

So far the evidence is against the Schumpeter-Galbraith thesis.
However, there is some evidence to support the thesis. Nelson, Peck,
and Kalachek found that firms with more than 5,000 employees
accounted for 87 percent of all industrial R&D expenditures. They
also found that "Larger firms also spend more on R&D as a fraction
of sales. In 1961 the giants—those employing more than 5,000
persons—spent an average of 5.2 percent of their sales on R&D; firms
in the 1,000 - 5,000 range averaged 2.2 percent and firms with less
than 1,000 employees, 2.0 percent."[14] In addition, they found that
for firms which employed more than 5,000 people there is no
tendency of the ratio of R&D to sales to increase as the firm
becomes larger.[15] This would imply that for firms with up to 5,000
employees there is additional R&D effort as a percentage of sales,
but past that level the trend does not continue.

These studies represent only a small sampling on this topic.
Further analysis would indicate that researchers have problems determining how to measure bigness, how to measure invention and
innovation, what years of study are the most appropriate, etc. Yet
even these conflicting studies allow us to make an important conclusion. Sometimes big business, even when accompanied by monopoly
power, provides important inventions and innovations and when
antitrust policy results in the division of this business, that creative
activity may be stifled. Likewise, not all big business is creative and
hence it is not valid to protect all monopolies on the grounds that
creativity will be stifled.

ADVANTAGES FROM ECONOMIES OF
SCALE

Firms may experience economies of scale in the long run, meaning that as they become larger their average costs decrease. This can
occur for two reasons: (1) As the firm becomes larger, the factors of

production become more specialized or (2) technological equipment can be used by a large firm that cannot be used in a small one.

If economies of scale exist, a number of effects on consumers can occur within the economy. Three general effects are worth enumerating for they affect the manner in which an antitrust case should be handled. While discussing them, we will assume that economies of scale were not attained at the expense of competition.

A. If economies of scale exist and the firm faces strong competitive pressure, the advantages of reduced costs can be passed on to the consumer. This will allow each consumer to increase his material well-being.

B. If economies of scale exist but the firm has no competitive pressures, it can continue to charge a monopoly price and pocket the cost savings itself. While this benefits the producer, it does little for consumer welfare.

C. If economies of scale exist up to the equilibrium quantity of the good produced, the firm, even if it is a monopolist, will charge a lower price and offer a greater quantity than the purely competitive firm. This is the case of the "natural monopoly" which we discussed earlier in this chapter.

If case "A" holds, the consumer benefits from economies of scale, and antitrust cases of this nature would be endorsed by the antitrust authorities as well as economists. If case "B" holds, the position of antitrust authorities would probably be neutral. Since the monopolist did not raise his price, consumers were not hurt as a result of the economies. If case "C" holds, the firm would probably be declared a public utility and put under the supervision of a regulatory board.

The problem is that instances do not always fall into one of the three cases because economies of scale are sometimes attained at the expense of competition. Imagine a situation where two competing firms merged together with resulting economies of scale. If the merger created no additional monopoly power, then consumers could benefit from the reduced costs by paying lower prices. On the other hand, if the merger created monopoly power, the consumer might have to pay a higher price even though costs were reduced.

No one will argue that some large firms experience economies of scale and when being large does not affect competition adversely, all economists would endorse it. Yet when bigness creates monopoly power, proper antitrust policy requires that the benefits from the economies be weighed against the harm resulting from the increased monopoly power. This is a difficult task.

A COST BENEFIT ANALYSIS

Some economists believe that the cost of making firms more competitive would exceed consumer benefits from the adjustment. Professor Arnold Harberger studied the question in the late 1920s and estimated that the cost to the consumer resulting from monopoly elements in the economy was 59 million dollars. He updated the figure into 1954 terms and found that the loss would be 225 million dollars or less than $1.50 for each individual in the United States.[16] Harold Hotelling performed a similar analysis in 1938 and arrived at about the same conclusion.[17] Based on these two estimates it seems reasonable to ask whether antitrust enforcement is worth the effort.

Only recently have estimates of the costs of monopoly been made that reverse the trend of the evidence. Howard Frazier, former President of the Consumer Federation of America said:

> Ralph Nader has estimated that the consumer is overcharged by $100 billion or more each year—some 20 percent of every dollar spent. Senator Hart has recently put the figure at 35 percent to 40 percent—that is between $170 billion and $230 billion per year.[18]

Neither source has explained in any detail their estimates' derivation which leaves reasonable doubt as to whether the statistics are creditable.

Professor Frederic M. Scherer recently estimated that the welfare loss was about $60 billion in 1966 or about 6.2 percent of national income.[19] The loss was attributed to the sum of (1) a misallocation of resources, (2) price distortions in the regulated sector of the economy, (3) additional costs of firms which are not under competitive pressure to regulate costs, (4) inefficiencies from a lack of cost control by defense and space contractors, (5) wasteful promotional efforts, (6) hauling costs associated with "distorted locational decisions," (7) inefficiency due to cartelization and (8) "operation at less than optimal scale for reasons other than differentiation serving special demands."[20]

Shortly after Scherer's estimate was published, consumer advocates used it as ammunition. However, Professor Scherer was careful to explain that the making of such an estimate was a "subjective task." Furthermore, he observed that:

> ... it seems improbable that the "true" combined social cost of monopoly, if it could be ascertained, would prove to be less than half or more than twice the estimated total

of 6.2 percent. Wherever the true figure lies within this range of uncertainty, the static inefficiency burden of monopoly does not appear to be overwhelming. But it is also not so slight that it can be ignored.[21]

Another measure of the harm resulting from monopoly power (although an indirect measure) is consumer prices. No one has determined, on the average, how much higher monopolistic prices are than competitive ones, but individual cases provide some insight. Charles E. Mueller, a man skilled in both law and economics, said that in a case involving price-fixing in the sale of stadium bleachers, prices dropped by 32 percent after the conspiracy was ended. After the termination of a price-fixing scheme among bakers in the state of Washington, prices declined almost 20 percent. Prices fell about 75 percent after a conspiracy in the fixing of prices for the antibiotic drug, tetracycline was ended.[22]

One of the sources of monopoly power is consumer brand attachment which is accomplished by advertising. Once consumers develop a strong brand attachment to a product, the producer gains monopoly power and can exercise it by charging higher prices. To see that higher prices result from brand attachment compare the prices charged for a "brand name" product with the prices charged by national chains who put their own name on a product. In many cases the product is produced for the chain by a leading company which also sells under its own brand name. Often the products sold to the chain are identical to those sold under the brand name. Table I contrasts prices charged by A&P, a national chain store, with prices charged by firms who have established some consumer attachment to their product. The prices are furnished by A&P and thus should not be taken as "scholarly proof." Nor should they be construed as an advertisement for A&P. The reader will notice that the prices charged by the "brand name" product range from 17.4 percent to 48.4 percent higher than the private-brand prices. Mueller concludes from this analysis that "on the average, 20 percent more [is paid] for the 'brand' products than for the functionally-equivalent but unadvertised private brand goods."[23]

The cost of eliminating monopoly is just as difficult to measure as the cost of allowing it. Assuming that the job is to be done through the use of antitrust laws, additional legislation would probably be necessary. In addition there would be a significant outlay for prosecutors, defendants' attorneys, and corporate and industry analyists. We have already seen that by dissolving big business, invention and

Table 1

Comparative Prices of Manufacturer Brand and Private Label Products, Selected Items, A&P Stores in Washington, D.C., June 10, 1970

Product	"Brand" Product	A&P "Private Label"	Price Difference	Percentage Difference in Price
Laundry Bleach	59¢	45¢	14¢	23.7%
(Gallon Bottle)	(Clorox)	(A&P)		
Scouring Pads	49¢	39¢	10¢	20.4%
(18 in pkg.)	(Brillo)	(A&P)		
Window Cleaner	33¢	27¢	6¢	18.2%
(8oz.)	(Windex)	(A&P)		
Aluminum Foil	65¢	46¢	18¢	27.7%
(18 in. x 25 ft. roll)	(Reynold's)	(A&P)		
Cleanser	2/37¢	2/25¢	12¢	32.4%
(18 oz.)	(Comet)	(Sail)		
Furniture Polish	95¢	49¢	46¢	48.4%
(7 oz. spray can-lemon)	(Pledge)	(A&P)		
Liquid Detergent	57¢	43¢	14¢	24.6%
(22 oz. plastic)	(Ivory)	(Sail)		
Spray Disinfectant	85¢	59¢	26¢	30.6%
(7 oz. can)	(Lysol)	(A&P)		
Golden Cream Corn	29¢	20¢	9¢	31.0%
(17 oz. can)	(Del Monte)	(A&P)		
Canned Dog Food	6/88¢	6/65¢	23¢	26.1%
(15½ oz. can)	(Ken-L-Ration)	(Daily)		
Mouthwash	89¢	59¢	30¢	33.7%
(14 oz. bottle)	(Listerine)	(A&P)		
(12 oz. bottle)	89¢	59¢	30¢	33.7%
	(Scope)	(A&P)		
Spray Deodorant	$1.19	69¢	50¢	42.0%
(7 oz. can)	(Right Guard)	(A&P)		
Liquid Shampoo	95¢	59¢	36¢	37.9%
(8 oz. bottle)	(Breck)	(A&P)		
Shave Cream	95¢	49¢	46¢	48.4%
(11 oz. can)	(Rapid Shave)	(A&P)		
Toothpaste	55¢	29¢	29¢	47.3%
(3.25 oz., with fluoride)	(Colgate)	(A&P)		
Instant Coffee	$1.15	93¢	20¢	17.4%
(6 oz. jar)	(Maxwell House)	(A&P)		
Instant Breakfast	75¢	49¢	26¢	34.7%
(6 envelope pkg.)	(Carnation)	(A&P)		
Pancake Mix	29¢	18¢	11¢	37.9%
(1 lb.)	(Aunt Jemima)	(Sunnyfield)		
Tomato Ketchup	2/59¢	2/43¢	16¢	27.1%
(14 oz. bottle)	(Heinz)	(Ann Page)		
Mayonnaise	79¢	49¢	30¢	37.9%
(Quart jar)	(Kraft)	(Ann Page)		

Source: A&P Advertisement, *Washington Post*, June 10, 1970, reprinted in *Antitrust Law and Economics Review*, III, (Spring 1970), 108.

innovation might be retarded as well as some advantages of economies of scale. And, unless the process is handled gradually there would probably be a significant impact on the general level of U.S. economic activity. Economic activity is based largely on incentives for business, and these would be retarded through mass antitrust prosecution.

We set out to determine whether the costs of monopoly exceeded the costs of ending monopoly. The studies cited do not really answer our question because neither cost can be measured. Yet something can be gained from the analysis. Remember that all of the studies of the costs of monopoly presented here were performed after antitrust legislation was passed. Thus they do not measure the cost of monopoly in the absence of antitrust legislation. Pre-legislation estimates would almost certainly be larger because, as we shall see in Chapter V, businesses were very monopolistic prior to the passage of the Sherman Act. It will be asserted here that in general antitrust legislation and prosecution has been worth the cost. The question that cannot be answered is, "Is it *economically* sound to *increase* antitrust prosecution?" Even if this question could be answered, another thorny question arises. "In what areas should antitrust prosecution be increased and in what areas should it be decreased?" Economists and lawyers do not agree on the answer to this question. Hopefully at the end of this book the student should have formulated an answer himself.

SUMMARY

In general, competition is preferable to monopoly because competitive pressure usually forces firms to provide their product at a relatively low price or to offer the consumer some other desirable inducement. Moreover, competition usually insures that resources are used in a more efficient manner than if competition were absent.

Despite these observations, it is not always true that competition is preferable to monopoly. Even though they may have monopoly power, large firms may be inventive and innovative. Additionally, they may be able to take advantage of economies of scale. In these instances monopoly power might be desirable if some of the benefits are passed on to the consumer. While the evidence does not suggest a strong case in favor of monopoly, it is sometimes advantageous and this fact should be considered in evaluating antitrust cases.

NOTES TO CHAPTER III

[1]This is true using partial equilibrium analysis. It is not necessarily true if general equilibrium analysis is used.

[2]This statement is not completely accurate. Since 1938 economists have wrestled with the idea of an individual who has gained from an adjustment being able to compensate a harmed individual such that society can still gain from the adjustment. Among the proponents of the "compensation principle" are Nicholas Kaldor, "Welfare Propositions in Economics," *Economic Journal*, XLIX (Sept., 1939), 549-552; J. R. Hicks, "The Foundations of Welfare Economics," *Economic Journal*, XLIX (Dec., 1939), 696-712; and Tibor Scitovsky, "A Note on Welfare Propositions in Economics," *Review of Economic Studies* (Nov., 1941), 71-88.

[3]Indifference curves show various combinations of two products that yield equal satisfaction.

[4]A budget constraint shows various combinations of two products that can be purchased with a given outlay of money. The slope of the budget constraint equals the ratio of the prices of the two goods.

[5]R. Lipsey and Kelvin Lancaster, "The General Theory of Second Best," *Review of Economic Studies*, XXIV, (1956-1957), 12.

[6]Quoted in Earl W. Kintner, *An Antitrust Primer* (New York: The Macmillan Company, 1964), p. vii.

[7]They usually argue in terms of less competition versus more competition as compared to our prior comparison of pure competition versus pure monopoly. For the remainder of this chapter we will adopt this comparison of more versus less competition.

[8]Joseph A. Schumpeter, *Capitalism, Socialism, and Democracy* (New York: Harper and Brothers, 1947), p. 82.

[9]J. Kenneth Galbraith, *American Capitalism* (Boston: Houghton Mifflin Co., 1956), p. 86.

[10]This argument assumes that a large number of firms have to exist in order to have strong competition. This need not be true.

[11]Frederic M. Scherer, "Firm Size, Market Structure, Opportunity, and the Output of Patented Inventions," *American Economic Review*, 55 (December 1965), pp. 1097-1125.

[12]Edwin Mansfield, "Size of Firm, Market Structure and Innovation," *Journal of Political Economy*, LXXI (1963), 565-568.

[13]John Jewkes, David Sawers, and Richard Stillerman, *The Sources of Invention* (London: Macmillan and Co., 1958), Chapter IV.

[14]Richard Nelson, Merton Peck, and Edward Kalachek, "The Concentration of Research and Development in Large Firms," in Edwin Mansfield, *Monopoly Power and Economic Performance* (New York: W. W. Norton & Co., Inc., 1968), p. 46.

[15]*Ibid.*

[16]Arnold C. Harberger, "Monopoly and Resource Allocation," *American Economic Review*, XLIII (May 1954), 77-87, quoted in Werner Sichel, *Industrial Organization and Public Policy, Selected Readings* (Boston: Houghton Mifflin Company, 1967), p. 391.

[17]Harold Hotelling, "The General Welfare in Relation to Problems of Taxation and of Railway and Utility Rates," *Econometrica*, VI (July 1938), 242-269.

[18]Howard Frazier, "Consumers and the FTC: It Makes a Difference Who Sits on It," *Antitrust Law and Economics Review*, III, No. 3 (Spring 1970), 40.

[19]Frederic M. Scherer, *Industrial Market Structure and Economic Welfare* (New York: Random House, 1970), p. 408.

[20]*Ibid.*

[21]Scherer, p. 408.

[22]Charles E. Mueller, "Rapping the 'System': Reform or Revolution?" *Antitrust Law and Economics Review*, III (Summer 1970), 29.

[23]Mueller, p. 29.

THE
NONECONOMIC
ASPECTS
OF ANTITRUST

SECTION III

Although the major objective of antitrust policy is to promote competition, the various antitrust laws were also designed to promote noneconomic objectives. Anyone who studies antitrust should be aware of these objectives and the reasons for them if he is to understand some court decisions that have been made in antitrust cases. Moreover, he should understand that antitrust is primarily the domain of the lawyer, and lawyers often have a different attitude toward antitrust prosecution than economists. These concepts are introduced in Chapter IV.

THE NONECONOMIC ASPECTS OF ANTITRUST

CHAPTER IV

While it is important to understand the concept of competition and how it applies to the antitrust laws, it is also important to realize that antitrust is not solely an economic phenomenon. Consequently, in this chapter, we will identify some noneconomic aspects of antitrust.

INTRODUCTION

Because the major objective of the antitrust laws is to promote competition, this book is primarily devoted to the study of competitive concepts. Thus far we have discussed the meaning of competition as well as its desirability. Before focusing on the antitrust laws in earnest, we must realize that antitrust is not exclusively a study of competitive phenomena. It involves a fundamental value judgment about the definition of monopoly itself. Furthermore, it is an interdisciplinary study composed principally of law as well as economics. Finally, the antitrust laws themselves have some noneconomic objectives. A clear understanding of all of these points will help the reader avoid the needless frustration and misunderstanding which could result if he makes the assumption that antitrust is solely a study of economics. We will consider each point in turn.

THE MEANING OF MONOPOLY

We have already discussed the concept that market structure affects the degree of monopoly held by a firm. Since the antitrust laws are designed to outlaw monopoly, the reader might automatically assume, based on this prior discussion, that monopolistic market structure itself evidences monopoly power and is outlawed. Yet not everyone comes to that conclusion. In browsing through antitrust cases the reader will encounter both structuralists and behavioralists. The structuralist, whether he be lawyer or economist, tends to define monopoly based on market structure. But the behavioralist believes that monopoly is only evidenced by the use of some specific business practice which restrains trade.

An example will make the distinction clear. Most structuralists believe that an oligopolistic industry is monopolistic in nature. Many would even contend that simply because of the market structure, the firms in oligopolistic industries should be charged with monopolization. The behavioralists will rarely adopt this viewpoint. Most would only initiate a charge of monopolization when one or more of the oligopolistic firms uses an anticompetitive practice and, for the behavioralists, anticompetitive practices do not include higher-than-competitive prices or output restrictions. But when one firm uses an exclusive dealing contract (where customers have to buy all of their requirements from it in order to buy any), or if one of the firms colludes with his neighbor to fix prices, then the behavioralists will step in.[1]

The behavioralist's tendency to treat practices rather than potential to engage in those practices is consistent with many points of law. Because there are a large number of drivers in the country, each of us faces potential harm, whether it be through frustration on the freeway, the problem of finding a parking space, or the potential for an accident. But the law does not outlaw driving unless one individual uses his automobile in a negligent manner such as speeding or running a stop sign. Besides the issue of consistency, there is another reason for behavioralists' unwillingness to outlaw market structure. Both the behavioralist and the average citizen feel there is something "unfair" about penalizing a firm for its size when the firm exhibits no anticompetitive practices.

Because behavioralists do not treat industry structure, a great controversy between them and structuralists has developed which will be seen frequently in our study of antitrust. Structuralists often claim that because behavioralists only treat specific anticompetitive practices, they deal with symptoms of problems instead of their root causes. An exclusive dealing arrangement, for example, can only be utilized when some degree of monopoly power (in economic terminology) exists. To get to the root of the problem, the power has to be eliminated, not its symptom.

ANTITRUST AND THE LEGAL PROFESSION

We must realize that antitrust is an interdisciplinary study composed of law as well as economics. Although each discipline is an integral part of the study, lawyers control the lion's share.[2] That is, the formulation and execution of the antitrust laws are the lawyers' domain and only by invitation do economists enter. Lawyers control legal journals, the presentation of economic testimony in antitrust cases, the formation of the antitrust laws themselves, and the objective established by the prosecution and the defense in any antitrust case.

This is a statement of fact not a complaint. Some economists have warranted exclusion. When invited to participate in policy formulation or antitrust adjudication, they have all too often presented graphs, mathematical equations, and *ceteris paribus* statements which proved their intellectual ability instead of their helpfulness. While these concepts can be very helpful in discussions between economists, they thwart meaningful communication between lawyers and economists. An understanding that antitrust activity is not a purely economic phenomenon just as it is not a purely legal phenomenon will help readers oriented toward law alone or economics alone to avoid needless frustration and misunderstanding. Lawyers and economists do not always agree on antitrust issues. Two major differences will be emphasized here: the attitude toward precedent and the attitude toward antitrust remedies.[3]

PRECEDENT

Most economists would argue that the competitive and anticompetitive effects of each specific practice should be analyzed with the objective of determining whether its net effect harms competition or promotes it. On the other hand, lawyers frequently use legal precedent to decide a case even when legal precedent is not helpful in finding the correct issues of fact. Precedent is legal analysis and decision in one case which is used to justify decisions in later cases. For example, if the Supreme Court decided that a merger which gave the acquiring firm 50 per cent of the market was illegal *per se*, then in subsequent merger cases involving 50 per cent or more of a market, that precedent probably will be presented by the prosecution and accepted by the Court as a valid argument. That is not to say that precedent is never rejected by the courts, but such occasions are rare.

There are two major advantages of using precedent. First, it adds certainty to the law. If a firm's lawyers know the precedent established concerning specific business practices, they can, with some degree of certainty, advise their client on what it can and cannot do. Second, when precedent was correctly established in an earlier case and is applicable to a later one, justice proceeds in later cases with minimum effort. <u>The economists criticize the use of precedent because the facts in any two cases rarely coincide.</u> Consequently, an appropriate decision in one case is not necessarily appropriate in another. Only a thorough economic analysis of each individual case will insure justice. The conflict in the attitude of lawyers and economists concerning the use of precedent was ably presented by Kenneth S. Carlston, Professor of Law at the University of Illinois.

> The lawyer seeks as a basis for decision analogous precedents in which the analogous elements unifying the precedent with the situation at hand may well be derived from wholly dissimilar contexts. The precedent then becomes the rule for decision. Whether the basic economic problems are grappled with in any one case accordingly tends to be fortuitous. . . . The basic assumption of the economist is that a solution of any problem demands the investigation, weighing and analysis of all relevant data and criteria.[4]

Some economists go so far as to contend that precedent is simply a crutch which the lawyer uses in lieu of thought. Yet, the lawyer's affinity for the use of precedent cannot be dismissed that lightly. In many cases, the lawyers arguing a case as well as the judges deciding it simply do not have the expertise to evaluate economic arguments. The majority of lawyers and judges have not had a basic course in principles of economics, much less a course in industrial organization or antitrust economics. And in their defense, they probably have not had time to learn the subject in any detail since their formal education. After all, many lawyers and judges have to plead and try cases ranging from property damage to murder, and given these diverse subjects, they cannot become experts in each discipline they encounter. The lawyers and commissioners of the Federal Trade Commission and of the Antitrust Division of the Department of Justice are the only segment of the legal profession able to completely specialize in antitrust. Therefore, they should be able to gain some expertise in economic concepts.

The fact that lawyers are sometimes not equipped with adequate economic tools is the fault of the economist as well as the lawyer. The lawyer who makes an attempt to understand economics will find that many economic tools are not sufficiently refined to make the type of determinations the adjudicative process requires. This is evidenced by the fact that almost every major case involves directly conflicting economic testimony from the expert witness economists for each side.

Closely associated with the lawyer's lack of economic knowledge is the great workload placed on lawyers and judges alike. The courts are so overburdened that they frequently take legal short cuts in lieu of detailed economic analysis. And in light of the fact that cases involving economic analysis can be very time consuming, their attitude is understandable. The *Sugar Institute* trial took one year, after which the judge spent fourteen months writing his opinion. The *Alcoa* trial took two years and two months and resulted in 58,000 pages of testimony from 153 witnesses. A trial involving A&P produced 45,000 pages of testimony and 7,000 exhibits.[5] What lawyer would not be tempted to take a legal short cut when pressed from below with voluminous economic evidence and pressed from above with yet other cases to be heard. Yet the critic would be correct in saying that short cuts do not always result in correct decisions.

ANTITRUST REMEDIES

There is yet another arena in which economists and lawyers come in conflict. Economists frequently argue that the only way to end monopoly power once and for all is to alter industry structure by breaking up companies. Yet throughout the remainder of the book, the reader will see that judges have been extremely reluctant to do this. They will prevent anticompetitive mergers and will stop anticompetitive practices, but rarely will they alter market structure. Several reasons may explain this. First, it is possible that judges realize that they are ill-equipped for economic analysis and consequently, they may not have complete confidence in their decisions. This doubt may make them hesitate to throw the book at the offender. Kingman Brewster, President of Yale University, stated that "Because of human scruples rather than in spite of them, it is unrealistic to expect identifiable officials to be willing to assume responsibility beyond their competence or commission."[6] There is yet another reason for judges' reluctance to break up firms. The courts were granted a tremendous amount of power with the passage of the antitrust laws. They have the power to completely restructure our economy if they so choose. There is a natural tendency for the recipient of that power to use it sparingly. As Dr. Brewster put it,

> ... legislatures may expect that by interpretation and construction the decision-maker will himself narrow his own mandate. Feasibility argues against bestowing or accepting the moral overload of unbridled power in any

individual or unrepresentative group to settle the fate of others in terms of some undefined "public interest."[7]

NONECONOMIC OBJECTIVES OF ANTITRUST

One of the most frequent criticisms of lawyers is that they sometimes argue and decide cases on the basis of some noneconomic objective of the antitrust laws. When, as sometimes happens, the lawyer or judge invents a new antitrust objective and then decides a case on that basis, the criticism is valid. However, all too often economists have failed to realize that Congress intended for the antitrust laws to have some noneconomic objectives. And whether or not the economists consider these to be valid, they are legitimate arguments that judges and lawyers use in arguing and deciding antitrust cases. However, the reader should not get the idea that noneconomic objectives are applied in all antitrust cases. Three of the most prevalent noneconomic objectives of antitrust are to decentralize power, to protect competitors, and to promote fairness in the market place. Each of these objectives will now be considered.

DECENTRALIZED POWER

Occasionally the courts have argued against the existence of large companies because they represent power. The use of this argument by the courts resembles the economists' view of monopoly as defined in terms of industry structure. In the *Columbia Steel* decision, Justice Douglas expressed this objective:

> Industrial power should be decentralized. It should be scattered into many hands so that the fortunes of the people will not be dependent on the whim or caprice, the political prejudices, the emotional stability of a few self-appointed men. The fact that they are not vicious men but respectable and social minded is irrelevant. That is the philosophy and the command of the Sherman Act. It is founded on a theory of hostility to the concentration in private hands of power so great that only a government of the people should have it.[8]

Do economists sometimes look disdainfully on large firms for the same reason? Economists would be against large firms when the industry is so structured that the firm can charge a higher-than-competitive price and restrict output. In contrast, the framers of the antitrust laws wanted to limit firm size because they thought that large firms inhibited the personal freedom of competitors and potential competitors.

THE PROTECTION OF COMPETITORS

The desire to promote the freedom of competitors takes us into the consideration of another noneconomic objective of antitrust. While most economists believe that the major purpose of the antitrust laws should be consumer protection, many judges and lawyers believe that the framers also designed the acts to protect the rights of competitors. Foremost among those to be protected were the small businessmen, an objective established in the Robinson-Patman Act and the Celler-Kefauver Act. Their protection sometimes conflicts with the objective of preserving competition because the protection of competition and the protection of competitors does not always call for the same policy. The distinction was observed by A. D. Neale, an Englishman who performed a thorough study of the antitrust laws of the United States.

> The economists, for example, who think that the courts should decide cases solely by reference to the causes of economic progress, not only run into legal difficulties but are bound to clash with the proponents of "small business," who sometimes seem to regard the preservation of small firms as antimonopolistic *per se*. Those who want the most competition are often at odds with those who want the most competitors.[9]

Why is the protection of competitors sometimes an objective of the antitrust laws? There are two major answers. First, small business has a very strong lobby which has pressed for special favors and received them from Congress. As Neale put it, "This cause may be seen in action in the hard-headed lobby pressures which have helped to secure the virtual exemption from the Sherman Act of resale price maintenance and which have fashioned the intricacies of the Robinson-Patman (price discrimination) statute."[10] But the protectionist attitude cannot be explained wholly or even primarily in terms of political pressure. It is largely based on the philosophy for which the United States was founded, the principle of freedom for the individual. Congress has interpreted that freedom to include the right of the individual, provided that he has the necessary financial resources, to be an entrepreneur rather than an employee. Of course when he is less efficient than big business there is a large problem to resolve.

Inefficiency could drive the small competitor out of business and deny him his personal freedom. On the other hand, protection of inefficiency through antitrust laws might cause the consumer to pay high prices. Some judges and lawyers interpret the acts to mean that small business should be preserved even at the expense of efficiency. Most economists would disagree. This is an argument that is discussed in some detail in Chapter XIV and Chapter XVI.

FAIRNESS

Some judges and lawyers also believe that Congress wanted the antitrust laws to promote "fairness" in the market place. They believe that the laws not only call for strong competition but also fair competition. What is meant by "fair" varies widely, but it generally means one of two things. It may mean that the laws are against competition which drives competitors out of business. Occasionally, it has meant a firm's not charging the highest price it can receive for a product. Two examples will make these meanings clearer. The courts have occasionally disallowed pricing below cost on the grounds that it will drive competitors out of business. Yet some economists would claim that this is competition of the greatest magnitude. Some courts have disallowed a tying contract in which a seller requires the customer to buy one product if he wants to buy some other product. Some economists consider this simply to be a means of extracting the profit-maximizing price from the consumer.

SUMMARY

If an economist is to be of any help in formulating appropriate antitrust policy or in aiding in antitrust litigation, he must continue to play his strong suit, economic analysis. He is no better a lawyer than the lawyer is an economist. If he believes that the lawyer's treatment of antitrust is improper, he must continue to express his complaint as well as his remedy. But he must, at the same time, understand that lawyers have many constraints placed upon them in formulating and executing antitrust policy. In the following chapters, we will use economic analysis to evaluate the lawyers' work, and we will often find that economic analysis suggests different policies than those derived by the lawyer. The first time students analyze antitrust they have a tendency to conclude that lawyers are rather unenlightened fellows who do not care about economic analysis. While this evaluation is sometimes correct, in the great majority of instances the constraints placed upon lawyers explain why their decisions differ from those of the economist.

NOTES TO CHAPTER IV

[1]For an excellent discussion of this issue see Edward S. Mason, "Monopoly in Law and Economics," *Yale Law Journal*, XLVII (1937-38), 34-49.

[2]In this chapter the term "lawyer" will include practicing attorneys, judges, Commissioners of the Federal Trade Commission and legislators. Legislators can be included because they are predominantly lawyers.

[3]It is impossible to discuss lawyers as an entity. Obviously, each lawyer is an individual and consequently has a different attitude toward what is proper antitrust policy. Therefore as we discuss the legal viewpoint, remember that we are talking in generalities.

[4]Kenneth S. Carlston, "Antitrust Policy: A Problem in Statecraft," *Yale Law Journal*, LX (1951), 1082.

[5]Mark S. Massel, *Competition and Monopoly: Legal and Economic Issues* (Washington: The Brookings Institution, 1962), p. 145.

[6]Kingman Brewster, Jr., "Enforceable Competition: Unruly Reason or Reasonable Rules?" *American Economic Review, Papers and Proceedings*, XLVI (May, 1956), 486.

[7]*Ibid.*

[8]*U.S.* v. *Columbia Steel Co.*, 334 U.S. 495, 536 (1948).

[9]A. D. Neale, *The Antitrust Laws of the United States of America* (Cambridge: Cambridge University Press, 1970), p. 431.

[10]*Ibid.*, p. 428.

THE SHERMAN ACT
SECTION IV

The Sherman Act was the first major piece of antitrust legislation passed in the United States. A knowledge of the provisions of the act as well as the events leading up to its passage are discussed in Chapter V. Because the act requires legal interpretation by the courts, a knowledge of its provisions alone will not give much insight into what it declared illegal. Therefore, in the remaining chapters in this section, the economics and the law of business practices which have been prosecuted under the provisions of the act are discussed. Price fixing and horizontal division of territories are analyzed in Chapter VI, vertical territorial arrangements in Chapter VII, resale price maintenance in Chapter VIII, and refusals to deal in Chapter IX. While mergers are business practices prosecuted under the provisions of the Sherman Act, they will not be considered until Chapter XIII just prior to an analysis of mergers under Clayton Act provisions.

THE DEVELOPMENT
OF THE SHERMAN ACT

CHAPTER V

The Sherman Act was the first major piece of antitrust legislation in the United States. In this chapter we will consider the reasons for its passage as well as its specific provisions. Additionally we will consider the procedure which is used for its implementation in specific court cases.

INTRODUCTION

The Sherman Act of 1890 was the first major piece of antitrust legislation in the United States. However, well before 1890, common law as well as some antimonopoly legislation controlled the latitude of business operations. Unfortunately, this early law was largely ineffective in retarding the development of monopoly power in the United States, and its ineffectiveness necessitated the passage of the Sherman Act. With this act came the development of the litigation process required to prosecute antitrust violators. It is important to establish the facts mentioned above and so in this chapter we will discuss:

A. The early law on monopolies;
B. The economic conditions prior to the passage of the Sherman Act;
C. The role of economists in the passage of the Sherman Act;
D. The major provisions of the Sherman Act;
E. The litigation process involved in prosecuting firms whose actions are in violation of the Sherman Act.

A knowledge of the early law and the economic conditions prior to 1890 will partially explain why this country has antitrust legislation. Knowing the major provisions of the Sherman Act and the litigation process used to implement the act will provide facts necessary for our forthcoming analysis of antitrust cases.

THE EARLY LAW ON MONOPOLIES

Common law is not legislated. Rather, it is a body of legal traditions which are developed and applied by judges through time.

Common law began in England and was adopted and further developed in the United States. This system is based largely on "precedent" which, as we saw in Chapter IV, is the use of prior legal decisions to serve as a logic or justification for later decisions. Although it was supplemented by some legislation, common law was the major tool for antitrust prosecution prior to 1890. Both the common law and the legislation were directed against three categories of business practices:

    A. forestalling, regrating, and engrossing;

    B. monopoly grants by royalty to firms;

    C. restraints of trade and conspiracies to monopolize.

FORESTALLING, REGRATING AND ENGROSSING

As early as 1263, there were three business practices which were outlawed by common law: forestalling, regrating, and engrossing. Forestalling is the act of purchasing goods that were en route to market with intent to resell them in the market. Regrating is the act of purchasing goods in a market with the sole intent to resell these goods within the same market. Regrating and forestalling differ only in the sense that the first involves buying prior to the time goods reach a market, and the latter involves buying in the market itself. Engrossing is the act of buying goods in large quantities at the wholesale level of distribution with intent to resell them at the same level.

In the thirteenth century, the Church considered wholesalers and retailers to be social outcasts because they did not produce a tangible product. Of course, this attitude was unwarranted. Why would a producer sell to a middleman instead of directly to the consumer? The answer is that the middleman provides some services to the producer. However, forestalling, regrating, and engrossing could create monopoly power by restricting supply and, as time passed, the courts put more emphasis on this argument as the reason for declaring the practices illegal. It is interesting to note that the law was strictly applied in times of economic depression and leniently applied in times of economic plenty and that common law was directed against these practices as late as 1844.

MONOPOLY GRANTS

Prior to 1602, the King and Queen of England had complete control over trade. One outlet for their power was the granting of "monopolies" or "patents." These gave a business the exclusive right to manufacture a product. Monopolies and patents were not always awarded for innovation and invention. Instead, they sometimes were distributed by royalty to good friends or to individuals willing to pay for them.

In 1602, the Queen's right to grant monopolies was challenged in *Darcy* v. *Allen*.[1] The Queen favored Darcy with a patent on playing cards. Allen, wishing to manufacture the cards, argued that the patent was unjust because it discriminated against him. Parliament agreed that it was illegal for the Queen to grant a monopoly by either selling a patent or giving it as a friendly gesture. Therefore, Darcy lost his patent rights. However, Parliament's decision was based more on a desire to rebuke the Queen than a desire to protect either the rights of Allen or the consumer. In fact, only a few years later, a monopoly was granted by Parliament itself to the Company of Card Makers. The Statute of Monopolies, passed in 1624 by Parliament, reiterated the idea that the Queen did not have the power to arbitrarily grant patents to favored companies.

RESTRAINTS OF TRADE AND CONSPIRACIES TO MONOPOLIZE

Common law denounced conspiracies to monopolize as well as restraints of trade. However, the courts never fully agreed on what constituted a conspiracy or a restraint. What is certain is that their interpretation of the law demonstrated a greater concern for the rights of businessmen than for those of the consuming public. For example, several court decisions outlawed monopoly power because it gave an unfair advantage to one firm over another and not because the consumer was harmed by the practice of monopoly. As Einhorn and Smith said, "Considerations of public interest were restricted to instances of an individual loss of support [income] rather than to market control. Thus the tendency of domestic courts to view contracts in restraint of trade as evidence of monopoly power required a modification of traditional law."[2]

In early common law all agreements wherein the parties contracted not to compete with one another were declared unlawful. However, in the 18th century, courts began to distinguish between "reasonable" and "unreasonable" restraints of trade. Reasonable restraints were limited to those that were ancillary to some justified business objective. In other words the restraint is necessary to enable a businessman to attain a justified objective. These restraints were allowed while unreasonable restraints of trade were declared illegal.

There are many cases in common law which can be used to illustrate the distinction between reasonable and unreasonable restraints of trade. One of the oldest cases was *Mitchel* v. *Reynolds*, decided in 1713.[3] Mitchel rented a bakery in central London from Reynolds for a period of seven years. Reynolds agreed that he would not reestablish himself as a baker in central London for the duration of the contract. If he violated the contract, he was liable to pay a sum of money to Mitchel. Reynolds did establish a bakery in central London and argued that he had this right because the contract he entered into was in restraint of trade. The court introduced a rule to determine whether the contract was reasonable. For a restraint of trade to be reasonable, the court thought that it must be *specific* on two counts: the geographical location of the restraint and the duration of the contract. Applying the rule, the court found that Reynolds was only restricted from competing in central London and then only for a period of seven years. The court upheld the contract.

The decision had merit, because when Mitchel rented Reynolds' bakery, he also was renting the good will which had been established by Reynolds. Had Reynolds been allowed to compete in close proximity to Mitchel, the good will would have been transferred back to Reynolds. The reader should note that although the decision appears to have been a just one, it was decided in terms of the rights of the two competitors, not the rights of the consumer.

In *Alger* v. *Thacker*, heard in 1837 in Massachusetts, the common law on reasonable and unreasonable restraints of trade was further clarified.[4] Alger and Thacker made an agreement in iron production similar to that of Mitchel and Reynolds. To decide the reasonableness of the contract, the court asked two questions: (1) Is the agreement voluntary or involuntary? (2) Is the agreement general or specific with respect to time and place? If all parties agreed to the contract, it was termed "voluntary." If all did not agree, then the contract was unreasonable. If the contract was a voluntary one, the courts then determined whether it was general or specific with regard to time and place. For example, if someone agrees never to sell iron goods, they have illegally made a general contract. If on the other hand, the contract only limits competition in a certain geographical area for a specified period of time, the arrangement would be allowed.

In *Pierce* v. *Fuller*, heard in 1811, we see a glimpse of concern for the consumer.[5] Pierce, the owner of a small independent stagecoach line, sold his capital (one horse and one stagecoach) to Fuller on the condition that Pierce would not compete on that route. Later, Pierce wanted to reopen his route and claimed that the contract was a restraint of trade. The court held for Fuller for two reasons. It reasoned that the contract was voluntary. It further reasoned that because the stage line was open for anyone except Pierce, competition (and presumably consumer welfare) need not be hurt.

Case decisions in the late 1800s demonstrated more concern on the part of the courts for consumer welfare. Even then, however, the record was mixed. In the case of *Central Ohio Salt Co.* v. *Guthrie*, several manufacturers of salt agreed to restrict production in order to raise prices.[6] The court said of their agreement: "It is no answer to say that competition in the salt trade was not in fact destroyed, or that the price of the commodity was not unreasonably advanced. Courts will not stop to inquire as to the degree of injury inflicted upon the public. . . ." In *Craft* v. *McConoughy* four grain dealers divided profits resulting from a secret combination to raise their prices.[7] The court stressed the degree of market control involved and held the agreement to be contrary to the public interest. The court took a different stand in *Shainka* v. *Scharringhausen*, heard in 1880.[8] Twenty-three owners of quarries in St. Louis agreed to fix prices. They defended their agreement as a protective device to end ruinous competition. The court allowed the arrangement, saying that the contract did not deprive anyone of employment, "unduly raise prices," or cause a monopoly.

No doubt common law suppressed monopoly power in the United States to some degree. However, several factors curtailed its ability to suppress the monopolistic firms that developed in the United States in the latter half of the 19th century. First, as we have already seen, common law showed only luke-warm concern for consumers. Its principal concern was the protection of property rights and therefore, it favored the businessman. Second, there was no agency responsible for public prosecution. Almost all anti-monopoly cases heard under common law involved harm to individual parties. Third, the penalties provided by common law were not stringent enough to deter monopolistic practices. Finally, common law decisions were conflicting, and, therefore, the law provided no real certainty for either business or the consumer. For all of these reasons, the United States needed to adopt antitrust legislation if it was to control the development of monopolies by using the legal process.

ECONOMIC CONDITIONS PRIOR TO 1890

Our country was founded on the principle of freedom. Therefore, it is not surprising that in its early years, the United States adopted a laissez faire attitude toward business. Firms with monopoly power prospered in those early years, and their power was amplified by the fact that most markets were localized; national or even regional markets were rare. Despite such power, the concentration of firms was not great enough to be considered a major problem prior to the Civil War. However, in the era following the Civil War, monopoly became a widespread social problem. In the short span of fifty years the country made the transition from a small agricultural economy to a large industrial one. The mass production accompanying this change significantly reduced the trade of small manufacturers and craftsmen. Manufacturing even displaced agriculture as the major source of income. This was prompted by the fact that the United States had all the necessary ingredients for rapid industrial development: raw materials, a large labor supply, inventions, and a developed transport system.

With the development of the economy came greatly increased competition. The transport system transformed local markets into regional and national ones, and some firms overexpanded such that their supply exceeded demand. Both situations resulted in "cut-throat" competition. Naturally, businesses did not care for the prospects of selling at or below costs, nor did they cherish the threat of bankruptcy which could result from such competition. Being inventive creatures, they were determined to find ways to "stabilize" the market. "Trusts" were one method used. Competitors assigned the voting stock of their companies to a board of trustees in exchange for trust certificates. This placed the control of competitors in the hands of trustees who could regulate competition among the firms. While trusts were certainly not conducive to consumer welfare, they did reduce businesses' competitive problems. The trusts were declared illegal under state antitrust law whereupon businessmen adopted the concept of the "holding company." Using this organization, competitors established a corporation authorized to hold their assets. In return for these assets, the corporation issued stock. In its organizational format, the holding company differed from the trust, but the result was the same—collusion between competing companies.

Trusts and holding companies were not the only practices that businesses used to create monopoly power. For example, the railroads used a discriminatory rate structure which gave unfair advantage to certain competitors. Many people believe that the most important factor explaining the development of Standard Oil of New Jersey was the fact that it secured lower rail rates than did its competitors. It is safe to say that during the latter part of the 19th century, businesses used every imaginable tool they could think of to destroy competition. One specific example of several thousand instances is worth citing. Professor Clair Wilcox said of National Cash Register Company that it

> set out deliberately to destroy its competitors. It hired their employees away from them. It bribed their employees and the employees of common carriers and telephone and telegraph companies to spy on them and disclose their business secrets. It spread false rumors concerning their solvency. It instructed its agents to misrepresent the quality of their goods, interfere with their sales and damage the mechanism of their machines in establishments where they were in use. It publicly displayed their cash registers under labels which read, "junk." It made, and sold at less than cost, inferior machines called "knockers," which it represented to be just as good as theirs.[9]

By the 1800s public opinion was vehement in its objection to monopolies. Besides the abuse of monopoly power, several additional factors prompted this attitude. First, popular writings against the monopolies flew off the presses. These were not always objective, but they did alert the public to the abuses of the monopolies. The effect was expressed by the economist, George Gunton, in 1888, when he said, "Indeed the public mind has begun to assume a state of apprehension, almost amounting to alarm, regarding the evil economic and social tendencies of these organizations."[10] Second, the political platforms of the national parties were directed toward the monopolies. In 1884, the Antimonopoly Party was formed, and it nominated Benjamin F. Butler for president. Throughout the campaign he denounced all forms of combinations, trusts and other forms of monopoly. The party argued for the impossible: the restoration to the public of monies taken away by monopolistic practices. Although the party did not win, it educated the public on the evils of monopoly. In 1888, both the Republicans and Democrats made the antimonopoly plank a major part of their platforms. By 1890 the evils of monopoly power and the disgust of the American people made the time ripe for antitrust legislation.

ECONOMISTS AND THE SHERMAN ACT

We have seen that by the late 1880s the country was replete with monopolistic elements. This environment provided the economists of the day with an ideal laboratory in which to study monopolistic elements and suggest ways to eliminate them. Surely, no one would have been in a better position than economists to guide the public in formulating antitrust legislation. It is, therefore, surprising to find that economists had little to do with the Sherman Act. In fact, with few exceptions, they were against antitrust legislation.

It is always dangerous to categorize people. Yet to a large degree, economists of the late 1880s fell into one of two schools of thought: laissez faire economics or Social Darwinism. The fundamental recommendation of both groups was to tolerate monopolies.

LAISSEZ FAIRE ECONOMISTS

Laissez faire economics was originated by the Physiocrats in the eighteenth century. It was developed by Adam Smith, David Ricardo, and John Stuart Mill and was still very popular in the period leading up to the Sherman Act. Its followers believed that the economy would function reasonably well if government did not interfere with its operation. The influence of individuals—both on the buying and selling side—would insure that society's welfare was maximized. The laissez faire attitude reached its peak in the writings of Frederic Bastiat who opposed all forms of government intervention in the operation of the economy. At the end of the 1800s, laissez faire economists were caught in a dilemma. They were opposed to private combinations which thwarted the free operation of the market. On the other hand, they were against government intervention because it reduced the free operation of the market. Faced with this dilemma, they reasoned that if the market were just left alone, it would solve its own problems. Professor Hans Thorelli, in his book *The Federal Antitrust Policy*, presented a thorough analysis of the attitudes of laissez faire economists prior to the Sherman Act.[11] In that analysis he cited some examples of the attitudes of these economists toward combinations. Speaking of the anthracite coal combination in Pennsylvania, the Reverend J. M. Sturtevand of Illinois College said the problem would solve itself if competition were allowed to operate freely. According to him, if the government would just take the protective tariff away from coal, competition would exist again. Concerning the monopolies in petroleum, he thought that consumers could search for new means of illumination. And to solve the monopoly problem in the railroad industry, he thought that more broad-minded railroad managers should be developed.[12] Some laissez faire economists actually endorsed monopolies because they thought that the advantages of bigness would offset any disadvantages resulting from the monopoly power that they held. Professor David Wells, in his book *Recent Economic Changes* published in 1889, said that combinations might provide certain economies while at the same time they could reduce the excesses of competition.[13] Optimistic attitudes such as these indicated a "wait and see" attitude which was not conducive to the development of social legislation.

SOCIAL DARWINISTS

A second group of economists, those that espoused Social Darwinism, reached the same conclusion as the laissez faire economists concerning government intervention. Herbert Spencer, an English social philosopher during the 1800s, believed that through time social structures progressed from simple to more complex forms. His philosophy has been called "Social Darwinism" because, for Spencer, evolution applied to social and business relationships as well as biological ones. For example, he thought that the gradual evolution of business would eliminate weak firms, resulting in the existence of only strong ones, or in his words, "survival of the fittest."[14] This evolutionary process would eventually lead society to utopia where, among other things, government functions would be nonexistent, only the "best" firms would exist, and man could exercise his "natural rights."

William Graham Sumner was the leading disciple of Herbert Spencer in the United States. Sumner, like Spencer, advocated the sacredness of private property and thought that the governmental functions should be negligible. He was not unmindful of the problems that trusts created for the people. However, he thought that the real cause of monopoly power was that firms had political power and that this power was used to develop monopoly power. His main objection to political power was its tendency to delay the evolutionary process in business. According to Sumner, the antimonopoly movement could not solve the problem. He thought that government regulations would result in more government control which would further delay the evolutionary process. His solution was one of the alternatives to antitrust discussed in Chapter I; Take away special advantages such as tariffs which have been granted by government. According to Spencer, "If there were no longer any legislative monopolies nor any legislative guarantee of natural monopolies, the only monopolies which would remain would be such as no one can abolish."[15] With this attitude it is certainly not surprising that the followers of Spencer and Sumner did not endorse legislation to end the trusts.

THE SHERMAN ACT

The outcry for social legislation came from writers for major newspapers, farmers who were hurt by the operation of the railroads, and labor unions. These groups put pressure on Congress to pass antimonopoly legislation. As a result, the Sherman Act was passed in 1890 with only one dissenting vote. Altogether it has eight sections; only two of them are of direct concern to us. Section 1 states: "Every contract, combination in the form of trust or otherwise, or conspiracy, in restraint of trade or commerce among the several states, or with foreign nations is hereby declared to be illegal." Section 2 says: "Every person who shall monopolize, or attempt to monopolize, or combine or conspire with any other person or persons to monopolize any part of the trade or commerce . . . shall be guilty of a misdemeanor. . . ."[16]

The reader may feel a little cheated after reading these provisions. What is really outlawed? Obviously, the act is so ambiguous that the reader does not know. Its interpretation is left largely in the hands of judges, and it is this fact that prompted Milton Handler, Professor of Law at Columbia, to say,

> The Sherman Law gave birth to no new principle. Congress merely affirmed its faith in competition as the principal regulating force in our economy by forbidding restraints of trade and monopolization in interstate and foreign commerce. These simple but pregnant terms were the entire intellectual stuff from which the jurisprudence of antitrust has been fashioned. Congress did not pause even to adumbrate the details; these were left to be filled in by the judiciary.[17]

ANTITRUST LITIGATION

In 1903, the Antitrust Division of the Department of Justice was established to enforce the Sherman Act. It is now composed of approximately 280 lawyers and 25 economists. Most of its actions originate with a customer's or competitor's complaint against a company, although the Antitrust Division does make some independent industry studies which suggest appropriate areas for prosecution. By no means do all complaints result in antitrust prosecution. Due to financial constraints and overburdened courts, the Antitrust Division must limit the number of cases. This automatically means that some firms are able to escape prosecution when they engage in anticompetitive practices.

Once the Antitrust Division decides to prosecute a company, it has to collect evidence. This is done by the Federal Bureau of Investigation because the Antitrust Division has no investigative agency of its own. If, after collecting materials, a business practice looks as though it should be prosecuted, the Antitrust Division begins the litigation process. If the case is a criminal one, the prosecutor representing the Antitrust Division must go to a grand jury to receive authorization for a trial.[18] If a grand jury rules in favor of a trial, the defendants may enter a plea of *nolo contendere* in a federal district court. In essence, this means that they admit no guilt but do not contest the charge against them. If the plea is accepted by a court, penalties may be imposed. If the charge is contested, the district court will hear the case. If the district court rules against him, a defendant may appeal a decision to the appropriate federal circuit court of appeal or in certain special circumstances directly to the United States Supreme Court. The government does not have the right to appeal a criminal case. If the appeal was heard by the court of appeals, and it upholds the district court's decision, defendants may petition the Supreme Court to review the case, but the Court does not have to hear the appeal. Only after the defendant has exhausted the right of appeal can a penalty be imposed. Presently, Sections 1 and 2 of the Sherman Act provide for criminal prosecution. Violations of these sections provide for imprisonment not to exceed one year and/or a fine not to exceed $50,000.

The Antitrust Division may bring a civil suit against a defendant.[19] The purpose of a civil suit is to provide remedies to end an anticompetitive act rather than deterring future violation by inflicting a fine or imprisonment. In a civil suit, the defendant has the right to take a "consent decree" at any time before a court gives the decision. Roughly 75 per cent of all Justice Department antitrust actions are ended this way. Acceptance of the decree by the defendant does not imply admission of guilt. However, it does mean that the firm will allow certain proscribed actions stated in the decree. These actions are negotiated between the defendant and the government. The defendant is in contempt of court if he does not abide by the terms of the decree.

If the defendant does not take a consent decree, the case is first heard in a district court. Either the government or the defendant may appeal a civil action to a court of appeals. Likewise, either party may petition the Supreme Court to review the case. Once a defendant has been found guilty, the court may impose one or more of several penalties. The firm may be enjoined from specific actions which have been found to be violations of the Sherman Act. For example, it may no longer be allowed to engage in price fixing, or exclusive dealing, or it may be prevented from a proposed merger with another firm. If a merger or other combination has already taken place, the firm may be ordered to divest itself of some of its assets or dissolve a business firm into several independent firms. The courts have wide latitude in providing a remedy which can restore competition in a market. However, we will later see that it is not always easy to find an appropriate remedy.

Economists play a very small role in the litigation process. They do not play any part in deciding which cases are to be prosecuted. Nor do they determine the strategy to be taken by the prosecutor. Their role is largely that of providing an analysis of the facts supplied to them by lawyers. Sometimes judges do use economists as advisors. For example, Karl Kaysen of Harvard University was appointed Judge Wyzanski's law clerk in the *United Shoe Machinery* case. While it is sometimes feasible, this advisory role presents a major problem because economists' advice is presented to the judge behind closed doors, and neither the defendant nor the prosecutor has an opportunity to present a rebuttal. This is one reason that economists are used infrequently as judicial advisors. In the last chapter we saw an even more fundamental reason explaining why economists are not warmly invited to take a large part in antitrust litigation. Lawyers fear that economists will interpret the law in an economic sense instead of a legal sense. Mark Massel paraphrased Judge Yankwich's opinion concerning the use of economists in antitrust litigation: " 'economic theories' would be brought into the proceedings and . . . an economist might speculate about the 'beneficial effect' of certain practices instead of confining his attention to the 'restraint.' "[20] Significant progress has been made of late to bring lawyers and economists closer together in antitrust proceedings.

SUMMARY

In this chapter we have seen why the Sherman Act was passed, the provisions of the act, and the process which antitrust litigation follows. However, we have also seen that the Sherman Act says little about what business practices are declared illegal. Only by analyzing specific cases can we discover the true antitrust policy of the Justice Department. In the next four chapters we will consider the economics as well as the legality of certain practices that have been placed under the jurisdiction of the Sherman Act. These practices are price fixing, division of territories, resale price maintenance, closed-territory distribution, and refusals to deal. While mergers are also prosecuted under the provisions of the Sherman Act, we will not consider them until Chapter XIII.

NOTES TO CHAPTER V

[1] 77 Eng. Rep. 1260 (1602).

[2] Henry A. Einhorn and William P. Smith, *Economic Aspects of Antitrust* (New York: Random House, 1968), p. 32.

[3] 88 Eng. Rep. 610 (1712); 88 Eng. Rep. 660 (1713).

[4] 19 Pick. 51 (1837).

[5] 8 Mass. 222 (1811).

[6] 35 Ohio St. 666 (1880).

[7] 79 Ill. 346 (1875).

[8] 8 Mo. App. 522 (1880).

[9] Clair Wilcox, *Competition and Monopoly in American Industry* (Washington: U.S. Temporary National Economic Committee, Monograph No. 21, 1940), p. 68. Quoted in Hans Thorelli, *The Federal Antitrust Policy* (Baltimore: The Johns Hopkins Press, 1955), p. 68.

[10] Oswald W. Knauth, *The Policy of the United States Towards Industrial Monopoly* (New York: Longmans, Green, 1914), p. 15.

[11] Hans B. Thorelli, *The Federal Antitrust Policy* (Baltimore: The John Hopkins Press, 1955).

[12] *Ibid.*, p. 110.

[13] *Ibid.*, p. 111.

[14] It was Herbert Spencer who coined this phrase, not as is commonly thought, Charles Darwin.

[15] Thorelli, p. 115.

[16] 26 Stat. 209 (1890).

[17] Milton Handler, *Antitrust in Perspective, The Complementary Roles of Rule and Discretion* (New York: Columbia University Press, 1957), p. 3.

[18] Criminal law is that portion of public law which is concerned with the welfare of the state as distinguished from the welfare of individual members of the state.

[19] A civil suit is one that is levied against a party not engaged in a criminal act. That is, he has not committed a crime against the state, but instead, a crime against individual members of the state.

[20] Leon R. Yankwich, " 'Short Cuts' in Long Cases," 13 F.R.D. 41 (1953), paraphrased in Mark S. Massel, *Competition and Monopoly* (Washington: The Brookings Institution, 1962), p. 166.

COLLUSIVE ARRANGEMENTS

CHAPTER VI

One of the most fundamental violations of the Sherman Act occurs when firms agree not to compete. Whether the agreement is overt or tacit it can eliminate competition and harm the consumer. The nature of such agreements as well as their effect on competition and the manner in which the courts have treated them are considered in this chapter.

INTRODUCTION

Active price competition between firms is essential to the maximization of consumer welfare. Therefore, both economists and antitrust authorities become concerned when price competition is suppressed, and such suppression is an illegal practice under Section 1 of the Sherman Act. We shall consider each of the following four instances in which price competition can be reduced or eliminated by firms:

1. Overt collusion among competing firms;
2. Tacit collusion among competing firms;
3. Base-point pricing; and
4. Trade association reporting practices.

It is important to emphasize that throughout this chapter we are concerned with *horizontal* price and territorial arrangements, i.e., arrangements between firms which compete at the same level of distribution. These should be distinguished from vertical price and territorial arrangements which will be considered in the later chapters on resale price maintenance and vertical territorial arrangements.

OVERT PRICE COLLUSION

It is not difficult to imagine a situation where friendly business competitors play golf together. Throughout their round they discuss their competitive business situation, and one of them suggests that if they eliminated price competition, they would increase their profits.

After some soul searching, their greed overcomes their sense of fair play, and they agree to raise their prices to a specified level. If they are the only competitors in the market, they will have effectively eliminated price competition which, under Section 1 of the Sherman Act, constitutes a conspiracy to monopolize. Their price fixing is termed "overt" because it involves either a written or verbal agreement.

The incentive for these businessmen to enter into the agreement may be strong. When they acted independently of one another, prices in the market were probably at a more competitive level. The sellers act as one after the agreement and thereby set a price similar to that charged by a monopolist. By so doing, they could increase their profits. Of course, consumers are hurt because they now have to pay a higher price for the product.

A simple model can be devised to demonstrate the arrangement. If they are to maximize profits, the collusive firms will act as though they were a pure monopolist. They will equate their collective marginal costs with the industry marginal revenue. This gives them the optimum price and quantity. The process is shown in *Figure I*. AR is the industry demand curve and corresponding to it is the industry marginal revenue curve, MR. The marginal cost curve for the combination, (ΣMC), is found by horizontally summing the marginal cost curves of each member. Equilibrium price is P_1, and the optimum quantity produced is Q_1. Because the firms act as a monopolist, this model is similar to that of the pure monopolist in Chapter II.

Not all firms in the combination will have identical marginal cost curves. Some will experience higher costs than others. If profits are to be maximized for the group as a whole, each firm must produce the quantity where its marginal cost equals the marginal revenue of the last unit sold by the combination. If one firm produced more than this level of output and experienced higher marginal cost, profits could be increased by transferring some production from this firm to others.

Naturally this model represents an ideal situation where all members of the combination have perfect knowledge about cost and demand and where they all try to maximize collective profits. The real world is not nearly so perfect. The price and the quantities produced are really determined through a bargaining process between members, and this process is largely a political one. Yet even though the model only approximates the real world, it does suggest two important considerations: First, the combination will *attempt* to act as a monopolist, and as a result, we can expect such an arrangement

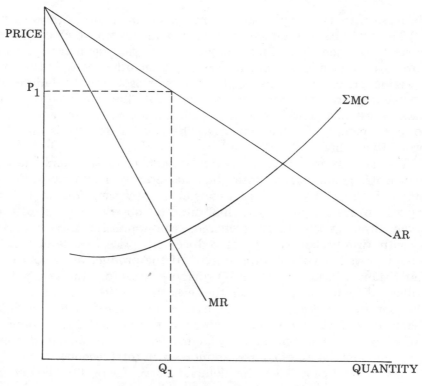

EQUILIBRIUM FOR COLLUSIVE FIRMS
FIGURE I

to increase the monopoly power of the firms involved. Second, most price-fixing arrangements must also involve some provision to curtail output. Excess supply will result if prices are raised above the competitive level without limiting output.

Although overt price-fixing arrangements sound easy to make, there are several stringent conditions that must be satisfied in order for them to be successful. (1) All competing firms must want to fix prices. Very few firms would charge high prices if a competitor charges a low price. The maverick of the group could make significant gains through its low pricing policy. (2) Frequent communication between members is necessary. Occasional adjustments generally have to be made to the agreement to reflect changes in economic conditions. Additionally, agreements may be very complicated when producers sell different types of products to different localities. When this is true, the agreements require frequent communication between conspirators. But since the agreements have to remain secret (because they are illegal), such communication is not always easy. (3) The firms have to police their agreement. A firm which charges a lower price than that of its competitors can gain significantly. This creates a tremendous tendency to cheat on other conspirators by lowering prices and is the single greatest reason for the failure of price-fixing arrangements. To be successful, the combination will have to establish both a means of policing the agreement and some form of penalty for the violators. The cost of doing this may be prohibitively high.

We have asserted that individual members of the combination have a strong incentive to cheat, but this assertion needs proof. For a moment, think of yourself as a consumer purchasing from an industry which has formed a combination. You observe that six of the seven firms in the industry charge a monopolistic price but the seventh firm (the cheater) has reduced his price to a level which would prevail if competition existed. If the product being sold is a fairly standardized one (which is usually the case for firms engaged in collusion), you would buy from the seventh firm. In economic terms, the maverick of the group has an extremely elastic demand schedule facing it so that a very small reduction in price will bring about a rather great increase in quantity demanded. Accompanying this increase in quantity is, of course, an increase in total revenue.

We have already seen the demand curve facing the cheater in Chapter II where Professor Sweezy's dd' curve was discussed. We noted then that the curve was drawn assuming that all competitors hold their price constant while the one firm we were analyzing reduced its price. You will remember that because of this assumption, the dd' curve was elastic. (4) It is not surprising that most successful price-fixing agreements occur only when there is a small number of competitors in the industry. Clearly the amount of communication and policing become unwieldy if a large number of firms are involved. (5) Finally, restricted entry into a market is generally a requirement for successful price fixing. If free and quick entry of new firms exists, market prices will soon be undercut by a new rival. Sometimes colluding firms retard entry of new firms by charging a price just low enough to provide a deterrent to new firms but still higher than the competitive price. But this reduces the monopoly profits that they can reap from their arrangement.[1] We will shortly see that this was done in the *Addyston Pipe* case.

The attitude of the antitrust authorities toward overt price collusion was established in three major antitrust cases: *Addyston Pipe and Steel Company* v. *United States; United States* v. *Trenton*

Potteries Co. et al.; and *United States* v. *Socony-Vacuum Oil Company.* We will consider each of these cases separately.

ADDYSTON PIPE

The *Addyston Pipe* case,[2] heard in 1898 by the Sixth Circuit Court of Appeals, represents a fascinating example of the intricacies of a price-fixing arrangement. Six pipe producers including Addyston agreed to fix prices and divide territories among themselves. They divided their market into three geographical areas: "free territory," "reserved cities," and "pay territory." All members of the combination engaged in legitimate competitive bidding in free territories. These territories were used where members of the combination faced strong competition from nonmembers. Since this market was a competitive one, it was not involved in the case. Each member of the combination had some cities in which it had been given the exclusive right to sell pipe. These were called "reserved cities." Other members of the combination submitted bids for contracts in these cities, but by prior agreement they always bid higher than the firm which had been assigned the territory. The firm assigned the reserved city would pay the other members a specified "bonus" per unit of the product sold. In "pay territories," the members of the combination would hold meetings to decide which one would be the successful bidder on a contract. This was determined by an internal bidding operation, with the firm agreeing to pay the highest bonus to the other members receiving the contract. The other members submitted phony high bids to the customer.

The combination hired an auditor who kept account of the business done by each firm. Twice a month he sent a statement to each member showing the shipments of each firm, the amount of the bonuses due on each shipment, and the distribution of the bonuses among the companies. This reporting system provided a means of policing the arrangement. Evidence showed that the members kept their prices just low enough to keep eastern competitors out of the market.

The defendants freely admitted the existence of the combination. However, they defended it by arguing that: (1) The prices that they charged the consumer were "reasonable"; (2) Their practices were not in violation of interstate commerce; (3) They did not create a monopoly because their tonnage was only 30 percent of the national output, their sales did not involve all states in the country, and their agreement was only for two years; (4) They adopted the arrangement to avoid ruinous competition. Their "shotgun defense" was an indication of the fact that the antitrust laws were still new, and the defense had little precedent on which to base its case.

The court denied all arguments of the defense. It did not find the prices to be "reasonable" but instead, higher than competitive. More importantly, it judged that whether or not prices were reasonable was a moot issue. The important thing was that the firms had the power to charge unreasonable prices if they wished. The court thought that the combination involved interstate commerce because producers in one state sold to customers in another state. In the most important part of the decision, the court agreed with the defense that following the tradition established in common law the Sherman Act provided for partial restraints of trade when they were ancillary to some good purpose. However, when they were designed simply to restrain competition and maintain prices, there was nothing to justify them. It reasoned that this particular arrangement was a restraint of trade. Whether or not it was reasonable could not be determined, and those who tried to make such a determination would "set sail on a sea of doubt." Finally, the court did not accept the threat of ruinous competition as a defense. The court ruled against the combination, and the Supreme Court affirmed their decision.

No doubt the court was correct in observing that one cannot determine a "reasonable" price. Furthermore, adoption by the courts of the principle of reasonable prices would require constant policing of business because in a dynamic economy a price that is judged reasonable today may not be acceptable tomorrow. But is price fixing always illegal? What is the court's policy in instances where ruinous price competition threatens the very survival of a large number of firms? The court hit upon this issue lightly in *Addyston Pipe*, but in *U.S.* v. *Trenton Potteries* and the *Socony Vacuum* cases it made a firm decision.

TRENTON POTTERIES

The *Trenton Potteries* case[3] is the leading case on overt price fixing because the Supreme Court established a firm rule with regard to the legality of the practice. Twenty individuals and twenty-three corporations were charged with fixing the prices of vitreous pottery used for bathroom fixtures. Together, the members of the combination sold over 80 percent of the product. The companies did not deny the charge of price fixing. Instead, they argued that the prices they charged were reasonable ones, and called numerous customers as witnesses to substantiate their defense. The witnesses were asked by the defense whether they had observed any competition among members of the combination, but the Court record states that the "offered evidence, in some instances, took the form of vague impressions or recollections of the witness as to competition, without specifying the kind or extent of competition."[4] The Court reasoned that the existence of competition should be proven by the use of relevant data. In any event, history does not tell us whether the prices charged by the combination were competitive ones or not. We do know that the arrangement was unsuccessful because of frequent cheating on the part of its members.[5]

In its decision, the Court said that not all restraints of trade were outlawed—only unreasonable ones. However, it did not consider overt price fixing to be a reasonable restraint of trade even if the prices charged were reasonable ones. To substantiate this point it argued that the interests of the consuming public were best protected by competition in the market place. Additionally, whether or not a price-fixing arrangement is successful in raising prices, it gives the combination power to control the market. It was unimportant to the Court whether or not the power was exercised.

The Court ruled that overt price fixing was illegal *per se*, meaning "in itself, without need to show more." Hence when a practice is termed "illegal *per se*," all the prosecutor has to do in a case is to show that the practice exists. He does not have to concern himself with the nature of the case or the effect of the practice on competition.

It is important here to emphasize the Court's concern with the mere existence of power, whether or not it is exercised. Imagine, for a moment, a large cinderblock dangling over your head. Someone controls the button which releases the block. He has controlled the button for over a month and has not yet given you a concussion. Therefore it can be said that he has been reasonable. Yet doesn't the existence of that block still bother you? It is this same reasoning that led the Court to decide that the existence of power was enough to declare a practice illegal. But does it make any difference how that power is attained? That question will have to be answered later when we consider whether a firm that has developed monopoly power by being the most efficient producer in a market should be prosecuted.

The most important part of the *Trenton Potteries* decision is that it declared overt price fixing illegal *per se*. For the idealist, this probably seems unjust because it is always conceivable that someday a justifiable form of price fixing may appear on the scene. Yet if a court hears the argument of even a justifiable arrangement and follows precedent, the practice will be outlawed. In a hypothetical world of zero court costs, the use of the *per se* rule is probably unjustifiable. However, since the great majority of price-fixing arrangements curb competition, it is an expedient and economical way to handle the practice. Moreover, it provides businesses with an unquestionable rule to follow.[6]

SOCONY-VACUUM OIL COMPANY

The *Socony-Vacuum Oil*[7] case is an interesting one because the price-fixing arrangement involved seems to have more justification than it did either in *Addyston Pipe* or *Trenton Potteries.* Several major oil companies in the midwest were charged with artificially raising the price of gasoline at both the wholesale and retail levels of distribution. They were able to raise this price by controlling the supply of gasoline.

The story goes back to 1926 when crude oil was produced in such large quantities that prices fell below the cost of production at marginal wells. When this happened, these wells, representing 40 percent of the nation's known oil reserves, had to be shut down. This was especially troublesome because of the high cost of putting wells back in operation. Oklahoma and Kansas restricted production, but their plan was defeated when major oil supplies were discovered in East Texas in 1930 which forced supply up and price down. Texas tried to curb production by setting quotas, but many firms produced more than their share. By 1933, the wholesale prices were again below the cost of production, and the federal government adopted the objective of returning the oil industry to a profitable level. It allotted an amount of crude oil that each refiner could process, and used other means of control so that the prices would rise to a profitable level. This arrangement became part of the National Industrial Recovery Act.

Later the section of the act concerned with price stabilization in the oil industry was declared unconstitutional by the Supreme Court. It was at that time that the individual oil companies began to take the problem into their own hands. Each major company selected one or more of the independent refiners that had excess gasoline and purchased its supply. Then they established a board to "recommend" prices for the excess gasoline. Evidence suggests that these prices were higher than prices that would have prevailed in the free market. Of course, by restricting supply the oil companies were able to raise prices at the jobber and consumer level of distribution. There was a steady increase in retail and wholesale prices from 1935 to 1936. There are other facts involved in the case, but those presented here represent the heart of the case heard by the Court. These facts demonstrate an attempt to raise prices, not by fixing them, but by controlling supply. They also indicate that the government seemed to have recognized the need for some sort of price stabilization program when it attempted to control prices itself. The case offered a good test of the Court's maintenance of its *per se* ruling.

The companies argued that their purchasing policy affected only minutely the rise in market prices during 1935. Instead, they attributed the rise to increasing demand, the passage of the Connally Act (which controlled excess supply by providing for state quotas in oil), and improved business conditions. They did not deny the existence of the plan to restrict oil, but the companies contended that even with the plan they had not gained enough power for aggressive price fixing, and that their objective was only designed to eliminate a "competitive evil."

The Supreme Court decided that there was conclusive evidence that the arrangement had increased prices. Concerning the defense's assertion that prices were only controlled to bring stability to the market, the Court reiterated the *Trenton Potteries* decision, saying that "the elimination of so-called competitive evils is no legal justification for such buying programs."[8] It further reasoned that:

> The reasonableness of prices has no constancy due to the dynamic quality of the business facts underlying price structure. Those who fix reasonable prices today would perpetuate unreasonable prices tomorrow, since those prices would not be subject to continuous administrative supervision and readjustment in light of changed conditions. Those who controlled the prices would control or effectively dominate the market. And those who were in that strategic position would have it in their power to destroy or drastically impair the competitive system.[9]

Once again, the Court showed that it was not going to get involved in the thorny question of what constitutes a "reasonable price." Moreover, they recognized the difficulties in policing pricing policies.

Finally, the Court said that it really did not make any difference whether the oil companies had the power to fix prices. The illegality arises from their entrance into a conspiracy to fix prices. This point was a legal issue, not an economic one. While Section 1 of the Sherman Act does not require a showing of specific intent to find guilt, we will see that the courts put a great emphasis on the attitude of the parties involved regardless of whether that attitude materializes into an action plan. This orientation on the part of the courts has caused some consternation in the ranks of economists, who are more concerned with the state of competition than the attitude of firms. On the other hand, the courts' concern with mental attitude is understandable. Attempted murder is illegal, and most of us would want it to be if the attempt were made on our life.

The Court left no question about the legality of overt price fixing—whether it involves control of supply or direct control of prices. It is illegal *per se*. The rule holds today, although some firms still engage in price fixing. In the late 1950s, for example, over thirty firms in the electrical equipment industry set the prices of their products. Many business executives found a home at the federal penitentiary as a result of government prosecution.[10]

TACIT COLLUSION

The reader is probably familiar with many examples of competing firms charging the same price for their product. The "sticker prices" on new Fords, Plymouths, and Chevrolets differ by only a dollar or two. Leading detergents have identical or almost identical suggested retail prices, all major cigarette brands sell for the same price, and state governments frequently find that bids submitted to them on a contract are identical. But similar or identical prices should not imply that these firms have engaged in overt collusion. A written or verbal contract is not usually required to induce identical prices in an oligopolistic industry. Instead, the firms tacitly agree that they will follow one another's prices rather than engage in price competition.

There are many types of tacit collusion. For the purpose of our analysis, we will consider three types: dominant-firm price leadership, barometric price leadership, and price leadership in lieu of overt collusion.[11] Each of these will be discussed separately, but there are two important points that should be made at the offset. (1) Such arrangements generally occur in oligopolistic industries where there are few sellers. (2) Monopoly power has to exist for tacit collusion to be successful. This implies that an identical pricing policy in an industry is a reflection of the existence of monopoly power, not a cause of monopoly power. This fact should be considered when selecting appropriate antitrust policy for tacit collusion.

DOMINANT-FIRM PRICE LEADERSHIP

Dominant-firm price leadership occurs in industries composed of one or more large firms (one of which is the "leader") and several small firms. The small firms sell such a small percentage of the total industry output that each one can sell its entire production without affecting price. The dominant firm, on the other hand, produces such a large output that it has a measurable effect on the price that can be charged in the industry. Sometimes the small firms are not as efficient as the large one, but this is not an essential requirement for dominant-firm price leadership. The practice has existed at one time or another in the rayon, tin can, and tractor industries among others.

Given its market power, the dominant firm will determine its optimum price. The smaller firms will charge the same price set by the leader, not only to maximize their profits but to escape the wrath of the dominant firm. The price chosen by the leader still will not be as high as the price charged by a pure monopolist because of a constraint resulting from the presence of the small firm.

A model can be constructed to represent the industry. Industry demand is shown in *Figure II* by AR. ΣMC is the summation of the small firms' marginal cost curves. Since the AR curve shows the quantity bought in the market at each price, and the ΣMC curve shows the quantity supplied by the small firms at each price, we can conclude that at price P, the small firms will provide the total amount needed by the consumer; there will be no market left for the dominant firm.

This suggests that the dominant firm's demand curve begins at price P. From point P to point R, the demand curve is derived from the horizontal difference between the marginal cost curve of the small firms and industry demand curve. At point R, the demand curve for the dominant firm becomes the industry demand curve, because the supply offered by the small firms is zero at that price. Corresponding to the average revenue curve of the dominant firm is its marginal revenue curve, MR_d. Following normal profit-maximizing procedure, the firm will equate its marginal cost, MC_d, with its marginal revenue, MR_d, and will produce quantity Q_1 and charge price P_1. The small firms will produce up to the point where their marginal cost is equal to the price P_1. (They do not have a separate marginal revenue curve because their output is too small to affect price. Their marginal revenue is P_1.) The total output of all of the small firms is Q_2.[12]

The reader is again reminded of the fact that the equilibrium price is lower than that of the pure monopolist. He should also remember that the pricing policy of the dominant firm creates no additional monopoly power. The policy simply represents the exercise of existing monopoly power. Both the dominant firm and the small firms are

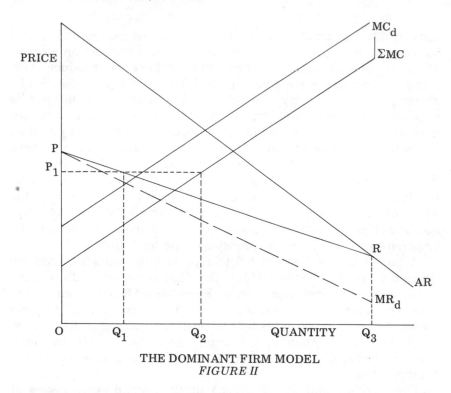

THE DOMINANT FIRM MODEL
FIGURE II

following an appropriate profit-maximizing policy, given the monopolistic structure of their industry. Moreover, they are doing it without overt collusion.

BAROMETRIC PRICE LEADERSHIP

Competitors follow a barometric price leader because they believe that its pricing policies best reflect market conditions. The leader is characterized by expertise in choosing the profit-maximizing price, and is generally chosen on the basis of its past performance. In the real world, economic conditions change daily. Therefore firms' optimum prices are constantly changing. Firms find their optimum prices by using the time-honored "trial and error method." To the extent that one firm in an industry is a better predictor of the optimum price than others, it provides a service to competitors by helping them find the optimum price. Moreover, we can say with little reservation that it provides a service to the consumer by finding the price where supply is equal to demand. In other words, all the barometric price leader does is to find the equilibrium price a little quicker than it otherwise might be found. If this is all that is involved, it does not even exercise monopoly power, much less create it.

It is not always easy to differentiate between a barometric price leader and a dominant-firm price leader or from price leadership in lieu of an overt conspiracy. However, Professor Markham suggested that a barometric price leader is a firm that is not immediately followed by his competitors in their choice of price. Moreover, barometric price leadership might be expected to change hands more frequently than dominant firm price leadership or price leadership in lieu of an overt conspiracy.[13]

ex.?

PRICE LEADERSHIP

Suppose there are three firms in an industry that have competed for many years. It is conceivable that through time they have developed an implicit understanding that they will all charge an identical price for their product and that they will attempt to make the price similar to that which would be charged by an individual monopolist. This situation represents price leadership in lieu of an overt conspiracy. The profit-maximizing price would be approximately the same as if the firms made a formal written contract between one another. The only difference between this arrangement and overt price fixing is that no contract, written or verbal, exists between the firms. The practice is often called "conscious parallelism" because the firms involved follow similar practices and are aware of their parallel activities. Their behavior is not limited to pricing policy. It may extend to include non-price competition such as financing terms, product service, etc. One instance of the arrangement was demonstrated by the "kinked demand" model presented in Chapter II.

Professor Markham has suggested several conditions that must be satisfied for such an arrangement to be successful. These are very similar to the conditions required for overt price fixing. They are:

(1) There must be few firms in the industry. A large number of firms increases the chances of having a maverick in the group that will undercut its competitors' price. We observed earlier in the chapter that it is crucial to a price agreement that all competitors follow the same pricing policy. Otherwise the price cutter can make excess profits at its competitors' expense.

(2) Entry of new firms into the industry must be restricted. Otherwise, new entrants could act as mavericks.

(3) The products sold by the competitors need not be identical, but they should be similar. If the products sold are not close substitutes,

each firm in the industry may believe that the optimum price for its product differs from the optimum price for the other firms' products.

(4) Demand must not be very elastic. If demand is elastic, a firm may be able to lower its price and increase profits even if its competitors also lower their price.

(5) Individual cost curves must be similar. Otherwise, each firm will choose a different profit-maximizing price.[14]

Tacit price fixing is usually implemented by a price leader. The leader need not be the largest firm, or the firm best able to predict the optimum price, and frequently the position of price leader changes hands.

The effect of tacit collusion is to increase prices to a monopolistic level. Therefore consumer welfare can be reduced as much as if overt price fixing existed, provided the oligopolists can tacitly agree on a monopoly price. From a policy viewpoint, however, the practice is a difficult one to control. The oligopolists are simply maximizing their profits, given their concentrated market structure. To charge any price other than the one tacitly agreed upon would be irrational behavior for them in the long run. Their situation is analogous to that of the pure monopolist. It charges a monopoly price because of its market structure; not because of unfair practices. Charging any other price would be irrational. Collusion without overt agreement appears in the rayon, cigarette, automobile, can, steel, and farm tractor industries, to name only a few. It is a very prevalent practice in the United States economy primarily because of the existence of a large number of oligopolistic industries.

AMERICAN TOBACCO COMPANY

American Tobacco Co. v. *United States*,[15] heard in 1945, was a landmark case on tacit collusion. The American, Liggett & Myers, and R. J. Reynolds tobacco companies were charged with conspiracy in restraint of trade, monopolization, an attempt to monopolize, and a conspiracy to monopolize under Sections 1 and 2 of the Sherman Act. The record showed that the list prices of the three companies were almost identical from 1923 to 1928 and were identical from 1928 to 1945. From 1928 to 1945, seven changes in price took place, and all the changes were identical for the three companies. The companies faced some competition from smaller cigarette manufacturers who sold low-grade tobacco at a lower price. When the sales of these cigarettes began to grow, the three major companies simultaneously cut their prices. The Court contended that the evidence showed that the price reduction was directed at the small companies and accomplished its objective. The price reduction occurred twice and each time, the sales of the low-priced cigarettes dropped off substantially.

The companies also followed parallel actions in bidding for leaf tobacco. No one company would purchase tobacco unless the other two companies were present at the auction. The companies put limitations on the maximum price that they were willing to pay, and no firm exceeded these ceilings. The ceilings for all three companies appeared to be identical. When one or two of the firms had purchased their requirement, they would remain at an auction to bid on tobacco so that the third firm would have to pay the ceiling amount for it. This prevented any one of the major firms from receiving a price advantage in the purchase of tobacco. The major companies also bid on cheaper tobacco leaves used for production by the other companies. They did not explain how they utilized this tobacco, but the court inferred that the purchase was designed to deprive the small manufacturers of the tobacco necessary for their production as well as to raise the cost of their tobacco.

The evidence presented against the tobacco companies was wholly circumstantial because there was no record of any communication between the firms concerning their parallel activities. The case is an important one because the court had to determine whether the Sherman Act was applicable to situations where there was no evidence of overt collusion. In a district court, a jury found that the circumstantial evidence was sufficient to declare the participants guilty of conspiracy. The Sixth Circuit Court of Appeals affirmed this decision as did the Supreme Court. The Supreme Court believed that the circumstantial evidence was enough to establish a conspiracy in restraint of trade, reasoning that "no formal agreement is necessary to constitute an unlawful conspiracy."[16] Moreover, it said that the firms had the power and intent to exclude competition and this alone was sufficient to find them guilty. It further argued:

> Authorities support the view that the material consideration in determining whether a monopoly exists is not that prices are raised and that competition is excluded but that power exists to raise prices or to exclude competition when it is desired to do so.[17]

The Court's emphasis on power implies that they used what has been called the "structure test" to determine the legality of the practice. This test seeks to detect a firm's monopoly power by virtue of its structure and the structure of its industry. The "abuse test," on the other hand, seeks to determine whether power has been used, not whether or not it exists.

Because in this case the Court used the "structure test" their decision represented an attack against the existence of oligopoly itself because it is the oligopolistic structure which induced the parallel action. And, by emphasizing the importance of the existence of power, the Court brought the large number of oligopolistic firms who follow parallel behavior under the scope of the Sherman Act.

Although the decision strengthened the Sherman Act, the penalty was not remedial. The companies were fined over a quarter of a million dollars, but they were given no guidelines to follow for future behavior. Since their practices were normal ones given the market structure in which they operated, the defendants said that they were "entirely without guide as to how they may lawfully avoid the creation of evidence of future Sherman Act violations against themselves, unless they cease business altogether." Must they always charge different prices? If so, one firm may gain a competitive advantage in the market and develop additional monopoly power. Should they intentionally follow a divergent policy even though that policy may give one firm an advantage over the others? These questions were left unanswered by the Court making it less surprising when the defendants reverted to their old parallel pricing policy shortly after the case was decided. William H. Nicholls said of their policy, "If there was illegal conspiracy before 1940, there is still illegal conspiracy today. Furthermore, if the economic power of the three major companies combined constituted illegal monopolization before 1940, it does so *a fortiori* at the present time."[18]

Nicholls discussed several appropriate remedies to stop the parallel actions of the tobacco firms. The ideas that follow are his. Dissolution of the firms is the obvious remedy. By dividing the three companies into many companies, the oligopolistic market structure would be eliminated, or at least reduced, because with a larger number of competing firms conscious parallelism would be made difficult. Nicholls found that the firms each had three to four manufacturing plants which could be easily divided into separate companies. Moreover, he believed that production costs would increase very little with a division.

However, each company produced a major brand cigarette (Chesterfield, Lucky Strike, and Camels). After the dissolution, the sellers of these three major brands would still be the leaders, and to remedy this problem the major brand names would have to be abolished. Nevertheless, a dissolution plan does not seem impractical. Historically, the government has been extremely reluctant to use this remedy, even though it is often the only one which gets to the heart of the problem. No doubt political pressure is one explanation for its reluctance. Regard for the property rights of companies is another reason. Finally, in the event that a purchaser cannot be found for new companies that are "spun off" from old ones, the government has to accept financial responsibility for the action. Consumer advocates are currently pressing their case against oligopolistic industries, and it is quite possible that the government will take a new look at the dissolution issue in the near future.

Professor Nicholls also suggested that a progressive tax could be placed on an individual firm's total expenditures for advertising. Advertising is one way of creating brand attachment and monopoly power. A reduction in advertising might reduce existing monopoly power held by oligopolistic firms or at least prevent the creation of new power. Another solution would be to reduce or eliminate the federal and state cigarette taxes. These taxes make up a large percentage of the total cost of cigarettes. Therefore, in order to reduce the retail price of its cigarettes by even a small percentage, a manufacturer has to reduce the wholesale price by a large amount. Nicholls cited an example which clarifies this point: " . . . at the present time, in a state levying a three-cent-per package cigarette tax in addition to the federal tax of seven cents, a manufacturer would have to cut his final net price by about 15 per cent to lower the retail price by five to six per cent (or one cent a package)."[19]

Although the *Tobacco* case was a landmark to antitrust, its effects on the economy have not been significant. One can only hazard a guess to explain why the antitrust authorities have not prosecuted more firms who follow practices similar to those of the tobacco companies. If they began prosecuting oligopolistic firms because of the firms' monopoly power, and used the only real remedy to solve the problem, dissolutionment, they would have to rework much of our economy. It would be a tremendous job. Yet the cry from increasingly powerful consumer advocates is for a reduction in the number of oligopolies, and so the task may be undertaken. Meanwhile the courts sometimes have to be satisfied with treating symptoms of monopoly power instead of eliminating it.

Before leaving our study of tacit collusion, a very important point should be made to clarify the law. In the absence of monopoly power courts have allowed price leadership. In 1927 in *United States* v. *International Harvester Co.*,[20] the court found that "The fact that competitors may see proper, in the exercise of their own judgment to follow the prices of another manufacturer, does not establish any suppression of competition or show any sinister domination. . . ."[21]

In a case decided after the tobacco case, two dairy companies in St. Louis, Peverly and St. Louis Dairy, charged identical prices. The Circuit Court found that:

> The milk as handled by appellants was a standardized product. Its cost items being substantially identical for both appellants, uniformity in price would result from economic forces. . . . We are clear that mere uniformity of prices in the sale of a standardized commodity is not in itself evidence of a violation of the Sherman Act.[22]

The decision was a surprising one in light of the fact that the parallel action of the two firms extended to credit terms, the provision of cooling equipment, and frequency of delivery. Yet it did not appear to extend to practices which affected the ability of other dairy firms in the area to compete.[23] Perhaps it was on this issue that the court could distinguish the dairy case from the tobacco case. The distinction is certainly not a clear one, and a firm facing charges of conscious parallelism today would have a difficult time trying to second-guess the court. Decisions subsequent to the dairy case have further clouded the law on tacit collusion.[24] In fact about the only conclusion that can be stated with certainty is that conscious parallelism is not, itself, evidence of guilt. In *Theater Enterprises, Inc.* v. *Paramount Film Distributing Corp. et al.*,[25] the court concluded that conscious parallelism is not sufficient evidence to demonstrate tacit collusion. More cases must be heard before one can say with certainty what the law is concerning tacit collusion. Phillips offered the best opinion on the current law when he said "The important questions . . . relate to the effectiveness of the organization in restraining rivalry and to the probable impact such restraint has on market performance."[26] This test implies that the "abuse test" may now be in vogue, despite the decision in the *Tobacco* case.

Not only is the law on tacit collusion unclear; it is inconsistent with the law on overt collusion. Economists have long been puzzled by the fact that tacit collusion is sometimes allowed by the antitrust authorities while overt collusion is never allowed. What is confusing is that the effect of both practices on prices is identical. Overt and tacit collusion differ mainly in the manner in which agreement between competing firms is reached, and to most economists the result seems more important than the nature of the contract. Just recently, the F.T.C. as well as Senators Hart and Harris have begun to make some inroads in attacking tacit collusion. The result of their effort is discussed in Chapter XV on monopoly and shared monopoly.

BASE-POINT PRICING

Base-point pricing is a practice which is usually implemented through overt or tacit collusion. But it is difficult to determine the appropriate antitrust policy for it because, depending on the circumstances, the practice may either increase or decrease competition. Base-point pricing is prosecuted either under Sections 1 and 2 of the Sherman Act, or Section 5 of the Federal Trade Commission Act. Prior to 1953 it was also prosecuted under the Robinson-Patman Act which deals with price discrimination, but a 1953 case ruled that base-point pricing did not involve price discrimination in a legal sense.[27]

To see how the practice works, imagine two steel companies vying for customers. One is located in Pittsburgh and the other in Birmingham. Assume each firm has identical costs of production and that their products are identical so that brand preference does not exist. Which firm will the consumer buy from? He will choose the firm that is closest to him because in this way he minimizes the cost of transporting the product. When purchasing heavy or bulky products, transportation cost is a major consideration for the buyer.

A model depicting the situation is shown in *Figure III*. The price of the product including the transportation cost is shown on the vertical axis, and distance is shown on the horizontal axis. One steel producer is located at point A, and another steel producer is located at point G. The letters B, C, D, E, and F represent cities between A and G where customers are located. AR and GS are the prices of A's and G's product excluding transportation costs. The lines RT and SV show the price of A's and G's product delivered to the various cities.

City D is located exactly half way between producers A and G. It follows from our assumptions that the steel producer at A will have a competitive advantage in selling to all customers located in cities between A and D, and firm G will have an advantage in selling to all customers located between D and G. City D is the only location in which the firms will compete without advantage because it is the only city to which both firms have equal transportation costs.

To increase sales to otherwise unreachable towns, the two firms may adopt *Single Base-Point Pricing.* This system is characterized by the choice of a common location by both firms from which all transportation costs will be quoted. This location is called a base point. It is usually a production point, but this is not always the case. Our two firms may elect to use town G as the base point. If this is the case, not only will the firm located in G use town G as the basis

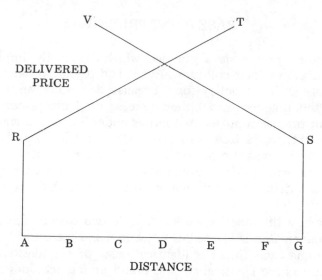

COST CURVES FOR TWO FIRMS LOCATED IN SEPARATE AREAS
FIGURE III

for determining its freight charge, but the firm located in A will also use G as the basis for the freight charge. Thus even if A sells to customers located in A, it will charge them a freight charge from G. Conversely, even if A has to ship its product to a buyer in town F, it will only charge the buyer a transportation charge from G to F, not from A to F. Actually, firm A adopts the same price curve that firm G has (SV in *Figure III*). Firm A has to absorb freight costs when it sells to cities E, F, and G, but makes an extra profit on shipping when it sells to cities C, B, and A. Because some customers pay for more freight than they receive, this extra profit to the firm is called "phantom freight." The system allows both steel firms to compete in all towns.

Single base-point pricing was first implemented by the U.S. Steel Corporation in 1901, and was called the "Pittsburgh Plus" system. Prior to 1901, Andrew Carnegie had a large number of steel plants which cut prices almost anytime price cutting was necessary to gain orders. This sparked intense competition in the industry. Carnegie's firm was purchased in 1901 by U.S. Steel, and the owners of U.S. Steel began quoting steel prices for all of their plants using Pittsburgh as the shipping origin. Competing firms followed suit by also quoting prices from Pittsburgh, regardless of their plant location.

A variation of this practice is Multiple Base-Point Pricing. Suppose our two firms, A and G, are located in the East, and they have a competitor located in Los Angeles. Clearly, customers in California would not buy from either firm A or G because of the high transportation cost involved. If A and G wanted to compete with the Los Angeles firm, they could adopt another base point—Los Angeles—in addition to point G. Customers closer to Los Angeles than point G would be charged freight from Los Angeles. Customers located closer to point G would be charged freight from point G. Firms may adopt a multitude of base points. For example, at one time the cement industry was reported to have 79 such points. Multiple base-point pricing has also been used in the pulp, sugar, and lead industries.

There are several important characteristics of firms that engage in single or multiple base-point pricing. (1) The product they sell is generally standardized so that the major consideration of purchasers is the price. (2) Transportation costs make up a large percentage of the total cost of the product because the product is usually heavy and/or bulky. Firms with small shipping costs do not use base-point pricing because they can generally absorb freight costs themselves and charge the same price to customers regardless of the customers' location. (3) Shipments frequently have to be made over long distances. (4) The market is oligopolistic so that firms are able to implement tacit or overt agreements among themselves concerning the base-point operation. Moreover, they may adopt base-point pricing in lieu of price competition because they realize that their competitive situation could break out into a price war if they used marginal cost pricing. (5) Firms frequently operate below capacity so that at times they find it advantageous to sell their product at or around its marginal cost. (6) The economics of production require that the plants be located in only a few areas in the country.[28]

These characteristics suggest two major reasons for the use of the practice. First, if firms are producing at less than full capacity, they may find it advantageous to increase sales by selling in distant territories either at or close to marginal cost. Second, the practice may simply be adopted in lieu of price competition. If this is the case, it represents a modification of tacit collusion to include an allowance for the existence of relatively high transportation costs.

Both single and multiple base-point pricing have mixed effects on consumer welfare. Probably the biggest objection to the practice is that it is discriminatory. Some customers would be able to purchase the product at less than they could if the basing formulas did not exist. Others, paying phantom freight, experience higher costs. Antitrust authorities generally object to any situation where prices charged differ without some cost justification. Economists, however, do not always support the thesis that price discrimination is harmful to the consumer. They reason that since individual utility functions cannot be measured, it is impossible to determine the net effect on consumer welfare when one group of consumers has to pay more for a product and another group pays less. Only when the two consumers compete with one another do economists become concerned. In that case, the use of price discrimination at one level of distribution may give a competitive advantage to a firm at a lower level of distribution. For example, if one auto manufacturer can buy steel at a lower price than other auto manufacturers, it might have a competitive advantage in the sale of automobiles. Single base-point pricing, however, insures that all customers in an area get the product at the same price because it takes away any locational advantage that a customer may have. Multiple base-point pricing does not insure uniform prices and may be injurious to competition.

Another objection to base-point pricing is that it tends to eliminate price competition. No doubt this is true, but there are two arguments that partially offset this disadvantage. First, although base-point pricing eliminates price competition, the customer usually has more sellers from which to choose. This can afford the consumer nonprice advantages. Suppose, for example, that a buyer is located near one steel plant. Other plants are far away, and only when base-point pricing is adopted by the steel industry would the customer be contacted by more than one firm. Although all the steel companies may charge the same price for their product, they may offer some other form of service to the customer in order to get his business. In this sense the customer may be better off than when he was supplied by one company. Of course, there is no guarantee that additional service will be provided. Second, base-point pricing is often used by companies to end cutthroat (hard) competition. Cutthroat competition may result in some firms being forced out of business while the remaining firms likely acquire additional monopoly power. Base-point pricing is one way to end this form of competition. Of course, the argument as well as the preceding one is equally applicable to any form of tacit or overt price collusion, and it was these arguments which were rejected by the courts in the overt price-fixing cases.

Some critics of base-point pricing argue that the practice causes unnecessary cross-hauling of products which is detrimental to the welfare of society. Their argument is sound. Without base-point pricing, consumers would probably buy from the firm nearest them, and the real cost of transportation as well as the use of energy resources would be minimized. However, with base-point pricing, customers have more incentive to purchase from the more distant plants which might cause real transportation costs to increase. Furthermore, base-point pricing may retard the search of producers for new industrial locations. Without some form of base-point pricing, they would tend to locate closest to the largest number of customers possible. Their incentive for doing this is to maximize profits, but in so doing, they minimize transportation costs. With base-point pricing, producers have less incentive to locate in a convenient area, and so the overall transportation costs may be higher than ordinary. Finally, base-point pricing may encourage the use of inefficient modes of transportation. Base-point rates are usually quoted from rate books of railroads because rail rates are standardized. As a result, producers generally use railroads even when more efficient methods of transportation are available.

The practice of base-point pricing certainly can have some detrimental effects on the welfare of the consumer. Therefore there are some good reasons for outlawing the practice. However, it is important to remember that producers must already have monopoly power in order to use base-point pricing. It follows that the elimination of the practice will not eliminate the monopoly power, but just an effect of that power. More importantly, if base-point pricing is outlawed, localized monopolies may develop, and producers may operate at less than full capacity.

Earlier we observed that base-point pricing can be prosecuted under the provisions of either Sections 1 and 2 of the Sherman Act, or Section 5 of the Federal Trade Commission Act. Section 5 states that "Unfair methods of competition in commerce, and unfair or deceptive acts or practices in commerce, are hereby declared illegal."[29] Most of the cases that we will review involving base-point pricing were prosecuted under the Federal Trade Commission Act. But because it involves tacit or overt collusion, base-point pricing also has been prosecuted under the Sherman Act. This is one of many instances where the Sherman and Federal Trade Commission Acts overlap.

CORN PRODUCTS REFINING COMPANY

Although base-point pricing was first used in the 1880s, it was not until 1945 that the courts made a decision concerning its legality. In *Corn Products Refining Co. v. F.T.C.*[30] the Supreme Court supported the Federal Trade Commission in contending that "... Petitioners' basing-point system resulted in discrimination in price among purchasers of glucose, and that the discriminations result in substantial harm to competition among such purchasers."[31]

The Corn Products Refining Company had two plants which manufactured glucose and corn syrup which were sold to candy manufacturers. One plant was located near Chicago, and the other was located at Kansas City. Freight was charged from Chicago for sales from either plant. The Court's decision was made wholly on the price discrimination issue. It did not consider the concept of tacit collusion because only one company was involved.

CEMENT INSTITUTE

In 1948, the Supreme Court heard an appeal concerned with base-point pricing in *F.T.C.* v. *Cement Institute.*[32] Several cement manufacturers were charged with maintaining multiple-base point schemes which resulted in uniform cement prices throughout the country. The Court ruled that adherence to a base-point pricing system was against the law, saying that:

> It seems impossible to conceive that anyone reading these findings in their entirety could doubt that the Commission found that respondents collectively maintained a multiple basing point delivered price system for the purpose of suppressing competition in cement sales. The findings are sufficient. The contention that they are not is without substance.[33]

This case brought tacit collusion in base-point pricing squarely under the law.

TRIANGLE CONDUIT AND CABLE COMPANY

In 1948, fourteen manufacturers of steel conduit were charged with multiple base-point pricing under Section 5 of the Federal Trade Commission Act.[34] The defendents contended that evidence of a conspiracy was wholly circimstantial. Moreover, they argued that their pricing system had no adverse effects on competition and was not oppressive. The court of appeals agreed that there was no evidence of a written or verbal contract between the defendants. However, it said that it was not necessary to find direct proof of an agreement. The mere fact that all of the defendants charged identical prices was enough for the court to infer a conspiracy. The court also held that competition was reduced: "Purchasers everywhere were unable to find price advantages anywhere; and purchasers at or near a place of production could not buy more cheaply from their nearby producer than from producers located at greater distances. . . ."[35]

The current law on base-point pricing is clear. If firms systematically match one another's price through the use of base-point pricing, their actions are illegal. The law is more stringent than the law on tacit collusion without base-point pricing. In the early 1950s, businesses did attempt to have Congress pass legislation to exempt base-point pricing from the law, but they were unsuccessful.

TRADE ASSOCIATION REPORTING PRACTICES

Most major industries have formed trade associations designed to promote the interests of their members. These organizations provide information dealing with the technology of the industry, form lobbies to promote the interests of their members, and acquaint their members with the economic conditions of the day. Although the associations are allowed by our antitrust laws, some of their practices violate the provisions of the Sherman Act. Trade association meetings provide a good gathering place for competitors. We already know that if the competitors make an agreement to fix prices at these meetings, their agreement would be illegal *per se*. But suppose that the association collects and publishes the prices charged by various competitors along with information related to their production costs, sales, inventory levels, etc. Does this practice affect competition?

Information about competitors' business operations can increase competition as well as consumer welfare. Firms are not expected to operate efficiently in a market where they have no knowledge of their competitors' actions. This would be analogous to playing a game of chess where one player has to guess his opponent's move and on the basis of a guess, make a counter move. On the other hand, too much information can foster the development of tacit collusion. Many of the industries that have trade associations are oligopolistic. Therefore they have some natural propensity to adopt parallel pricing arrangements. But parallel pricing is not easy to implement if there are more than four or five firms in an industry. It is even more difficult to implement if there are different types and grades of products being sold, and if a firm does not know the prices charged by its competitors. However, the publication of price lists and other information can aid in reducing these problems. Moreover, such business reporting can provide a means of policing an overt conspiracy to determine whether any member has cut prices. It is easy to see why the publication of price lists and other information by trade associations has been scrutinized carefully by the antitrust authorities.

Since it is recognized that price lists and other information can promote competition, such publications should not always be disallowed. Some way must be devised to separate the lists designed to aid the competitive process from lists which retard it. Kaysen and Turner have constructed a set of criteria. They found that the undesirable lists are those which include:

1. Agreements by competitors to abide by their price list;
2. Reporting of offers, even though sales are not always made on the basis of these offers;
3. Identification of individual buyers and sellers;
4. Refusals to make the information available to buyers as well as sellers;
5. Opening competitor's books to each other;
6. Reporting prices without some time lag.[36]

Kaysen and Turner reasoned that these characteristics promote parallel pricing rather than competition.

AMERICAN COLUMN AND LUMBER COMPANY

The courts have recognized both the good and bad aspects of association publications. However, separating information which is detrimental to competition from that which can promote it has been difficult. *American Column and Lumber Company* v. *United States*[37] was the first major antitrust case involving the publication of information by trade associations. Hardwood manufacturers which produced about one-third of the national output took part in an "open competition" plan. They sent daily reports of sales and deliveries to the secretary of their association. Each month they filed information related to price lists, their level of production, and their inventory of hardwood. The secretary then sent reports to the members summarizing this information. Moreover, the members met periodically to set up pricing and output policies which would secure high profits. Attendance at the meetings was voluntary. The case was not hard to decide because by holding the meetings, the members revealed their true intent. The Supreme Court found that the arrangement surpassed steps which promote competition. Justice Clarke, speaking for the majority of the Court, stated:

> Genuine competitors do not make daily, weekly, and
> monthly reports of the minutest details of their business to
> their rivals, as the defendants did; they do not contract, as
> was done here, to submit their books to the discretionary
> audit, and their stocks to the discretionary inspection of
> their rivals, for the purpose of successfully competing with
> them; and they do not subject the details of their business
> to the analysis of an expert, jointly employed, and obtain
> from him a "harmonized" estimate of the market as it is,
> and as, in his specially and confidentially informed judg-
> ment, it promises to be.[38]

Three judges disagreed with the decision. Justice Brandeis argued
that a redeeming virtue of the plan was that the information was
made available to customers. He also said that the evidence did not
show that the defendants charged uniform prices. He thought that
the information provided in the reporting plan was simply designed
to provide market information.

AMERICAN LINSEED OIL COMPANY

In 1923, the Supreme Court heard a similar case, *United States* v.
American Linseed Oil Company.[39] The reporting plan involved was
almost identical to that of the lumber association, but in this arrangement the members were required to attend monthly meetings and
were prosecuted by the association if they did not give a full report
of their transactions or if their output level resulted in low prices.
The Supreme Court declared the practice illegal.

MAPLE FLOORING

The Court endorsed the reporting system used in *Maple Flooring
Manufacturers Association et al.* v. *United States*,[40] heard in 1925.
The association collected and published information dealing with the
members' sales, prices, stocks, average costs, and freight charges. The
members also held periodic meetings, but the record showed that
they did not discuss prices. Moreover, members' prices were not
uniform. The Supreme Court said that information concerning the
cost of production, the cost of transportation, the production level,
the amount of stock and the prices at which a commodity was
actually sold were "legitimate subjects of inquiry and knowledge in
any industry." It further said that it would allow the publication of
this information by trade associations as long as there was no

evidence of agreement among the members to follow one another's prices and no evidence of parallel action.

SUGAR INSTITUTE

In the *Sugar Institute v. United States*,[41] heard in 1936, the question of whether members could religiously adhere to published prices was a major issue. The institute published information very similar to that in *Maple Flooring*. However, the members of the Sugar Institute agreed that they would not deviate from announced prices. Chief Justice Hughes endorsed the specific reporting system of the institute, but he outlawed the requirement that the firms adhere to their announced prices. Justice Hughes reasoned that changing competitive conditions might make price variations appropriate. Yet, because of the agreement to sell at quoted prices, members would be unable to adjust prices. The decision is a clear one: while the printing of some trade information is acceptable, requiring strict adherence to it is not.

TAG MANUFACTURERS INSTITUTE

In *Tag Manufacturers Institute et al. v. Federal Trade Commission*,[42] a court of appeals endorsed the publication of information by the institute. The arrangement was similar to the ones we have discussed except that members had to notify the institute within 24 hours if their prices deviated from the list prices. The court of appeals found there was no agreement to sell at list price, and they noted that frequently the members sold at less than list price.

There have been many recent cases on the subject, but these have not changed the law regarding the publication of information by trade associations. The associations are allowed to publish most but not all of the information concerning their business activities. (Current prices identified by buyer would probably be disallowed, for example.) However, the members must not discuss the level at which they believe prices should be set. Nor should the association require that members adhere to their list prices. In fact, members who rarely cut prices below their quoted level may find that the courts construe their pricing policy as evidence of conspiracy.

DIVISION OF TERRITORIES

Unethical firms with a penchant for monopoly profits may decide that price fixing is not as effective in ending competition as they want it to be. After all, it does not necessarily stop nonprice competition and, as we have already seen, there is a tremendous incentive for firms to cut their prices below the prescribed level in order to make additional profits. Therefore colluding firms may elect to divide the total market among themselves so that they do not compete in any way with one another. The effect of such an arrangement is to create a virtual monopoly for each firm in an assigned territory. The customer can expect to pay a monopoly price for the product he purchases.

Territories can be divided in several ways.

(1) Geographical division is the most common method. Firms simply slice the country into various sections, and each firm claims an exclusive right to sell in a section.

(2) The firms might divide the country into classes of customers. For example, one firm might sell exclusively to government accounts while another firm sells to private customers.

(3) Markets can also be divided into percentage shares. Each member would be allowed to sell anywhere, but his total sales would be limited to a certain per cent of the industry output.

(4) The market can be divided in terms of the uses to which the product will be put. One firm, for example, may sell chemicals to fertilizer companies while another firm will sell the same chemicals to pharmaceutical companies.

In the first part of this chapter, we studied *Addyston Pipe and Steel Company* v. *United States.* Although we considered it in the context of overt price fixing, the reader will remember that the companies also divided territories among themselves. The court considered the price-fixing scheme and the division of territories as a unit; it did not differentiate between the legality of each practice. However, it is safe to say that division of territories would have been outlawed even if the price-fixing arrangement was not involved.

A provision to divide territories was considered in *Timken Roller Bearing Co.* v. *United States.*[43] The government had charged that Timken Roller Bearing Company conspired with British Timken, Ltd. and Societe Anonyme Francaise Timken to divide the world market in the sale of anti-friction bearings. Even though the three companies were jointly owned, the arrangement was thought to be anticompetitive by the Supreme Court. Timken Roller Bearing Co. argued that its arrangement was merely incidental to its "joint venture" with the other companies. Additionally, it thought that the division of territories merely represented an exercise of the company's right to license the trademark "Timken." The Court thought that these arguments did not justify the arrangement since a restraint of trade was established.

It was not until 1972 that the courts determined that horizontal division of territories was *per se* illegal. This decision was made in *U.S.* v. *Topco Associates, Inc.*,[44] a case that we will analyze in Chapter VII.

SUMMARY

The courts have taken a very critical view of collusive arrangements between firms. Price fixing, division of territories, and base-point pricing are illegal. Tacit collusion is also illegal when the firms using it have significant monopoly power. However, the courts have not been willing to break up firms engaged in tacit collusion, and therefore no remedial penalties have been envoked. Tacit collusion exists in many parts of our economy today and represents perhaps the greatest "loop hole" in our antitrust laws. Trade associations are allowed, but they are prevented from distributing information which promotes parallel pricing behavior.

NOTES TO CHAPTER VI

[1]For a detailed analysis of pricing arrangements for overt or tacit collusion see Joe S. Bain, "A Note on Pricing in Monopoly and Oligopoly," *American Economic Review*, XXXIX, (1949), 448-464, reprinted in Heflebower and Stocking, *Readings in Industrial Organization and Public Policy* (Homewood, Ill.: Richard D. Irwin, Inc., 1958), pp. 220-235.

[2]175 U.S. 211 (1899).

[3]47 S. Ct. 377 (1927).

[4]47 S. Ct. 377, 383 (1927).

[5]See Almarin Phillips, *Market Structure, Organization and Performance* (Cambridge, Mass.: Harvard University Press, 1962), pp. 161-176 for an interesting analysis of the case.

[6]See Almarin Phillips, "A Critique of the U.S. Experience with Price Fixing Agreements and the Per Se Rule," *Journal of Industrial Economics*, VII (1959), 13-32 for good arguments against the use of the *per se* rule.

[7]60 S. Ct. 811 (1940).

[8]60 S. Ct. 811, 843 (1940).

[9]60 S. Ct. 811, 843 (1940).

[10]It is interesting to note that individuals engaged in many of the professions have engaged in overt price fixing with immunity from the antitrust laws. Among them are doctors, stock brokers, real estate brokers, funeral directors, and lawyers. They have argued that price competition may reduce the quality of the services they provide. Although their argument has some convincing aspects, no one has been able to prove, at least to this author's satisfaction, that their professions differ markedly from others which provide an important service to the public. In the last few years the Justice Department has initiated a number

of actions against these professions, and it is doubtful that their price fixing activity will continue for long.

[11]The terminology is that of Jesse W. Markham, "The Nature and Significance of Price Leadership," *American Economic Review*, XLI (1951), 891-905.

[12]This model was presented by James M. Henderson and Richard E. Quandt, *Microeconomic Theory, a Mathematical Approach*, 2nd ed. (New York: McGraw-Hill Book Company, 1971), pp. 249-250.

[13]Markham, p. 897.

[14]Markham, pp. 901-903.

[15]66 S. Ct. 1125 (1945).

[16]66 S. Ct. 1125, 1139 (1945).

[17]66 S. Ct. 1125, 1140 (1945).

[18]William H. Nicholls, "The Tobacco Case of 1946," *American Economic Review*, XXXIX (1949), 284-96, reprinted in Heflebower and Stocking, Editors, *Readings in Industrial Organization and Public Policy* (Homewood, Ill.: Richard D. Irwin, Inc., 1958), p. 112.

[19]Nicholls, p. 116.

[20]274 U.S. 693 (1927).

[21]274 U.S. 693, 709 (1927).

[22]Peverly Dairy Co. v. United States, 178 F. 2d 363, 368-69 (1949).

[23]Phillips, *Market Structure, Organization and Performance*, p. 62.

[24]See *C-O-Two Fire Equipment Co.* v. *U.S.*, 197 F. 2d 489 (1952), *Morton Salt Company* v. *U.S.*, 235 F. 2d 573 (1956), and *U.S.* v. *Eli Lilly & Co.*, Crim no. 173-58 D.N.J. (1959), summarized in Phillips, *Market Structure, Organization and Performance*, pp. 61-73. In deciding these cases the courts used legal "nit-picking" in deciding which forms of conscious parallelism were acceptable and which were not.

[25]346 U.S. 537 (1954).

[26]Phillips, *Market Structure, Organization and Performance*, p. 73.

[27]*F.T.C.* v. *National Lead Company*, 352 U.S. 419 (1953).

[28]All six characteristics were presented by Carl Kaysen, "Basing Point Pricing and Public Policy," *The Quarterly Journal of Economics*, XLIII (1949), 289-314.

[29]38 Stat. 717 (1914).

[30]324 U.S. 726 (1945).

[31]324 U.S. 726, 730 (1945).

[32]68 S. Ct. 793 (1948).

[33]68 S. Ct. 793, 809 (1948).

[34]*Triangle Conduit and Cable Co.* v. *F.T.C.*, 168 F. 2d 175 (1948).

[35]168 F. 2d 175, 180 (1948).

[36]Carl Kaysen and Donald F. Turner, *Antitrust Policy: An Economic and Legal Analysis* (Cambridge, Mass: Harvard University Press, 1959), p. 150.

[37]42 Sup. Ct. 114 (1921).

[38]42 S. Ct. 114, 120 (1921).

[39]262 U.S. 371 (1923).

[40]45 S. Ct. 578 (1925).

[41]297 U.S. 629 (1936).

[42]43 F.T.C. 499 (1947).

[43]341 U.S. 593 (1950).

[44]319 F. Supp. 1031 (1970); 92 S. Ct. 1126 (1972).

VERTICAL TERRITORIAL ARRANGEMENTS   CHAPTER VII

When producers use independent businessmen to sell their product, they frequently attempt to control some of the operations of the businessmen. In this chapter the economics as well as the legality of assigning specific territories to them is considered.

INTRODUCTION

Vertical territorial arrangements, resale price maintenance and refusals to deal are discussed in this and the next two chapters. While their use is not limited exclusively to the practice of franchising, they frequently constitute part of a franchise agreement. The franchisee selling a supplier's product is an independent businessman in the sense that he provides capital and is responsible for the operation of his business. But he agrees in his contract to meet certain standards established by the supplier. The supplier, in turn, provides some managerial and technical assistance in addition to selling his products to the franchisee for resale. Such an agreement is often better for a supplier than selling directly to final consumers. It reduces the amount of capital required. Additionally, suppliers often find that a small independent businessman with an attachment to the community in which he sells will generate greater sales than a representative hired by the supplier. Yet because the franchisee is the supplier's representative, it is crucial that he be an effective one. It is for this reason that suppliers often attempt to control some activities of their franchisees. The extent of that control allowed under the provisions of the antitrust laws will be explored by analyzing vertical territorial arrangements.

Vertical territorial arrangements need little introduction to the student of business and economics. Everyone has heard of an "exclusive franchise," a dealer who is the "exclusive representative" for a product in a geographical area, or a dealer who has "primary responsibility" for the sale of a product. Advertisements often contain one or more of these words to impress the consumer with the dealer's ability to satisfy his needs.

All truly vertical territorial arrangements (V.T.A.'s) have three major characteristics: First, they are initiated by a supplier of a product; second, they are designed to allocate customers among dealers, either geographically or by some other customer characteristic; third, they reduce or eliminate intrabrand competition. That is, they reduce or eliminate competition between dealers selling the same-brand product.

V.T.A.'s can be divided into three major categories according to the degree to which they restrain intrabrand competition. The categories are exclusive franchising, territorial security arrangements, and closed-territory distribution.

Exclusive franchising is a method of distribution whereby a supplier grants to each of his dealers sole responsibility for promoting the supplier's product in an assigned territory. Only one dealer is allowed to locate in the territory, called a "zone of influence." In return for the supplier's concession, the dealer is expected to actively promote the supplier's product in the zone. It is important to observe that, although the arrangement puts a restraint on the physical location of dealers, it places no restraint on the territory in which a dealer may sell the product. A dealer may send his salesmen to other dealers' zones of influence. Also, customers are allowed to shop freely from one dealer to another. Most customers do not even know that zones of influence exist.

Like exclusive franchising, territorial security arrangements involve the granting of an exclusive right to locate in an assigned area. However, they further limit intrabrand competition by providing that the dealer may not sell outside of his territory. Thus, dealers operating under territorial security clauses are not allowed to send salesmen to other dealers' zones of influence. Customers, however, are allowed to shop freely between dealers. Whether or not territorial security provisions differ in practice from exclusive franchising depends on the importance of dealers' sales contracts outside of their zone of influence. If dealers normally do not sell outside of their zones, the two arrangements are, in practice, identical.

Closed-territory distribution grants to a dealer the exclusive right to sell to customers residing in an assigned area. The agreement provides that a dealer must refuse sale of the product to any consumer who has his residence outside of the dealer's assigned area or to any business which is located outside of the assigned area. Customers cannot travel freely between dealers. The arrangement precludes any shopping by customers among dealers of the same brand unless a private consumer has two or more residences which are located in more than one of the dealers' territories, or a firm is located in more than one of the dealers' territories.

So that the reader clearly understands the nature of the practice, an example may be helpful. Suppose two automobile dealers are located in a town, and they sell the same brand. If the company supplying the automobiles chose to use closed-territory distribution, it could assign the western part of the town to dealer A and the eastern part of town to dealer B. Should a customer from the west come into dealer B's showroom to purchase a car, he would be told that he must buy that brand of car from dealer A. It can readily be seen that the practice eliminates intrabrand competition. Closed-territory distribution is not always used to allocate customers geographically. Instead it might be used to segregate them by some characteristic other than their location. For example, one dealer selling patent medicine may be assigned all the hospital accounts and another dealer may be assigned all drugstore accounts.

Closed-territory distribution differs in degree but not in kind from territorial security agreements. If, under territorial security agreements, no customer would go to a dealer other than the one in the territory in which the customer resided, there would, in practice, be no difference between the two arrangements. There can be variations of closed-territory distribution which are designed to retain customer good will and make up for oversights on the part of dealers. These variations include provisions for reimbursing offended dealers for the loss of profit from an improper sale as well as various expenses which may be incurred by him, such as serving or honoring warranties on products sold by other dealers.

REASONS FOR VERTICAL TERRITORIAL ARRANGEMENTS

As the reasons that would prompt a supplier to adopt one of the vertical arrangements are considered, it is very important to remember that the arrangements are vertical. They are unlike the horizontal division of territories that were discussed in Chapter VI.[1]

It is not immediately clear why a supplier would wish to restrict intrabrand competition. It would seem that if the supplier sold to all representatives willing to carry his product, and if there was strong competition among them, he would maximize demand for his product and earn greater profits than he otherwise could. An increased number of outlets would increase the total amount of advertising, the customer convenience of buying the goods, the number of service outlets, and the degree of price competition. One cannot claim that competition between representatives grows in direct proportion to their number, but there is a correlation between the number of sales outlets available to the consumer and competition. Why, then, would a supplier use one of the V.T.A.'s? There are four possible answers to this question. The arrangements might be used:

   A. To increase the monopoly power of a supplier's dealers so that the supplier can extract profits from them;
   B. To increase the monopoly power of the supplier;
   C. To increase the profits of the supplier and his dealers by providing dealers with the means to engage in price discrimination;
   D. To increase the supplier's efficiency as well as the efficiency of his dealers.

INCREASED MONOPOLY POWER OF DEALERS

Many lawyers and economists believe that V.T.A.'s are used by a supplier to increase the monopoly power of his dealers. The practices do give additional monopoly power to dealers by reducing intrabrand competition. However, it is not obvious that a supplier would want his dealers to have this power. A supplier would not grant V.T.A.'s to his dealers unless he was in some way compensated for the provision. There is, however, a sound theoretical economic reason explaining why dealers could offer a large enough payment to induce their supplier to provide them with one of the vertical arrangements. When we study vertical integration in Chapter XIII, we will see that joint profits of a supplier and his dealers are maximized if they act as a vertically integrated firm when they establish the retail price of their product. To maximize joint profits without vertical integration, the supplier could act with some degree of monopoly power in setting the retail price of their product. Since the joint profits of the supplier and his dealers are maximized by such an arrangement, it follows that the dealers could adequately compensate their supplier for transferring his monopoly power to them and still increase their own profits. Although the argument is theoretically sound, it is doubtful whether suppliers would act in this way since the arrangement would be complicated to administer.

INCREASED MONOPOLY POWER OF SUPPLIERS

V.T.A.'s might be used by a supplier to induce dealers to carry the supplier's full line of products to the exclusion of those of competing companies. In other words, V.T.A.'s might be a means of implementing exclusive dealing arrangements. Additionally, they might be used as part of a horizontal arrangement to divide territories. The use of the practices in either of these ways affects interbrand competition and might increase the monopoly power of the supplier.

That it could be advantageous to obtain dealers specializing exclusively in the supplier's product is fairly obvious. It is discussed in Chapter XII but for now it is enough to know that dealers would not have divided allegiance between different brands and hence the possibility of their substituting other brands would be eliminated. If, in addition, the dealers have a good reputation in their areas, or have some locational advantage, the benefit would be increased because these choice dealers would be foreclosed to competitors.

V.T.A.'s might also be used as part of a collusive arrangement to divide territories so that no supplier's dealer competes with another supplier's dealer. For example, one supplier handling brand X may assign all of his dealers V.T.A.'s in the western part of a town, and another supplier handling brand Y may assign all of his dealers territories in the eastern part of a town. In this case the arrangement is horizontal as well as vertical. By using V.T.A.'s in this manner suppliers can increase their monopoly power and their profits. This arrangement is equivalent to horizontal division of territories resulting in the reduction or elimination of interbrand competition.

PRICE DISCRIMINATION

It is a common characteristic of imperfectly competitive markets that demand elasticities vary among different classes of customers. Because of the differing elasticities, it might pay a supplier to engage in price discrimination.[2] This simply means the setting of prices in different markets which are not proportional to the costs of serving these markets. It is essential to price discrimination that markets in which different prices are charged be kept separate. Closed-territory distribution is one feasible way to do this. In other words, if customers in market A are charged a certain price and customers in market B are charged a higher one, B customers must not be allowed to move freely to A in order to purchase products. Obviously, if there is free movement between the areas, all customers will go to A and the price discrimination will be defeated.

INCREASED EFFICIENCY

In antitrust litigation, suppliers have claimed that V.T.A.'s make them or their dealers more efficient in the selling of their products.

Three ways in which the arrangements might be used to increase efficiency are:

A. To induce dealers to provide certain forms of product promotion;

B. To increase the number of customers that dealers contact;

C. To provide cost reductions for dealers and their supplier.

Provision of Adequate Product Promotion

Suppliers sometimes argue that they must offer potential representatives some freedom from intrabrand competition in order to obtain the kind of representation they need. In this case "kind" may take the dimensions of quantity of capital, technical "know how," sales experience, or quality and quantity of advertising. This special representation is especially desirable if the supplier's product is one which requires specialized selling or servicing techniques which the supplier must control in order to protect his reputation. If the supplier is able to induce his dealers to provide these special services, he may be able to achieve a higher sales volume because he may be able to offer consumers a more desirable product.

Two examples will clarify this idea. An extreme example of the need to provide some form of V.T.A. existed in the Sandura case.[3] Sandura sold a laminated plastic floor covering and served about four per cent of the market. Before 1950 it experienced production problems which resulted in yellowing of the material. Also, some of the flooring became unlaminated while in stock. As a result, the company had a difficult time obtaining dealers and nearly failed. After correcting its production techniques, the company resorted to the use of closed-territory distribution in order to obtain dealers. The prospect of having no intrabrand competition lured dealers who might not otherwise have handled the product.

The Bendix Company, maker of automatic washing machines, also claimed it needed V.T.A.'s to obtain the type of representation it needed. When the automatic washing machine was first introduced it required frequent adjustment and detailed instructions for new buyers. Many retailers expressed a desire to handle the product, but Bendix only wanted representatives who were willing to demonstrate the product, educate buyers on the proper use of the unit, and establish an adequate service department. To obtain the desired representation Bendix promised dealers freedom from intrabrand competition.

There is good reason to believe that the promise of freedom from intrabrand competition is sometimes essential to induce the dealer to promote the product in certain ways. Without the promise of some freedom from intrabrand competition, the dealer is less assured that some forms of product promotion will bring adequate returns to him. A lack of adequate returns lessens his incentive to provide such services. Consider the case of a hypothetical dealer, Reinarman, who has specialized salesmen, spacious sales rooms, and actively promotes his product through advertising. Next to Reinarman is dealer Pratt who does not advertise, has untrained representatives, and uses an old building to house his facilities. Both dealers sell the same product. Since Pratt's promotional costs are lower, he can offer the product at a lower price. Potential consumers might become acquainted with the product through Reinarman's advertising and product demonstrations. Yet, to the extent that customers shop for the lowest price, they will go to Pratt for their purchase. Reinarman's superior effort is beneficial to the supplier in that it increases demand for his product. It is also beneficial to Pratt in that it increases the demand for his product. The problem is that Reinarman's superior facilities do not fully benefit Reinarman. Therefore, he is not likely to continue providing the effort that his supplier desires. This is a simple case of Reinarman's conferring an external economy on Pratt. Many externalities are difficult to internalize but this is not. If the supplier denies Pratt the right to compete with Reinarman, all the benefits resulting from Reinarman's efforts will accrue to Reinarman, and he will be more likely to provide the service that the supplier wants.

Increased Customer Contacts

Another reason that a supplier might wish to use V.T.A.'s is that without one of the practices, the duplication of sales effort by dealers competing for the same large accounts might reduce the sales effort directed toward smaller, less profitable accounts. Consequently it might reduce the supplier's sales. Expressed more precisely, sales effort of dealer A in dealer B's territory might increase the probability of sales in B's territory, but there may be a greater reduction in the probability of sales in A's territory. In such a situation, the optimum allocation of sales resources for the dealer would differ from the optimum allocation for the supplier. V.T.A.'s can reduce the degree to which dealers compete for accounts. Hence duplication of sales effort is reduced. White Motor, for example, argued that:

> . . . to obtain the maximum number of sales of trucks in a given area, the White Motor Company has to insist that its distributors and dealers concentrate on trying to take sales away from other competing truck manufacturers in their respective territories rather than on cutting each other's throats in other territories.[4]

Providing Cost Reductions

Certain cost reductions might accrue to the supplier who restricts the number of dealers representing him. First, with a reduced number of dealers, there is a reduced selling cost. Fewer dealer contacts have to be made by a supplier, and there are more sales per contact. Second, V.T.A.'s might allow each dealer to sell a greater volume of the product. To the extent that the dealer experiences economies of scale in distribution, he may be able to offer the consumer lower prices, or he may experience an increase in his profits. Evidence does tend to indicate that there can be increasing returns in distribution. For example, Charles E. Edwards found in his study of the automobile industry that substantial economies of scale were at the local dealer level, and "volume per dealer was important in the ultimate unit cost of putting a car in the hands of the consumer."[5]

EFFECTS OF VERTICAL TERRITORIAL ARRANGEMENTS

In this section of the chapter the effects of the three forms of V.T.A.'s on consumer welfare will be considered. More specifically, we will consider the arguments of two opposing schools of thought. One school argues that the practices restrict the degree of intrabrand competition and reduce consumer welfare while the other school argues that the practices, *when truly vertical in nature*, will never decrease consumer welfare.

THE INTRACOMPETITOR ARGUMENT

The first school of thought—we will call its proponents the "intracompetitors" for the sake of identification—argues that the use of V.T.A.'s reduces intrabrand competition. Therefore they believe that the practices should be disallowed by the courts. To demonstrate the harm resulting from the practices they would point to a consumer who is not able to patronize his favorite dealer. As a result, this consumer may have to pay a higher price for the product, use facilities that he likes less, or may even be forced to buy a different brand of the product. That some customers are hurt by the reduction or elimination of intrabrand competition is undeniable. Even though they have the option of switching brands, they may have a strong attachment to their old brand. Furthermore, if one believes that intrabrand competition gives benefits to the consumer that pressures from other-brand dealers cannot bring about, then a strong presumption exists in favor of maintaining strong intrabrand competition for the sake of consumer welfare.

THE INTERCOMPETITOR ARGUMENT

Another school—the "intercompetitors"—argue that if V.T.A.'s are truly vertical, they might increase overall consumer welfare, or at a minimum they cannot reduce it. The argument they present is more detailed than the "intracompetitor" argument, but it deserves careful consideration because it applies to some other alleged anti-competitive practices that we will analyze in later chapters. Their argument is based on one major theme: V.T.A.'s can never be used to increase monopoly power; at worst they transfer such power from one level of distribution to another level. The supplier of a particular brand of product already has a monopoly in the sale of that brand. By virtue of this power, he can control the price and output of his product. The use of V.T.A.'s cannot increase his monopoly power. Monopoly power can be extended only if interbrand competition is curbed.

The effect of V.T.A.'s on economic efficiency will be considered in each of the instances for which the practice might be used: to increase the monopoly power of dealers, to increase the monopoly power of the supplier, to implement price discrimination, and to increase consumer welfare.

INCREASED MONOPOLY POWER OF DEALERS

When a supplier transfers monopoly power to his dealers no additional monopoly power is created. Other things being equal, the effect of the arrangements on the price paid by the consumer would be the same as if the supplier integrated to the retail level of distribution. Monopoly power is not increased (unless foreclosure is involved), and thus there is no reason to suspect that the arrangements affect consumer welfare adversely.

INCREASED MONOPOLY POWER OF THE SUPPLIER

It has been shown that V.T.A.'s might be used by a supplier to insure that dealers carry the supplier's full line of products to the exclusion of those of competing companies. However, there is no reason to expect that competition is reduced in all instances or even in the majority of instances in which exclusive dealing arrangements are used. Nor is there reason to assume that a large percentage of instances exist in which vertical territorial restraints are used by suppliers to induce their dealers to carry products exclusively. Antitrust cases do not reveal one instance in which V.T.A.'s were used with this effect. Even if they are used to gain exclusive dealing, it is the exclusive dealing clause that affects competition and hence consumer welfare. V.T.A.'s are merely a means to that end. Therefore it is the exclusive dealing provision that should be evaluated by the courts and the Federal Trade Commission.

When V.T.A.'s are used to divide territories between suppliers, no supplier's dealer competes with another supplier's dealer. Competition is eliminated between suppliers, and a decrease in consumer welfare will probably result. Courts have considered horizontal division of territories illegal *per se*. But the intercompetitors would say that if V.T.A.'s are found to be part of an agreement to divide territories horizontally, the horizontal conspiracy, not the V.T.A., should be declared illegal under Section 1 of the Sherman Act.

PRICE DISCRIMINATION

It has been shown that V.T.A.'s might be used by a supplier to engage in price discrimination. The basic problem in analyzing price discrimination is that it is difficult to determine its net effect on consumer welfare when a product is sold to a final consumer. The practice will harm consumers with lower elasticities of demand by increasing the price they pay. On the other hand, customers with higher elasticities of demand will gain. The optimum price in their territories will be lower than if an "average" price were chosen for all dealers selling the supplier's product. To evaluate the net effect on society, we have to turn to a rule established by Joan Robinson in the 1930s. She said that "When some output would be produced even if discrimination were forbidden, it is only possible to say definitely whether price discrimination is damaging to the interests of the customers, as compared with a single price monopoly, if we identify ourselves with one or another group of customers."[6] Paraphrasing Mrs. Robinson, it is impossible to determine the effects of this form of price discrimination on consumer welfare unless we are willing to make value judgments to determine the more worthy group of consumers. We have no justification to disallow V.T.A.'s if they are used to implement price discrimination at the retail level.

INCREASED EFFICIENCY

We have seen that V.T.A.'s might be used by a supplier to make his dealers more effective in promoting the supplier's product. Specifically, the practices might be used to induce dealers to provide certain forms of product promotion, to increase the number of customers that dealers contact, and to provide cost reductions for dealers and their suppliers. By doing this, the use of V.T.A.'s can increase the efficiency of dealers and thus increase consumer welfare. Each of the three instances mentioned above will be considered.

PROVISION OF ADEQUATE PRODUCT PROMOTION

A supplier would not offer V.T.A.'s unless he thought the arrangements improved the product package. It is to the supplier's advantage to have his dealers offer the most desirable package to the consumer. When the supplier sells directly to the consumer, he seeks the package (including promotion, service, demonstrations, etc.) that the consumer desires most. By doing this, he maximizes his profits. The situation is not different when he sells through an independent dealer. The supplier and his dealers maximize their joint profits by offering the most desirable package to the consumer. Thus, if customers generally prefer a low product price without service as compared to a higher product price with service, it is to the supplier's advantage to see that his dealers offer that product package. Likewise, it is not to the supplier's advantage for his dealers to offer a product without service and product information if customers prefer to have service and information and pay a higher price.

INCREASED NUMBER OF CUSTOMERS CONTACTED

The use of V.T.A.'s to increase the number of customers contacted can increase consumer welfare by increasing the number of alternatives available to them. If certain customers were not offered the product by any dealer prior to the use of V.T.A.'s, these customers clearly would gain, provided they desired the product. Furthermore, the addition of one more dealers contacting customers might increase the pressure on existing dealers selling other brands to offer a better price or other customer inducement.

REDUCE COST

It has been shown that the use of V.T.A.'s may reduce unit costs of distributing a product for both the supplier and his dealers. If this happens, it may pay the dealer to sell a larger quantity of the product at a lower price.

THE INTERCOMPETITOR SCHOOL: A SUMMARY

The members of the intercompetitor school argue that it is appropriate to declare V.T.A.'s legal *per se*. The practices, themselves, cannot rationally be used to increase monopoly power; at most, they transfer monopoly power from one level of distribution to another level. Furthermore, the practices can be used by suppliers to increase consumer welfare. In fact, unless they are used to implement price discrimination, exclusive dealing, or are a part of a horizontal conspiracy, the supplier would use them only if they enabled him to offer a better product package to the consumer. Even when they are used to engage in price discrimination, there is no reason to outlaw them. One cannot determine the effects of price discrimination on consumer welfare.

If V.T.A.'s are used to implement a horizontal conspiracy to divide territories, monopoly power probably would be increased. The intercompetitors would agree that the horizontal conspiracy should be declared illegal. Also, if V.T.A.'s are used to induce dealers to handle a product exclusively, monopoly power might be increased. Hence the intercompetitors would agree that the exclusive dealing provisions should be judged under Section 3 of the Clayton Act.

THE LEGALITY OF VERTICAL TERRITORIAL ARRANGEMENTS

So far we have been able to evaluate the three major forms of V.T.A.'s as an entity because they differ in degree, not in kind. However, legal decisions indicate that the courts see a significant difference between the practices. Thus each practice must be considered separately while we discuss the legality of V.T.A.'s.

THE LEGALITY OF EXCLUSIVE FRANCHISING

Bausch & Lomb

Beginning with *United States* v. *Bausch & Lomb Optical Company* there has been general agreement among the courts that exclusive franchising is allowable if it is ancillary to some acceptable business practice.[7] The *Bausch & Lomb* decision is known primarily for the ruling on resale price maintenance, but it is relevant to our study because it involved the granting of exclusive selling rights to Soft-Lite, a dealer for Bausch & Lomb's pink-tinted eyeglass lenses. Although the practice reduced intrabrand competition, Judge Rifkind recognized that it was used to promote Bausch & Lomb's products. He said:

the main purpose of the contract is to provide a source of supply for Soft-Lite. The restraining covenant is for the protection of the purchaser who is spending large sums to develop his good will and enlarge the public patronage of a relatively new article of commerce. The arrangement, though not a partnership in legal form, is functionally a joint enterprise in which one will produce and the other market the commodity.[8]

Rifkind also observed that strong interbrand competition existed between Bausch & Lomb's product and other competing lenses, and that competition had become even more intense because of the exclusive franchising arrangement.

Schwing Motor Co.

In two cases involving exclusive franchising, the legality of the practice was upheld, and the court's attitude further clarified. In *Schwing Motor Company* v. *Hudson Sales Corporation*, two franchised dealers for Hudson cars in Baltimore sued Hudson and a Hudson dealer for treble damages resulting from the loss of their dealerships.[9] Hudson had discontinued their franchises so that it could issue an exclusive franchise to another dealer in the Baltimore area. The Maryland District Court ruled that while the granting of exclusive representation established a territorial monopoly in the sale of a specific brand, it did not foreclose strong competition in the automobile industry because of the existence of rival brands. The law was further clarified when the court said that had Hudson dominated the market in the sale of automobiles, the finding might have been different. In the absence of market domination the manufacturer was permitted to grant a dealer a local monopoly in the sale of his brand.

Webster Motor Co.

A similar complaint was lodged in *Packard Motor Company* v. *Webster Motor Car Company*.[10] The largest of three Packard dealers in Baltimore told Packard that it would stop handling Packard automobiles unless it was granted an exclusive franchise. Packard decided to give the franchise to the representative and informed Webster Motor Car Company, among others, that its franchise would be discontinued. Webster then brought suit against Packard. The district court found in favor of Webster. Reversing the decision, the court of appeals reasoned that since interbrand competition was so fierce and since Packard was small relative to its competitors, the restraint on interbrand competition was not unreasonable. Chief Judge Edgerton went so far as to say that exclusive franchising was always legal when not part of a scheme to monopolize. "When an exclusive dealership is not part and parcel of a scheme to monopolize and effective competition exists at both the buyer and seller levels, the arrangement has invariably been upheld as a reasonable restraint of trade. In short, the rule was virtually one of per se legality."[11]

In summary, the law on exclusive franchising permits the practice when the defendant can demonstrate that its use is designed to bring about some justifiable business purpose (such as acquiring dealers and adequate dealer services), exists in an environment of strong interbrand competition, and does not have as its objective an increase in monopoly power.

Less lenient criteria have been urged by the Attorney General's National Committee to Study the Antitrust Laws. The committee suggested that three criteria should be used to determine the legality of exclusive franchising.[12]

1. the percentage of the market that is controlled by the franchise;
2. the strength of interbrand competition; and
3. whether the action is ancillary to a reasonable business practice or whether it is the result of a desire to monopolize.

The student will see in Chapter XIII that these criteria are similar to those used to evalute horizontal and vertical integration.

THE LEGALITY OF TERRITORIAL SECURITY ARRANGEMENTS

Before studying the courts' position on territorial security arrangements, it is important to remember that there is only one major difference between these arrangements and exclusive franchising. Territorial security arrangements prohibit dealers from selling in another dealer's territory. However, they do not prohibit customers from shopping between dealers. It might seem that the difference between the arrangements is insignificant, but the courts do not think so.

General Cigar   1932

In the *General Cigar* case, territorial security was likened to horizontal market division and resale price maintenance, an analogy of lasting importance.[13] General Cigar had divided its total market among forty-six independent wholesalers. Although there was no formal agreement, its distributors accepted the territories as assigned and cooperated in confining their sales activities. The decision of the Federal Trade Commission is of little importance, for the case was dismissed without opinion. But Commissioner McCulloch, in his dissent, presented an argument against territorial security arrangements which even today is the principal legal argument against the practice. Essentially, McCulloch's thesis corresponds to the arguments of the intracompetitors. He said that territorial security does not differ from horizontal market division, a practice which is illegal *per se*. He reasoned that an agreement between competitors is a violation of the Sherman Act. He further said that vertical agreements have the same effect as if dealers had agreed among themselves to divide territories. From this, he concluded that vertical territorial arrangements should also be illegal under the Sherman Act.

Boro Hall

1941

In *Boro Hall* v. *General Motors* the district court rejected McCulloch's analogy and presented a clear decision on the legality of security clauses.[14] Boro Hall, a Chevrolet dealer, had been assigned a zone of influence by General Motors. However, the agreement actually took the form of a territorial security arrangement when General Motors denied Boro Hall the right to establish a used car outlet and the right to solicit customers outside of its assigned territory. The district court, in finding for General Motors, said that a special relationship existed between General Motors and its dealers. According to the court, G.M. had given dealers the right to use its trademarks and good will, and there was nothing unreasonable about restricting the area in which the good will and trademarks were utilized. Moreover, the court found that such an agreement, if disallowed, might bring about conflict between dealers and harm General Motors' business interest. We can only guess from the court record that this statement meant that intrabrand competition might hurt General Motors' sales program.

The court of appeals interpreted the agreement between G.M. and its dealers not as involving absolute territorial security but as merely restricting placement of outlets to where they would not "unduly prejudice" other Chevrolet dealers. Because the case was reduced to one involving exclusive franchising, the reasoning of the *Schwing* and *Packard* decisions was used to find in favor of G.M. The law on territorial security arrangements was still undecided.

Snap-On Tools

After the *Boro Hall* decision, there were no important cases on territorial security until the early 1960s because the Justice Department had placed pressure on manufacturers to abstain from this practice. Snap-On Tools was one company willing to try the practice in spite of the pressure. The company manufactured a full line of tools and sold them through independent "vendors on wheels" operating from walk-in trucks which carried a stock of the tools most frequently bought. Snap-On had agreed with its dealers to restrict the territory within which and the customers to whom the dealers might sell.

The hearing examiner for the Federal Trade Commission stated that the rule of reason should be applied in each case of this type to determine whether the practice would be "reasonably likely" to have a substantial adverse effect on competition. Applying that rule, he found that the practice of providing territorial security to dealers was the only way that Snap-On could adequately promote its product other than through vertical integration. He also observed that strong interbrand competition existed and thought that the lack of intrabrand competition would not be harmful to the consumer.

On appeal, the Seventh Circuit Court of Appeals thought the examiner had made a mistake.[15] It said that intrabrand competition was the "essence of competition," and the existence of strong interbrand competition was considered to be immaterial to the decision. The commission sent the case back to the examiner for reconsideration. He once again considered the evidence and dismissed the case. The commission again reversed the examiner's decision and issued a cease and desist order to Snap-On. The *Snap-On* decision is important for one reason. The commission did deny the analogy with horizontal market division drawn in *General Cigar*. It said that a practice is not illegal *per se* just because it restricts intrabrand competition.

Topco

The fact that territorial security arrangements are not *per se* illegal was reiterated in a district court decision in *United States* v. *Topco Associates, Inc.* However, that decision was reversed by the Supreme Court.[16] Topco was a cooperative owned by twenty-five independent grocers. Its primary purpose was to purchase grocery products in large quantities and sell them to the grocers under various brand names owned by Topco. This allowed the grocers to sell a private-brand product which put them on equal footing with large national chains which also had their own private brands. Usually private brands can be sold at a lower price, and yet they yield a greater profit than those processed and sold under the name of a nationally advertised brand. Topco used two forms of territorial security arrangements. Some grocers were assigned an exclusive territory. This prohibited any other grocer from selling Topco products in the territory. Other grocers were assigned coextensive territories where they shared their exclusive arrangement with one or more grocers. Some Topco products were sold to grocers in nonexclusive territories where anyone could sell Topco products.

The government contended that the territorial security arrangements were illegal *per se*. To support its argument it noted that intrabrand competition would be diminished or eliminated. Topco, on the other hand, argued that the arrangement promoted competition because it placed the grocers on an equal footing with the large national grocery chains. Moreover it thought that unless the territorial security arrangements were permitted, grocers would be reluctant to promote Topco products.

The District Court for the Northern District of Illinois permitted Topco's practice. It noted that it was difficult to determine whether Topco's use of territorial security arrangements diminished intrabrand competition. But it thought that the relevant question was "whether the antitrust laws prohibit practices by a cooperative buying organization which may reduce competition between its members to compete more effectively with national chains whose private label brands are sold exclusively through their own outlets."[17] Part of the reason for its decision was based on the court's observation that if a national chain did the same thing, there would be no prohibition. This is an important point because quite frequently the courts have used a double standard in franchising cases. That is, they have permitted integrated companies to do that which a nonintegrated company is prohibited from doing.

The Supreme Court overturned the district court's decision. Because Topco's customers were also its owners, it treated the arrangement as a horizontal one and declared it *per se* illegal. It recognized that the benefit of increased interbrand competition might outweigh the detriment from decreased intrabrand competition, but thought itself in no position to determine the net effect on competition.

> If a decision is to be made to sacrifice competition in one portion of the economy for greater competition in another portion this too is a decision which must be made by Congress and not by private forces or by the courts. Private forces are too keenly aware of their own interests in making such decisions and courts are ill-equipped and ill-situated for such decision-making. To analyze, interpret, and evaluate the myriad of competing interests and the endless data which would surely be brought to bear on

such decisions, and to make the delicate judgment on the relative values to society of competitive areas of the economy, the judgment of the elected representatives of the people is required.[18]

While the *Topco* case did involve a possible horizontal combination it is doubtful whether territorial security arrangements which are purely vertical in nature will be allowed in the future. As long as the courts believe that a truly vertical arrangement can create monopoly power, they will continue to conceive the judgment process as the weighing of intrabrand and interbrand competition. And this is something they are not willing to do.

In his dissent, Justice Burger presented some interesting arguments against the Court's adoption of the *per se* rule, its failure to look at the economics of territorial security arrangements, and the effect of the Court's decision. Justice Burger's words speak for themselves.

The goal sought [by Topco] was the enhancement of the individual members' abilities to compete, albeit to a modest degree, with the large national chains which had been successfully marketing private label lines for several years. The sole reason for a cooperative endeavor was to make economically feasible such things as quality control, large quantity purchases at bulk prices. . . . All these things, of course, are feasible for the large national chains operating individually, but they are beyond the reach of the small operators proceeding alone.[19]

In the face of the District Court's well-supported findings that the effects of such a rule [declaring the practice illegal] will be adverse to the public welfare, the Court lays down that rule without regard to the impact which the condemned practices may have on competition. . . . I question whether the Court is fulfilling the role assigned to it under the statute when it declines to make this determination; in any event, if the Court is unwilling on this record to assess the economic impact, it surely should not proceed to make a new rule [the *per se* illegal rule] to govern the economic activity.[20]

The majority overlooks a further specific determination of the District Court, namely, that the invalidation of the restraints here at issue "would not increase competition in Topco private label brands." Indeed, the District Court seemed to believe that it would, on the contrary, lead to the likely demise of those brands in time. And the evidence before the District Court would appear to justify that conclusion.[21]

THE LAW OF CLOSED-TERRITORY DISTRIBUTION

There are two major cases concerned with closed-territory distribution. They are *White Motor Company* v. *United States*[22] and *United States* v. *Arnold Schwinn & Co., et al.*[23]

White Motor Co.

White Motor used closed-territory distribution in two ways. First, it reserved for itself sales to federal and state government. Second, its dealers and distributors were assigned customers geographically. That is, its distributors were only allowed to sell to certain dealers, and its dealers were only allowed to sell to specified final consumers. The effect of the arrangement was to completely eliminate intrabrand competition.

White argued that closed-territory distribution was needed to increase the number of customers contacted by its dealers. It also argued that the practice was used so that its dealers would make "vigorous" and "energetic" efforts in promoting its product. The company argued that it reserved all federal and state accounts for itself because it wanted to be certain that the best possible prices and services were provided to these accounts and "the only sure way to make certain something really important is done right is to do it for oneself." As presented, White's argument for reserving government accounts is not a sound one. If dealers were unable to compete with White for government accounts, the dealers would eventually have directed their activities to other accounts. They would not have to be told not to compete. However, White's contention can be formulated in a more plausible manner. The company might have wished to eliminate intrabrand competition for government accounts for the same reason it wanted to eliminate competition between its dealers. If dealers were not allowed to compete for such accounts, White would have been assured that it would receive all the returns from its sales activities. As a result, it might have been able to contact more government accounts and more actively promote its product.

In the district court, both forms of closed-territory distribution were found in violation of Sections 1 and 3 of the Sherman Act. The district court found that the practice was illegal *per se* because that court made no attempt to distinguish White's practices from horizontal division of territories. On appeal, the Supreme Court gave a detailed decision. It first ruled that the *per se* ruling by the lower court was improper in a case of this nature because the "true test of legality is whether or not the restraint is such as merely regulates and perhaps thereby promotes competition or whether it as such may suppress or even destroy competition."[24] Since this was the first case the Court had heard involving closed-territory distribution, it reasoned that there was insufficient knowledge of the economic effect of the practice.

Before the case was returned to the district court for more detailed study, Justice Brennan presented some questions that he thought the lower court should ask when reconsidering the case. He cautioned the lower court not to be too quick in finding an analogy between closed-territory distribution and horizontal restraints. The former, he said, may promote interbrand competition by providing intensive product promotion and inducement for dealers to represent a new product. He also thought that it could promote advertising and customer service. Brennan thought that the main criterion in judging White's reservation of government accounts for itself should be the dealers' ability to compete with White for these accounts. If the dealers could not compete, then the allocation of customers would not restrain trade. However, if there was competition between White and its dealers, it could be inferred that the practice had been "designed, at least in part, to protect a noncompetitive pricing structure in which the manufacturer in fact does *not* always charge the lowest prices."[25]

The decision of the Court could certainly be judged an honest one. Furthermore, Justice Brennan raised some important questions which might have put the lower court on the right track in its deliberation. However, White Motor chose to take a consent decree. As a result there was no definite decision on the legality of closed-territory distribution. but interpreted by some as precedent.

Schwinn

In 1962 the Schwinn Bicycle Company was charged with using closed-territory distribution because Schwinn had assigned dealers to its distributors. A lower court found Schwinn guilty of violating Section 1 of the Sherman Act.

The Supreme Court recognized that the restriction was vertical. It also recognized that Schwinn adopted the practice to allow it to compete more effectively, "Schwinn sought a better way of distributing its product; a method which would promote sales, increase stability of its distributor and dealer outlets, and augment profits."[26] It would seem fair to deduce from this statement that the Court recognized that the practice increased interbrand competition. Despite this observation, the Court found Schwinn's use of closed-territory distribution *per se* illegal. It gave two reasons for its decision, neither of which had anything to do with economics. First, it observed that the district court had invalidated a horizontal agreement among Schwinn's distributors. Given this fact, the Court reasoned that it would be "illogical and inconsistent" not to strike down all of Schwinn's territorial restrictions. Thus, although the Court had observed in another part of its decision that horizontal and vertical territorial restrictions are different, it did not make that distinction in deciding the case.

The second reason given for its decision was that Schwinn, in attempting to control the method by which its product was marketed after it had been sold, violated the "ancient rule against restraints on alienation." Simply stated, the Court thought that the company had violated common law by controlling a product which, according to the Court, it had no legal right to control after it had relinquished title to the goods. The Court did recognize that had Schwinn sold on consignment (maintaining title to the goods) the decision might have been different.

The best critique of this decision came from two dissenting Justices of the Court: Justice Stewart and Justice Harlan. They reiterated that "the evidence supports the District Court's finding that the ultimate effect of [Schwinn's] policies was to embrace rather than undermine or destroy competition."[27] Then they stated that the decision of the Court appeared to be inconsistent with its stand in *White* because "the Court does not cite or discuss any new data that might support such a radical change in the law."[28]

The Justices then questioned the two justifications given by the Court for its decision. Remember that the Court first observed that it would be inconsistent to disallow horizontal division of territories and to allow Schwinn's territory allocation. Stewart and Harlan answered that it would not be at all inconsistent to allow one type of arrangement and disallow the other. The former arrangement was horizontal in nature. "By contrast, the restrictions involved in the franchising methods now before us are quite different in nature, as the Court points out elsewhere in its opinion."[29] Concerning the application of the rule against restraints on alienation to vertical arrangements, the Justices answered:

> The state of the common law 400 or even 100 years ago is irrelevant to the issue before us: the effect of the antitrust laws upon vertical distributional restraints in the American economy today. The problems involved are difficult and complex and our response should be more reasoned and sensitive than the simple acceptance of a hoary formula.[30]

Richard McLaren, former Assistant Attorney General for Antitrust, offered the most logical reason for the Court's aborting economic principles.

> The real reason for the adoption of a *per se* rule is that the Court simply does not have time to administer a rule of reason in this kind of case. Consider these facts. The *Schwinn* record was composed of 23 thick volumes, and it was filed only a little more than 60 days before the oral arguments which were heard on April 20. Decision came down on June 12. I question that any of the justices were able to read the record in that length of time, much less analyze it and apply the rule of reason.[31]

Most students of antitrust disagree with the methods the Court used to reach its decision in the *Schwinn* case. Essentially, the Court ran away from the very issues it had raised in the *White* decision. But certainly the decision does clarify the current position of the Court with regard to closed-territory distribution. The practice is illegal whenever it is used after a supplier has sold his product.

SUMMARY

In this chapter, three types of vertical territorial arrangements have been identified. The three types—exclusive franchising, territorial security arrangements, and closed-territory distribution—differ according to how much intrabrand competition is eliminated. The economics of the arrangements has also been discussed. Two general schools of thought exist concerning the effect of the practices on consumer welfare. One school, the intracompetitors, points to the loss of intrabrand competition resulting from the use of the practices. They note that some consumers might be harmed if intrabrand competition is reduced, and thus they believe that the practices should not be allowed by the courts. Another school of thought, the intercompetitors, agrees that the practices reduce or eliminate intrabrand competition. But they point to the fact that their use could increase interbrand competition and thus increase consumer welfare. Therefore, they believe that the courts should allow vertical territorial arrangements. When the arrangements are used as part of a horizontal conspiracy to divide territories or when they are used to gain exclusive representation, the intercompetitors believe that the exclusive dealing clause and the conspiracy should be judged as such by the courts.

Courts have allowed exclusive franchising. They reason that although intrabrand competition might be reduced, the practice can help the supplier promote his product and hence increase overall competition. Territorial security arrangements appear to be illegal *per se*, but courts hearing cases involving the practice seem torn between the arguments of the intercompetitor school and those of the intracompetitor school. Closed-territory distribution is illegal *per se*, a decision based on noneconomic issues. The courts have never determined the effect of closed-territory distribution on competition.

NOTES TO CHAPTER VII

*Much of this chapter is taken from an earlier article. Russell G. Warren, "Economics of Closed-Territory Distribution," *Antitrust Law and Economics Review*, II (Winter 1968-69), 111-124.

[1]It is conceivable that V.T.A.'s might be used as part of a horizontal conspiracy to divide territories. This use is considered later in the chapter.

[2]Price discrimination is discussed in detail in Chapter XVI.

[3]*Sandura Co.* v. *F.T.C.*, 339 F. 2d 847 (1964).

[4]*White Motor Co.* v. *United States*, 194 F. Supp. 562, 578 (1963).

[5]Charles E. Edwards, *Dynamics of the United States Automobile Industry* (Columbia: University of South Carolina Press, 1965), pp. 230-231.

[6]Joan Robinson, *The Economics of Imperfect Competition* (London: Macmillan and Co., LTD., 1933), p. 204.

[7]45 F. Supp. 387 (1942).

[8]45 F. Supp. 387, 398 (1942).

[9]138 F. Supp. 899 (1956); aff'd 239 F. 2d 176 (1956).

[10]135 F. Supp. 4 (1955).

[11]243 F. 2d. 418, 420-421 (1956).

[12]*Attorney General's National Committee Antitrust Report* (Washington: U.S. Government Printing Office, 1955), p. 28.

[13]16 F.T.C. 537 (1932).

[14]37 F. Supp. 999 (1941).

[15]321 F. 2d 825 (1963).

[16]319 F. Supp. 1031 (1970); 92 S. Ct. 1126 (1972).

[17]319 F. Supp. 1031, 1042-1043 (1970).

[18]92 S. Ct. 1126, 1135 (1972).

[19]92 S. Ct. 1126, 1136-1137 (1972).

[20]92 S. Ct. 1126, 1139-1140 (1972).

[21]92 S. Ct. 1126, 1141 (1972).

[22]83 S. Ct. 696 (1963).

[23]35 L.W. 4563 (June 13, 1967).

[24]83 S. Ct. 696, 701 (1963).

[25]83 S. Ct. 696, 708 (1963).

[26]*U.S.* v. *Arnold Schwinn & Co., et al.*, 35 L.W. 4563 (June 13, 1967).

[27]35 L.W. 4563, 4568 (June 13, 1967).

[28]35 L.W. 4563, 4569 (June 13, 1967).

[29]35 L.W. 4563, 4570 (June 13, 1967).

[30]35 L.W. 4563, 4571 (June 13, 1967).

[31]Quoted by Thomas M. Scanlon, *Antitrust Law Journal Section of Antitrust Law Proceedings of the National Institute on Prices and Pricing*, XLI (October, 1971), 25.

R
N

itories in which
, also frequently
r their products.
this practice are
analyzed in this chapter.

INTRODUCTION

Resale price maintenance is similar to vertical territorial arrangements. The only major difference is that instead of assigning territories to his dealers a supplier specifies a minimum price which the independent dealers selling his product must charge. For example, a supplier of razor blades might specify that each of the independent retailers selling his product charge at least $.98 for a package of blades. The effect of the arrangement is usually to eliminate intrabrand price competition. Of course, retailers are still free to engage in nonprice competition.

REASONS FOR RESALE
PRICE MAINTENANCE

As in cases involving vertical territorial arrangements, it is difficult to see why suppliers would wish to eliminate price competition between their dealers. Fierce price competition should increase product sales which usually would raise the supplier's profits. Consequently, for a supplier to adopt resale price maintenance (R.P.M.), the loss of profits resulting from the elimination of price competition must be less than the increase in profits resulting from some other activity incompatible with price competition. ~~Four~~ Five of the most prevalent reasons explaining the use of R.P.M. are:

A. R.P.M. is adopted to eliminate "loss leader" selling.
B. R.P.M. is used to maintain product image.
C. R.P.M. is adopted to insure that customers are provided with adequate service.

D. R.P.M. is part of a cartel arrangement between suppliers or dealers.

E. R.P.M. is used to insure that the supplier who uses independent dealers to represent him receives the same rights as a vertically integrated firm.

Each of these arguments will be considered in turn.

LOSS LEADER ARGUMENT

A "loss leader" is a product which is sold at a lower price than usual to attract customers to a store in order to increase demand for all of the products in the store. The price charged may be below cost, at cost, or it may exceed cost but still be less than that normally charged by competitors. To understand the concept of loss leader sales, assume that a popular brand of razor blades usually sells for $1.29 a package. One retailer advertises packages at $.50, presumably to get customers into his store. If he is selling the product above cost, he can make a profit on it and will be perfectly happy if the customer buys nothing but razor blades. However, if he is selling the blades at or below cost he would offer the inducement only to get customers to purchase other products along with the blades. In other words, the major purpose of selling loss leaders is to promote other product sales.

Some suppliers contend that the use of their product as a loss leader is harmful to their business. One way in which such sales may harm a supplier is that they may reduce the number of retail outlets willing to represent him. Suppose one retailer, Albert, continually uses product A as a loss leader. Other retailers find that in order to match Albert's price they must either take a loss or just break even on the product. Consequently, they lose interest in promoting the product or may even drop it completely. Note, however, that this argument is valid only when the product is continually used as a loss leader. When it is a loss leader for only a short period of time, representation should not fall off significantly. This argument is also only valid when the loss leader is sold at or below cost. If a retailer sells the product above cost, he is simply engaging in price competition, and competing stores should be able to meet his price and still make a profit on the sale of the product.

PROTECTION OF PRODUCT IMAGE

The lack of consumer knowledge about products often causes buyers to gauge the quality of a product by its price. This practice demonstrates the lack of real information about many products available to consumers and not consumer ignorance. Despite the law of demand (which says as price decreases the quantity demanded of a product increases) consumers' demand may increase when price is raised. In such an instance, charging a high price is a form of product promotion. Conversely, when products are sold at a low price, their image may deteriorate and sales may decline. Suppliers may wish to have their representatives use R.P.M. to preserve product image. Of course, this argument is only valid when price competition does not exist throughout a range of competitive products. Suppose that Exenons and Buratons are two brands of watches of similar quality which are produced at approximately the same cost. If Exenons are sold at a relatively high price because of the monopoly power of dealers, consumers may get the idea that Exenons are better watches. But if both brands sell at a similar price because of strong interbrand competition, the consumer will have to decide which brand has greater quality on the merits of the watches. And if all brands sell under conditions of significant price competition, those selling at a higher price might truly reflect difference in quality.

PROVISION OF SERVICE

Many proponents of R.P.M. have argued that the practice is needed to induce retailers to provide consumer services. Presumably this service could take the form of presale demonstrations, advertising, installation services, warranties to protect the consumer after he has purchased the product, and consumer credit. Their argument is based on the idea that if a retailer is required to sell at a price which affords him too little profit, he will not be able to provide such services. R.P.M. does insure that the retailer receives a sufficient mark-up on the product he is selling, and he is therefore better able to provide these services than if he sold at a lower price.

This argument has been rejected by many economists. They contend that even with a higher price there is no assurance that the services will be offered by the retailer. Instead of providing service, the retailer may prefer to take a larger profit. Furthermore, they believe that if consumers really preferred a product which is accompanied with service, the retailers would offer the product at a higher price without the use of R.P.M. Conversely, if consumers prefer to buy products from discount houses instead of stores which provide services (and charge a higher price), they obviously do not want the services. Therefore the market mechanism will satisfy the consumer's desires by providing: either a lower-priced product without services or a higher-priced product with service. The mere fact that R.P.M. has to be enforced implies that the consumer would prefer the discount house.

Professor Lester G. Telser discussed this argument against R.P.M. and concluded that it is not necessarily sound. That is, consumers who wish to purchase a product at a higher price and receive services may not be able to unless R.P.M. is used.[1] The argument is almost identical to the one presented in the last chapter to explain the use of vertical territorial arrangements. Customers tend to receive service from retailers that offer it but then purchase products from discount houses. They may, for example, discover information about a product and get a demonstration of the product from some retailer. After receiving these presale services they go to a discount house to buy the product. Obviously, if many consumers do this, the retailer will not be able to provide the services for very long, and the consumers who want services will find that they do not have that alternative open to them. The McGraw Electric Company affirmed this argument when it said,

> During the last Christmas season [1951], we found it quite impossible to carry out our seasonal promotion plans in the San Francisco area. This was due to the deep price cutting of one chain organization. Other stores, large and small, refused to meet these extremely low prices and, of course, would not cooperate in our merchandising plans. All dealers are reluctant to participate in merchandising expenditures aimed at creating willingness to buy if some other dealer, large or small, is able to get a free ride by selling at cut prices relying on the good will and acceptance which he has not helped to create.[2]

To counteract "free riding," Telser observed that some services may be sold individually to the consumer. For example, a consumer may be charged for a product warranty, for installation costs, and for product service. However, it is extremely difficult to charge a consumer for product advertising or even product demonstrations. Others have argued that if it is not advantageous to have discount houses represent a supplier, he should simply refuse to deal with them. But in Chapter IX we will see that refusals to deal are illegal except in rare circumstances. Therefore, R.P.M. may in fact be necessary to induce retailers to provide some services. Telser suggested that his argument is especially true for products which are unfamiliar to the majority of consumers and which cannot be promoted solely through national advertising by the supplier.[3]

EQUITY ARGUMENT

Some proponents of R.P.M. argue that it is not equitable to allow vertically integrated companies to control the price of their product at successive levels of distribution while disallowing this control when a supplier sells through independent representatives.[4] It is true that the antitrust laws frequently have a double standard. The supplier using independent dealers usually has less control than a vertically integrated firm. Yet, from an economic viewpoint, there is no difference in the effect of selling through vertically integrated firms rather than independent dealers. From an equity viewpoint this argument is sound. Moreover, the existence of a double standard may promote vertical integration.

CARTEL ARRANGEMENTS

R.P.M. is sometimes used to implement horizontal agreements between suppliers or dealers. For example, one supplier may suggest to his competitors that they fix the wholesale price of their product. To insure that prices are also fixed at the retail level (so no supplier gets an advantage) they may impose R.P.M. on their dealers. Likewise, dealers having strong bargaining power vis à vis their supplier may attempt to force him to adopt R.P.M. Whether instigated by suppliers or dealers, this use of R.P.M. constitutes a horizontal arrangement just as tacit or overt price fixing does. Whether the agreement is tacit or overt, the effect is detrimental to consumer welfare. Evidence suggests that in a large number of cases this has been the reason for the use of R.P.M. Retail druggists, not manufacturers, were one of the most prominent groups who argued for the passage of the several R.P.M. laws. Nor does one have to look very far to find instances of dealers using coercion to force a manufacturer to adopt R.P.M. In 1935, the Pepsodent Company, after using R.P.M. for a number of years, suddenly dropped the practice. Subsequently the Northern California Retail Druggists Association told Pepsodent that "They would have the toughest time any salesman had had in any territory. We passed a resolution at our meeting . . . and we sent that resolution to every member in California in which we urged and advised them to discontinue the sale of any product that had cancelled their fair-trade contract."[5] As a result of this pressure, Pepsodent not only reinstated R.P.M. but also donated $25,000 to the fair-trade lobby.

THE POLICY TO EVALUATE RESALE MAINTENANCE

Where R.P.M. is part of a horizontal conspiracy among the dealers or suppliers to fix prices, the provision rightly falls under Section 1 of the Sherman Act and should be declared illegal. Of course, it is not really the R.P.M. provision which is illegal. The horizontal conspiracy is the harmful practice. The majority of economists contend that R.P.M. should be illegal because many of these arrangements are horizontal; they are forced upon manufacturers by colluding dealers.

Suppose, however, that R.P.M. is truly a vertical arrangement in which one supplier, independent of all other suppliers selling a similar product, and isolated from dealer pressure decided to adopt it. Should it be allowed or disallowed? There are two schools of thought on the answer to this question. Some economists correctly observe that the use of R.P.M. raises prices and on the basis of this information conclude that it should be outlawed. Another group of economists argue that it should always be allowed. Their argument is virtually identical to that used by the "intercompetitors." They would say that a supplier would not use R.P.M. unless its use increases his profits. All things being equal, it would be more profitable for his dealers to engage in fierce price competition. This would increase the quantity demanded of his product and presumably increase his profits. If consumers really preferred nonservice discount houses to service dealers, the suppliers would not protect the service dealers with a R.P.M. provision. But if the reverse were true, the provision of R.P.M. may be essential to preserve service. Certainly a part of the product package may include advertising of a noninformative, brand-attachment nature. But advertising of this nature has not been outlawed by the Justice Department or the Federal Trade Commission, and it would be inconsistent to outlaw it only when it is financed through the use of R.P.M.

It is probably true that many, if not most instances of R.P.M. are part of horizontal conspiracies and that only rarely is the practice a truly vertical one. Because of the rarity of vertical instances, it might be convenient to declare R.P.M. illegal *per se*. This is especially true in light of the fact that it is very difficult for the courts to separate the instances where the use of R.P.M. is vertical in nature from the instances where it is part of a horizontal arrangement. But technically it would be incorrect to do so, for when R.P.M. is a vertical arrangement it may simply be a method of competition.

THE LEGALITY OF RESALE PRICE MAINTENANCE

DR. MILES MEDICAL COMPANY

The first major antitrust case involving R.P.M. was *Dr. Miles Medical Company* v. *John D. Park & Sons Company*, heard by the Supreme Court in 1911.[6] Dr. Miles Medical Company manufactured and sold proprietary medicines to jobbers and wholesale druggists who in turn sold to retail druggists. Dr. Miles specified resale prices for the jobbers as well as for the retail druggists. All of its products were sold under a consignment contract which provided that the drugs remained the property of Dr. Miles until they were sold under the provisions of the resale price arrangement. Additionally, wholesalers were only allowed to sell to retailers who had signed Dr. Miles' contract.

Dr. Miles argued that specifying resale prices insured that its jobbers and retail druggists received a fair profit. It also said that the resale prices were designed to protect Dr. Miles' good will. Four hundred jobbers and over twenty-five thousand retailers had signed contracts in agreement with the resale price arrangement. John D. Park & Sons was a wholesale drug company which had not signed the agreement. Park & Sons purchased Dr. Miles' products from jobbers who had violated their agreement with Dr. Miles. Park, in turn, sold the product to drug retailers at "cut-rate" prices. The retail druggists then sold the product to the final consumers at low prices.

The Supreme Court said that the major question before it was whether Dr. Miles had the right to make restrictive agreements. The defense argued that it had the right to specify resale prices for two reasons. First, it had a secret process which it used to manufacture its product, and although the process was not patented, Dr. Miles contended that it had the same right of protection as did patented processes. One of these rights was the setting of resale prices. Second it contended that since it manufactured the product it had the right to control the prices.

Directing itself to the first defense, the Court claimed that the patent laws did not allow a producer to control his product after he had sold it. And the fact that the Court considered Dr. Miles' agreement as a restraint of trade made it even more opposed to the postsale extension of the patent rights. The Supreme Court also did not agree with Dr. Miles' second defense that since the company produced the product it should be able to control its sale all the way to the retail level. The Court affirmed the right of a supplier to maintain control of a product to the retail level through the use of contracts with subsequent sellers of the product. However, when the contracts are in restraint of trade the practice is illegal. Dr. Miles' contracts were considered to have as their "sole purpose the destruction of competition and the fixing of prices [which are] injurious to the public interest and void. They are not saved by the advantages which the participants expect to derive from the enhanced price to the consumer."[7]

Justice Holmes was the only dissenter in the case. His argument in favor of the arrangement is similar to that which would be presented in defense of any truly vertical arrangement. He said, "I suppose that the reason why the contract is held bad is that it is part of a scheme embracing other similar contracts, each of which applies to a number of similar things, with the object of fixing a general market price. This reason seems to me inadequate in the case before the court."[8] In other words, the arrangement does not fix the price of all proprietary medicines at any one level of distribution. Therefore it can be distinguished from cases where horizontal price fixing is involved. Holmes further argued that in vertical arrangements the producer is best able to determine the needs of society.

> I think that at least it is safe to say that the most enlightened judicial policy is to let people manage their own business in their own way, unless the ground for interference is very clear. I cannot believe that in the long run the public will profit by this court permitting knaves to cut reasonable prices for some ulterior purpose of their own, and thus impair, if not to destroy, the production and sale of articles which it is assumed to be desirable that the public should be able to get.[9]

Justice Holmes presented a perceptive analysis of the situation. His argument approximates the statement that truly vertical arrangements will be made by producers only when they somehow make the product package better for consumers.

The Supreme Court's decision in the *Dr. Miles* case was reiterated in numerous R.P.M. cases. To overcome the judicial ruling, many companies petitioned Congress and state legislatures for the right to adopt R.P.M. More as a result of political pressure than enlightened economic reasoning on the part of legislatures, they gradually received that right. Several states soon granted exemption from the vertical-price prohibitions when goods were produced and sold within state boundaries. However, these provisions did not satisfy companies because they applied only to intrastate trade. By 1937, R.P.M.

lobbies were able to convince Congress that it should exempt R.P.M. on goods involved in interstate commerce. The Miller-Tydings Act amended the Sherman Act and the Federal Trade Commission Act to that effect.[10] However, the act was only valid in states which passed legislation approving R.P.M. Subsequent to the passage of the Miller-Tydings Act, forty-five states passed legislation allowing the use of R.P.M. Vermont, Missouri and Texas as well as the District of Columbia did not endorse the practice.

Even with the legislative endorsement of R.P.M., producers experienced difficulties when they used the practice. The Miller-Tydings Act was unclear as to whether suppliers could impose R.P.M. on all dealers or only on dealers who signed a resale price agreement. The issue was a major one because if nonsignatory dealers were allowed to set their own prices, signatory dealers would be at a competitive disadvantage.

SCHWEGMANN BROTHERS

The decision in *Schwegmann Brothers* v. *Calvert Corp.* clarified the law.[11] Schwegmann Brothers was a large retailer in New Orleans who sold Calvert's liquor. The retailer refused to sign a R.P.M. contract with Calvert and undercut the prices charged by other liquor stores who had signed the contracts. The liquor supplier sued Schwegmann, contending that even though he had not signed an agreement, Schwegmann was bound to follow the prescribed resale prices. The Supreme Court upheld Schwegmann's position stating that if a dealer did not sign the agreement, he was not obliged to follow the resale prices. In the majority opinion, Justice Douglas stated that had Schwegmann been forced to abide by the arrangement it would have been horizontal in nature. This decision threatened the use of R.P.M. so much that its supporters took their problem back to Congress for a solution. Their prayers were answered when, in 1952, Congress passed the McGuire Act.[12] This act amended the Federal Trade Commission Act to require that nonsigners must abide by R.P.M. where such provisions are established by a producer and endorsed by state law.

EASTMAN KODAK CO.

Subsequent court decisions limited the provisions of the Miller-Tydings Act. In *Eastman Kodak Co.* v. *Federal Trade Commission,* the commission decided that unless a product was in "free and open competition" with other brand products, a supplier could not specify resale prices.[13]   Kodak had established resale prices on "Koda-chrome" and "Magazine Cine-Kodak Film." The court found that neither type of film faced strong interbrand competiton.

McKESSON AND ROBBINS, INC.

In *United States* v. *McKesson and Robbins, Inc.*[14] the Court made it clear that a supplier may not set resale prices when he is in competition with another firm handling the same brand product. McKesson and Robbins was a manufacturer and a wholesaler of drug products. The drug company established resale prices on McKesson and Robbins products which were to be charged by independent wholesalers as well as by McKesson and Robbins' own wholesale outlet. The Court likened this arrangement to horizontal price fixing and declared the practice illegal. It said that "the crucial inquiry is whether the contracting parties compete with each other. If they do, the Miller-Tydings and McGuire Acts do not permit them to fix resale prices."[15]   In their dissenting opinion, Justices Harlan, Frankfurter and Burton argued that the purpose of any R.P.M. agreement is to eliminate intrabrand competition. Therefore even if McKesson and Robbins did not have its own wholesale outlet, competition would have been eliminated at the wholesale level. It makes no difference "between whom the eliminated competition would have existed had it not been eliminated."[16]

To find the key to the issue, one has to ask whether it would be monopolistic for a manufacturer to fix prices at the wholesale level of distribution if he were one of the wholesalers. The answer is "no," because in so doing he creates no additional monopoly power. If, in fixing resale prices, his sole purpose is to eliminate price competition between his wholesale operation and independent wholesalers, he already has that option as the sole manufacturer of a specific brand product. He may either handle all of the wholesale operations required to distribute his product or raise the price he charges the independent wholesalers. Therefore it makes no difference if while setting resale prices, a manufacturer also engages in business at successive levels of distribution.

MASTERS MAIL ORDER CO.

Another issue involved in R.P.M. is whether a mail order house located in a state which disallows R.P.M. is allowed to sell its products in other states where competitors are required to maintain prices. This question was answered in *General Electric Co.* v. *Masters Mail Order Co.*[17]   Masters was a mail order company located in the

District of Columbia. Because the District of Columbia had never validated R.P.M. agreements, Masters was not required to sell at manufacturers' resale prices. Masters sold to residents of New York State, where R.P.M. agreements were legal. Consequently, consumers in that state were able to buy at lower prices from Masters than from retailers in their own state. To complicate the issue further, Masters' parent company was located in New York, and it often accepted orders for Masters' products. Obviously, the arrangement hurt New York retailers and defeated the purpose of General Electric's resale price agreements, so G.E. sued Masters. The major question before the court was whether the Miller-Tydings Act (when validated by state law) applied to goods which were sold at a certain location (in this case, the District of Columbia) or whether it applied to the place where the contract to buy was made (New York State). The court decided that "Congress was concerned with the place where resales occurred [the District of Columbia], rather than the place where the retailer's owners resided and exercised supervision over operations [New York State]."[18]   The result of the decision was to provide retailers with a means to circumvent the Miller-Tydings Act. Mail order houses may locate in states which do not permit R.P.M. and sell at cut-rate prices to customers located in states which endorse R.P.M. even if the mail order houses contract to sell the goods in the R.P.M. state.

SUMMARY

We have seen that even with congressional support, proponents of resale prices have not acquired total freedom in the use of R.P.M. The popularity of the practice declined throughout the 1950s and 1960s for a number of reasons. Several states have declared that R.P.M. is not constitutional, and other states have passed laws nullifying the McGuire Act's provisions. Frequently, retailers have refused to abide by R.P.M., and many producers have decided that it was not worth the effort to prosecute them. This is especially true when the retailer involved is a large one which the producer cannot afford to lose. Finally, several courts have failed to enforce R.P.M. The practice is still in frequent use, but its legality is not a certain thing.

NOTES TO CHAPTER VIII

[1]Lester G. Telser, "Why Should Manufacturers Want Fair Trade?" *Journal of Law and Economics*, III (1960), 86-105.

[2]Brief in support of H.R. 6925 for McGraw Electric Co., 11 (1952); Quoted in Ward S. Bowman, "The Prerequisites and Effects of Resale Price Maintenance," *University of Chicago Law Review*, XXII (1955), 837.

[3]Telser, p. 95.

[4]This argument is applicable to all vertical arrangements which fall short of vertical integration.

[5]Carl H. Fulda, "Resale Price Maintenance," *The University of Chicago Law Review*, XXI (1954), 192-193.

[6]31 S. Ct. 376 (1911).

[7]31 S. Ct. 376, 384-385 (1911).

[8]31 S. Ct. 376, 386 (1911).

[9]31 S. Ct. 376, 386 (1911).

[10]50 Stat. 693 (1937).

[11]341 U.S. 384 (1951).

[12]66 Stat. 631 (1952).

[13]158 F. 2d 592 (1946).

[14]76 S. Ct. 937 (1956).

[15]76 S. Ct. 937, 942 (1956).

[16]76 S. Ct. 937, 944 (1956).

[17]244 F. Supp. 681 (1957).

[18]244 F. Supp. 681 (1957).

REFUSALS TO DEAL CHAPTER IX

Can a producer legally refuse to have certain independent businessmen represent him? Under what conditions? Does such a practice create monopoly power? These are the subjects discussed in this chapter.

INTRODUCTION

The term "refusal to deal" usually refers to a situation in which a firm refuses to sell to certain customers. Often the firm refuses to sell to customers who do not abide by R.P.M. The practice itself is not illegal. Within the bounds of the provisions of the civil rights laws, every seller has the right to choose his customers just as every buyer has the right to choose the firm he patronizes. However, when a refusal to deal accompanies some illegal practice or when the intent of the seller using it is to create monopoly power, it violates the provisions of Sections 1 and 2 of the Sherman Act as well as Section 5 of the Federal Trade Commission Act.

At the offset we must understand that a seller's refusal to deal with a customer always indicates that the seller has some degree of monopoly power. Because he is undifferentiated from his adversaries, the pure competitor would never refuse to deal unless his supply had been exhausted, customers had a questionable credit rating, or if the sale would be unprofitable.[1] But a firm with some degree of monopoly power might refuse to sell in order to increase prices, receive exclusive representation, or foreclose markets to competitors.

ARGUMENTS FOR OUTLAWING

Two major arguments have been levied against the use of refusals to deal. The arguments suggest that the practice may:
A. Foreclose markets to competitors;
B. Coerce customers to adopt some practices which they otherwise would not endorse.
Each of these arguments will be considered. However, a refusal to

deal is, by itself, not anticompetitive. Only when it is used in conjunction with some anticompetitive practice can it be harmful. Therefore, the concept will only be discussed briefly here because the real issue is the use of the anticompetitive practices that may be accompanied by refusals to deal.

FORECLOSURE OF MARKETS

The use of a refusal to deal may create monopoly power by foreclosing markets to competitors in a manner similar to that which we will encounter in our discussion of vertical integration. To understand this, assume that a monopolistic firm agrees to sell its good to customers only if they boycott the goods of a competitor. If customers agree and the foreclosure is significant, the competitor might be forced out of business. Ultimately, this gives the monopolistic firm even more monopoly power. Of course, the reader will recognize that the real problem here is not the refusal-to-deal clause but the existing monopoly power which enables the firm to foreclose markets. Should this use of a refusal-to-deal be disallowed? The answer is "no" if we treat fundamental problems instead of their symptoms. The problem here is the already existing monopoly power of the supplier. If he did not have that power, the refusal-to-deal would be futile. Therefore the power should be eliminated unless there is some reason which makes this solution impractical.

Suppose that several suppliers form a combination and agree to sell only to customers refusing to buy from other suppliers. Does the existence of a combination alter the prior conclusion that refusals-to-deal should not be outlawed? The answer is still "no." The horizontal combination creates the problem by uniting firms which formerly competed. It is this horizontal combination, not the refusal-to-deal, which should be outlawed.

COERCION OF CUSTOMERS

Sometimes independent dealers have to accept resale price maintenance, exclusive representation, or some other provision in order to purchase from the supplier. If they do not accept the provision, the supplier will refuse to deal with them. Should this be illegal? While the supplier's dictation of such terms indicates his power in bargaining with the dealers, his refusal to deal should not be outlawed. Presumably, if dealers agree to the arrangement, they believe that its benefits exceed its harm. The forced provision may be more than the buyers would like to concede, but not more than they are willing to concede. The refusal-to-deal is simply a bargaining tactic, and even outlawing the practice will not equate the dealers' and suppliers' bargaining power. If the terms are to be evened up, the monopoly power of the supplier must be reduced. Otherwise, the supplier will find some other way to exercise his power.

COURT ANALYSIS OF REFUSALS-TO-DEAL

The courts have distinguished between refusals-to-deal which are used by a horizontal combination of suppliers and those used by only one supplier. The distinction is an important one because the collusive agreement creates monopoly power while the truly vertical arrangement merely represents an exercise of existing monopoly power. The first three cases presented here deal with refusals-to-deal by horizontal combinations of suppliers.

PARAMOUNT FAMOUS LASKY CORPORATION

One of the first antitrust cases involving a horizontal combination of firms using refusals-to-deal was *Paramount Famous Lasky Corporation et al.* v. *United States.*[2] Paramount Famous Lasky Corporation and nine other corporations produced and distributed 60 per cent of the motion pictures in the country. They acted in concert by requiring that their customers (motion picture theatres) sign a standardized contract. If a customer did not agree to the contract, the defendants would refuse to deal with him. The companies were charged under the provisions of Section I of the Sherman Act with "an alleged combination and conspiracy to restrain interstate commerce in motion picture films."[3]

The defense claimed that the regulations established in the contracts were reasonable and that Paramount's use of the contract had not brought about a significant number of complaints. In further defense of the contract's reasonableness, they argued that it had evolved after six years of discussion and experimentation. The Supreme Court denied the defense. It claimed that the contract's slow evolution did not demonstrate its reasonableness. More importantly, the Court ruled that the Sherman Act had been designed to prevent acts which suppressed competition, and this particular act "directly tends to destroy the kind of competition to which the public has long looked for protection."[4]

Although the Court did not actually consider the economics of the arrangement, its decision was economically correct and consistent with the antitrust decisions on overt price fixing. Any customer who wanted to buy from Paramount or the other defendants had no choice in the terms of the contract. Nor did the customer have a significant number of alternative suppliers from which to lease its films. The Court came very close to making a *per se* illegal ruling in its deliberation.

FASHION ORIGINATORS' GUILD

Fashion Originators' Guild of America, Inc., et al. v. *Federal Trade Commission* is an important case because it demonstrates how the use of refusals-to-deal by a horizontal combination can reduce competition by foreclosing a significant market to competitors.[5] The Guild consisted of 167 manufacturers of women's garments as well as manufacturers, converters, and dyers of textiles from which the garments were made. These manufacturers claimed that they created original and distinctive designs for women's clothes. However, other garment manufacturers who were not members of the Guild copied the designs and sold them at lower prices.

The Guild manufacturers realized that their original creations were not copyrightable or patentable. They also realized that the patent and copyright laws afforded them no protection against "style piracy." In order to stop the piracy, they only sold to retailers who agreed not to buy clothing manufactured by pirate companies. Their arrangement was effective because most retailers needed the Guild manufacturers' products. Its members sold more than 38 per cent of all women's garments which wholesaled at $6.75 and up and more than 60 per cent of those wholesaling at $10.75 and up. According to the Court, "Competition and the demand of the consuming public make it necessary for most retail dealers to stock some of the products of these manufacturers."[6] The combination went beyond the mere exclusion of pirate manufacturers. It prohibited its members from participating in retail advertising, it regulated sales discounts, it prohibited selling at retail, it regulated days on which special sales could be held, and it prohibited members from selling to retailers who conducted their business in residences. Therefore, the arrangement suppressed many forms of non-price competition.

In earlier hearings, a lower court had refused to consider evidence supporting the "reasonableness" of the refusal-to-deal. The Supreme Court defended this attitude because the situation created by the Guild was analogous to horizontal price fixing, and "the reasonableness of the methods pursued by the combination to accomplish its unlawful object is no more material than would be the reasonableness of the prices fixed by unlawful combination."[7] The fact that the Guild was protecting itself against piracy was even an unacceptable defense because "that situation would not justify petitioners in combining together to regulate and restrain interstate commerce in violation of federal law."[8] The Court's decision not to analyze the justifications for the refusal-to-deal implied that refusals-to-deal were illegal *per se* when they were used by a horizontal combination. Of course, the Court was not really attempting to outlaw refusals-to-deal. Its attack was on the horizontal arrangement.

KLOR'S INC.

In a more recent case, *Klor's Inc.* v. *Broadway-Hale Stores, Inc.,*[9] the Supreme Court reiterated its *per se* ruling against refusals-to-deal. In fact, the Court labeled refusals accompanied by a collusive arrangement illegal *per se* regardless of their effect on competition. The case involved Klor's, an appliance store, and Broadway-Hale, a neighboring department store. According to the prosecution, Klor's was as well equipped as the department store to represent appliance suppliers. However, Broadway-Hale used its monopolistic buying power to persuade General Electric, RCA, Admiral, Zenth, Emerson, and other manufacturers to refuse to deal with Klor's. Broadway-Hale did not deny the charge, but it did contend that the deletion of Klor's from the market had no effect on the degree of competition in the area. There were hundreds of appliance stores located only a few blocks away which sold many competing brands of appliances. The district court agreed with that contention as did the court of appeals. They both considered the situation to be a "purely private quarrel."

Although the Supreme Court agreed that competition had not been harmed, it found other reasons for reversing these earlier decisions. The Court claimed that there were certain practices which, because of their character alone, were forbidden by both common law and the Sherman Act. Moreover, "as to these classes of restraints. . . . Congress had determined its own criteria of public harm and it was not for the courts to decide whether in an individual case injury had actually occurred. Group boycotts, or concerted refusals by traders to deal with other traders, have long been held to be in the forbidden category."[10] This statement clarifies the Court's position on refusals-to-deal used by collusive firms. They are illegal *per se.*

It is disappointing that the courts have not clearly segregated the legality of refusals-to-deal from the legality of collusive agreements. However, most economists would agree with the court decisions provided that the collusive behavior, not the refusals-to-deal, is singled out as the anticompetitive practice.

THE ABSENCE OF
HORIZONTAL COMBINATIONS

Four major cases involving truly vertical instances of refusals-to-deal are: *U.S.* v. *Colgate and Company*,[11] *U.S.* v. *A. Schrader's Son, Inc.*,[12] *F.T.C.* v. *Beech-Nut Packing Co.*,[13] and *U.S.* v. *Parke, Davis and Company.*[14] All of these cases involved refusals-to-deal used as tools to obtain dealer adherence to resale price maintenance in states where it was not sanctioned by law.

COLGATE

Colgate was charged under the provisions of the Sherman Act with refusing to sell to dealers who would not adhere to Colgate's prescribed resale prices. Although Colgate did not place its refusal-to-deal or its resale pricing arrangements in a contract, it is clear that the company refused to sell to erring customers. Colgate distributed circulars showing the prices to be charged, it requested that offending dealers promise that they would not undercut the prices again, and it requested that complying dealers report offending dealers. The government contended that through the use of the arrangement Colgate had suppressed competition on the retail level.

The Supreme Court found the major question to be "how far one may control and dispose of his own property."[15] In answer to the question it stated:

> In the absence of any purpose to create or maintain a monopoly, the [Sherman] act does not restrict the long recognized right of trader or manufacturer engaged in an entirely private business, freely to exercise his own independent discretion as to parties with whom he will deal; and, of course, he may announce in advance the circumstances under which he will refuse to sell.[16]

In upholding Colgate's right to refuse to deal, the Court seemed to think that it was important that Colgate's price maintenance provision was not included in the contract between Colgate and its dealers. It distinguished between the decision in this case and the illegality decision in the *Dr. Miles Medical Company* case by noting that Dr. Miles had contracts which "undertook to prevent dealers from freely exercising the right to sell."[17] Of course, so did Colgate, but its contracts were not in writing. The Court's decision that it was acceptable to refuse to deal with retailers who did not abide by resale prices, as long as the supplier's policy was announced and not part of a contract, was later called the "Colgate Doctrine." The doctrine had a very short life, largely because it offered a loophole for firms wishing to use resale price maintenance.

A. SCHRADER'S SON, INC.

In *U.S.* v. *A. Schrader's Son, Inc.*, the District Court for the Northern District of Ohio found an inconsistency in the Supreme Court's decisions in *Dr. Miles Medical Company* and *Colgate*. Schrader's was a manufacturer of valves, valve parts, pressure gauges, and various other accessories used for automobile tires. In selling its products to jobbers, retail dealers, and tire manufacturers, it required minimum resale prices, and it placed the resale price maintenance provision in its contracts. Evidence indicated that Schrader's refused to sell to buyers who would not abide by these prices.

Understandably, the district court did not understand how the Supreme Court could declare Dr. Miles' resale practice illegal *per se* and allow Colgate's practice. The district court judge stated:

> Personally, and with all due respect, permit me to say that I can see no real difference upon the facts between the Dr. Miles Medical Company Case and the Colgate Company Case. The only difference is that in the former the arrangement for marketing its product was put in writing, whereas in the latter the wholesale and retailer dealers observed the prices fixed by the vendor. This is a distinction without a difference. The tacit acquiescence of the wholesalers and retailers in the prices thus fixed is the equivalent for all practical purposes of an express agreement.[18]

The district court relied on the *Colgate* precedent and allowed the scheme.

Claiming that there was a difference between *Colgate* and *Schrader's*, the Supreme Court overturned the district court's decision. In writing the Majority Opinion, Justice McReynolds held that there was an obvious difference between

> The situation presented where a manufacturer merely indicates his wishes concerning prices and declines further dealings with all who fail to observe them, and one where he enters into agreements—whether express or implied from a course of dealing or other circumstances—with customers throughout the different states which undertake to bind them to observed fixed resale prices.[19]

While the Court found a difference between the written agreement in *Schrader's* and the oral one in *Colgate*, there is certainly no difference in the effect of the two arrangements on competition. To the economist, the reasoning of the *Schrader's* decision is as tortured as that of the Mad Hatter in *Alice in Wonderland*. In any event, the Court certainly clarified the Colgate Doctrine when it implied that firms using refusals-to-deal to enforce resale price maintenance provisions could not put their price agreements in writing.

BEECH-NUT PACKING CO.

In *F.T.C.* v. *Beech-Nut Packing Co.*, the *Colgate* decision was further clarified by the Supreme Court. Beech-Nut, a manufacturer of chewing gum and food products, required its wholesalers and dealers to abide by resale prices. It never wrote the resale price maintenance agreements into a contract, but it was tacitly understood that Beech-Nut refused to deal with any wholesaler or retailer who violated the pricing arrangements. The Federal Trade Commission had declared the practice illegal, but a court of appeals decided that Beech-Nut, by not having a formal contract with wholesalers and retailers, met the requirements of the Colgate Doctrine. The Supreme Court overturned this decision. What did Beech-Nut do that Colgate did not do? They used "improper" methods to obtain compliance with the resale price maintenance arrangement. In other words, they not only said that they would refuse to deal with customers who did not abide by resale price maintenance; they also established a system using complying dealers to detect violators. The Court said:

> In its practical operation it necessarily constrains the trader, if he would have the products of the Beech-Nut Company, to maintain the prices "suggested" by it. If he fails so to do, he is subject to be reported by special agents, numerous and active in that behalf, or by dealers whose aid is enlisted in maintaining the system and the prices fixed by it. . . . From this course of conduct a court may infer—indeed, cannot escape the conclusion—that competition among retail distributors is practically suppressed, for all who would deal in the products are constrained to sell at the suggested prices.[20]

From its observation, we can conclude that the Supreme Court meant to allow refusals-to-deal to enforce resale price maintenance only when the resale price maintenance clause was not part of a written agreement (from the *Schrader's* decision) and only when the supplier uses no detection methods (from the *Beech-Nut* decision). Of course, the distinction in economics between arrangements which use devices to detect violators and those which do not is meaningless.

One wonders whether there is really a distinction in law or whether the Court simply tried to cover its tracks in the *Colgate* decision.

At this stage of our analysis, it might be useful to ask how the Court found itself in a position of having to play the "word game" to backtrack on its *Colgate* decision. "Second guessing" is dangerous, but one explanation for the Court's conduct seems plausible. The *Colgate* case really involved two practices, refusals-to-deal and resale price maintenance. At the time, the Court thought that a firm should have the right to refuse to deal, and it allowed Colgate's practice. Later, it became apparent to the Court that in upholding refusals-to-deal, it permitted resale price maintenance. Had the Court analyzed resale price maintenance by itself in *Colgate* as it did in *Dr. Miles*, it probably would have found the practice to be anticompetitive. It then could have allowed the refusal-to-deal, but not the resale price maintenance provision. By this, two goals are accomplished. The right of a seller to choose its buyers could be allowed because, by itself, it cannot create monopoly power. And the "anticompetitive" resale price maintenance provision could be disallowed. But the Court did not separate the two practices, and what resulted was a decision which constantly had to be explained and modified.

PARKE, DAVIS AND COMPANY

When resale price maintenance was legalized in the 1930s, the courts had less occasion to consider the legality of refusals-to-deal. However, in 1960, one firm attempted to use resale price maintenance in Virginia, a state which, at that time, had not passed a law permitting the practice. The defendant, Parke, Davis, used refusals-to-deal to gain dealer compliance. It manufactured roughly 600 pharmaceutical products which it marketed through drug wholesalers and retailers. Retailers either bought from drug wholesalers or made large quantity purchases directly from Parke, Davis. The company said that it would only deal with those drug wholesalers which charged specified prices to retailers.

During the summer of 1956, several drug retailers in Richmond, Virginia and Washington, D.C. sold some Parke, Davis products below the suggested price. At that time Parke, Davis' attorney notified them that the company could refuse to sell to them unless they again observed the suggested minimum prices. Because he was mindful of earlier antitrust decisions, the lawyer was careful to state that, "we can lawfully say 'we will sell you only so long as you observe such minimum retail prices' but cannot say 'we will sell you only if you agree to observe such minimum retail prices.'"[21] He was trying not to imply that Parke, Davis and its dealers had entered into an agreement to control prices. Parke, Davis also told its wholesalers that it would refuse to deal with them if they sold to retailers who undercut prices.

Several retailers refused to give any assurance that they would not undercut prices, and these retailers even continued to advertise prices below the suggested level. Dart Drug Company in Richmond was one of these mavericks, and consequently its drug supply was shut off. Dart protested to Parke-Davis because a large competitor, Peoples Drug chain, also had advertised cut prices but had not been terminated. Peoples had drugstores throughout Virginia and the Washington, D.C., area. Parke, Davis received compliance from Peoples, but five other retailers in the Richmond area continued selling at less than the suggested prices from stocks they had on reserve.

In August, Parke, Davis decided to change its policy. It attempted to get price cutters to stop advertising their low prices. In return, Parke, Davis agreed to supply them. The suspension of advertising lasted only one month before one retailer broke the advertising deadlock and others followed. The supplier then gave up its refusal-to-deal provision as well as its attempts to constrain advertising.

The case is particularly interesting because it represents a non-monopolistic firm's attempt to force something on retailers which they did not want. The retailers obviously either thought that Parke, Davis was excessively dependent on them or that they could operate successfully without Parke, Davis' supplies. Had the supplier held more monopoly power, the retailers probably would not have violated the resale pricing policy.

The Supreme Court declared Parke, Davis' policy illegal. Its decision was totally consistent with the modified Colgate Doctrine. It reiterated the right of a company to simply state its refusal-to-deal policy, and then refuse to sell to firms which do not comply. However, it agreed with the government that Parke, Davis went beyond this policy.

> The Government contends, however, that subsequent decisions of this Court [subsequent to *Colgate*] compel the holding that what Parke Davis did here by entwining the wholesalers and retailers in a program to promote general compliance with its price maintenance policy went beyond mere customer selection and created combinations or conspiracies to enforce resale price maintenance in violation of Sections 1 and 3 of the Sherman Act.[22]

Describing the means Parke, Davis used to "entwine" the wholesalers and retailers, the Court continued:

Parke Davis used the refusal to deal with the wholesalers in order to elicit their willingness to deny Parke Davis products to retailers and thereby help gain the retailers' adherence to its suggested minimum retail prices. The retailers who disregarded the price policy were promptly cut off when Parke Davis supplied the wholesalers with their names. The large retailer who said he would "abide" by the price policy, the multi-unit Peoples Drug chain, was not cut off. In thus involving the wholesalers to stop the flow of Parke Davis products to the retailers, thereby inducing retailers' adherence to its suggested retail prices, Parke Davis created a combination with the retailers and the wholesalers to maintain retail prices and violated the Sherman Act.[23]

In its decision, the Supreme Court went through another tortured attempt to reconcile the prior decisions it had made on refusals-to-deal. Its arguments are interesting, but do little to resolve the issue. It is enough to say that the Court's treatment of refusals-to-deal represents a bleak void in logical jurisprudence which is best forgotten.

SUMMARY

The law on refusals-to-deal is clear, if not well thought out. A firm may refuse to deal with the customer if: (1) No anticompetitive practice is placed in a written contract; (2) The firm does not use customers to gain compliance with a specified practice; (3) When a supplier encounters a violating customer, it simply refuses to sell. As we have said before, throughout the legal history of refusal-to-deal cases the major problem was probably that the courts confused refusal-to-deal clauses with resale price maintenance. However, it does seem fair to say that it was the resale price maintenance provision that they were trying to declare illegal, not the refusal-to-deal. Moreover, if refusals-to-deal are designed to get dealer compliance on a legal practice, the refusal-to-deal would be allowed.

NOTES TO CHAPTER IX

[1]Comment, "Refusals to Sell and Public Control of Competition," *Yale Law Journal*, LVIII (1949), 1121.
[2]282 U.S. 30 (1930).
[3]282 U.S. 30, 36 (1930).
[4]282 U.S. 30, 43 (1930).
[5]312 U.S. 457 (1941).

[6]312 U.S. 457, 462 (1941).
[7]312 U.S. 457, 468 (1941).
[8]*Ibid.*
[9]359 U.S. 207 (1951).
[10]359 U.S. 207, 211 (1951).
[11]250 U.S. 300 (1919).
[12]252 U.S. 85 (1920).
[13]257 U.S. 441 (1921).
[14]362 U.S. 29 (1960).
[15]250 U.S. 300, 305 (1919).
[16]250 U.S. 300, 307 (1919).
[17]250 U.S. 300, 308 (1919).
[18]252 U.S. 85, 97 (1920).
[19]252 U.S. 85, 99 (1920).
[20]257 U.S. 441, 454-455 (1921).
[21]362 U.S. 29, 33 (1960).
[22]362 U.S. 36, 37 (1960).
[23]362 U.S. 36, 45 (1960).

CLAYTON AND FEDERAL TRADE COMMISSION ACTS

SECTION V

The Clayton and Federal Trade Commission Acts were passed in 1914. These are major pieces of antitrust legislation which greatly augmented the provisions of the Sherman Act. In Chapter X the two acts as well as their amendments are introduced. Then, because a knowledge of court decisions is necessary to understand the implications of these acts, specific practices prosecuted under the provisions of the Clayton and Federal Trade Commission Acts are discussed. Tying contracts are analyzed in Chapter XI, exclusive dealing arrangements in Chapter XII, mergers in Chapters XIII and XIV, monopolization and shared monopolies in Chapter XV, and price discrimination in Chapter XVI.

CLAYTON AND FEDERAL TRADE COMMISSION ACTS

CHAPTER X

The provisions of the Federal Trade Commission and Clayton Acts, the reasons for their enactment and the procedures for their implementation are analyzed in this chapter.

INTRODUCTION

The Clayton Act and the Federal Trade Commission Act are introduced in this chapter. These are two major pieces of antitrust legislation which today are used more often than the Sherman Act. The reasons explaining the need to pass the acts are discussed here as well as their major provisions. However, since the real interpretation of any antitrust act is developed through case analysis, in *Chapters XI to XVI*, the application of the acts to anticompetitive practices are considered.

THE FAILURE OF THE SHERMAN ACT DURING ITS EARLY YEARS

When the Sherman Act was passed in 1890, most critics of big business thought that their problems were over. They did not have to wait long to find that the act was to be extremely ineffective in its early years. From 1897 to 1917, the United States economy experienced rapid natural growth, but at the same time massive "artificial" growth was realized through mergers and consolidations. In a style reminiscent of the period in which they wrote, J. M. and J. B. Clark described the tremendous combinations.

> The mere size of the consolidations which have recently appeared is enough to startle those who saw them in the making. If the carboniferous age had returned and the earth had repeopled itself with dinosaurs, the change made in animal life would have scarcely seemed greater than that which has been made in the business world by these monster-like corporations.[1]

It was not just the existence of large firms that bothered the critics of big business. They thought that the firms' actions were detrimental to strong and weak competitors alike. For example, the large firms would sometimes sell at a loss to drive their competitors out of business. Given their large war chests it was easy to do this.[2] Then, when competitors left the market, the large firms could raise prices and extract monopoly profits from consumers. Historians of the period claimed that such practices forced many small business- men out of business or forced them to merge with the large firms.[3]

There were a number of faults with the Sherman Act and early Sherman Act litigation which allowed big business to develop. First, even if a firm was found guilty of monopolization by combining with other firms, the antitrust remedy was frequently insufficient. Some- times the courts issued dissolution decrees to break up a large combination, and the stock of the newly created firms was issued to the individuals who had previously held stock in the combination. Had each stockholder received the stock of only one newly created firm there would have been no problem. However, each stockholder usually received stock in a number of competing firms. This set the stage for collusive activities.

A second problem was that in early Sherman Act litigation the courts interpreted the statute as requiring specific evidence of intent to monopolize in order to find a firm guilty. Intent is difficult to prove, and therefore many monopolistic firms could not be touched. Third, except for private suits, all antitrust charges were initiated by the Department of Justice. Because the attorney general reported to the president, prosecution became a political football. Those presi- dents who wanted strong antitrust enforcement got it. But more importantly, antitrust lay dormant during the administration of presidents who were attuned to the desires of business. As Congress- man McGillicuddy of Maine observed in a partisan speech:

> As to the enforcement of the antitrust laws by Republican officials for the past 16 years, it is putting it mildly to say that they were at least indifferent. At times the Sherman antitrust law was deliberately ignored and practically con- sidered a dead letter.[4]

Fourth, the Department of Justice did not have lawyers trained in antitrust matters. Therefore, because of inept prosecution, the gov- ernment lost many cases that it should have won. This was not completely the lawyers' fault. The department did not have a sepa- rate investigative division for antitrust, nor did it have a division of economics to help with the presentation of economic concepts.

Finally, there was a definite need to clarify just what the Sherman Act declared illegal. The courts gradually performed this job, but the task was great, and many anticompetitive practices were allowed while the courts developed their philosophy toward the Sherman Act.

Although public pressure for a new antitrust law evolved gradually, the real impetus was developed in the Presidential Campaign of 1912. All three parties included antitrust planks in their platforms. The Democrats called for provisions outlawing specific practices, the Progressive Party called for the formation of an agency which would supervise antitrust enforcement, and the Republicans were in agreement with both ideas. The Republicans added that it was important to clarify the antitrust laws to provide businessmen with guidelines concerning what constituted acceptable business practices. President Wilson emerged as the winner of the campaign, and he was a major catalyst in prompting the passage of both the Federal Trade Commission Act and the Clayton Act.

FEDERAL TRADE COMMISSION ACT

Because of the growth of large businesses and a need to centralize the antitrust attack against them, there was a common understanding among legislators that an agency was needed to direct the fight against anticompetitive practices. Moreover, new antitrust laws were needed to clarify and extend the provisions of the Sherman Act. In his message to Congress on January 20, 1914, President Wilson began his attack on the trust movement by calling for the formation of an administrative agency to examine and control business practices. Later that year the Federal Trade Commission Act was passed establishing a new antitrust law and an administrative agency to enforce it.[5] The bulk of this act deals with the formation of the Federal Trade Commission (F.T.C.) and the powers given to it. Section 5 of the act provides antitrust legislation because "unfair methods of competition" are declared illegal. By not enumerating specific illegal practices, the commission's jurisdiction could be expanded as new anticompetitive practices developed. Had Congress outlawed specific practices the act probably would have quickly become obsolete.

Section 5 was designed to supplement the Sherman Act. Unlike the former legislation which required a restraint of trade to find guilt, the Federal Trade Commission Act only requires a lessening of competition. This wording allows the commission to prosecute practices which are not great enough to become violations of the Sherman Act. Moreover, because the F.T.C. is free to interpret "unfair methods of competition" it can proceed against violations of the Sherman Act. This explains why many Sherman Act cases discussed earlier in this book were also prosecuted under Section 5 of the Federal Trade Commission Act.

The Federal Trade Commission Act calls for five Commissioners appointed by the president with the advice and consent of the Senate. These members have staggered seven year terms, and at no time are more than three of them from the same party. Today the commission is comprised of eleven regional offices and nine functional divisions. Each of the nine divisions has separate areas of responsibility. Several of the more important divisions are the Office of Policy Planning and Evaluation, the Bureau of Competition, the Bureau of Consumer Protections, and the Bureau of Economics. The Office of Policy Planning and Evaluation determines where the commission can best employ its resources to serve the public interest. This division also evaluates and coordinates the work of the other divisions. Antitrust law enforcement is the responsibility of the Bureau of Competition. Its basic function is to discover and cure anticompetitive practices which are violations of the Clayton Act or Section 5 of the Federal Trade Commission Act.

An important function of the bureau has been to clarify the antitrust laws by offering a set of guidelines for business to follow. A major subdivision of this bureau is the Compliance Division which acts as a policing unit to insure that the commission's decisions are implemented. The Bureau of Consumer Protection is involved with the study and the regulation of practices which are believed to be deceptive or unfair.

The Bureau of Economics is composed of three divisions. The Division of Economic Evidence provides assistance to the Bureaus of Competition and Consumer Protection in their investigations. The Division of Industry Analysis conducts economic studies of industries and the effects of specific business practices. Finally, the Divison of Financial Statistics compiles a quarterly statistical publication for all manufacturing industries.

The Federal Trade Commission is given many powers for the investigation of businesses. Several excerpts taken directly from Section 6 of the act will give the reader an idea of the breadth of these powers.[6]

1. To gather and compile information concerning, and to investigate from time to time the organization, busi-

ness, conduct, practices, and management of any corporation engaged in commerce.

2. To require . . . corporations engaged in commerce . . . to file with the commission in such form as the commission may proscribe . . . reports or answers in writing to specific questions. . . .

3. Whenever a final decree has been entered against any defendant corporation in any suit brought by the United States, the commission must investigate upon its own initiative, of the manner in which the decree has been or is being carried out. . . .

4. Upon the direction of the president or either house of Congress, to investigate and report the facts relating to any alleged violations of the antitrust acts by any corporation.

5. Upon the application of the attorney general to investigate and make recommendations for the readjustment of the business of any corporation alleged to be violating the antitrust acts in order that the corporation may thereafter maintain its organization, management, and conduct of business in accordance with the law.

6. To make public from time to time such portions of the information obtained by it . . . except trade secrets and names of customers, as it shall deem expedient in the public interest; and to make annual and special reports to the Congress and to submit therewith recommendations for additional legislation.

7. To investigate . . . trade conditions in and with foreign countries where associations, combinations, or practices of manufacturers, merchants, or traders, or other conditions, may affect the foreign trade of the United States, and to report to Congress thereon, with such recommendations as it deems advisable.

Section 8 furthers the investigative powers of the F.T.C. by providing:

That the several departments and bureaus of the government when directed by the president shall furnish the commission, upon its request, all records, papers, and information in their possession relating to any corporation subject to any of the provisions of this Act.[7]

Finally, in Section 9, the commission is given the power to secure information from the documents of any firm being investigated as well as the right to subpoena witnesses. All of these powers clearly give the F.T.C. the ability to obtain a true picture of business conditions and operations. Moreover, they enhance the commission's ability to construct cases against violators of antitrust laws.

Since we will be studying antitrust cases prosecuted by the Federal Trade Commission, it is important to understand the flow of cases within the Commission. The F.T.C. can initiate an investigation any time it is warranted. Businessmen, members of Congress, other government agencies, trade associations, and private citizens may report anticompetitive practices in letters to the commission. These letters are called "applications for complaint." Each application is reviewed by the commission to determine whether the practice cited involves interstate commerce, the public interest (rather than the interest of individuals), and a violation of a law that the F.T.C. administers. If a practice does satisfy these criteria, an investigation is initiated.

In its investigation the commission will either require the firm involved to submit a special report concerning its operations or submit the case to a regional office for personal investigation. Upon completion of the investigation, the commission will close the case if there is a lack of evidence, obtain a voluntary assurance that the party involved will discontinue its illegal practices, or issue a formal complaint and a "cease and desist" order. Voluntary assurance that an anticompetitive practice will be discontinued is accepted when the commission feels that the party involved will act in good faith and that the public interest will be protected. However, a formal complaint and a cease and desist order will be utilized in most cases.

Upon issuance of the formal complaint, the case, like Sherman Act cases, can be settled by a "consent decree." The reader will remember from Chapter V that this is a written agreement by the party involved which establishes procedures to stop the questioned practice or alter it in such a manner that the public interest will be protected. This decree can be entered into at any time prior to a final Supreme Court decision. The consent decree will be reviewed by the commission and if acceptable, placed on the public record for thirty days. During this time interested persons can file their comments with the commission. These comments are taken into consideration when the commission decides whether to accept the decree or begin formal procedures against the party involved.

If either the firm or the F.T.C. does not agree to the consent decree, the firm is brought to trial by the issuance of a formal complaint. The case is first heard by an F.T.C. administrative law judge (previously called hearing examiner) in public hearings. His decision is handed down within ninety days of the completion of the hearings. This decision can be appealed to the commission by either party but if it is not, the commission will either accept the administrative law judge's decision or modify it in some manner. When the judge's decision is appealed, the commission hears the arguments and then decides whether to issue a cease and desist order or alter the charges. The respondent then has sixty days to comply with the commission's decision or appeal it to a U.S. district court. Ultimately the case can be appealed to the Supreme Court if that Court is willing to hear it.

WHEELER-LEA ACT

In 1938, the Federal Trade Commission Act was amended by the Wheeler-Lea Act.[8] Although this revision mainly deals with false advertising, it also strengthens the commission's enforcement power. Prior to this act, the commission had no recourse of its own if a cease and desist order was violated. The Wheeler-Lea Act gave the commission the power to levy a $5,000 fine per violation if an order was ignored. Later, this fine was increased to $5,000 per day per violation.[9] The Wheeler-Lea Act also reworded Section 5 to declare "unfair or deceptive acts or practices in commerce" illegal. For example, the Wheeler-Lea Act amended Sections 12 to 15 of the Federal Trade Commission Act to declare false advertising of foods, drugs, cosmetics, and curative or corrective devices illegal. This gives the commission the right to enjoin any practices injurious to consumers even if competition is not harmed.

When a violation of the Wheeler-Lea Act is found, the commission has the right to halt the practice by applying for a court injunction. This injunction lasts until the commission has completed its investigation, held a hearing, and made a final decision. If the findings do prove that false advertising or a deceptive act or practice is injurious to the consumer's health, the act provides that the case can be submitted to the attorney general for prosecution as a criminal offense.

CLAYTON ACT

The Clayton Act was another part of President Wilson's legislative package to control business practices.[10] Preventitive measures are emphasized in this act rather than the punitive actions which had developed from court interpretations of the Sherman Act. The legislators wanted to attack monopoly in its "incipiency" thereby preventing the development of monopoly power. They did this by making illegal specific practices thought to be used by businesses to harm competition. The practices are not declared *per se* illegal but only illegal when they "substantially lessen competition or tend to create a monopoly." Thus the Clayton Act has a built-in rule of reason. The most important of the practices prohibited in the act are price discrimination (in Section 2), exclusive dealing and tying contracts (in Section 3), acquisitions of competing companies (in Section 7), and interlocking directorates (in Section 8). Either the Justice Department or the Federal Trade Commission can bring suit under the provisions of the Clayton Act. This is the only act over which both agencies have joint jurisdiction. Only the Justice Department can bring suit under the Sherman Act, and only the Federal Trade Commission can use the Federal Trade Commission Act. Because each outlawed practice is important to an understanding of antitrust, the provisions outlawing each will be discussed individually.

PRICE DISCRIMINATION

At the time Congress passed the Clayton Act large businesses sometimes employed price-cutting policies to harm unwanted competitors. It was this price discrimination which Congress wanted to outlaw in Section 2 of the Clayton Act. That section states:

> . . . it shall be unlawful for any person engaged in commerce, in the course of such commerce, either directly or indirectly, to discriminate in price between different purchasers of commodities, which commodities are sold for use, consumption or resale . . . where the effect of such discrimination may be to substantially lessen competition or tend to create a monopoly in any line of commerce.[11]

The original Clayton Act allowed price differentials when it was cheaper to sell to one customer than another. Moreover, the F.T.C. and the courts did not spend much time determining whether a price reduction was fully justified by a savings in cost. Additionally, the original provision was only directed toward price discriminators who harmed their own competitors through cutthroat pricing. It was not until 1929 that the act was applied to price discrimination which hurt competitors at a lower level of distribution.[12] Many critics of the original act thought that it allowed too many loopholes for the price discriminator. By 1936, discontent with Section 2 was so widespread that the Robinson-Patman Amendment to Section 2 was passed by Congress.[13] No longer could price discrimination which hurt a disciminator's customer avoid the law. The practice is outlawed when it lessens competition "in any line of commerce." Anyone who receives an illegal discrimination in price is also in violation of the act. The Robinson-Patman Act does recognize the three defenses for a price discriminator which were in the original Clayton Act. A price decrease is defensible when different qualities of goods are sold or when a price is lowered in "good faith to meet an equally low price of a competitor." The third defense deals with cost justification. Previously, this had been a popular defense, but it was severely limited by the revision. Price differentials are to "make only due allowances for differences in the cost." A supplier can not justify lowering the price per unit by a quarter if he is only saving a dime per unit in costs.

EXCLUSIVE DEALING ARRANGEMENTS AND TYING CONTRACTS

The courts have considered tying contracts and exclusive dealing arrangements to be a violation of the Sherman Act. Although these practices could be regulated in this way, they are also included in Section 3 of the Clayton Act. This section states that if, at any time, the effect of an exclusive dealing arrangement or tying contract "may be to substantially lessen competition or tend to create a monopoly in any line of commerce," the practices are illegal.

ACQUISITION OF COMPETING COMPANIES

Many critics of the Sherman Act thought that it did not adequately retard merger activity. Therefore, the original Section 7 was designed to put more teeth into merger prosecution by providing that:

> . . . no corporation engaged in commerce shall acquire, directly or indirectly, the whole or any part of the stock or other share capital of another corporation engaged also in commerce, where the effect of such acquisition may be to substantially lessen competition between the corporation whose stock is acquired and the corporation making the acquisition, or to restrain such commerce in any section or community, or tend to create a monopoly in any line of competition.[14]

Section 7 excluded an important means of promulgating a merger. There was no provision to prohibit the acquisition of the physical assets of a firm. This loophole allowed mergers to continue because, although corporations were not permitted to use stock acquisitions to effect a merger, they could make an outright purchase of a firm's assets, thereby avoiding the provisions of the Clayton Act. There was yet another problem with Section 7. As it read, the section implied that only horizontal mergers were outlawed under the Clayton Act provisions. Vertical as well as conglomerate mergers were excluded.

Because Section 7 did not provide an effective weapon to fight mergers and because the Sherman Act merger decisions had been very lenient, the Justice Department and the F.T.C. prodded Congress to enact new legislation. In 1950, the Celler-Kefauver Act amended Section 7 of the original Clayton Act.[15] As revised, the new Section 7 states:

> No corporation engaged in commerce shall acquire, directly or indirectly, the whole or any part of the stock or other share capital and no corporation subject to the jurisdiction of the Federal Trade Commission shall acquire the whole or any part of the assets of another corporation engaged also in commerce, where, in any line of commerce in any section of the country, the effect of such acquisition may be substantially to lessen competition or to tend to create a monopoly.[16]

By including the acquisition of physical assets in the revision, the Justice Department and the F.T.C. closed an important merger loophole. Moreover, because of the wording of the amendment, all mergers, whether vertical, horizontal, or conglomerate, can be prosecuted under the new Section 7. It is also important to note that the new Section 7, like the original Clayton Act, is designed to stop monopoly power in its incipiency. Moreover, in contrast with the Sherman Act, the Clayton Act does not require that firms intend to create monopoly power in order to find a violation.

INTERLOCKING DIRECTORATES

The provisions of Section 8 of the Clayton Act deal with interlocking directorates. These exist when a person is a director of two or more competing firms. The main provision of Section 8 states:

> . . . no person at the same time shall be a director in any two or more corporations, any one of which has capital, surplus, and undivided profits aggregating more than $1 million engaged in whole or in part in commerce . . . if such corporations are or shall have been therefore by virtue of their business or location or operation, competitors, so that the elimination of competition by agreement

between them would constitute a violation of any of the provisions of any of the antitrust laws.[17]

The framers of the Clayton Act rightly thought that if one person was a director of two or more competing firms, it would be a simple matter to initiate collusive behavior.

SUMMARY

Taken at face value, the Clayton Act, the Federal Trade Commission Act, and their various amendments clearly gave the country a tougher antitrust policy and an impressive agency to implement it. Because it is not nearly as vague as the Sherman Act, businesses and courts alike have a much better idea of what is allowed and what is disallowed. Moreover, for those individuals who demanded a tough treatment of anticompetitive practices, the Clayton Act provided it. By declaring monopolistic practices illegal in their incipiency, the act required only a showing that if the practices were allowed to continue they might create additional monopoly power. Like the Sherman Act, however, it is difficult to judge the operation of antitrust laws on the basis of the wording of statutes. Therefore, in the next six chapters we consider the application of the law to tying arrangements, exclusive dealing arrangements, horizontal, vertical, and conglomerate mergers, monopolization and price discrimination.

NOTES TO CHAPTER X

[1]J. B. Clark and J. M. Clark, *The Control of Trusts* (New York: The Macmillan Company, 1912), pp. 14-15.

[2]Whether it was rational will be discussed in *Chapter XIV*.

[3]See, for example, Ida M. Tarbell, *The History of The Standard Oil Company*, Vol. II (New York: The Macmillan Company, 1952), pp. 31-62; Eliot Jones, *The Trust Problem in The United States* (New York: The Macmillan Company, 1927), pp. 100, 151-153.

[4]51 Cong. Rec. 9260 (1914).

[5]38 Stat. 717 (1914).

[6]38 Stat. 717, 721-722 (1914).

[7]38 Stat. 717, 722 (1914).

[8]52 Stat. 111 (1938).

[9]64 Stat. 20, 21-22 (1950).

[10]38 Stat. 730 (1914).

[11]38 Stat. 730 (1914).

[12]*Van Camp & Sons* v. *American Can Co.*, 49 S. Ct. 112 (1929).

[13]49 Stat. 1526 (1936).

[14]38 Stat. 730, 731-732 (1914).

[15]64 Stat. 1125 (1950).

[16]64 Stat. 1125, 1125-1126 (1950).

[17]38 Stat. 730, 733 (1914).

computers   1 product   monopoly power

cards   Complementary product: sold in competitive market

               (in use)   "meters" elasticity of demand for 1st product

TYING ARRANGEMENTS

Most readers have encountered situations where they must purchase goods jointly. If they want good A they must buy good B. Such an arrangement is termed a "tying contract." In this chapter we determine whether the arrangement creates monopoly power as well as its legality under the provisions of the Clayton Act.

INTRODUCTION

Students tapped into one national honor society found that they were required to purchase either a gold key or a lapel button to receive a membership certificate. This is an instance of a tying contract or tying arrangement. It is characterized by the sale of one good (the tying good) conditional on the consumer's agreement to purchase one or more other goods (the tied goods). Where such arrangements can be explained by economies of joint production they usually are not objectionable. The tying of steering wheels and cars, houses and land, and a chapter on tying arrangements with a chapter on resale price maintenance rarely bothers anyone. However, when the arrangements cannot be explained in terms of economies of joint production, they cause consumer animosity. Moreover, since firms might use tying arrangements to create monopoly power, they have been placed under the provisions of Section 1 of the Sherman Act and Section 3 of the Clayton Act.

Tying arrangements are a form of exclusive dealing when they require that for a consumer to receive one good, he must buy his requirements of some other good from the same producer. Because tying and exclusive dealing are similar, this chapter and the one that follows on exclusive dealing overlap. Yet tying arrangements do differ from exclusive dealing arrangements in enough ways to warrant separate consideration of the two subjects.

THE ECONOMICS OF TYING ARRANGEMENTS

A number of reasons have been presented to explain why firms adopt tying arrangements, and an understanding of them is helpful in formulating appropriate antitrust policy. The explanations can be divided into three classifications:

Jo

    A. Tying arrangements may be used to create monopoly power;
    B. Tying arrangements may be used to exercise existing monopoly power;

false   ? C. Tying arrangements may be used to coerce customers into buying something they do not want.

Each of these will be considered separately.

THE CREATION OF MONOPOLY POWER

In one sense, it is inappropriate to consider whether tying arrangements create monopoly power and whether such power results in harm to consumers. Their use by a producer is almost always impractical unless the producer already has some monopoly power in the sale of the tying good. Therefore, if consumer harm results from their use, the already-existing monopoly power is the fundamental cause. To understand this, imagine a situation where a manufacturer using tying arrangements does not have monopoly power in the sale of the tying good. One producer of pencils and paper clips requires customers to purchase his paper clips if they wish to purchase his pencils. Customers' reactions to this arrangement would be both immediate and severe; they would no longer purchase from the pencil manufacturer because they would have a large number of other brands available to them. Only when a large number of alternatives do not exist can the practice be used. This suggests that if tying contracts are harmful to the consuming public, the fundamental cause of this harm is the existence of monopoly power, and the fundamental solution would be the elimination of this power.

To declare tying arrangements illegal would be to treat a symptom of the problem instead of the problem itself. Of course, it is not always practicable to eliminate monopoly power. Diseconomies may result from reducing the size of a firm, and benefits to the public resulting from monopoly power such as those which stem from a patent right granted for invention or innovation may be lost. In the following analysis it will be assumed that one or both of these barriers to the elimination of monopoly power exist, for only then is the discussion meaningful.

The use of tying arrangements may create monopoly power in two ways. First, the arrangements may be used to create economic leverage. Second, they may foreclose markets to competitors. These arguments deserve careful consideration for they appear to be valid arguments in favor of outlawing tying contracts.

Can Co. extract all rent in 1st market, sell in 2nd at competitive price?

Economic Leverage

Many critics of tying contracts believe that they are used to create "economic leverage," which is defined as the use of monopoly power in one market (the market for the tying good) to create monopoly power in a second market (the market for the tied good). To understand leverage, consider the following hypothetical example. Suppose that because of its patent rights, Synergetics Limited is the only producer of data processing machines. Wishing to extend its monopoly power to cover data-processing cards, the company stipulates that it will rent its machines only to customers who agree to purchase its cards. Although Synergetics does not have a patent on the cards and although the cards can be produced equally well by a number of manufacturers, Synergetics' tying arrangement may create a monopoly in the sale of the cards.

It is incorrect to assume that all tying arrangements involve economic leverage. Therefore it is important to be able to separate instances where monopoly power is created from instances where it is not. Reduced output in the tied-good market is the best indicator of the creation of monopoly power. In earlier sections of this book, the ability of a firm to charge a higher price has been the major indicator of increased monopoly power, but this test is inappropriate for tying arrangements. If a producer reduces the price of his tying good, and its tied good is a complement, the profit-maximizing price of the tied good would probably be raised because of the increase in the quantity demanded for the tying good. Yet this higher price does not automatically indicate increased monopoly power in the tied-good market. Therefore restriction of output is the appropriate indicator. When the use of a tying contract results in a reduction of the output of the tied good as compared to the situation where the producer sells the good separately and chooses the profit-maximizing price for each of them, monopoly power has been created.[1] If, on the other hand, there is no reduction in the output of the tied good as compared to the situation where the producer sells the goods separately and chooses the profit-maximizing price for each of them, no monopoly power is created.

Producers adopting tying arrangements to gain economic leverage may create monopoly power in the market for the tied good if the tied good and the tying good are complements which are used by consumers in variable proportions. The example of Synergetic machines and cards fits this description; the cards and the machines are complements in that they are consumed together. Moreover, the two products are used in variable proportions. Complementary goods have interrelated demands such that the quantity sold of any one of them depends not only on the price of the good itself but also on the price of its complements. The demand for Synergetic cards, for example, depends on the price of Synergetic machines. This relationship implies that for every price charged for a good there is a separate demand curve for its complementary goods, and this idea suggests that it is not wise for a producer of two or more complementary goods to set the price of each good independent of the price he charges for the others.[2] After considering the relationship between the two goods, the producer may even discover that it pays him to sell one product at or below cost. This may stimulate enough demand to permit him to charge a higher-than-normal price for his complementary product and more than compensate for his reduced profit on the first good. But when a producer decides that selling one product at a relatively low price will increase his profits, he must be certain that consumers do not purchase the lower-priced good from him and then purchase its complement from his competitors. To protect himself he may adopt a tying arrangement by stipulating that if the consumers are to purchase the low-priced good (tying good) from him they must also purchase the high-priced good (tied good).

Because the producer is now charging a higher price for the tied good than he would if he priced each good independent of the other, output might be reduced in the tied-good market. If this is the case, leverage exists, monopoly power has been created, and the producer would be able to get a greater profit from the tied sales than he would receive if he independently priced each product. A graphical example makes this point clear.[3] Suppose that a firm produces two complementary goods, A and B. The firm has a monopoly in the sale of A, but B is sold in a competitive but not a purely competitive market. Additionally, assume that the goods are related such that a 50 cent increase in the price of B decreases the amount of A sold by 100 units, and a 50 cent increase in the price of A decreases the amount of B sold by 200 units. Prior to using a tying arrangement (when the goods were priced independently) the firm found that the profit-maximizing price for A was $4.00, and the profit-maximizing price for B was $2.00, the competitive price. Given these prices, the firm sold 2,000 units of A and 3,700 units of B. The amount of A and B sold as well as the prices are shown in *Figures I-A* and *I-B*. The reader will note that in the sale of A, the firm was on the demand curve marked P_B = $2.00 (indicating that the price of B was $2.00). In the sale of B, the firm was on the demand curve marked P_A = $4.00 (indicating that the price of A was $4.00).

Now suppose that the firm requires its customers to buy good B if they wish to buy good A. The firm now charges $3.50 for A which

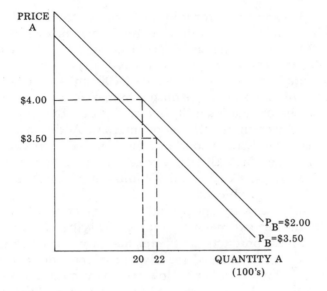

FIG. I-A

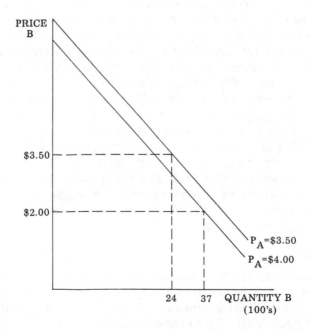

FIG. I-B

DEMAND RELATIONSHIPS BETWEEN COMPLIMENTARY GOODS

shifts the demand curve for B upward relative to its location when A was $4.00. The firm finds that the profit-maximizing price for B is now $3.50 which shifts the demand curve for good A downward relative to its location when B was $2.00. *Figures I-A* and *I-B* show the final equilibrium position where 2400 units of B are sold and 2200 units of A are sold. The output in market B has been decreased relative to the original quantity indicating that the firm has created monopoly power in the tied-good market. Additionally, provided that the cost per unit is constant, the firm has increased its profits relative to the first situation when it determined the profit-maximizing price for each good without considering the relationship between the two products.

It is fairly easy to understand why the creation of monopoly power in the second market requires the tying of complementary products. Unless products are complementary, their demand is unrelated, and the price charged for any one of them does not affect the quantity sold of the other.[4] However, why must the products be consumed in variable proportions? Cannot monopoly power be created by tying goods which are used in fixed proportions? The answer is "no" because profits cannot be increased in this manner. To see why, consider the following example. Gloves are consumed in fixed proportions. Very few people would wish to use a right hand glove without using a left hand glove. Therefore, consumers think of the two products as one. Considered as a package, there is a maximum amount that an individual is willing to pay for the two gloves. Suppose it is seven dollars. One glove could be sold at two dollars and the other glove at five dollars, but the maximum amount received is still seven dollars. And if a producer tries to sell the first glove at two dollars and the second glove at six dollars, he will find that the consumer will no longer purchase from him because he has exceeded the seven dollar limit. It is irrational to tie goods which are consumed in fixed proportion because there is no way that the arrangement can increase profits as compared to a situation where the two goods are sold separately.

Foreclosure

A second way tying arrangements may be used to create monopoly power is to foreclose markets to competitors. Many economists who have studied tying contracts have concluded that the price of the tying good is usually lowered, and the price of the tied good is usually raised as a result of the contract. Yet because the lowering of the price of the tying good has created additional demand for the tied good, the output of that good may be increased. To the extent that this is true, markets are foreclosed to competitors. Although not all foreclosure is detrimental, there is something particularly mischievous about this instance of foreclosure. When tying arrangements foreclose the market for the tied good they do so not because the firm is a better competitor in that market but because of its monopoly power in the tying-good market. Very few people can fault a firm which gains 25 per cent of a market because it is the most competitive firm in that market. However, people can fault a firm which gains 25 per cent of a market because it has a dominant position in another market. And the distinction between the two cases is relevant to the formulation of sound antitrust law because in the situation involving competition the firm was able to obtain its market share because it offered customers more than its competitors did. In the second situation—the one involving the tying arrangements—it did not necessarily offer its customers more than did its competitors.

The degree to which a firm can foreclose a market through the use of tying contracts depends mainly on two variables. (1) The degree of monopoly power in the tying-good market and (2) the number of uses for the tied good. If a firm has significant monopoly power in the tying-good market, it may be able to take away a substantial share of the tied-good market from its competitors. If the tied good has a number of uses which can be performed without the tying good, a large number of customers will not be foreclosed to competition.

Although the foreclosure argument may be valid, it is not without at least one pitfall. A firm may lose some of its market share in the tying good when it adopts a tying arrangement. If, for example, General Motors required that consumers who purchase its cars also finance the cars through the General Motors Acceptance Corporation, many customers might find it advantageous to buy from another automobile manufacturer; a case of negative foreclosure in the tying-good market. However, although this is an interesting observation, the fact that the manufacturer may lose sales in the tying good does not salve the wounds of competitors and, more importantly, customers in the tied-good market. Therefore, it is relevant to analyze competition in that market alone. And where a substantial share of that market is foreclosed, competitors and, ultimately, competition might be hurt.

THE EXERCISE
OF MONOPOLY POWER

It is important to warn the reader not to jump to the conclusion that monopoly power is created in the tied-good market every time complements used in variable proportions are tied. There are reasons explaining the use of tying arrangements which do not involve the creation of monopoly power. In fact, in many instances of tying arrangements it would be impossible for a producer to develop monopoly power in the tied good. M. L. Burstein suggested this when he asked the rhetorical question,

> . . . can it sensibly be accepted that G. S. Suppiger Co. tied salt to its salt-dispensing machinery as a part of a scheme to monopolize the American salt market? Did Morgan Envelope Co. tie its toilet paper to its dispenser as part of a grand scheme to monopolize the American bathroom tissue market? Why do we see again and again in the court report cases involving the tying of rivets, staples, windshield wipers, repair parts, varnish, etc. when the tying monopolist's share of the market for the tied product remains miniscule?[5]

Alternative explanations all involve an attempt by firms to extract a higher payment from the customer than that which could be received if the tying product and the tied product were sold separately. Four ways of doing this will be considered.

A. Tying arrangements might be used to implement price discrimination.
B. Tying arrangements might be used to avoid maximum-price legislation.
C. Tying arrangements might be a means of sharing risks with consumers.
D. Tying arrangements might protect the product image of the tying product.

Each of these will be considered in turn, but throughout the analysis it is important to remember that the intent of firms using tying contracts for these reasons is not to create new monopoly power. However, this does not deny that market foreclosure may be incidental to these uses of tying arrangements, and monopoly power may be created when foreclosure is substantial.

Price Discrimination

It might be profitable for a firm to engage in price discrimination if it sells or rents products to customers with differing elasticities of demand. By charging higher prices to customers with a low elasticity of demand, a firm may increase its over-all profits. One of the greatest problems encountered by firms using price discrimination is the determination of customers' elasticity of demand. A tying arrangement is helpful in doing this if a producer sells at least two products which are complementary and which are consumed in variable proportions because sales of tied products may provide an indication of the elasticity of demand for the tying product. If it is true that heavy users of the tying product have a lower elasticity of demand for the tying product than light users, the tied product could be sold at a higher-than-competitive price, and the tying product could be sold at a lower-than competitive price. This arrangement would cause heavy users of the tying good to pay more for the combined products than light users. Consider the Synergetic machine/Synergetic card situation to see a hypothetical example of this practice. The machine could be rented at a relatively low price, and the price of the cards might be relatively high. The sale of the cards would provide a metering device to determine the degree of machine utilization, and a relatively large amount of money from the sale of cards could be extracted from those who use the machine heavily. Conversely, a relatively small amount from the sale of the cards would be received from those who use the machine infrequently.

Two questions might occur to the reader at this stage of the analysis. First, why doesn't the producer simply charge higher rent to heavy users of the machine? Second, why doesn't the company place a meter on the machine instead of using cards to measure intensity of use? The answer to the first question hinges on the degree of difficulty in estimating consumers' demand for the tying good prior to its use. Customers may not know how much they will utilize the tying product, and even if they did know, it would be difficult to get such information from them if their answer affects the rental fee or price. The problem of estimating the level of utilization is especially complicated in situations where the tying good will be used for a number of years. Concerning the second question, the degree of product utilization cannot always be metered, although metering is feasible in the Synergetic example. Many meters can be tampered with. Additionally, a meter cannot be attached to all types of goods. Of course, even the use of tied products to measure consumption of the tying product is problematic, and such arrangements must be continually policed to see that customers do not substitute another product for the tied good.

Firms which use tying arrangements to implement price discrimination attempt to utilize their existing monopoly power, not to create additional monopoly power. They use the tying arrangement to receive the maximum possible price for their tying good. If they could meter their tying product without a tying arrangement they would receive as much profit. The fact that the arrangement may increase the output of the tied good and hence foreclose markets to competitors is purely incidental to this use of tying arrangements. Nonetheless, if the foreclosure is substantial it may incidentally reduce competition in the tied-good market.

Avoidance of Maximum-Price Legislation

Tying contracts may provide a means to avoid maximum-price legislation. When the government specifies maximum allowable prices for some good but not for others, firms may find it profitable to tie two goods to avoid the price legislation. The classic example of this situation occurred during World War II when the government established a maximum price for whiskey. Since the price was less than that which consumers were willing to pay (the profit-maximizing price), companies tied unregulated rum to the sale of whiskey. By making the purchase of whiskey conditional on the purchase of rum and by charging a higher-than-competitive price for the rum, sellers were able to maximize their profits. Of course, the users of this practice probably had no intention of increasing their monopoly power. Their sole intent was to extract the profit-maximizing price from consumers, but this does not deny possible foreclosure of markets to rum makers who were not also in the whiskey business.

Risk Sharing

Tying arrangements may be used by firms to reduce the risk their customers encounter in purchasing products. If a customer buys a durable product which is used as a factor of production, the amount that he is at most willing to pay for the product is the discounted value of its future expected returns. But a risk factor must be considered in computing this value because the customer will rarely know the rate of return on the factor of production. If the customer is a risk averter, the maximum price he will pay would be less than the expected value of the factor. But if the seller of the factor is willing to reduce the customer's risk by sharing it, the seller will be able to receive a higher price. To reduce risk, the seller might rent the durable product to the customer instead of selling it. He could set the rental fee at a relatively low level and use a tied complementary product sold at a higher-than-competitive price to meter the customer's use of the durable product. This arrangement reduces the customer's risk by reducing the amount of money he will have to pay if he has limited use for the durable product. On the other hand, if the customer finds that he has extensive use for the durable product, the seller will receive an excess profit on the sale of the tied product. The Synergetic machine/Synergetic card example could describe this case.

Burstein noted that the arrangement is also applicable to franchise operations.[6] The firm selling franchises could offer them at a relatively low price to reduce the risk of the prospective franchisee. In return, the franchisor could require that the franchisee purchase all of the products sold in the franchised outlet from him. By offering the franchise at a relatively low price, the franchisor shares the risk with the franchisee, but to compensate the franchisor, he is allowed to share the rewards. *backwards*

It is important to remember that this use of tying arrangements is not designed to create additional monopoly power; it is solely designed to increase the profit that the firm is able to receive from the sale of the tying good. If the seller were able to find an alternative way to share risk with the buyer which did not involve tying arrangements, he could earn as much profit. Of course, foreclosure in the tied-good market may be incidental to this arrangement.

Protection of Good Will

Some firms have defended their use of tying arrangements by arguing that they need them to protect the image of their tying product. This argument is applicable to situations where the use of an inferior product in conjunction with a superior product will decrease the value of the superior product. It can be understood by returning to the Synergetic machine/Synergetic card example. If an inferior data processing card is fed into a Synergetic machine, the card may impede the operation of the machine, customers may blame the inadequate performance on the machine, and this can result in a permanent reduction in the demand for it. To solve the problem Synergetic Limited might tie its cards to its machines to insure that proper inputs are used.

Even though maintenance of product good will is important, this argument is not one which should be accepted at face value. There are good reasons to expect producers of machine inputs to sell products which are conducive to the successful operation of machinery, even if the machinery is not theirs. It should also be important to the machinery user to utilize only those inputs which will readily be accepted by machinery. Why would a seller of machinery have to require that his customers use only satisfactory inputs? Wouldn't they use them without coercion? In most situations the answer is "yes." Of course, there may be a few situations where the interests of the buyer and seller do not coincide, and in the rare case when consumers are ignorant about the quality of machine inputs, a tying arrangement might be necessary to protect the consumer from himself.

COERCION

Some critics of tying arrangements argue that the arrangements may coerce consumers into purchasing something they do not want. But there is nothing unfair to the consumer about this form of coercion, because the consumer is never forced to pay more for a product than it is worth to him. To see this, assume that 15 cents is the most a consumer is willing to pay for a pencil. If a pencil manufacturer charges 15 cents for his pencil he has effectively eliminated all consumer's surplus, but he has done nothing unfair. He is simply charging the profit-maximizing price. Now suppose that the producer ties paper clips to the sale of his pencil. In effect he is now charging more for the pencil because in addition to paying for the pencil, the consumer must purchase another product. If the consumer thinks the paper clips are worthless, the maximum price that the producer would be able to get for the clips and the pencil together is still 15 cents. If the paper clips have some value to.the consumer, the maximum amount of money that the producer can receive for the two products is 15 cents plus the value of the clips. Whether or not the paper clips have any value to the consumer, one thing is clear: it is impossible for a producer to receive an amount of money in excess of the consumer's valuation of his good.

This analysis suggests that tying contracts should not be outlawed merely because they coerce consumers into buying something they do not want. Firms can receive no more than their profit-maximizing price for a good, and a law which prohibits them from charging this price would be foolish because it would force the firm into irrational behavior. The fact that a firm may choose to exercise part of its existing monopoly power through the use of tying contracts in lieu of charging a higher price for the tying product does not excuse the foolishness of such a law.

Of course, unlike our example, the profit-maximizing price may be an excessively high one due to the existence of monopoly power. But as we have said numerous times before, the solution to that problem is to treat the power, not the symptom. Furthermore, this argument is not altered if the power exists because of a patent right. The right gives the seller the ability to charge a higher-than-competitive price. But, unless leverage or foreclosure is involved, the use of a tying arrangement is no worse than charging the consumer the highest possible price. And if the tying arrangement is outlawed because the monopoly power cannot be eliminated, the firm involved can still try to extract the most the consumer is willing to pay.

CRITERIA FOR EVALUATION

Numerous reasons which do not involve the creation of additional monopoly power can be offered to explain the use of tying arrangements. Moreover, it would be ludicrous to assume that most instances of tying arrangements in the United States have been designed to create monopoly power. On the other hand, tying arrangements may create such power in the tied-good market if the tied goods are complementary goods which are used in variable proportions. Moreover, even if firms using tying contracts do not intend to create monopoly power, that power may develop if a substantial share of the tied-good market is foreclosed to competitors. These observations suggest that proper antitrust adjudication requires one to look at the circumstances surrounding each individual tying arrangement.

Despite the fact that tying arrangements do not always create monopoly power and despite the fact that they are not always harmful to the consuming public, economists have mixed feelings concerning how they should be evaluated by the courts. Burstein and Fergerson have suggested that the arrangements should be declared illegal *per se*.[7] They reasoned that by outlawing tying contracts the potential gain from existing monopoly power will be limited. Donald Turner has suggested that they be declared illegal *per se* because they deny competitors access to some markets.[8] Ward S. Bowman, Jr., has suggested that a rule of reason be used to evaluate them and that they be declared illegal only when they result in the creation of additional monopoly power.[9] Each of these three arguments is based more on a different philosophy toward the purpose of the antitrust laws than a different economic analysis of tying contracts. For example, if, as Turner argued, the protection of competitors is a valid objective of antitrust then the arrangements should be *per se* illegal when they foreclose markets. If, as Burstein suggests, an objective of antitrust is to prevent firms from exercising existing monopoly power, then tying contracts should be *per se* illegal.

At this point, the reader may decide how antitrust cases involving tying arrangements should be adjudicated. If he adopts the *per se* illegal approach, evaluating antitrust cases will be a simple matter. But if he decides that a rule of reason is the appropriate means of evaluating tying arrangements, he will need some criteria to determine whether tying arrangements create monopoly power. Several important ones are suggested here, which are derived from the preceding economic analysis.

One of the most important criteria is the degree of monopoly power a firm has in the tying-good market. If it has little power, it probably will be unable to create monopoly power in the tied-good market. The pencil manufacturer, discussed in an earlier section of this chapter, would be unable to increase his monopoly power in the sale of paper clips because consumers have a large number of alternative sellers who do not tie clips to their pencils. Another consideration in determining the legality of tying arrangements is the percentage of the tied-good market which is foreclosed. Of course this criterion is not really different from the first one because the percentage of the market foreclosed will be dependent on how much power a firm has in the tying-good market. But where foreclosure is significant, monopoly power may be created. Foreclosure is more likely when a firm has monopoly power in the tying good, and there are few alternative uses for the tied good except in conjunction with the tying good. A company which ties its ink to its mimeograph machine would probably not foreclose a significant share of the ink market to its competitors because there are a large number of alternative uses for ink.

A third criterion is the reason given by a firm for using tying arrangements. If the arguments given do not involve the creation of monopoly power and if they are plausible within the context of the market in which the firm operates, the tying arrangements can be looked upon more favorably than otherwise. Where, for example, tying arrangements are genuinely needed to protect the good will of a company and where such arrangements do not involve the creation of monopoly power, there is no reason to disallow them. A final criterion concerns the ease with which a firm may enter the tying-good market. The tying of data processing machines and data processing cards need not harm card producers if they are able to produce machines. However, if patents block the entry of new machine producers, there is a likelihood that the card producers will be harmed.

CASES INVOLVING TYING ARRANGEMENTS

UNITED SHOE MACHINERY CO.

In 1918 the Supreme Court heard its first major case involving tying arrangements, *United States* v. *United Shoe Machinery Co. et al.*[10] United Shoe resulted from an 1899 merger of seven producers of machinery used in shoe production.[11] The firm produced a large number of different shoe-processing machines, some of which were patented. Most of its machines were leased to shoe manufacturers, and the leases tied much of the shoe-producing machinery manufactured by United Shoe. For example, the company often stipulated that one of their machines could be used by a lessee to process shoes only if their other machines were also used to process them. Additionally, the company often required that its supplies be purchased as inputs for its machinery, and royalties were to be paid to United Shoe when shoes were produced on competitors' machinery.

The firm was charged under Sections 1 and 2 of the Sherman Act. In the Majority Opinion, Justice McKenna considered whether the tying arrangements represented the legitimate use of the company's patent rights or an illegal extension of monopoly power. McKenna recognized that a patent right is, by definition, a restraint of trade but it is one which is granted by the government to foster invention. He did not believe that United Shoe's use of tying arrangements was an illegal extension of that right. McKenna was not impressed with the government's argument that tying arrangements coerce customers into buying something they do not want. The Justice said that:

> It approaches declamation to say that the lessees were coerced to their making. And, as we have said, there was a benefit to the lessee. It is easy to say that the leases are against the policy of the law. But when one tries to be definite one comes back to the rights and obligations of the parties. There is no question in this case of the use of circumstances to compel or restrain; the leases are simply bargains, not different from others, moved upon calculated considerations, and whether provident or improvident are entitled nevertheless to the sanctions of the law.[12]

The Majority Opinion gave little consideration to the rights of competitors who might have had markets foreclosed to them. In his dissenting opinion, Justice Day gave their rights careful consideration. He argued that the arrangements restricted the free flow of interstate commerce and created monopoly in the shoe machinery business. To support his claim he noted that every time United Shoe received a patent on one piece of machinery, that patent along with the tying arrangements gave the firm monopoly power in the production of all shoe machinery for the length of the patent right (17 years). According to Day, the practical result of the arrangements was to exclude other shoe machinery producers from the industry.

In a later case, United Shoe was charged with monopolization under Section 3 of the Clayton Act.[13] This second case reached the Supreme Court in 1922, and this time Justice Day delivered the

Majority Opinion of the Court. Day emphasized that Section 3 of the Clayton Act,   •

> so far as precedent makes it unlawful for persons engaged in interstate commerce in the course of such commerce to lease such machinery, supplies, or other commodities, whether patented or unpatented. . . . Upon the condition, agreement, or understanding that the lessee thereof shall not use or deal in the machinery, supplies, or other commodities of any competitors of the lessor, where the effect of such lease, agreement, or understanding may be to substantially lessen competition and tend to create a monopoly.[14]

This was an important statement because it differentiated the method used by courts to determine the legality of tying arrangements in Sherman Act cases from the method used in Clayton Act cases. In the 1918 Sherman Act case, the Supreme Court had the burden of determining whether United Shoe had the right to use its patents in one market to create monopoly power in a second market. At that time the Court concluded that tying arrangements represented a legitimate use of patent rights. In the 1922 Clayton Act case, Day noted that the Clayton Act specifically said that tying arrangements represented a legitimate use of patent rights only when their use did not create monopoly power in the tied-good market. Thus, in determining the legality of tying arrangements under the provisions of the Clayton Act, the Court's only major consideration was whether the arrangements created monopoly power.

Day believed that United Shoe had created monopoly power. To demonstrate this he pointed to the fact that United Shoe had a dominant position in the shoe machinery industry (around 95 per cent of the market). Although he did not say that this dominance resulted from the use of tying arrangements, he implied as much. He believed that their use practically forbade users of United Shoe's machinery from buying equipment from other manufacturers, and the fact that United Shoe had a dominant position in the market suggested to him that competition must necessarily have been lessened and that the tying arrangements tended to create a monopoly.

United Shoe argued that its customers had an alternative to the tying arrangements. They could purchase United Shoe's equipment instead of renting it, and if they selected this option they would not be subject to the tying arrangements. Existence of this alternative suggests that United Shoe might have been using the tying arrangements as a means of sharing risks with its customers, but Day did not consider the purchase agreements to be a valid defense of the nature of the leasing arrangements. He thought, but did not prove, that the price of the equipment might have been so high as to prohibit its purchase. Even if such was not the case, he thought that tying arrangements should be analyzed without regard to the purchase agreements. Consumer coercion was not an issue in this case. Instead, the finding of guilt was based on lessening of competition through foreclosure. Whether or not the company did create monopoly power in the tied-good markets is unknown, but the dominant position of the company, and the large number of products involved in the tying arrangement suggests guilt.

IBM

The next major case was *International Business Machines Corporation* v. *United States.*[15] IBM was charged under the provisions of Section 3 of the Clayton Act with using tying arrangements to create monopoly power. IBM rented tabulating machines to customers only when they agreed to use IBM's data processing cards in the machines. IBM's only competitor in the production of tabulation machinery and cards was Remington Rand. (IBM produced 81 per cent of the card output and Remington Rand had 19 per cent of the output.) Remington Rand also tied the sale of its cards to the leasing of its tabulating equipment. Because its business practice was identical to IBM's, it agreed with the government to accept the ruling in the IBM case.

IBM offered two major arguments in its behalf. First, it contended that its tying arrangements were legal because of the patent rights it held on the production of the machinery and the cards. The Majority Opinion of the Supreme Court, delivered by Justice Stone, rejected this argument. Stone returned to the 1922 *United Shoe Machinery* case, saying that in that decision the Court specifically said that tying arrangements could not legally be based on patent rights when the result of such arrangements was to create monopoly power. And Stone thought this particular arrangement did create monopoly power. He said that IBM specifically forbade the use of competitor's cards and that this has "operated to prevent competition and to create a monopoly in the production and sale of tabulating cards suitable for the appellant's machines."[16] Referring to IBM's share of the market in card production and the sheer dollar volume of business it did in that market, he contended that IBM's monopoly power was substantial.[17]

IBM also argued that its tying arrangements were adopted to preserve its product image. The company reasoned that if inferior cards were placed in its machine, inaccuracies in the function of the machine could hurt the reputation of the company. While Stone said that antitrust law was not designed to hurt IBM's image, he argued that the tying arrangement was not necessary to preserve it. Other companies, he contended, would be able to produce cards of equal quality. In fact, the government had been allowed to lease IBM machines without buying IBM cards. It produced its own cards and successfully used them in the machines.[18]

Although the Court did not actually prove that IBM's monopoly power resulted from its use of tying arrangements, the arrangements were suspect. The company had a dominant position in the tying-good market, and its argument concerning good will was at best a weak one. It offered no substantial argument in its behalf, and the arrangement used by both IBM and Remington Rand deterred the entry of card manufacturers into the market. The Supreme Court found IBM guilty, and that company as well as Remington Rand was ordered to stop its arrangements.

INTERNATIONAL SALT

International Salt[19] is perhaps the most important case involving tying arrangements because the Supreme Court declared tying arrangements *per se* illegal when they lessened competition substantially.[20] The salt machine manufacturer was charged under Section 3 of the Clayton Act and Section 1 of the Sherman Act with using tying arrangements to create monopoly power. The company was the nation's largest producer of commercially used salt, and in addition, it had patents on two machines which were used to process salt. One of the machines, the "Lixator," dissolved rock salt into a brine used in industrial processes. The other machine, the "Saltomat," injected salt during the canning process. These machines were leased to customers, provided that the customers agreed to purchase all salt tablets used in the leased machines from International Salt.

The Supreme Court wasted no time in getting to the heart of the issue. Delivering the Majority Opinion of the Court, Justice Jackson stated that any arrangement which forecloses competitors from a substantial market is unreasonable *per se*.[21] Volume of business was chosen as the major indicator to determine whether International Salt had foreclosed a substantial share of the tied-good market. Since the firm sold about $500,000 worth of salt for use in its machines, the Court concluded that a substantial share of the market had been foreclosed. This determination of guilt based on the sheer dollar volume of business done was called "quantitative substantiality" by the Court.

International Salt offered several defenses. It argued that if any of its competitors offered to sell the salt to its customers at a lower price, the customer would be free to buy from the competitor unless International Salt matched the price. The Court was not impressed with this argument. Justice Jackson noted that, "A competitor would have to undercut appellant's price to have any hope of capturing the market, while appellant could hold that market by merely meeting competition. We do not think this concession relieves that contract of restraint of trade. . . ."[22] Jackson's reasoning is correct because although the modified arrangement provided customers with some degree of protection, it still placed competitors at an unfair disadvantage. In order to get salt business they must undercut International Salt's price, not merely meet it. Nor did International's arrangement provide for nonprice competition. International Salt also argued that it used tying arrangements to insure that only high-quality salt was used in its machines. Since International remained under obligation to repair and maintain its machines, the company thought that it was reasonable to require that its customers use high-quality inputs. Jackson said that it was reasonable for the company to require its customers to use high-quality salt in its machines, but it was not necessary to specify that International's salt be used. Instead, the company could simply require that salt with a minimum sodium chloride content of some level be used in the machine.

While International may have been guilty of creating monopoly power in the tied-good market, the Court certainly did not prove it. Even though the use of the Doctrine of Quantitative Substantiality provided an easy way to determine guilt it did not necessarily provide correct determination of guilt. The subject of quantitative substantiality will be discussed further in Chapter XII on exclusive dealing contracts. However, it is important to present a major criticism of the doctrine at this point. Perhaps the best criticism comes from Milton Handler, Professor of Law at Columbia University. Handler said of the doctrine,

> The exclusion of competitors from a substantial number of outlets may seriously handicap them in their competition. Conversely, it may have no anticompetitive tendency or effect if suitable alternative channels are open to them in adequate number. To ascertain such tendency or effect demands of judges nothing more than the ordinary

skill of their calling. It does not require them to divine whether competition were to flourish more with the use of their competitive techniques. The issue is of limited dimension and is essentially no different than any other question of fact in antitrust or other fields of law.

The Court's test, however, shuts the door to this modest factual inquiry. The number and character of the avenues of distribution employed by or opened to competitors are ignored. Attention is centered entirely on whether the volume of commerce tied up by the exclusives, even though temporary, is "substantial." To make matters worse, the Court's conception of substantiality borders on the frugal. It embraces all but the most insignificant transactions. In a case dealing with the problem of tying restrictions in the lease of patented machines, the Court held that an annual sales volume of $500,000 of salt was not "insignificant" or "insubstantial" . . . if $500,000 worth of business is held substantial on an absolute basis, or 2% to 6.7% of the relevant market on a comparative basis the "substantial lessing of competition" standard is reduced to the level of a *per se* invalidation of exclusives save in *de minimis* situations.[23]

The result of the International Salt case was that tying arrangements were declared illegal *per se* under the provisions of the Clayton Act when a company does a significant dollar volume of business in the sale of the tied-good. And in this case, $500,000 in sales was judged as a significant dollar volume. The Court did leave two major questions unanswered. First, was a patent in the tying good required for the Court to apply this stringent test? Second, did International Salt really create monopoly power? Since the Court denied International Salt the right to prove that competitive salt machines were available, we will never know the answer to the second question.

TIMES-PICAYUNE PUBLISHING COMPANY

In another case, the Justice Department prosecuted the Times-Picayune Publishing Company under the provisions of Sections 1 and 2 of the Sherman Act.[24] Since the Sherman Act was involved, the case makes another important distinction between tying-arrangement litigation involving the Sherman Act and litigation involving the Clayton Act.

The New Orleans publishing company owned and operated a morning mewspaper, the "Times-Picayune" and an evening newspaper called the "States." The Court record indicated that the two papers had individual formats and reached different readers. Their sole newspaper competitor was an evening paper called the "Item." The publishing company adopted a "unit selling plan" which required that advertisers who wished to purchase advertising space in the morning paper also had to advertise in the evening paper. Similar plans were used by many newspapers throughout the country.

A district court disallowed the practice, but the Supreme Court thought it was legal. To establish the test that the Court used, Justice Clark noted that guilt under the provisions of the Clayton Act required a showing that firms using tying arrangements have a monopolistic position in the market for the tying good *or* do a substantial volume of business in the tied good. However, Justice Clark thought that the Sherman Act test was not so stringent. Under its provisions, Clark thought that firms using tying arrangements must have *both* a monopolistic position in the tying-good market and restrain or intend to restrain a substantial volume of commerce in the tied-good market.

Clark set out to show that the Times-Picayune passed the Sherman Act test. To determine whether the publishing company had a dominant position in the tying-good market, Clark first defined the relevant market as newspaper advertising. He then found that the Times-Picayune had about 40 per cent of newspaper advertising linage in the tying-good market. This estimate defined the tying-good market to include all three New Orleans' newspapers because the Court thought that advertisers did not distinguish between evening readers and morning readers. Based on its definition of the relevant market, the Supreme Court concluded that the Times-Picayune did not have a dominant position in newspaper advertising. In contrast, the district court had decided that the morning newspaper (The Times-Picayune) was a distinct market. This market definition gave the Times-Picayune 100 per cent of the tying-good market.

The Supreme Court's definition of the tying-good market to include the tied good was a curious one which has been criticized by many lawyers and economists. One good critique was offered by Dirlam and Kahn who contended that the share of the market should have been based on circulation, not advertising linage.[25] A newspaper sells readers to advertisers. Therefore the important thing to the advertiser is the number of readers the paper reaches, not the amount of advertising handled by a paper. A large number of readers gives the paper monopoly power. A large number of advertisers is merely a reflection of monopoly power or some other fact. The Times-Picayune had 46 per cent of the total newspaper circulation in New Orleans (as compared to 40 per cent of New Orleans advertising linage). Dirlam and Kahn also said that even if the relevant market share of the tying good was defined as the combined morning and evening papers of the publishing company, and the relevant market was linage, its share was 78 per cent of that market. Finally, Dirlam and Kahn considered the major error to be the Court's adding up of the morning and evening markets to get the share of the market for the tying good. They argued that it was Times-Picayune's monopolistic position in the morning paper which gave it the ability to use economic leverage. And the inclusion of the evening paper distracted the Court such that in determining the market share it did not recognize the fact that the morning paper was the "power base."

Finding no monopoly in the tying good, the Court set out to determine whether the unit plan had created monopoly power in the tied good. In doing this, the Court said that either intent to create monopoly power or the creation of monopoly power itself was enough to declare tying arrangements illegal. The Court concluded that the Times-Picayune did not create, nor did it intend to create monopoly power in the tied-good market.

The Court analyzed classified and general display advertising to determine the effect of the unit plan on the Item's advertising sales. Since the unit plan for general display advertising did not go into effect until 1950, the Court had only one year of information on which to base its findings. Classified advertising had been sold under the unit plan since 1935 so there were a number of years on which to base that analysis. Study of classified advertising disclosed that from 1940 to 1950, the Item's share of the market had declined from 23 per cent of the total market to approximately 20 per cent. Taking the very slight downward trend into account, the Court concluded that the unit plan merely reallocated advertising from the Times-Picayune to the States. Moreover, in absolute terms, the Court thought that the Item flourished. "The ten years preceding this trial marks it [the Item's] more than 75 per cent growth in classified linage."[26]

In its analysis of general display advertising (where only one year's information was available), the Court found that in 1949 the Item had 49 per cent of the linage in the evening market. By the end of 1950 the share had dropped to 42 per cent. The Item's share of the overall market (morning and evening newspapers) had dropped two per cent. A comparison of the share-of-the-market figures in the evening market and the overall market, indicated that there was a shift of general display advertising from the Times-Picayune to the States. The Court concluded that competition was not hurt either in the acquisition of advertisers for classified ads or for general display advertising. Where the Item's share of the market dropped, the Court thought that the drop was insignificant. Moreover, the Court was impressed with the fact that in absolute terms the Item had done well. By 1950, its circulation was at an all-time high and its profits were high.

The real danger of the Court's share-of-the-market test is the same danger encountered in most experiments involving a social science: there is no controlled experiment. What would the Item's share of the market have been if the Times-Picayune had not used the unit plan? What would the Item's profits have been? Only when this information is known (and it cannot be known) can one say for certain whether the unit plan hurt competition.

Justices Burton, Black, Douglas, and Minton dissented. They argued that the relevant market for the tying good was morning newspapers, and since the Times-Picayune was the only morning newspaper, it had 100 per cent of the market. In addition to finding monopoly power in the sale of the tying good, they used the coercion argument as a reason for disallowing the unit plan. Justice Burton stated that, "Insistence by the Times-Picayune upon acceptance of its compulsory combination advertising contracts makes payment for, and publication of, classified and general advertising in its own evening newspaper an inescapable part of the price of access to the all-important columns of the single morning paper."[27]

Whether or not the Times-Picayune really foreclosed a substantial share of advertisers to the Item depended on the degree to which typical advertisers wanted to reach consumers. If their objective was to reach all consumers in the New Orleans area, they would have advertised in all three papers, and advertisers would not have been foreclosed to the Item. If they just wanted to advertise in one paper and were indifferent between morning and evening newspapers, the Item would have been aided by the Times-Picayune's use of the unit plan. Had advertisers wanted space in both a morning and an evening newspaper but not both evening newspapers, some advertisers would have been foreclosed to the Item. Neither the government nor the defense offered statistics covering the desired degree of advertising saturation.

Despite the fact that the Court may have left some important questions unanswered, it did undertake a reasoned attempt to determine the effect of the Times-Picayune's unit plan on competition, and their attempt is to be applauded. It represents a significant intellectual advance over the *International Salt* case. Of course, the

Times-Picayune decision does not overturn the precedent established in *International Salt* because *Times-Picayune* involved the Sherman Act while *International Salt* involved the Clayton Act.

The major reasons the Times-Picayune wanted to use the unit plan are unknown. On the basis of the Court record, several suggestions can be made. First, it would be cheaper for the publishing company to provide advertising in one newspaper when the type has already been set for their other newspaper. However, a tying arrangement does not appear necessary to induce advertisers to accept both papers. A simple price reduction for joint advertising would do the trick, and the publishing company used this approach for a number of years prior to its adoption of the unit plan. Second, the tying arrangement might have been a way of exploiting the Times-Picayune's monopoly in the morning newspaper. Monopoly profits could be extracted from the advertiser who had a strong desire to advertise in the morning paper. Finally, the practice might have been a real attempt by Times-Picayune to foreclose markets to the Item and eventually drive its competitor out of the market. Ultimately, the Times-Picayune Publishing Company did purchase the Item.

NORTHERN PACIFIC RAILWAY COMPANY

The next Sherman Act case involving tying arrangements was *Northern Pacific Railway Company* v. *United States*, heard by the Supreme Court in 1958.[28] The case was important in establishing precedent because the Supreme Court backtracked on its *Times-Picayune* decision. Northern Pacific Railway had large land holdings adjoining its tracks which had been granted by the Government between 1864 and 1870 to encourage rail construction. Northern Pacific leased or sold much of the land under the stipulation that the buyer or lessee use Northern Pacific Railway to ship all commodities purchased or manufactured on the land. The arrangement was similar to that made by International Salt in that Northern Pacific allowed buyers or lessees to use other transportation only if competitors could undercut its prices. This tying arrangement, called "preferential routing," appeared to be a meaningful restraint because the Court found that alternative means of transportation existed for a large portion of the lessees.

The Court's reasoning was largely devoid of economic analysis. Northern Pacific's practice was declared illegal without an analysis of the share of the market Northern Pacific held in the tying good or the percentage of the tied-good market foreclosed to competitors. To reach its finding, the Court simply asserted that Northern Pacific had dominance in the tying good. In fact, it claimed that "this host of tying arrangements is itself compelling evidence of the defendant's great power at least where, as here, no other explanation has been offered for the existence of these restraints."[29] To demonstrate competitive harm in the tied-good market the Court claimed that "So far as the Railroad was concerned, its purpose obviously was to fence out competitors, to stifle competition. While this may have been exceedingly beneficial to its business, it is the very type of thing the Sherman Act condemns."[30] The lack of economic analysis was based on the Court's opinion that the practice was so unreasonable that it should be *per se* illegal. "In short we are convinced that the essential prerequisites for treating the defendant's tying arrangements as unreasonable 'per se' were conclusively established below [in the District Court] and that the defendant has offered to provide nothing there or here which would alter this conclusion."[31]

What happened to the precedent established in the *Times-Picayune* case that argued for the use of a rule of reason in judging tying arrangements under the provisions of the Sherman Act? The reader will remember that in that case the Court claimed that to find guilt, the government must show that the firm using a tying arrangement has both a monopolistic position in the tying-good market and restrained or intended to restrain a substantial volume of commerce in the tied-good market. The Court said of their decision in the *Northern Pacific* case that "While there is some language in the Times-Picayune opinion which speaks of 'monopoly power' or 'dominance' over the tying product as a necessary precondition for application of the rule of per se unreasonableness to tying arrangements, we do not construe this general language as requiring anything more than sufficient economic power to impose an appreciable restraint on free competition in the tied product."[32] And apparently an assertion of "sufficient economic power," not proof, was enough to find guilt since, as Justice Harlan pointed out in his dissent, figures concerning Northern Pacific's power in the tying-good market did not prove monopoly power.

The decision did make one important legal distinction which clarified the law concerning unpatented goods which are used to tie other goods. The Court said that whether or not the tying good was patented was irrelevant to its decision. "The defendant attempts to evade the force of International Salt on the ground that the tying produce there was patented while here it is not. But we do not believe this distinction has, or should have, any significance."[33]

FORTNER ENTERPRISES

The precedent established in the *Times-Picayune* decision was further weakened in *Fortner Enterprises, Inc.* v. *United States Steel Corporation.*[34] U.S. Steel Homes Credit Corporation provided loans of over $2,000,000 to Fortner Enterprises for land development. The terms of the loans were exceptionally attractive in that U.S. Steel provided 100 per cent financing for both the land and the erection of homes. Additionally, the loans were provided at lower-than-competitive interest rates. However, U.S. Steel did require that Fortner Enterprises build prefabricated houses manufactured by U.S. Steel on each of the lots bought with the loan. Subsequently Fortner claimed that the houses were sold at unreasonably higher prices by U.S. Steel and were defective.

A district court judge dismissed the suit. Following the precedent established in *Times-Picayune*, he concluded that U.S. Steel neither had sufficient monopoly power in the loan market nor had foreclosed a substantial volume of commerce in home building. While he did not compute the market percentages involved, it is fairly obvious that the $2,000,000 borrowed by Fortner was a negligible percentage of the total money borrowed yearly in the country for home construction. Moreover, the number of U.S. Steel houses sold to Fortner was a negligible percentage of the total number of houses being constructed in the country.

The Supreme Court reverted to the quantitative substantiality test to determine whether U.S. Steel had monopoly power in the tying good. By the simple assertion that $2,000,000 was not "paltry or insubstantial" it found that monopoly power was present. To further document its conclusion, the Court reiterated the fact that sufficient monopoly power to prove guilt exists even though "the power falls far short of dominance." The Court then said that U.S. Steel had some power in the tying good arising from its lenient credit terms. According to the Court, these terms might have resulted from economies or the fact that savings and loan associations are prevented from offering 100 per cent financing. The terms induced Fortner to buy homes for at least $400 more than that charged by U.S. Steel's competitors. Therefore the Court concluded that U.S. Steel had sufficient monopoly power in the tying good market. It is possible to paraphrase the Court's reasoning by saying that since U.S. Steel was offered a price reduction on financing, it had monopoly power in that market.

The quantitative substantiality test was also used to show that U.S. Steel foreclosed a substantial share of the home-building market. While the Court did not contend that a large percentage of the market was foreclosed, it asserted that in dollar terms, the $9,100,000 foreclosed in 1960-1962 was substantial.

U.S. Steel contended that Fortner suffered no harm because it had the right to buy credit and homes elsewhere if it chose. The fact that it bought from U.S. Steel evidenced the fact that the "package" of loans and homes was offered at a lower price than that offered by competitors. In short, "the offering of favorable credit terms is simply a form of price competition equivalent to the offering of a comparable reduction in the cash price of the tied product." The Court's response was simply that the "seller can achieve his alleged purpose, without extending his economic power, by simply reducing the price of the tied product itself." This, according to the Court, is superior because it does not involve foreclosure and, furthermore, does not erect new barriers to entry. This reasoning was derived from the fact that the new entrant in the home-construction business might require funds to lend to his buyers if he is to be able to compete with U.S. Steel.

Can U.S. Steel's arrangement be distinguished from vigorous price competition in the home-building market? Unless evidence of foreclosure, or leverage or the erection of entry barriers is present, there is no reason to expect a distinction. Certainly the Court didn't demonstrate that a difference existed.

In his dissenting opinion, Justice White contended that the Court made an improper decision. His reasoning deserves repeating. After properly noting that no harm can result from tying arrangements unless the firm using them has monopoly power in the tying product, he asked,

> In this case, what proof of any market power in the tying product has been alleged? Only that the tying product—money—was not available elsewhere on equally good terms, and perhaps not at all.

> There was nothing unique about U.S. Steel's money except its low cost to petitioner. A low price on a product is ordinarily no reflection of market power. It proves neither the existence of such power nor its absence, although absence of power may be the more reasonable inference. One who has such power benefits from it precisely because it allows him to raise prices, not lower them, and ordinarily he does so.

> A low price in the tying product—money . . . is especially poor proof of market power when untied credit is available

elsewhere. In that case, the low price of credit is functionally equivalent to a reduction in the price of the houses sold. Since the buyer has untied credit available elsewhere, he can compare the house-credit package of U.S. Steel as competitive with the price of the untied credit plus the cost of houses from another source. . . . The same money which U.S. Steel is willing to risk or forgo by providing better credit terms it could sacrifice by cutting the price of houses. There is no good reason why U.S. Steel should always be required to make the price cut in one form rather than another, which its purchaser prefers.[35]

The Court did not prove the existence of monopoly power, and it left an important question unanswered. Frequently the purchase of a product and the provision of credit are perfect complements. Without credit, the purchase cannot exist. For these buyers the products are analogous to our prior example of right and left hand gloves, or in other words, goods consumed in fixed proportion. In our discussion of that example, we concluded that the producer of both cannot extract from the buyer any more money than he is willing to pay for the two goods separately. Thus unless foreclosure or leverage is involved, no monopoly power is created. Of course we also concluded that the practice of tying two goods consumed in fixed proportion was also irrational. Why did U.S. Steel tie houses to money? Perhaps this unasked and unanswered question led the Court to believe that monopoly power existed.

CHICKEN DELIGHT

In another recent case on tying contracts, the courts applied the Sherman Act to franchising.[36] Chicken Delight franchised home delivery and pick-up food stores. Its major product was prepared chicken which was cooked in a patented mix. Chicken Delight did not charge its franchisees a franchise fee or a royalty on sales. Instead, in exchange for the license granting the franchise, it required franchisees to purchase a specified number of cookers and fryers and to purchase certain packaging supplies and mixes. The prices for these purchases were higher than for comparable products sold by competing suppliers.

Chicken Delight offered several defenses on its behalf. The most interesting argument was that the tying arrangement was a means of metering output and collecting revenue based on the quantity of the franchisees' sales. This logic is consistent with the price discrimination argument presented earlier in the chapter. To this, the court of appeals said that there was no authority for justifying a tying arrangement for this reason. Apparently, the court was not willing to establish that authority.

Chicken Delight also argued that the tied goods were necessary to protect the quality of their chicken. The court was careful to note that this was not an issue which could be dismissed lightly. A franchisor has to protect his good will so that the product always is what it purports to be. However, the court thought that the only situation in which the protection of good will necessitated the use of a tying contract was when specifications for substitute products were so detailed that they could not be provided by alternative suppliers. In the district court, the jury had decided that the cooking machinery, paper, and dip and spice mixes could be supplied by alternative suppliers if Chicken Delight established specifications for them. Moreover, the specifications would ensure the protection of Chicken Delight's good will. Based on all of these observations, the court of appeals affirmed the district court's decision and disallowed the use of the tying arrangement. This decision represents the first major instance where tying arrangements were disallowed when used by a franchisor to protect product quality and brand image [37] If this decision is upheld in subsequent cases it will have far-reaching effects on the whole franchise system used in the United States.

JERROLD ELECTRONICS

Not all recent cases involving tying arrangements under the provisions of the Clayton Act and the Sherman Act have been declared illegal. One case is worth a brief analysis because it indicates that courts sometimes have been willing to accept defenses of tying arrangements when the courts believe that the defenses are reasonable.

In *United States* v. *Jerrold Electronics Corporation*, a district court thought that protection of good will was a valid defense for Jerrold's tying its community television antenna systems with its antenna service. [38] Jerrold was a relatively new producer of antenna for community television stations. Its product had not been fully tested in the field and was a sensitive piece of equipment. Consequently, Jerrold feared that if the antennae were serviced by the stations or by other firms, they might not be adjusted to perform at capacity. Less than optimum performance could ruin Jerrold's image. The ourt thought that the tying of the antennae with antenna service was justified provided that the arrangement was maintained only during the early years of the company's development.

SUMMARY

It is clear that the courts have not looked favorably upon tying arrangements. In fact, it is almost certain that a firm using them will be found in violation of either the Sherman Act or the Clayton Act. In the *Times-Picayune* decision the Supreme Court did attempt to determine the effect of the practice on competition, but this approach is rare. Most courts have assumed that tying arrangements are so inherently harmful that they have declared them illegal *per se*. Theoretical economic analysis does not suggest that such a rule is appropriate. There are valid reasons for the use of tying arrangements, and even if the arrangements are harmful to competition, it is the already-existing monopoly power of the firm using them which is the real problem. Yet, as we have seen numerous times before, the courts are unwilling to remedy the existence of that power and instead, have continued to treat its symptoms. Nevertheless, many economists would agree that the courts do little harm to competition by declaring tying arrangements illegal *per se*. The *per se* illegal rule does save time which perhaps could be put to better ends.

NOTES TO CHAPTER XI

[1]This test of leverage was suggested by Ward S. Bowman, Jr., "Tying Arrangements and the Leverage Problem," *Yale Law Journal*, LXVII (1957-58), 19-36.

[2]For a detailed analysis of this point see Martin J. Bailey, "Price and Output Decisions by a Firm Selling Related Products," *American Economic Review*, XLIV (March, 1954), 82-93.

[3]This example comes from Ward S. Bowman, p. 26.

[4]This assumes that the income effect of a price reduction is insignificant.

[5]M. L. Burstein, "A Theory of Full Line Forcing," *Northwestern University Law Review*, LV (February, 1960), 63-64.

[6]Burstein, p. 72.

[7]Burstein, p. 93, and James M. Fergerson, "Tying Arrangements and Reciprocity: An Economic Analysis," in Werner Sichel, *Industrial Organization and Public Policy, Selected Readings* (Boston: Houghton Mifflin Company, 1967), pp. 298-300.

[8]Donald F. Turner, "The Validity of Tying Arrangements Under the Antitrust Laws," *Harvard Law Review*, LXXII (1958-59), 50-75.

[9]Bowman, pp. 19-36.

[10]247 U.S. 32 (1918).

[11]The legality of the merger was also attacked in the 1918 case but that analysis will not be considered here.

[12]247 U.S. 32, 35 (1918).

[13]*United Shoe Machinery Corporation* v. *United States*, 42 Sup. Ct. 263 (1922).

[14]42 Sup. Ct. 263, 264 (1922).

[15]298 U.S. 131 (1936).

[16]298 U.S. 131, 136 (1936).

[17]298 U.S. 131, 136 (1936).

[18]There is good reason to believe that the government was able to reproduce the cards. IBM cards have the same dimensions as the old dollar bill. In fact, they were originally cut from dies from the U.S. Mint because the dies had exacting dimensions.

[19]*International Salt Company, Incorporated* v. *United States*, 332 U.S. 392 (1947).

[20]This is an odd use of the term *"per se"* because this *per se* ruling is contingent upon the proof or the assumption that competition is reduced. See W. L. Baldwin and David McFarland, "Some Observations on 'Per Se' and Tying Arrangements," *Antitrust Bulletin*, VI (July-December, 1963), 433-439.

[21]There has been some argument over whether or not Jackson's decision really declared tying arrangements illegal *per se*. For example, Dirlam and Kahn suggested that either Justice Jackson did not mean what he said or that he meant that tying arrangements were *per se* illegal only when they involve "deliberate exclusion by exercise of coercion," Dirlam and Kahn, *Fair Competition: The Law and Economics of Antitrust Policy* (Ithaca, New York: Cornell University Press, 1954), pp. 97-98.

[22]322 U.S. 392, 397 (1947).

[23]Milton Handler, *Antitrust in Prospective, the Complimentary Roles of Rule and Disgression* (New York: Columbia University Press, 1957), pp. 36-37.

[24]*Times-Picayune Publishing Company* v. *United States*, 354 U.S. 594 (1953).

[25]The following analysis is that of Dirlam and Kahn, pp. 106-108.

[26]345 U.S 594, 620 (1953).

[27]345 U.S. 594, 628 (1953).

[28]356 U.S. 1 (1958).

[29]356 U.S. 1, 8 (1958).

[30]356 U.S. 1, 8 (1958).

[31]356 U.S. 1, 8 (1958).

[32]356 U.S. 1, 12 (1958).

[33]356 U.S. 1, 9 (1958).

[34]394 U.S. 495 (1969).

[35]394 U.S. 495, 503 (1969).

[36]*Siegel* v. *Chicken Delight, Inc.*, 448 F. 2d 43 (1971).

[37]See *Bernard Susser* v. *Carvel Corporation*, 332 F. 2d 505 (1964) for the conventional viewpoint of the courts toward tying arrangements used in conjunction with a franchise arrangement.

[38]187 F. Supp. 545 (E.D. Pa., 1960).

EXCLUSIVE DEALING ARRANGEMENTS

CHAPTER XII

In this chapter we consider the economics of an arrangement which gives a supplier the exclusive right to sell to a customer. Specifically we consider why a supplier would utilize such an arrangement, the effects of the arrangement on competition, and the attitude of the courts toward the practice.

INTRODUCTION

An exclusive dealing arrangement gives a supplier the exclusive right to sell to a customer for some specified period of time. In return for the arrangement, the customer who serves as a dealer for the product might receive an exclusive franchise. Other inducements include price reductions, rebates, a promise of a steady supply of products or some type of financial aid. We saw in Chapter IX that a powerful supplier may even be able to obtain an exclusive dealing agreement by simply refusing to sell to dealers unless their purchases are exclusive. The practice falls under the prohibitions of the antitrust laws because the supplier using them forecloses markets to suppliers of competing products.

In economic terms exclusive dealing contracts may resemble tying contracts because the customer may have to buy his total needs from a supplier if he wants any of that supplier's product. There is also a similarity to vertical integration where, through acquisition, customers may be foreclosed to suppliers. These similarities enable us to use some of the economic concepts presented in prior chapters for our analysis of exclusive dealing. We can also expect a similarity in the court's treatment of these practices. Like tying arrangements, exclusive dealing arrangements are prosecuted under the provisions of Section 3 of the Clayton Act. Although less likely, they may also be prosecuted under Sections 1 and 2 of the Sherman Act.

REASONS FOR EXCLUSIVE DEALING ARRANGEMENTS

There are a number of good reasons for suppliers and dealers to enter into exclusive dealing contracts. Like vertical integration, the arrangements can be explained by:

A. Reduced cost for the supplier and the dealer;
B. Improved product promotion and customer service;
C. Increased certainty of supply and demand;
D. Foreclosure of markets to potential and existing suppliers.

Since many of the exclusive dealing contracts are between suppliers and independent dealers, these reasons will be discussed in that context. However, the following analysis is also applicable to most other supplier-customer relationships.

COST SAVINGS FOR THE SUPPLIER AND DEALER

A supplier has two major alternatives when distributing his product through independent dealers. He may have a large number of dealers represent his product along with the products of competitors, or he may have his product represented exclusively.[1] The first alternative usually gives him representation in a large number of outlets and will probably be used if the product is a "convenience good." The second alternative, the use of an exclusive dealing arrangement, usually restricts his representation to a few outlets. There are advantages and disadvantages to both approaches, but one advantage of the exclusive outlet is that it usually reduces the supplier's cost. He has fewer dealers to call on, less records to keep, and less credit problems. If it reduces the supplier's cost, exclusive dealing could cause a reduction in the price he charges for his product provided that he faces sufficient competitive pressure.

The dealer can also receive some cost savings from exclusive dealing arrangements. Anyone having experience with a multi-brand outlet such as a drugstore, knows that much of the owner's time is spent talking to a host of product representatives, adjusting to the different business records used by each of the companies, arguing over which company gets the optimum display space, keeping a large inventory, and paying the bills of the various suppliers. Cost can be reduced somewhat if the owner purchases from a few middlemen representing a number of suppliers, but it can be reduced even more if only one company is represented.

IMPROVED PRODUCT PROMOTION AND
CUSTOMER SERVICE

In the chapters on vertical territorial arrangements and resale price maintenance we learned that suppliers will sometimes use those practices so that their dealers will concentrate on the promotion and servicing of the supplier's product. We also learned that product promotion and service is especially important if the supplier's product is one requiring specialized selling or servicing techniques. But a supplier may decide that a vertical territorial arrangement or resale price maintenance is not really required. Simply having a dealer represent the supplier's products exclusively might be sufficient to receive the desired promotional effort and product service.

CERTAINTY OF SUPPLY AND DEMAND

Sometimes, during product shortages, customers are unable to purchase needed products. When an exclusive dealing contract is coupled with a contract in which a supplier agrees to provide the buyer's needs for a specified period of time, the customer will not have this problem. One argument demonstrating the need of a buyer to know that a product will be available to him was recognized by the district court in *United States* v. *American Can Co.*[2] In that case, the customers were users of metal cans who had signed agreements with American Can to purchase exclusively for a period of five years. The district court noted that "The canners are subject in many instances to the whims of nature over which they have no control. They are, therefore, required to have available a supply of tin containers, fluid in amount, and appropriate from the technological and marketing viewpoints."[3] By reviewing the problems faced by service station operators during the gasoline shortage, the reader can easily grasp the importance of insured supply. Independent dealers without exclusive contracts faced an especially grave shortage which threatened their livelihood.

FORECLOSURE OF POTENTIAL AND
EXISTING SUPPLIERS

In the chapters on vertical integration and tying arrangements we examined the nature of market foreclosure as well as its potentially adverse effect on competition. By foreclosing markets to competing suppliers, exclusive dealing arrangements can also create this adverse effect. For example, suppose that there is a particularly effective dealer in a market, a dealer that has some locational advantage, or a dealer in a market which is not large enough to support many dealers. If a dealer having one or more of these characteristics signs an exclusive dealing contract with a supplier, that dealer will be foreclosed to other suppliers for the duration of the contract. More importantly, the arrangement might create monopoly power for the supplier, harm competing suppliers, and harm consumers. One example of this occurrence was cited by Senator Phillip Hart in Congressional hearings.

Among witnesses heard were representatives of two independent Pennsylvania motor oil companies, Kendall Refining Company and Penzoil Company. They testified as to the difficulties of attempting to compete with Ford Motor Company which recently has entered the motor oil business. Two of the largest major oil companies, American and Humble, apparently have an agreement whereby they supply Ford with oil under the Ford private brand name, Rotunda. Ford in turn sells this oil to its franchised dealers. According to these witnesses, their distributors had lost considerable oil gallonage to Ford through the economic leverage exercised by Ford over its franchised dealers. They stressed the fact that their companies—as well as many other oil companies—produced an oil of equal if not better quality than Rotunda.[4]

If the exclusive dealing contract is accompanied by a price concession, it will be especially difficult for another supplier to lure the customer away. Imagine that there is a supplier who normally sells his product to dealers at $60 a unit but who offers it at $50 if a customer buys the product exclusively. If a customer normally purchased 1,000 units of the product yearly, his total bill would be $50,000. Now suppose that a relatively small supplier who can provide only 600 units yearly asks the customer for his business. What price could the small supplier charge if the customer is to pay no more than he did with the exclusive contract? The customer will have to buy at least 400 units from the old supplier at $60 a unit so that total bill would be $24,000. If the customer is to pay no more than he had paid ($50,000), the new supplier's total bill could not exceed $26,000. This means that he would have to sell his 600 units at no more than $43.43 a unit. This requires that he be able to undercut the price of his established rival by a significant amount in order to enter the market.

By no means are the majority of exclusive dealing arrangements designed to achieve foreclosure. But under conditions where foreclosure is substantial, monopoly power can be created by blocking market access to existing and potential firms. The market conditions in which exclusive dealing can successfully foreclose markets will be discussed shortly.

CRITERIA FOR EVALUATION

The only harmful effect of exclusive dealing is that it may foreclose markets to competitors. But since all foreclosure is not harmful to competition, the task of the antitrust authorities is to determine what amount of foreclosure is acceptable and what amount is harmful. Hale and Hale identified the instances in which exclusive dealing arrangements may be harmful to competition.[5] They suggested that the foreclosure of markets to competitors will harm competition when markets are too small to support a number of dealers or when capital is limited or investors are unaware of the potential return from new outlets. The first condition is based on the idea that the foreclosure of dealers in a market in which demand is relatively small may effectively exclude suppliers from that market because even if they could finance new dealers themselves, the demand would not be large enough to support them. The second condition emphasizes the idea that even if the market could support additional dealers, it might be foreclosed to the supplier if his capital is limited or if he is unaware of the potential return from constructing a new outlet.

William Lockhart and Howard Sacks presented nine criteria to separate allowable instances of exclusive dealing from instances in which the practice is anticompetitive. Some of these deserve careful consideration. First, they suggested that a case appraisal should determine the share of the market foreclosed to competitors. Where a large share of the market is foreclosed, the presumption is that competition will be harmed. Second, they would consider the extent to which other suppliers in the market use exclusive dealing arrangements. If only one supplier uses them, less customers will be foreclosed than if they are used by all or almost all suppliers. Third, they would consider the duration of the exclusive dealing arrangement. As a general rule, the longer the contract, the greater is the probability that competition will be harmed. Fourth, they would consider whether the exclusive dealing provision could reduce suppliers' or dealers' cost. Where it does, they would look upon it more favorably than otherwise. Fifth, they would consider whether the exclusive dealing arrangement provides a more certain source of supply and whether this was important to the customer. Sixth, they would determine whether exclusive dealing arrangements induce foreclosed suppliers to develop their own outlets. Where they do this, competition may ultimately be enhanced.[6] A much more stringent test is presented by Dirlam and Kahn. Throughout their book they attack Lockhart and Sacks' criteria because:

> To require convincing proof of even a "reasonable possi-
> bility" of over-all deleterious consequences, involving a
> tenuous comparison of unpredictables, weakens the prohi-
> bition of practices that experience and logic demonstrate

tend to have certain anti-competitive effects (whatever their influence on the market as a whole).[7]

Dirlam and Kahn believe that the state of economic knowledge has not progressed enough to provide an objective standard with which to determine the effect of most arrangements on competition. Given this premise, they believe that courts should not get into the business of allowing practices which, although they may have benefits, also have harms. There is no way to precisely weigh the harms against the benefits. Their test is a simple one. They would allow exclusive dealing if it helps a new firm gain a foothold. Presumably this would be the only instance in which the practice would be allowed because "the primary purpose [of litigation] is still to define the act, not to evaluate market structure or performance."[8] Whether the argument of Lockhart and Sacks or the argument of Dirlam and Kahn is preferable depends on the degree of faith one has in economic science as well as one's interpretation of the purpose of the antitrust laws. The two adversaries presented their arguments almost twenty years ago and since then little has happened to economic knowledge or the philosophy of the antitrust laws which can help us make our choice.

A CASE ANALYSIS

STANDARD FASHION CO.

One of the earliest antitrust cases directed against exclusive dealings was *Standard Fashion Co.* v. *Magrane-Houston Co.*, decided in 1922 by the Supreme Court.[9] Standard Fashion was a manufacturer of patterns for women's and children's clothing, and Magrane-Houston was a retail outlet for patterns in the city of Boston. In 1914, Magrane-Houston agreed to represent Standard Fashion's patterns exclusively. In return it was able to purchase the patterns at a discount of 50 per cent and was allowed to return discarded patterns to the manufacturer at a small discount. The contract was for a two year period with a continuance after that initial period until either party gave the other a three months' notice that the contract was to be terminated. On July 1, 1917, Magrane-Houston discontinued the sale of Standard Fashion's products without notice and began selling the patterns of a rival supplier. Shortly thereafter, Standard Fashion charged the retail outlet with breach of contract.

The Supreme Court considered the major issue before it to be: "Does the contract of sale come within the third section of the

Clayton Act, because the covenant not to sell the patterns of others 'may be to substantially lessen competition or tend to create a monopoly'?"[10] The Court observed that Section 3 of the Clayton Act was designed to curb restraints of trade in their incipiency. Therefore, in order to declare them illegal, the Court thought that it was enough to demonstrate that exclusive dealing arrangements "may" restrain trade. Applying this test, the Court found that Standard Fashion and two other pattern companies controlled 40 per cent of the retail outlets in the country. It also found that in some small markets the company had a virtual monopoly, and that even in large cities Standard Fashion's exclusive dealing arrangements might promote the adoption of additional exclusive dealing arrangements by other firms and result in the monopolization of most of the pattern business. Based on these observations, Standard Fashion's use of exclusive dealing was declared illegal.

Certainly, if the "reasonable possibility" test was appropriate, the Court was correct in its decision. Furthermore, the observation that if many pattern manufacturers engaged in exclusive dealing, monopoly power would be increased is also correct and is an important criterion in evaluating exclusive dealing arrangements. But the Court's test was certainly not based on economic analysis. There may have been some good business purpose for the use of the arrangements, since the specifics of the contract were designed to insure that Magrane-Houston represented Standard Fashions in a thorough manner.

This case is more important for the Court's interpretation of the Clayton Act than for the legality of the specific practice involved. The Court's method of applying the act in this case has been followed in numerous Clayton Act decisions and is worth reiterating here. Louis B. Schwartz, Professor of Law at the University of Pennsylvania, has paraphrased the interpretation of the act as follows:

> The import of the *Standard Fashion* case may then be stated as follows: A general inquiry of Sherman Act scope into the effect of the exclusive supply contract is not called for by the Clayton Act; the door is kept open for some showing of circumstances which might legalize the use of these devices [exclusive dealing arrangements]; the circumstance of paramount import is the relative standing in the industry of the person who uses the device; if he be among the leaders, then no demonstration of virtues of the contract or actual effects of its use will overcome the substantial potentiality of competitive impairment derived from the combination of large size and restrictive con-

tracts. In this connection large size does not mean complete dominance in the Sherman Act monopoly sense, but
only a place among the leaders of the industry.[11]

We will see this interpretation of the act applied in most of the
exclusive dealing cases that follow, as well as in many Clayton Act
cases involving other business practices.

STANDARD STATIONS

Standard Oil Co. of California and Standard Stations, Inc. v.
United States was a landmark case involving exclusive dealing arrangements.[12] The case reached the Supreme Court on appeal from
the U.S. District Court for the Southern District of California. Like
the *Standard Fashion* case, it involved a violation of Section 3 of the
Clayton Act. Standard Oil sold its products to its own service
stations, independent stations, and industrial users. Being the largest
oil company in the California area, it sold 23 per cent of the taxable
gallonage. Its sales to independent stations were under scrutiny in
this case.

Standard utilized two types of exclusive dealing arrangements in
selling to independent stations. In one type, dealers were required to
purchase their total requirements of gasoline and other petroleum
products as well as tires, tubes, and batteries. The second type only
bound dealers to purchase their total requirements of petroleum
products. 8,187 dealers had agreed to one form of exclusive dealing
arrangement or the other. Their contracts were for varying periods of
time, but the majority were for one year. These, however, could be
terminated "at the end of the first six months of any contract year,
or at the end of any such year, by giving to the other at least 30 days
prior thereto written notice."[13]

In its decision, the Court recognized that exclusive dealing arrangements may have a valid business purpose:

> In the case of the buyer, they may assure supply, afford
> protection against rises in price, enable long-term planning
> on the basis of known costs, and obviate the expense and
> risk of storage in the quantity necessary for a commodity
> having a fluctuating demand. From the seller's point of
> view, requirements contracts may make possible the sub-
> stantial reduction of selling expenses, give protection
> against price fluctuations, and—of particular advantage to a
> newcomer to the field to whom it is important to know
> what capital expenditures are justified—offer the possi-
> bility of a predictable market.[14]

It further recognized that the benefits resulting from such a contract may outweigh the harms and therefore the *International Salt* decision utilizing the quantitative substantiality test was not applicable to exclusive dealing. The Court even recognized that if it were to analyze the competitive effects of a particular exclusive dealing arrangement in detail, it would use various economic criteria such as:

1. Whether competition has flourished under the agreements;
2. The duration of the contracts;
3. Whether the defendant is an established firm or a newcomer;
4. The defendant's degree of market control.

Did it use these criteria? The Court said that it was incapable of using them to determine whether the arrangements affected competition favorably or unfavorably.

> To demand that bare inference be supported by evidence as to what would have happened but for the adoption of the practice that was in fact adopted or to require firm prediction of an increase of competition as a probable result of ordering the abandonment of the practice, would be a standard of proof if not virtually impossible to meet, at least most ill-suited for ascertainment by courts.[15]

How was the case decided? The Court used a combined share-of-the-market/quantitative substantiality test because:

> the qualifying clause of Section III is satisfied by proof that competition has been foreclosed in a substantial share of the line of commerce affected. It cannot be gainsaid that observance by a dealer of his requirements contract with Standard does effectively foreclose whatever opportunity there might be for competing suppliers to attract his patronage, and it is clear that the affected proportion of retail sales of petroleum products is substantial. In view of the widespread adoption of such contracts by Standard's competitors and the availability of alternative ways of obtaining an assured market, evidence that competitive activity has not actually declined is inconclusive. Standard's use of the contracts creates just such a potential clog on competition as it was the purpose of Section III to remove wherever, were it to become actual, it would impede a substantial amount of competitive activity.[16]

Standard's contracts involved 6.7 per cent of total gasoline sales. This, coupled with the fact that all of the other major suppliers used exclusive dealing arrangements, was enough for the Court to find the arrangements illegal. The exclusive dealing arrangement involving 2 per cent of the market in tires and batteries was, surprisingly, also struck down.

The case was decided by a vote of five to four. Justice Jackson wrote a dissenting opinion in which he represented himself, Justice Warren, and Justice Burton. Justice Douglas wrote a separate dissenting opinion. The Jackson dissent was based on the contention that even though the exclusive dealing arrangement covered a substantial number of outlets and products, that did not automatically make it anticompetitive. Jackson admitted his regret that the Clayton Act required the Court to determine whether a practice was an unfavorable effect on competition. But given the wording of the act, Jackson thought that the Court ought to hear the relevant economic evidence and weigh it. "This is a tedious process and not too enlightening, but without it, a judicial decree is but a guess in the dark. That is all we have here [in the decision of the Court] and I do not think it is an adequate basis on which to upset long-standing and widely practiced business arrangements."[17]   Jackson did not think that Standard's exclusive dealing arrangement decreased competition. Moreover, he thought that it might be necessary in order for a supplier to obtain dealers who provide customers with adequate supplies of petroleum products and promote them in a desirable manner. True, this was not proved in the case but Jackson's point was that until the government substantiated its case by showing competitive harm, the defendant was innocent.

Douglas' argument was based on the double standard that companies may engage in vertical integration but may not engage in exclusive dealing. He attacked the members of the Court by pointing to the relative ease with which they had allowed big businesses to merge. He also observed that one of the reasons that there were a large number of independent service stations in the country was that the major oil companies were allowed to use exclusive dealing arrangements. This gave them many of the advantages they would have if they merged vertically to the retail level. If, however, exclusive dealing arrangements were outlawed, vertical integration would prevail. "The method of doing business under requirements contracts at least keeps the independents alive. They survive as small business units. The situation is not ideal from either their point of view or that of the nation. But the alternative which the Court offers is far worse from the point of view of both. The elimination of these requirements contracts sets the stage for Standard and the other oil companies to build service-station empires of their own."[18]

Expectedly, Lockhart and Sacks did not agree with the Court's method of arriving at its decision. They admitted that economic analysis has not advanced so far as for it to be able to render a conclusive prediction that the elimination of Standard's exclusive dealing arrangement would increase competition. However they believed that it could give a more accurate answer than the simple share-of-the-market test utilized by the Court.

> Concededly, the present limitations of economic analysis, plus the great expense of full-dress investigations of economic effects of a given exclusive arrangement, will make it impossible in many cases to prove definitely the precise effect of the practice on competition, or whether its elimination will increase competition. But the statute does not require such perfection. It makes no suggestion that "conclusive proof" is required. It merely requires a showing that the effect of the challenged practice "may be" to substantially lessen competition or *tend* to create a "monopoly." A careful analysis of the various economic factors bearing upon this issue should enable a court to decide a case on the basis of something more than a pure guess, and in view of the wording and purpose of the statute, more does not seem required.[19]

Also expectedly, Dirlam and Kahn supported the Court's refusal to use economic tests. While agreeing that exclusive dealing arrangements have both positive and negative effects, they pointed to the tremendous problem of weighing these effects against one another. Addressing their comments to Lockhart and Sacks, they asked,

> Do they imply . . . that the Supreme Court should have had to decide whether there are too many gas stations on the West Coast and weigh against this possible waste the economic benefits of competition among the excessively numerous dealers? Or to decide what portion of these offsetting consequences were properly attributable to exclusive dealing, and strike a balance between these, before deciding whether Standard might legally exert its leverage to close a substantial market to competitors? Would such a procedure make the law clearer to businessmen, as the critics of antitrust demanded, and diminish the uncertainties of the law as now interpreted?[20]

AMERICAN CAN

In 1949, the District Court for the Northern District of California heard a case involving both exclusive dealing arrangements and tying contracts.[21] American Can was charged under the provisions of Sections 1 and 2 of the Sherman Act and Section 3 of the Clayton Act. The trial lasted for 117 days and is recorded in more than 7,000 pages of testimony. American was a producer of metal cans as well as closing machines used to put lids on the cans. It, together with its major competitor, Continental Can Co., manufactured 70 per cent of all cans and approximately 80 per cent of all cans made for sale.[22] American accounted for 47.9 per cent of the sanitary cans and 52.2 per cent of the general line cans sold. Both American and Continental were also the two largest producers of can closing machines, and virtually all of their can customers leased their machines. There were only two other manufacturers of these machines.

American sold the great majority of its cans (92 per cent) through exclusive dealing contracts. It offered a quantity discount for customers who signed the contracts and claimed that most customers preferred to deal with only one can manufacturer. Its contracts had been for different durations, but in 1946 they were all standardized at five years. American only leased its closing machines to customers who purchased its cans exclusively. The machines were leased at a nominal fee which often did not even cover American's costs. This pricing policy obviously afforded little opportunity for firms to enter the closing can industry and is a major explanation for the fact that the industry was so concentrated. American controlled 50 per cent of the market, and Continental had 36 per cent of the market. This left only 14 per cent for independent manufacturers.

In its decision, the district court stressed the fact that American was a dominant firm with a large share of both the can market and the closing machine market. In 1916 the company had been declared a monopoly by a district court, but the 1916 court thought that dissolution was too drastic a remedy. The 1949 district court thought that the tying arrangements had given American a great amount of its monopoly power. It found that the market for the two independent closing machine manufacturers was limited to customers supplied by the small can makers. The canner who bought from American or Continental would not purchase a closing machine as long as he could lease it from them at low rental rates. The court also thought that American's dominant position could be attributed to its exclusive dealing arrangement. This was especially true when the arrangements were accompanied by price reductions or quantity discounts for those customers who dealt exclusively. In short, according to the court, both the tying arrangement and the exclusive dealing arrangement appeared to foreclose a substantial share of the market, and thus they were declared illegal under Section 3 of the Clayton Act as "unreasonable restraints of trade." They were also declared illegal under Sections 1 and 2 of the Sherman Act as "attempts to monopolize trade and commerce."

The manner in which the court decided the case was almost wholly consistent with the *Standard Fashion* and *Standard Stations* decision. In *American Can*, the court contended that "Substantiality of restraint or tendency to create monopoly is established by (a) the market foreclosed,—here represented by the controlled unit,—and (b) the volume of controlled business, totalling here in value $68,000,000.[23] This combined share-of-the-market/quantitative substantiality test did not completely displace other considerations. The court did analyze the advantages and disadvantages of the arrangements but found that its conclusions from this analysis were not "determinate."

Unlike many antitrust decisions, this one provided a remedial penalty. The American and Continental Can Companies were ordered to limit their exclusive dealing arrangements to one year. Moreover, customers who owned a number of factories were permitted to contract with American and Continental to buy cans for some of their factories on an exclusive dealing basis while permitting other of their factories to buy from competing can suppliers. The companies were no longer allowed to use their tying contracts and were ordered to sell their closing machines at relatively low prices. The companies were also to end their volume discounts for customers who entered into exclusive dealing contracts.

James W. McKie studied the can industry three years after the court's decision. He concluded that although a dissolutionment proceeding would have brought about more spectacular changes in the industry, the court's solution did increase competition.[24] He found that American and Continental had sold over 75 per cent of their closing machines and that after the transition period was over, independent manufacturers would be better able to market their machines. After the exclusive dealing arrangements had been limited to one year, he found that many large packagers who operated several canneries used a number of brands of cans and even split their requirements within a plant. Even the two major companies, American and Continental appeared to be in a state of "intense rivalry." They competed strongly for annual exclusive dealing contracts and also competed in the development of new technology. The smaller can manufacturers established "themselves on a more secure footing and have also been edging into the market of both the leaders."[25] While no new entrants have appeared, "the threat of entry from the buying side has been intensified."[26] That is, users of cans had strongly considered manufacturing their own containers.

J. I. CASE CO.

United States v. *J. I. Case Co.* involved exclusive arrangements between Case and its independent dealers.[27] Case was a manufacturer and distributor of farm machinery. It sold a complete line of this machinery and had an independent organization of 3,783 dealers. Some dealers bought farm machinery under the provisions of an exclusive dealing arrangement which forbade them from selling other brands of farm machinery. The exclusive provision was an oral agreement, and the contracts were negotiated yearly. Some of the dealers contended that the exclusive dealing arrangements were achieved by Case by the use of coercion. Case was charged under the provisions of Section 1 of the Sherman Act and Section 3 of the Clayton Act. The government contended that through the use of exclusive dealing arrangements the company had a significant impact upon the farm machinery market by foreclosing approximately 1,050 dealers from other machinery suppliers.

The District Court of Minnesota admitted that there was no evidence of the fact that outlets had been restricted by Case's policy with its dealers and no evidence that farmers were denied a complete choice of different brands of farm machinery. Instead, the government argued that "each dealer should have the right to buy from every farm machinery manufacturer and distributor who desires to sell, and that there should be no restriction on the right of any farm machinery manufacturer to sell to anyone who may desire to buy."[28]

Case had about seven per cent of the farm machinery at the end of 1948, and its share of the market had grown steadily from 1944 to 1948. This percentage did not impress the court as being a significant share of the market. It did recognize that Case intended to obtain dealers who would devote the majority of their time to Case's products, but the court was not certain that it was Case's objective to use coercive tactics to force dealers to handle its products exclusively. Buttressing its position, the court pointed to the fact that a survey of 4,854 dealers and former dealers uncovered only 108 dealers who contended that coercive tactics had been used. Additionally, it pointed to the fact that a large number of Case dealers carried other brands. Where dealers might have been foreclosed to other suppliers, the court noted that the foreclosure was only for a period of one year and that this period of time was not unreasonable. The court found Case innocent.

TAMPA ELECTRIC

The stringent test used in the *Standard Stations* case was modified somewhat in *Tampa Electric Company v. Nashville Coal Company*.[29] Tampa was an electric utility located in Tampa, Florida. In

1955 it constructed a new generating plant known as the Francis J. Gannon Station. Until the station was completed, every electrical generating plant in peninsular Florida burned oil. Tampa elected to experiment with coal in the first two generating units constructed at the Gannon Station. To supply these units it contracted with Nashville Coal for its full requirements of coal for a period of twenty years. A minimum price was established at $6.40 per ton, subject to an escalation clause based on labor cost and other factors. Shortly before the first delivery of coal was to be made, Nashville Coal advised Tampa Electric that the arrangement was illegal under the antitrust laws and that it would not deliver the coal. Both the district court and the court of appeals found the contract to be in violation of the Clayton Act. In their decisions they attempted to determine how significant the foreclosure was. That analysis led them to the conclusion that because the contract involved approximately $128,000,000 it was not " 'insignificant or insubstantial' and that the effect of the control would 'be to substantially lessen competition,' in violation of the Act."[30]

The Supreme Court observed that to reach a fair decision it was important to determine the relevant market. To do this, it said that the line of commerce and the geographical area of effective competition must be defined. Then, the Court must determine whether the competition foreclosed by the exclusive dealing arrangement constituted a substantial share of the market. The reader will see shortly that this three step test to determine market share is very similar to that utilized in determining whether mergers reduce competition. The similarity of the tests is understandable since vertical mergers and exclusive dealing arrangements are almost identical in their effect on the market. In light of the *Standard Stations* decision, however, it is surprising to hear the Supreme Court say:

> To determine substantiality in a given case, it is necessary to weigh the probable effect of the contract on the relevant area of effective competition, taking into account the relative strength of the parties, the proportionate volume of commerce involved in relation to the total volume of commerce in the relevant market area, and the probable immediate and future effects which pre-emption of that share of the market might have on effective competition therein. It follows that a mere showing that the contract itself involves a substantial number of dollars is ordinarily of little consequence.[31]

Certainly, the Court's statement rejects the quantitative substantiality rule and requires a detailed share-of-the-market analysis. For its analysis, the Court assumed that the relevant product market was bituminous coal. When looking at the relevant geographical market, it observed that Nashville Coal contended that if the relevant market were defined as Georgia and Florida, Tampa Electric's contract would foreclose 18 per cent of the market. Alternatively, the Court found that "By far the bulk of the overwhelming tonnage marketed from the same producing area as serves Tampa is sold outside of Georgia and Florida, and the producers were 'eager' to sell more coal in those states."[32] Given this large geographical market, less than one per cent of the market was foreclosed through the contract. Not only did the Court find the market share "insignificant," it also concluded that the arrangement was made for good business purposes. "We seem to have only that type of contract which 'may well be of economic advantage to buyers as well as to sellers.' . . . it 'may make possible the substantial reduction of selling expenses, give protection against price fluctuations, and offer the possibility of a predictable market.' "[33] Based on its conclusions, the decision of the court of appeals was reversed.

The facts in the *Tampa Electric* case do differ from those in *Standard Stations* in that a smaller market share was foreclosed, and exclusive dealing was used in a less oligopolistic market. But even given these differences, the Court certainly modified its approach to the antitrust questions involved in exclusive dealing arrangements.

SUMMARY

We can expect future courts to rely heavily on the share-of-the-market/quantitative substantiality test and firms which have a dominant position in their industry adopt exclusive dealing arrangements at their own risk. The criteria used by the courts to evaluate the legality of a particular instance of exclusive dealing are much more similar to those suggested by Dirlam and Kahn than to the criteria offered by Lockhart and Sacks.

NOTES TO CHAPTER XII

[1]There are, of course, intermediate degrees of representation between having a large number of dealers represent him and having exclusive dealing arrangements.

[2]87 F. Supp. 18 (1949).

[3]87 F. Supp. 18, 21 (1949).

[4]Phillip Hart, "Distribution Problems Affecting Small Business," *Hearings Before the Subcommittee on Antitrust and Monopoly of the Committee on the*

Judiciary, United States Senate (Washington: U.S. Government Printing Office, 1966), p. 698.

[5]G. E. Hale and Rosemary D. Hale, *Market Power: Size and Shape Under the Sherman Act* (Boston: Little, Brown and Company, 1958).

[6]William B. Lockhart and Howard R. Sacks, "The Relevance of Economic Factors in Determining Whether Exclusive Arrangements Violate Section 3 of the Clayton Act," *Harvard Law Review*, LXV (April, 1952), 913-952.

[7]Joel B. Dirlam and Alfred E. Kahn, *Fair Competition: The Law and Economics of Antitrust Policy* (Ithaca, New York: Cornell University Press, 1954), p. 49.

[8]*Ibid.*, pp. 118-119.

[9]258 U.S. 346 (1922).

[10]258 U.S. 346, 355 (1922).

[11]Louis B. Schwartz, "Potential Impairment of Competition—The Impact of Standard Oil Co. of California v. United States on the Standard of Legality Under the Clayton Act," *University of Pennsylvania Law Review*, XCVIII (November 1949), 23.

[12]337 U.S. 293 (1949).

[13]337 U.S. 293, 296 (1949).

[14]337 U.S. 293, 306-07 (1949).

[15]337 U.S. 293, 310 (1949).

[16]337 U.S. 293, 314 (1949).

[17]337 U.S. 293, 322 (1949).

[18]337 U.S. 293, 319-320 (1949).

[19]Lockhart and Sacks, p. 939.

[20]Dirlam and Kahn, p. 184.

[21]*United States* v. *American Can Co.*, 87 F. Supp. 18 (1949).

[22]Although Continental did not come to trial, it agreed to accept any decision made against American short of dissolutionment.

[23]87 F. Supp. 18, 22 (1949).

[24]James W. McKie, "The Decline of Monopoly in the Metal Container Industry," *American Economic Review Proceedings*, XLV, No. 2 (May 1955), 499-508.

[25]*Ibid.*, p. 507.

[26]*Ibid.*

[27]101 F. Supp. 856 (1951).

[28]101 F. Supp. 856, 860 (1951).

[29]365 U.S. 320 (1961).

[30]365 U.S. 320, 325 (1961).

[31]365 U.S. 320, 329 (1961).

[32]365 U.S. 320, 331 (1961).

[33]365 U.S. 320, 334 (1961).

HORIZONTAL AND VERTICAL MERGERS UNDER THE PROVISIONS OF THE SHERMAN ACT

CHAPTER XIII

> Merger activity makes up a significant part of antitrust prosecution. In this chapter the economics of horizontal and vertical mergers are considered, and rules are established to determine whether such mergers are anticompetitive. Additionally, we determine the legal attitude toward the mergers under the provisions of the Sherman Act.

INTRODUCTION

There are three general types of mergers: horizontal, vertical, and conglomerate. Horizontal and vertical mergers can be prosecuted under the provisions of either the Sherman or Clayton Acts, but conglomerate mergers can be prosecuted only under Clayton Act provisions. In this chapter, the economics of horizontal and vertical mergers will be discussed as well as two Sherman Act cases directed against them. The reader will recognize the fact that we are returning to the Sherman Act in the midst of chapters on the Clayton Act. This is done so that we might consider all merger activity in two sequential chapters. The economics of conglomerate mergers and Clayton Act cases concerning all three types of mergers will be discussed in Chapter XIV. The contents of this chapter give only a limited description of the legality of horizontal and vertical mergers under the Sherman Act.

A merger is simply the unification of various companies under one management, and it may be implemented in two major ways. First, mergers may be implemented through the outright purchase of the assets of one company by another. Second, acquisition can also be achieved by purchasing the stock of another company.

An extremely large number of mergers have occurred in the United States. Chronologically, most have occurred from 1895 to 1904, during the 1920s, and from 1948 to the present. Between 1895 and 1904, Ralph Nelson found that approximately 3,000 firms disappeared as a result of mergers.[1] Professor Jesse Markham estimated that from 1919 to 1930 mergers eliminated approximately 12,000 firms.[2] Between 1945 and 1965, 11,668 mergers occurred,

241

and an additional 4,933 took place between 1966 and 1968.[3] Two fundamental conclusions can be drawn from this data: (1) merger activity has been extremely prevalent in the United States and (2) a large number of mergers have not been prosecuted by the Justice Department and the Federal Trade Commission.

HORIZONTAL MERGERS

A horizontal merger is one that unifies firms at the same level of distribution. Because the firms are on the same level, they sell identical or at least similar commodities. For example, the unification of steel companies is a horizontal merger, and a merger between an aluminum company and a steel company might also be considered horizontal because, for certain uses, the two firms sell competing products.

ANTICOMPETITIVE ASPECTS

A horizontal merger reduces the number of competitors in an industry and consequently, monopoly power might be created. A striking example of the creation of monopoly power through merger occurred in the pipe industry. The reader will remember from Chapter VI that the six companies involved in the *Addyston Pipe and Steel Co.* case were found guilty of price fixing. Subsequent to the Court's decision, they merged and became the largest manufacturer of cast iron pipe in the United States. The merger allowed them to resume their anticompetitive practices.[4]

Whether or not a horizontal merger creates monopoly power depends upon whether a sufficient number of competitive firms remain in the industry after the merger. To visualize this, consider an industry that is initially monopolistically competitive. Suppose that once a month two firms in the industry merge. As the months pass, some competitors are eliminated, and there will be change in the market structure. The remaining firms will have a larger share of the market, and at some point in time the industry will become oligopolistic. Later, firms will probably adopt conscious parallelism in their actions, and finally there will be a pure monopoly. We would not notice a dramatic change in market structure with each merger, but through time the change would become apparent, and consumer welfare would be reduced. At what stage should the mergers be stopped if consumer welfare is to be maximized? To be perfectly safe the mergers probably should not be allowed at all because the greater the number of firms in an industry, the greater are the chances that firms in the industry will charge a competitive price. However, if economies of scale result from the mergers, perhaps some of them should be allowed. For example, as long as the market structure remains monopolistically competitive, one might not mind giving up some firms. If the industry were already an oligopolistic one, but only marginally so, then one might be willing to allow mergers until a tendency toward conscious parallelism is suspected. The point is that one cannot determine an optimum number of firms which is correct for all industries so one cannot say that mergers should always be disallowed if less than, say, fifteen firms exist in an industry.

CRITERIA FOR EVALUATING

The answer to the question, "Can you reduce by one the number of firms in an industry without creating additional monopoly power?" depends on: (1) the structure of the industry, measured in terms of the degree of market concentration, and (2) the performance of firms in the market. Therefore, market structure and market performance are appropriate criteria with which to judge horizontal merger cases. Each of these criteria will be considered separately.

The degree of concentration in an industry reflects the market structure of that industry. Concentration is the control of a large proportion of economic resources in an industry by a small number of firms. The degree of concentration refers indirectly to the degree of control which these firms have. The number of firms in an industry is a crude measure of the degree of concentration. This figure gives a rough indication of whether the market is oligopolistic, monopolistically competitive, or purely monopolistic. Therefore, such information is helpful in determining the effect of a horizontal merger on monopoly power.

But dependence on this figure alone can be dangerous. Suppose there are fifty companies in an industry. On the basis of this information, you would say that the industry is monopolistically competitive. But if one of the firms produces over 60 per cent of the industry output, it probably has significant monopoly power. A concentration ratio is a better measure of market structure because it expresses the quantity of sellers as well as their relative size. The most common version of the ratio shows the market share of the four largest companies in an industry. Market share is usually measured by sales, the level of production, the number of employees, or the dollar value of shipments. Most of the ratios use shipments to measure market share because such statistics are readily available from the Department of Commerce. *Table I* shows four-firm concentration ratios for a number of industries. The ratio can be modified to include eight, sixteen, or any number of companies in the industry which the analyst wishes to include. Sometimes the data is depicted on a concentration curve which shows the number of firms in an industry on the horizontal axis (ranked from the largest to the smallest firm) and the market share (shipments, employees, or some other measure of market share) on the vertical axis.[5] *Figure I* depicts a concentration curve.

Probably the greatest problem in the use of concentration ratios is deciding how to define an industry. All firms that compete should be grouped together because, in deciding horizontal merger cases, the relevant question is, "Do a sufficient number of competitors remain after the merger?" If the merger is between New York bus companies, do we count all bus companies in the country as part of the industry? Obviously the answer is "no" because a bus company located in St. Louis does not compete in New York. But bus companies and subways compete to some degree. Therefore, perhaps New York subways should be included in the industry. Likewise, it

TABLE I

Four-Firm Concentration Ratio For
Selected Domestic Industries

PRODUCT CLASS	Four-Firm Concentration Ratio* (%)
Passenger Cars	98
Cigarettes	82
Metal Cans	81
Bottled Liquors	67
Glass Containers	63
Aircraft	55
Household Refrigerators	62

*Shipments are used to determine the share of the market.

Source: Senate Subcommittee on Antitrust and Monopoly of the Committee on the Judiciary, *Concentration in American Industry* (Washington: U.S. Government Printing Office, 1957), pp. 166–174, reproduced in Ralph L. Nelson, *Concentration in the Manufacturing Industries of the United States* (New Haven, Conn.: Yale University Press, 1963), p. 6.

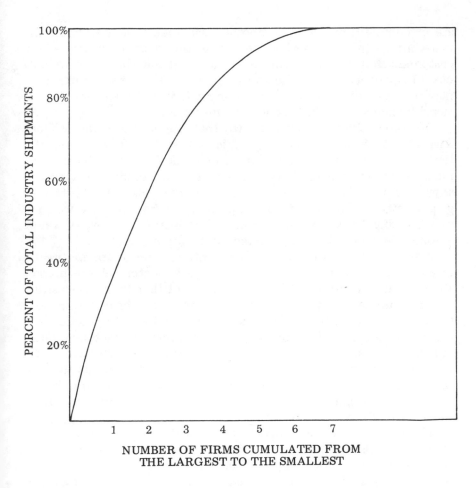

FIGURE I
CONCENTRATION CURVE

might even be appropriate to include New York taxis in the ratio. The point is, for a concentration ratio to be helpful in deciding antitrust cases, it must include all firms in strong competition with one another. This implies that before constructing such an index, it is important for the analyst to identify the strong competitors of merging companies. In both legal and economic terminology this job is called "determining the relevant market," where "relevant market" means the group of competitors with which merging firms compete. To determine any relevant market, the analyst must find the "relevant product market" which represents the group of products which are in competition with one another. He then must determine the "relevant geographic market" which is the geographic area where customers shop for the group of products. It may be as narrow as a city block or as wide as the world. Ghetto customers, for example, may only be able to buy in their immediate vicinity whereas international businessmen shop throughout the world.

Of course the reader will realize that the nature of the product itself affects the size of the geographic market. New York transportation is, by definition, limited to the market of New York. The money market is worldwide because the commodity is identical anywhere it is found. The value of a product also affects its geographic market. We would not shop far away from home if we were only looking for a box of hair pins, but in the purchase of a new automobile we would tend to extend our shopping area.

It is important to realize that concentration ratios are not precise measures of monopoly power. They are indicators of the market structure of an industry. Only to the extent that the market structure is a major determinant of the monopoly power of a firm does the ratio give us a useful indicator of that power. In practice, the concentration ratio concept has been an important factor in determining the legality of horizontal mergers. But the courts have used a modified form of the ratio. They determine: (1) the market share of the merging firms, and (2) the number of remaining firms in the industry. Both figures give a crude measure of the competition facing the merging firms.

There is no specified market share which is acceptable to the courts. What is acceptable varies from case to case and from court to court. However, guidelines have been developed outside the courtroom. For example, Donald Turner and Carl Kaysen suggested that any acquisition of a competitor which results in the control of more than 20 per cent of the market should be disallowed.[6] George Stigler believed that every merger which gives a firm one fifth or more of the market should be illegal. Mergers giving the acquiring firm five to ten per cent of the market should be allowed, and mergers involving between ten and twenty per cent of the market should be judged on the merits of the case.[7] In 1968, the Department of Justice published guidelines which it has used to determine whether merging firms will be prosecuted.[8] Its guidelines used both the share-of-the-market concept and the concentration ratio. If the Justice Department found that an industry had a four-firm concentration ratio of 75 per cent or more, it said that it would challenge horizontal mergers in that industry involving the following market shares:

Acquiring Firms	Acquired Firm
4%	4% or more
10%	2% or more
15% or more	1% or more

In industries with four-firm concentration ratios of less than 75 per cent, the Justice Department said that it would challenge horizontal mergers involving the following market shares:

Acquiring Firms	Acquired Firms
5%	5% or more
10%	4% or more
15%	3% or more
20%	2% or more
25% or more	1% or more

The Department of Justice also stated that even if a merger creates economies of scale, it would not consider the economies to be a justification for horizontal mergers unless "exceptional circumstances" were involved. This implies that the Justice Department does not wish to get involved in weighing costs and benefits resulting from a merger. But it must realize that strict adherence to its guidelines can harm the consuming public by blocking a merger that creates substantial cost reductions. Numerous lawyers and economists, including the Stigler Task Force appointed by President Nixon, have been critical of the guidelines and have recommended a less stringent set of criteria to determine the legality of horizontal mergers.

The rules of Kaysen and Turner, Stigler, and the Justice Department imply that bigness is badness, but this is not necessarily true. A firm with a large market share can be quite competitive. However, the use of simple rules to determine the legality of horizontal mergers is understandable, if not academically correct. The courts can never hope to know with certainty the results of a merger. They can only make their "best guess" of the effects on consumer welfare, and simple rules aid them in making this guess. Moreover, there is at least one good reason to disallow bigness. The larger a firm becomes, the greater is the chance that it has monopoly power. Even if that power is not exercised, it is bothersome because it represents a potential threat to the consumer. The problem of size was eloquently discussed by Thomas Carver in 1915. He said:

The larger the corporation, the greater is its power, either for good or for evil, and that makes it especially important that its power be under control. If I may use a homely illustration, I will take the common house cat, whose diminutive size makes her a safe inmate of our household in spite of her playful disposition and her liking for animal food. If, without the slightest change of character or disposition, she were suddenly enlarged to the dimensions of a tiger, we should at least want her to be muzzled and to have her claws trimmed, whereas if she were to assume the dimensions of a mastadon, I doubt if any of us would want to live in the same house with her. And it would be useless to argue that her nature had not changed, that she was just as amiable as ever, and no more carnivorous than she always had been. Nor would it convince us to be told that her productivity had increased and that she could now catch more mice in a minute than she formerly could in a week. We would be afraid lest, in a playful mood, she might set a paw upon us, to the detriment of our epidermis, or that in her large-scale mouse-catching she might not always discriminate between us and the mice.[9]

MARKET PERFORMANCE

We have seen that one way of predicting the effect of a horizontal merger on monopoly power is to analyze industry structure. This approach rests on the assumption that market structure reflects the state of competition in an industry. The problem is that there is not a perfect correlation between an increase in concentration and an increase in monopoly power. In terms we have used before, a decrease in the number of firms in an industry from six to five will increase the concentration ratio, but it need not increase monopoly power. Therefore, courts will have a better chance of arriving at a correct decision if in addition to analyzing market structure they also analyze market performance. Market performance means the degree to which firms attempt to compete and the degree to which they strive to be efficient. The concept is not independent of market structure because structure affects performance. However, given a certain market structure, firms still have latitude in choosing the degree of market performance, and even firms in a very highly concentrated industry may be efficient and highly competitive. The following criteria are helpful in evaluating the effects of a horizontal merger on market performance.

(1) It is possible that the merger of two small firms can permit the now larger company to increase its competition vis à vis its larger

competitors. We saw in Chapter I that John K. Galbraith introduced the idea of large size offsetting large size and called it Counterveiling Power.[10] The concept could also be based on the principle that monopoly power could develop in one firm to combat the effects of monopoly power in another competitive firm. For example, it is conceivable that General Motors would face stronger competition if Chrysler Corporation and American Motors merged. The structure test would no doubt indicate that such a merger should be disallowed, yet the merger might increase the industry performance.

(2) Another indicator of the effect of a merger would be whether the remaining firms in an industry are dynamic. If the remaining firms abstain from conscious parallelism and insist on valid competition, and if they attempt new ways of improving and marketing their product, then the merging firms will find that they are unable to charge a monopolistic price or engage in collusive activities with their competitors.

(3) If the acquired firm is facing bankruptcy, the merger may salvage economic resources and jobs. Moreover, because the acquired firm would have gone out of business anyway, the merger does not reduce the number of competitors in the industry. The issue of whether it is desirable to save a firm from bankruptcy has no easy answer. Congress proved that it was a difficult task when they engaged in the lengthy 1971 debate on whether to save the Lockheed Aircraft Company. For our purposes, it is enough to say that saving a company from bankruptcy benefits society in some ways and, as a result, should be a consideration in horizontal merger cases.

(4) Ease of entry into an industry has a significant effect on whether a merger creates monopoly power. If new companies are able to enter an industry quickly and at a low cost, they could effect the resulting loss of a competing firm through merger. For example, the American Can Company found that free entry inhibited its attempt to create monopoly power. The company purchased almost all of the can manufacturers in the United States. It then raised prices, whereupon new firms entered the industry. Although American Can tried to purchase the new entrants, it found the cost prohibitive. The company then tried to purchase some of its competitors' output in order to restrict supply and also found that cost prohibitively high. It finally gave up the struggle and became accustomed to competition.[11]

(5) Economies of scale may result from horizontal mergers, and the advantages from these might offset any acquired monopoly power. Economies of scale can be defined as a reduction in per-unit costs following business expansion. Horizontal mergers will increase

the size of a firm in one of two ways. First, they might simply increase the number of plants in which the product is produced. If Firm A, which has three plants, and Firm B, which has one plant, merge, then the new firm has a total of four plants, none of which is any larger than before the merger. Second, a horizontal merger may not increase the number of plants, but instead, it may increase the size of the plants. After the merger, Firm B might move its resources into Firm A's building. Since horizontal mergers can increase the size of a firm in two ways, two resulting types of economies might arise: *plant scale economies* which result from the increase in the size of a plant and *multiplant economies* which result from an increase in the number of plants.

As early as 1776, Adam Smith discussed the benefits resulting from plant scale economies: increased specialization can take place, managerial costs can be spread over a greater volume of output, and more efficient factors of production can be substituted for less efficient ones. It's more difficult to conceive of multiplant economies. Certainly some economies might result from unified management, and the costs of getting the product to the consumer might be reduced when a company has a large number of plants spread throughout the market. Additionally, some savings might result from purchasing raw materials in large quantity.

No one doubts that plant scale and multiplant economies can exist. But do firms have to be very large in order to minimize their production costs? Professor Joe S. Bain has explored the question for both plant scale economies and multiplant economies. Concerning plant scale economies, he obtained estimates of the size of the optimal plant for twenty leading manufacturing industries in the United States. In only three of the twenty cases did the optimal-sized plant's share of the market reach 10 per cent or more.[12] This suggests that a large concentration ratio is not usually a requirement for economies of scale, although it is important for some industries such as those involving automobile and typewriter production. Bain performed a similar study for multiplant economies. For the same twenty industries, he found that such economies were small in six industries and insignificant in six others (he could not derive estimates for eight of the twenty industries). Bain concluded that large size is generally not necessary for multiplant economies.

A more recent study suggests that concentration and productivity are positively correlated. Bock and Farkas studied 417 manufacturing industries using data from the 1963 *Census of Manufacturers.* They concluded that on the average the industries with the highest productivity tended to have high concentration ratios. They also concluded that when the courts disallow mergers in highly concentrated industries they may lower productivity rates.

> These relations [between concentration and productivity] suggest that where the indicated correspondence between productivity and concentration holds for an individual industry, raw data on concentration or company size are not necessarily reliable indicators of anticompetitive behavior. And this, in turn, suggests that if antitrust policy were to rely heavily on such raw data, the resulting enforcement program would run the risk of lowering productivity rates below those that would be reached if criteria were aligned with a wider array of relevant industry and company facts.[13]

Since Bain's conclusions conflict with those of Bock and Farkas, and because the conclusions of many other studies have also been conflicting, it is dangerous to make a general statement concerning the correlation between concentration and economies of scale. But the purpose of our analysis is not to conclude that concentration is always required for efficiency. The point is that it may be required in some industries. This is why a judicial appraisal of economies of scale in each merger case seems to be an important ingredient in determining the legality of a horizontal merger.

Just recently, Professor Oliver Williamson concluded that where significant economies result from a merger, society can gain even when the merger results in a substantial increase in monopoly power.[14] His graphical analysis of the trade off involved is shown in *Figure II*. AC_2 represents the average cost of a firm before the merger, and AC_1 represents the average cost after the merger. Prior to the merger we will assume that the firm charged price P_1. Since the merger resulted in an increase in monopoly power, we will assume that the post-merger price is P_2. The dead weight loss is shown by the area ABC.[15] The gain to the producer through the cost savings is represented by the area P_1 BDE. To determine the overall effect on society (the consumer and the producer), the two areas have to be compared. Williamson found that if the elasticity of demand was 2, a cost reduction of 4 per cent would offset an increase in price of 20 per cent. That is, if a merger reduced cost by 4 per cent, it would have a beneficial effect on economic welfare as long as any resulting monopoly power did not cause a price increase in excess of 20 per cent. He concluded that "a merger which yields nontrivial real economies must produce substantial market power and result in relatively large price increases for the net allocative effects to be negative."[16] Of course, in this instance the consumer is

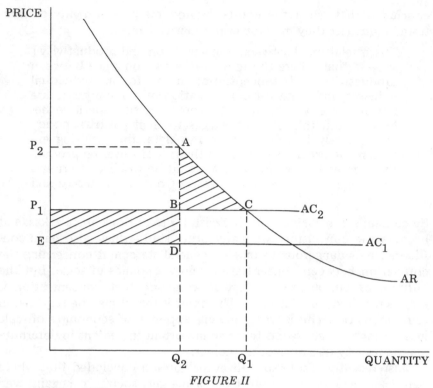

FIGURE II

Source: Oliver Williamson, p. 21.

THE WELFARE ASPECTS OF HORIZONTAL MERGERS
AND ECONOMIES OF SCALE

hurt, and the courts might not be impressed with the fact that the producer's benefits exceed the consumers' loss.

A SUMMARY

A structure test utilizing concentration ratios and share-of-the-market data can give insight into the probable effect of a merger on monopoly power. However, it is also important to consider the performance of firms in the industry where the merger takes place. If a merger increases the concentration in an industry without any offsetting advantages, it should be disallowed if economics is the sole criterion by which it is evaluated. Where it somehow makes the merging firms more efficient without creating monopoly power, it should be allowed. Where it creates monopoly power as well as increased efficiency, the courts could weigh the advantages and disadvantages of the merger. Yet this is a difficult task because it requires a subjective decision. The details of the courts' analysis of horizontal mergers will be seen later in this chapter and in Chapter XIV.

VERTICAL MERGERS

Vertical mergers (sometimes referred to as vertical integration) unify firms at successive levels of distribution. For example, if a steel company, an automobile manufacturer, and an automobile dealer merged, their activities would encompass three levels of distribution, such that a product from one level of distribution would become a factor of production at a succeeding level. Because firms contemplating a vertical merger are not competitors of one another, it is difficult to see how such mergers could harm competition. After all, competition involves horizontal, not vertical relationships. We will find that vertical mergers can decrease competition only when they have some effect on, or are affected by horizontal relationships. This point will be clarified by considering both the favorable and the unfavorable effects of vertical mergers.

THE FAVORABLE EFFECTS

Professor J. J. Spengler demonstrated that vertical mergers having no horizontal effects will increase economic welfare. His argument is worth reviewing because it suggests that the legal presumption should be in favor of allowing vertical mergers. Assume that an automobile manufacturer purchases its steel requirements from an independent steel company. Both the steel company and the auto manufacturer have some degree of monopoly power. The steel company will equate its marginal cost to its marginal revenue to determine the price that it charges the auto manufacturer. As a consequence of its monopoly power, that price will include a monopoly profit. This equilibrium position is shown in *Figure III*. AR_s is the demand curve for steel, and MC_s is the steel manufacturer's marginal cost curve. The producer equates his marginal revenue (MR_s) with his marginal cost (MC_s), charges price P_1 for his steel, and produces quantity Q_1.

Now let's turn our attention to the automobile manufacturer's pricing policy. The demand curve of his customers is shown by AR_a and his marginal revenue curve by MR_a. MC_a represents his marginal

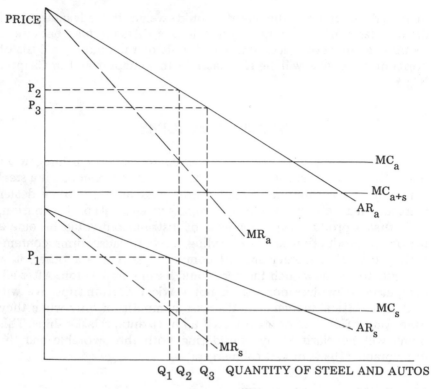

FIGURE III

THE RELATIONSHIP BETWEEN VERTICALLY RELATED COMPANIES

cost which includes the cost of steel. The auto manufacturer will equate his marginal revenue with his marginal cost, charge price P_2, and produce quantity Q_2.

Now let the auto manufacturer purchase the steel company. The auto manufacturer will receive steel from the same plant, but now the plant is his. The auto manufacturer's marginal cost still includes the cost of steel, and it should also include a normal return on the operation of the steel plant. However, there is no reason for it to include the monopolistic surcharge that the steel producer received prior to the merger. Because the surcharge has been eliminated, the auto manufacturer's new marginal cost curve is MC_{a+s}, <u>which is lower than the old marginal cost curve by the per-unit amount of the monopolistic surcharge.</u> The auto manufacturer will equate his marginal revenue with his new marginal cost, charge his customers P_3 for automobiles, and produce quantity Q_3. Consumer welfare has been increased because the price has been reduced. Moreover, Spengler demonstrated that if the auto manufacturer's demand curve is elastic, the profits of the vertically integrated company are greater than the combined profits of the steel and auto producer before they merged. Thus, when a vertical merger does not create monopoly power, it can be expected to increase consumer welfare as well as the profits of the merged firms.

Spengler's conclusions are based on the assumption that the vertical merger does not create additional monopoly power. But when the merger does create monopoly power, it might decrease consumer welfare. Several arguments have been presented by economists and lawyers to explain the manner in which vertical integration creates monopoly power, and each of these will be discussed. But a preliminary remark is in order. Running through all of the arguments is a central theme which is important in the formulation of appropriate antitrust policy; the possibility of anticompetitive effects resulting from a vertical merger is remote as long as the firm has a small percentage of the market at each successive level of distribution. Vertical mergers cannot create monopoly power unless the companies already have monopoly power prior to their merger.

ANTICOMPETITIVE EFFECTS

Critics of vertical mergers have argued that they affect competition adversely. Specifically, they argue that:
A. Vertical mergers foreclose markets to competitors;
B. Vertical mergers squeeze the profits of competitors;
C. Vertical mergers give the integrated firm a competitive advantage by eliminating the middleman;
D. Vertical mergers retard the entry of new firms into an industry.

Although not all of these arguments are valid, they deserve careful consideration.

Foreclosure

One argument against vertical mergers is that they may foreclose raw materials or customers to nonintegrated firms. To understand this, consider the following situation depicted in *Figure IV*. There are three suppliers of raw materials, A, B, and C. They sell to two producers, I and II. These producers sell their products to dealers e, f, and g. Each producer has three sources of raw materials and three dealers representing him. Now suppose that producer I merges with supplier A and dealer e. The effect of the arrangement is to foreclose

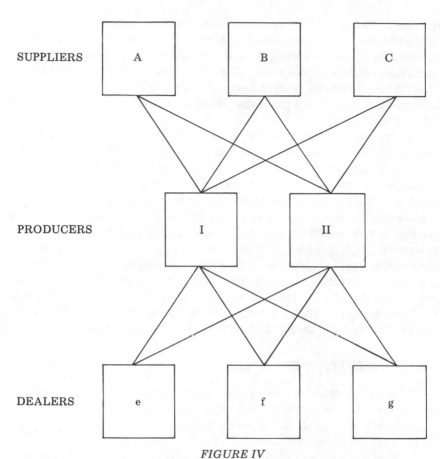

FIGURE IV

RELATIONSHIP BETWEEN SUPPLIERS, PRODUCERS AND DEALERS

one supplier and one dealer to producer II, provided that the integrated firm does not wish to supply producer II or sell producer II's products at the dealer level. This can significantly harm the producer if there are not a sufficient number of remaining suppliers or dealers, or in other words, if the integrated supplier and dealer have monopoly power at their levels of distribution.

Profit Squeezing

There are other ways in which vertical mergers can harm competition. The integrated firm might continue to sell raw materials to producer II. If there is strong competition in that market, no adverse effect will result from the vertical merger because producer II will be able to buy the raw materials at a competitive price. However, where competition at the supplier level is weak, the integrated firm might engage in "profit squeezing." This means the integrated firm charges independent producers a high price for raw materials but sells its final product at a relatively low price. Essentially, the integrated firm is using one division to subsidize another division and, in so doing, squeezes the profits of its competitors.[17] If the squeeze is severe, it might force the independent producers out of business. Even if it is a relatively mild squeeze, it might prohibit them from expanding.

Once again, it is important to remember that the practice will not work if the integrated firm faces strong competition in the raw materials market, or if there is relatively free entry into that market. It is also important to note that vertical integration is not really a requirement for the squeeze. Presumably, the high price charged for the raw materials is a profit-maximizing price which is high by virtue of the monopoly power at the supplier segment of the integrated firm. It would not pay the supplier segment to charge a price for raw materials higher than the equilibrium price. Therefore, the high price would probably prevail even if the vertically integrated firm was not trying to squeeze the prices of its competitors. It would prevail even if vertical integration was not involved. Even the fact that the integrated firm sells its final product at a relatively low price should not imply that it does this as a result of the vertical merger. Independent firms can also sell at or close to their marginal cost, and numerous instances of this practice have occurred in our economy. What is happening is that the integrated firm is using the monopoly power that it has at one level of distribution to gain monopoly power at another level of distribution. But this does not alter the fact that the integrated firm, like the independent firm, is losing money or just breaking even at the producer level of distribution. The only difference between the position of the integrated firm and that of the independent firm is that the integrated firm may be able to hold out longer because it receives a source of funds from the sale of raw materials.

Elimination of the Middleman

Another argument against vertical mergers is that the producing segment receives an advantage by being able to purchase its raw materials at cost from its supplying segment. This is a variation of the fallacious "eliminating the middleman" argument. The integrated firm has an investment in the segment which produces raw materials. Unless it is willing to forego a return on that phase of its operation, it must consider the return on investment as a cost and include it in the determination of the price of its product. It is true that its cost does not have to include a monopoly surcharge, and that point was the core of the Spengler argument discussed earlier in this chapter.

Increased Cost of Market Entry

Vertical mergers may increase the difficulty and cost of entry for new firms and hence may increase the monopoly power of existing firms. This occurs in industries where most, if not all competitors are vertically integrated so that they provide their own raw materials and/or have their own dealers. If vertical integration exists on a grand scale, raw materials and dealers may be inaccessible to the nonintegrated firm. Therefore, a new entrant would have to be vertically integrated, and a vertically integrated firm is more expensive to finance than a business limited to one level of distribution.

A Summary

In summary, vertical mergers can be used to increase monopoly power if the merging firms already have monopoly power on at least one level of distribution. If there is not a sufficient number of alternatives to an independent producer, vertical mergers may foreclose raw materials and customers to it. They can also provide a source of funds (existing from monopoly profits at one level of distribution) with which to subsidize the operations at another level of distribution. Finally, if there are a large number of vertically integrated firms in an industry, new entry into the industry may be difficult.

THE POLICY FOR EVALUATING
VERTICAL MERGERS

We have seen that any monopoly power that is developed through vertical mergers depends on already existing monopoly power. Therefore, one plausible antitrust remedy would be to always allow vertical mergers and increase antitrust enforcement vis à vis horizontal monopoly power. This, like the treatment of conscious parallelism, would require mass restructuring of firms, and at the present time our antitrust agencies are not willing to undertake that mission. The mere fact that some instances of vertical integration create monopoly power in our economy is evidence that the government has allowed monopoly power to develop at the various levels of distribution.

Since mass restructuring will probably not be adopted by the Justice Department in the near future, criteria for judging vertical merger cases should be considered. These criteria are not significantly different from those which were introduced in the discussion of horizontal mergers because they are designed to determine whether a vertically integrated firm has monopoly power at at least one level of distribution. They center around the two concepts of market structure and market performance.

Market Structure

Vertical integration cannot foreclose markets or suppliers to competitors if a sufficient number of markets and suppliers remain at each level of distribution after the merger. Nor can a vertically integrated firm earn monopoly profits at one level of distribution if a sufficient number of competitors are in the industry. Therefore, it is important to determine the market share of firms contemplating a vertical merger and/or the concentration ratio in the respective industries. Where firms have a large market share, or where the concentration ratio is high in their industry, there is a possibility that vertical mergers will be harmful to the consuming public. Kaysen and Turner would disallow any vertical merger in which a firm has 20 per cent of the market at any one level of distribution.[18] The Department of Justice Guidelines recommend that a vertical merger be prosecuted if a firm having 10 per cent of the market at any one level of distribution purchases a firm having 6 per cent or more of the market at another level. The Guidelines add that the existence of economies of scale will be accepted as a defense only under unusual circumstances.[19]

Market Performance

While the appraisal of market structure is one important criterion in judging vertical mergers, market performance is an equally important consideration. There are several ways in which vertical mergers might increase market performance: (1) By unifying successive levels of distribution, they may reduce costs. Vertical mergers may insure a more steady supply of raw materials which, in turn, can reduce costs. Also, by placing the various stages under one management, vertical integration can sometimes improve firms' ability to produce optimum quantities. For example, if dealers and a manufacturer are under the same management, the manufacturer can receive quick information feedback from his dealers concerning expected demand for the product and adjust his output accordingly. Economies might also occur if the vertically integrated firm puts a series of successive production processes under the same roof. Professor Bain cited the example of putting the making of pig iron, the conversion of iron into steel, and the shaping of the steel into semifinished products all in one plant. This resulted in a considerable saving in the fuel requirement for heating the iron and steel.[20] No doubt, vertical integration can cause cost savings but there is far less reason to expect them to result from vertical integration as compared to horizontal integration.

There are other performance criteria that should be considered by a court in judging a vertical merger case. (2) If the acquired firm faces bankruptcy, the merger could salvage economic resources. (3) Ease of entry into the industry is a consideration, although most vertical integration tends to retard entry. (4) Vertical mergers in dynamic industries can be expected to have less effect on monopoly power than those which occur in industries where the firms do not wish to compete with one another.

MAJOR CASES

By analyzing two important antitrust cases we can get a limited view of the courts' attitude toward mergers prosecuted under the provisions of the Sherman Act. We will find that the courts use similar criteria to evaluate both horizontal and vertical mergers. The court rulings indicate that they have used some of the economic concepts discussed earlier in this chapter.

Horizontal and vertical merger cases are also considered in Chapter XIV dealing with Clayton Act cases. Because most horizontal and vertical mergers are prosecuted under the Clayton Act today, Sherman Act cases are important only for historical perspective. Therefore we will consider only two such cases: *Yellow Cab* and *Columbia Steel*.

YELLOW CAB COMPANY

In *United States* v. *Yellow Cab Co.*, the defendants were charged with creating a vertical merger in restraint of trade.[21] It is an important case because it was one of the first to involve vertical mergers. Morris Markin, the president of the Checker Cab Manufacturing Company, gained control of the three largest taxicab companies in Chicago. Additionally, he had acquired cab companies in New York City, Pittsburgh, and Minneapolis. Markin required that his companies purchase Checker cabs, which resulted in the foreclosure of 86 per cent of the Chicago cab market to other automobile manufacturing, 15 per cent of the New York City market, 100 per cent of the Pittsburgh market, and 58 per cent of the

Minneapolis market. Around 5,000 automobiles were sold to these cab companies each year. The Court did not attempt to determine the share of the taxi market nor the share of the overall automobile market foreclosed by Checker. No doubt, 5,000 cars would be an insignificant percentage of the total number of automobiles sold in the country. Instead, the Court found that the absolute number of 5,000 automobiles was sufficient evidence that competition had been restrained. It reasoned that: "Its relative position in the field of cab production has no necessary relation to the ability of the appellees to conspire to monopolize or restrain, in violation of the Act, an appreciable segment of interstate cab sales. . . . By excluding all cab manufacturers other than CCM [Checker] from that part of the market represented by the cab operating companies under their control, the appellees effectively limit the outlets through which cabs may be sold in interstate commerce."[22] Surely the definition of "market share" in terms of the absolute number of units sold leaves much to be desired. The decision implied that any vertical merger which forecloses any market, no matter how insignificant, is illegal if there are no offsetting advantages resulting from the merger.

COLUMBIA STEEL COMPANY

United States v. *Columbia Steel Company* involved both a horizontal and vertical merger.[23] It overturned the *Yellow Cab* decision. Columbia Steel, a division of U.S. Steel, operated in the western part of the United States where it produced rolled steel and also fabricated steel. U.S. Steel was considering the purchase of Consolidated Steel Corporation, a fabrication company which bought rolled steel from suppliers and processed it. Thus, the proposed consolidation involved both a vertical merger (because Consolidated could take Columbia's rolled steel and fabricate it) and a horizontal merger (because Consolidated competed with Columbia in the fabrication of steel).

The government's attack against the vertical aspects of the merger was based on the fear that the purchase of Consolidated would foreclose a market to other producers of rolled steel. If the nation was defined as the relevant geographical market, Consolidated purchased 1/2 of one per cent of the rolled steel in the country. If the market was defined to include only the western market (composed of eleven states), it purchased 3 per cent of the rolled steel. Rolled steel comes in different forms, and Consolidated used "plates" and "shapes." If the market is narrowed to include just these two types of rolled steel, Consolidated purchased 13 per cent of the plates and shapes in the western market. The Court decided that all steel manufacturers were capable of producing plates and shapes, therefore it was not necessary to define the market that narrowly. It believed that the western market was the relevant one and hence found that the merger could foreclose three per cent of the market to other producers of rolled steel.

The government's attack relied heavily on the Court's analysis in the *Yellow Cab* decision. It argued that the foreclosure of Consolidated to other steel manufacturers was an illegal restraint of trade because the government claimed that the *Yellow Cab* decision made vertical mergers illegal *per se* when any appreciable market is foreclosed. Addressing itself to this argument, the Supreme Court said that vertical mergers were illegal when an unreasonable restraint was involved, but that they were not illegal *per se*. Moreover, it found that the foreclosure of three per cent of the market was insignificant. Nor could the Court find any evidence that U.S. Steel intended to create monopoly power through the merger. In short, the vertical aspects of the merger were allowed by the Court.

Concerning the horizontal aspects of the merger, the Court made what it called the "doubtful assumption" that the two firms would have 24 per cent of the western market in the sale of fabricated steel. This market share is a little misleading because the two firms made different types of structural steel products in their fabrication plants. In deciding the legality of the merger, the Court did not "think the dollar volume was in itself of compelling significance; we look rather to the percentage of business controlled, the strength of the remaining competition, whether the action springs from business requirements or purpose to monopolize, the probable development of the industry, consumer demands and other characteristics of the market."[24] On the basis of this reasoning they allowed the merger. If the figure is correct, 24 per cent of the market is a significant share. But it did not appear to be significant to the Court.

Justice William O. Douglas was one of four judges who dissented in the case. He would have disallowed the merger because of the dollar volume of business involved. Douglas argued that the effect of the acquisition was "for control of a market for which United States Steel has in the past had to compete but which it no longer wants left to the uncertainties that competition in the west may engender."[25] Using the quantitative substantiality test he found that Consolidated purchased five million dollars worth of rolled steel a year, and he did not consider that dollar value to be insignificant. Nor did he consider the foreclosure of three per cent of the market insignificant. As we have said in prior chapters, there is some doubt that the mere dollar value of purchases is a good test of monopolization, but Justice Douglas did have a point. U.S. Steel was large and no doubt it had monopoly power. Should that power be allowed to increase through a merger—no matter how small the increase was? Douglas' decision foreshadowed the attitude adopted by the courts that have heard more recent cases under the Clayton Act.

SUMMARY

Based on our limited analysis of horizontal and vertical merger cases under the provisions of the Sherman Act, a few conclusions can be drawn. First, the courts use a rule of reason. Second, the courts determine whether the firms have acquired monopoly power. This may be done with a share-of-the-market test. Just because firms have a large share of the market does not imply that they are guilty of monopolization. For example, the Supreme Court did not think that control of 24 per cent of the market in the sale of fabricated steel amounted to monopolization.

Largely as a result of the lenient interpretation given to vertical as well as horizontal mergers in *Columbia Steel*, Congress amended Section 7 of the Clayton Act to strengthen the laws against merger.

NOTES TO CHAPTER XIII

[1]Ralph L. Nelson, *Merger Movements in American Industry, 1895-1956* (New York: National Bureau of Economic Research, 1959), pp. 28—29.
[2]Jesse W. Markham, "Survey of the Evidence and Findings on Mergers," in the National Bureau of Economic Research Conference Report, *Business Concentration and Price Policy* (New York: National Bureau of Economic Research, 1955), pp. 168-69. Quoted in F. M. Scherer, *Industrial Market Structure and Economic Performance* (Chicago: Rand McNally and Company, 1970), p. 106.
[3]Scherer, p. 107.
[4]Fritz Machlup, *The Political Economy of Monopoly: Business, Labor and Government Policies* (Baltimore: The Johns Hopkins Press, 1952), p. 105.
[5]Another name for a concentration curve is a Lorenz Curve.
[6]Carl Kaysen and Donald F. Turner, *Antitrust Policy* (Cambridge: Harvard University Press, 1959), p. 133.
[7]George J. Stigler, "Mergers and Preventive Antitrust Policy," *University of Pennsylvania Law Review*, CIV (November, 1955), 178-84.
[8]Press Release Accompanying U.S. Department of Justice, *Merger Guidelines* (May 30, 1968), paragraphs 3-8.
[9]Thomas Nixon Carver, *Essays in Social Justice* (Cambridge: Harvard University Press, 1915), p. 332. Quoted in Walter Adams, "Is Bigness a Crime?" *Land Economics*, XXVII (November, 1951), 291.
[10]John K. Galbraith, *American Capitalism: The Concept of Countervailing Power* (Boston: Houghton Mifflin, 1956).

[11]G. E. Hale and Rosemary D. Hale, *Market Power, Size and Shape Under the Sherman Act* (Boston: Little, Brown and Company, 1958), p. 74.

[12]Joe S. Bain, *Barriers to New Competition: Their Character and Consequences in Manufacturing Industries* (Cambridge, Mass.: Harvard University Press, 1956), pp. 78, 80, and 84. Quoted in William N. Leonard, *Business Size, Market Power and Public Policy* (New York: Thomas Y. Crowell Company, 1969), pp. 28-29.

[13]Betty Bock and Jack Farkas, *Concentration and Productivity: Some Preliminary Problems and Findings* (Washington: National Industrial Conference Board, Inc., 1969), p. 5.

[14]Oliver E. Williamson, "Economies as an Antitrust Defense: The Welfare Trade-Offs," *American Economic Review*, LVII (March, 1968), 18-35.

[15]Dead weight loss is the net loss to society of consumer's surplus (the loss to the consumer minus the gain to the producer) resulting from a price increase. The area ABC does not take into account any gains resulting from the cost reduction.

[16]Williamson, p. 23.

[17]This argument is also levied against conglomerate mergers and is considered in *Chapter XIV*.

[18]Kaysen and Turner, p. 133.

[19]Press Release Accompanying U.S. Department of Justice, *Merger Guidelines* (May 30, 1968), paragraphs 3-8.

[20]Joe S. Bain, *Industrial Organization* (New York: John Wiley & Sons, 1968), p. 177.

[21]67 S. Ct. 1560 (1947).

[22]67 S. Ct. 1560, 1565 (1947).

[23]68 S. Ct. 1107 (1948).

[24]68 S. Ct. 1107, 1124 (1948).

[25]68 S. Ct. 1107, 1129 (1948).

MERGERS AFTER 1950 UNDER THE CLAYTON ACT

CHAPTER XIV

Here we study the legal attitude toward horizontal and vertical mergers under the provisions of Section 7 of the Clayton Act. Moreover we analyze the economics and law of conglomerate mergers.

INTRODUCTION

In Chapter XIII we discussed mergers prosecuted under the provisions of the Sherman Act. Although Section 7 of the Clayton Act also had prohibitions against unlawful mergers, most cases from 1890 to 1950 were prosecuted under the Sherman Act. Because the Clayton Act only applied to acquisitions of stock and not physical assets and because most antitrust authorities thought that it was inapplicable to vertical mergers, it was ineffective until it was amended in 1950.

In 1950, the Celler-Kefauver Act amended Section 7. Since that year, this provision has become the major vehicle used by antitrust authorities to attack mergers. Before considering the application of Section 7 to merger cases, it is important to clarify the purpose of the revised statute. In *Brown Shoe*, a case that will be considered below, the Supreme Court outlined its interpretation of the revised Section 7.[1] According to the Supreme Court, the legislation was designed to:

1. Retard the development of economic concentration;
2. Protect small businesses;
3. Apply to the acquisition of assets as well as the acquisition of stock;
4. Apply the Clayton Act to vertical and conglomerate mergers as well as to horizontal mergers;
5. Prohibit monopoly power in its incipiency;
6. Use more stringent tests than were used under Sections 1 and 2 of the Sherman Act;
7. Allow mergers which increased efficiency as long as they do not increase monopoly power;
8. Leave the interpretation of the word "substantially" up to the courts;

9. Allow probability of anticompetitive effects, not certainty, to be sufficient in declaring a merger illegal.

These nine points represent a fair reading of Congress' intentions when it formulated the revised Section 7. Of course most of these provisions are not enumerated in Section 7 itself.

The economic validity of some of the provisions have been questioned by many economists. Why protect small businessmen when their absence does not impede competition? What is wrong with concentration if it has no anticompetitive effects? How do you define "incipiency"? We will analyze these questions within the context of the antitrust cases that will be presented. Some economists argue that the courts have improperly answered the questions. However, in all fairness to the courts, it is important to remember at the offset that when the courts make a decision which violates principles of economic theory, economists should not be too quick to attack them. Given the mandate of Congress, the courts do not have absolute latitude in formulating antitrust policy. Some of the economists' attacks on court decisions should be redirected toward Congress. Of course, the courts do have some latitude in structuring the various tests to determine whether firms "substantially lessen competition" under the provisions of the Clayton Act.

In the first part of this chapter, court cases involving horizontal and vertical mergers under Section 7 will be presented. The economics of these arrangements were presented in Chapter XIII.

MAJOR CASES

DU PONT-GENERAL MOTORS

U.S. v. *E. I. du Pont de Nemours & Co.* was a vertical merger case decided by the Supreme Court in 1957.[2] Between 1917 and 1919, du Pont acquired 23 per cent of General Motors' stock. Because du Pont supplied automotive finishes and fabrics to General Motors, the government contended that du Pont foreclosed a substantial share of the market to competitors. Several issues make this an interesting case. First, the government was attempting to disallow a merger that had taken place forty years prior to the hearing. Second, this was the first merger case heard under Section 7 of the Clayton Act since 1930. Third, it was the first vertical merger case ever heard under the provisions of Section 7, because the F.T.C. had thought that this section was not applicable to vertical mergers. Finally, although this case was heard under the old Section 7 of the Clayton Act (because the case was initiated prior to 1950), the Supreme Court's decision foreshadowed its attitude toward the interpretation of new Section 7.

After deciding that the old Section 7 was applicable to vertical acquisitions, the Court set about determining the relevant market for finishes and fabrics. Du Pont contended that its finish sales to G.M. constituted only 3.5 per cent of all sales of finishes for industrial uses, and that its fabric sales to G.M. constituted only 1.6 per cent of the total market for the type of fabric used in the automobile industry. The Court considered finishes and fabrics used in automobiles to be distinct products. Given this narrow definition, the Court found that du Pont supplied 67 per cent of G.M.'s finishes in 1946 and 68 per cent in 1947. Moreover, it supplied 52.3 per cent of the fabrics that G.M. used in 1946 and 52.3 per cent of those used in 1947. Extending its analysis to the whole automobile industry, the Court concluded that du Pont supplied almost one-half of the automotive finishes and fabrics market.

To determine whether the acquisition substantially lessened competition, the Court simply observed that du Pont had a substantial share of the relevant market. And although it recognized that "considerations of price, quality and service were not overlooked by either du Pont or General Motors" it thought that "du Pont purposely employed its stock to pry open the General Motors market. . . ."[3] The Court did not determine the competitive harm to other finish and fabric suppliers or the availability of the G.M. market to them. As a result, its evaluation was performed in a manner similar to the method it had used to evaluate exclusive dealing cases. That is, it used a modified quantitative substantiality test, where size of G.M. plus share of the market supplied by du Pont constituted evidence of competitive harm. The Court also established what is called the "Backward-Sweep Doctrine" where mergers of the past can be prosecuted today by the courts if they have anticompetitive effects today. Du Pont purchased G.M. stock between 1917 and 1919, and the Court found that the merger had anticompetitive effects in 1957. It ordered du Pont to divest itself of its G.M. stock.

BROWN SHOE

Brown Shoe[4] was the first important merger case involving the new Section 7 of the Clayton Act. In fact it is one of the most important decisions in the history of antitrust because it clearly established the criteria used under the new provisions of the Clayton Act. Brown Shoe Co., the third largest shoe company by dollar volume, merged with Kinney Shoe Co., the eighth largest shoe company by dollar volume. The two firms were horizontally and vertically related because each firm produced shoes and owned retail shoe stores.

The Court first defined the relevant product market as men's, women's, and children's shoes. For the vertical aspects of the case, it defined the geographical market as the nation. For the horizontal aspects of the case (merger of retail outlets), it defined the relevant geographic market as cities with a population exceeding 10,000 persons where both firms competed. The Court was also careful to establish a very important point of law: If competition was harmful in any "significant market" the merger could be outlawed. In other words, if the merger monopolized sales in children's shoes but not in men's and women's shoes, that was enough to declare it illegal. Alternatively, if it monopolized sales in Chicago but in no other cities, that was enough to declare it illegal.[5] Of course, if it found a monopoly in any one market, the Court's remedy need not be total divestiture but simply divestiture of the assets in the market where monopoly power was created.

The vertical aspects of the merger were first considered by the Court. After defining the relevant market, it found that Brown owned 470 shoe outlets or 2.1 per cent of the shoe stores in the country. Kinney owned more than 350 stores, constituting 1.6 per cent of the market. The government feared that Brown would force its shoes into Kinney's outlets and foreclose a market to competitors. It was the foreclosure of 1.6 per cent of the market that the government was worried about.

The Court reasoned that the foreclosure involved was less than that which would constitute a violation of the Sherman Act but more than insignificant. Since it reasoned that the percentage of the market foreclosed could not be decisive in this particular case, it thought it appropriate to undertake an examination of "various economic and historical factors." The following reasoning led the Court to declare the vertical aspects of the merger illegal:

1. The Court applied the quantitative substantiality test, noting that Brown was the fourth largest manufacturer in the shoe industry with large dollar volume of sales;
2. Vertical mergers were analogous to tying arrangements because Brown could force its shoes into Kinney's outlets;
3. The Court detected a trend toward vertical integration in the shoe industry and it thought that if this continued, the industry would eventually become concentrated. "Congress was

desirous of preventing the formation of further oligopolies with their attendant adverse effects upon local control of industry and upon small business."[6] It is important to emphasize that the Court did not contend that the industry was oligopolistic at the time of its hearing. It contended that if firms are allowed to continue to merge it may become oligopolistic.

The government attacked the horizontal aspects of the merger at the retail level, not at the manufacturing level. The Court accepted the relevant geographic markets as "those cities with a·population exceeding 10,000 and those metropolitan areas in which both Brown and Kinney retailed shoes through their own outlets." Because the markets involved were numerous, the district court used samples to determine the effects of the merger on competition, and the Supreme Court accepted this approach. The national share of the market of the two producers was only five per cent. However, in thirty-two cities, the share of the market for women's shoes exceeded 20 per cent and in six cities, the share of the market for children's shoes exceeded 40 per cent. In Dodge City, Kansas, the share of the market for women's shoes was over 57 per cent and for children's shoes, over 40 per cent. While these shares are impressive, the Court returned to the five per cent figure in formulating its decision. On the basis of the five per cent share it disallowed the merger because, if the trend toward merger continued, monopoly power would eventually develop.

> If a merger achieving 5 per cent control were now approved, we might be required to approve further merger efforts by Brown's competitors seeking similar market shares. The oligopoly Congress sought to avoid would then be furthered and it would be difficult to dissolve the combinations previously approved.[7]

The fact that the merged company might be more efficient and drive small, less efficient businessmen out of business played a part in the Court's decision. While it contended that the preservation of competition, not competitors was the objective of the act, it stated that

> ... we cannot fail to recognize Congress' desire to promote competition through the protection of viable, small, locally owned business. Congress appreciated that occasional higher costs and prices might result from the maintenance of fragmented industries and markets. It resolved these competing considerations in favor of decentralization. We must give effect to that decision.[8]

This is one of the most interesting value judgments made throughout the development of antitrust precedent. The small businessman should be preserved even if the consumer has to pay for it. Of course, the judgment is really that of Congress, not that of the Supreme Court.

This decision represents a major change in the Court's attitude toward horizontal and vertical mergers: Merging firms with small market shares found their merger illegal; protection of the small businessman was established as a goal of antitrust policy; trends toward market concentration were to be stopped at the very beginning; quantitative substantiality was indirectly applied to merger cases. Certainly the Court had moved away from determining whether a particular merger affected competition adversely and into the realm of projecting trends and determining their effect on the social and economic structure of the United States.

The approach brought cries from many economists in the form of articles attacking the economics of the decision.[9] The following are typical of the arguments levied against the Court's decision:

1. Even if each firm in the market obtained 5 per cent of the total market, oligopoly would not exist;
2. The argument that "if you allow Brown's merger, eventually you will have an oligopoly" is analogous to saying that since the baby grew one foot this year it will eventually be 20 feet tall;
3. The Court was over zealous in its evaluation of foreclosure. Even if Brown foreclosed Kinney's total market, it would gain only one per cent of the market;
4. The Court failed to give proper attention to economies resulting from the merger. One of the reasons Kinney wanted the mergers was to buy shoes at a lower price;
5. The economies argument and the foreclosure argument used by the courts were in conflict. According to the Court, the merger was both bad because Brown might "force" Kinney and because Kinney wanted to be "forced."[10]

These arguments are all sound. It is probably true that the Court was over zealous in finding that Brown's merger created monopoly power. However, the Court's point was that the development of oligopolistic tendencies had to be stopped somewhere. The real difference between the arguments posed by the critics of the decision and the arguments posed by the Court is the issue of determining the point where the trend is to be stopped. Should it be stopped when each firm in an industry has five per cent of the market? Ten per cent? Precisely, what part should the existence of merger economies play in the answer to those questions? The line between competition and oligopoly is a very thin one. As we said in Chapter XIII, competition does not necessarily require the existence of a large number of competitors. It requires only that a sufficient number of firms exist. But the determination of what is sufficient would be difficult for the best economist and probably impossible for the Court. It is no surprise that economists are able to cry, "You stopped the merger movement too early. There are more economies to be reaped without any additional cost to competition!" It also would be no surprise if courts asked economists where to stop. The *Columbia Steel* decision was probably too lenient and the *Brown Shoe* decision too harsh. Somehow the acreage in between the two decisions has to be cultivated.

PHILADELPHIA NATIONAL BANK

In *U.S.* v. *The Philadelphia National Bank et al.*, the Supreme Court reiterated its intent to reduce the national trend toward market concentration.[11] Philadelphia National Bank was the second largest bank in the Philadelphia metropolitan area and the twenty-first largest bank in the nation. It wanted to merge with the Girard Trust Corn Exchange Bank, the third largest bank in the metropolitan area. Together the two banks would have been the largest in the four county metropolitan area with 36 per cent of the area banks' total assets, 36 per cent of the deposits, and 34 per cent of the net loans. Both banks had become rather large through mergers. As a result of this as well as the mergers of other banks, the number of banks in the four county area had been reduced from 108 in 1947 to 42 at the time of the hearing. Since 1950, PNB had acquired nine banks and Girard had acquired six.

The district court had allowed the merger. It reasoned that the merger had no anticompetitive effects, even given the fact that the four county Philadelphia metropolitan area was the relevant geographic market. Moreover, the district court did not believe the metropolitan area was the relevant market. It agreed with the defense that the market was the northeastern United States because in making large loans, banks competed throughout this area.

The Supreme Court thought that the relevant geographic market was the Philadelphia metropolitan area. It observed that large borrowers and depositors may find it practical to perform their banking business outside of the area. But very small customers probably use banks in their immediate neighborhood and medium-sized customers fall somewhere in between. The Court reasoned that the relevant geographic market should not be so constrained that it centers on local neighborhoods or so broad that it includes large geographical areas which service only the largest customers. Instead, a compromise should be reached, and the Court's compromise was the four county metropolitan area of Philadelphia. The Court agreed with the district court that the relevant product market was "commercial banking." It distinguished the loans made by commercial banks from those offered by small loan organizations by noting that these organizations generally charge a higher interest rate. It separated the savings deposit services offered by commercial banks from those offered by various other savings outlets by noting that some customers appear to have a "settled customer preference" for deposits in commercial banks.

Having defined the relevant geographic area and product market, the Court set about determining whether the effect of the merger "may be substantially to lessen competition in any line of commerce in any section of the country."[12] It based its decision on the share of the market which was held by the merged firms. Choosing 30 per cent as the benchmark, the Court stated that, "Without attempting to specify the smallest market share which would still be considered to threaten undue concentration, we are clear that 30 per cent presents that threat."[13] In justifying its simple share-of-the-market test, the Court explained that litigation using detailed economic studies would place businessmen contemplating mergers in a position where they could not determine, with any reasonable degree of certainty, the legality of their merger. Additionally, the Court thought that Congress did not wish it to pursue a "too-broad economic investigation."[14] Finally, it reasoned that Congress wished the Clayton Act to retard concentration, and market share was a good test of concentration.

> We think that a merger which produces a firm controlling an undue percentage share of the relevant market and results in a significant increase in the concentration of firms in that market is so inherently likely to lessen competition substantially that it must be enjoined in the absence of evidence clearly showing that the merger is not likely to have such anticompetitive effects.[15]

PNB presented a number of considerations to justify its merger and negate the share-of-the-market test. It had argued that the merger was made so that it could follow its customers to the suburbs and retain their business. The Court observed that this could be done by opening new branches; mergers were not necessary. The bank also argued that the merger would aid it in competing with large out-of-state banks. The Court said that anticompetitive effects in one market cannot be justified by competitive effects in another market. The Court was probably aware of the fact that the weighing of the positive and negative effects would be a difficult task. Finally, PNB argued that having a larger bank in Philadelphia would bring business to the area and stimulate economic development. The Court said that it was beyond its competence to evaluate the effects of the merger on the development of the metropolitan area. Moreover, it thought that Congress intended to outlaw mergers which decreased competition even when they had some positive effects.

VON'S GROCERY

The Supreme Court decided *U.S.* v. *Von's Grocery Co.* almost solely on the fact that there had been a move toward concentration in the grocery industry.[16] It looked only lightly at the share-of-the-market test that had been used in *Philadelphia National Bank* and considered other economic considerations to be irrelevant. The case involved a horizontal merger between Von's Grocery and Shopping Bag Food Stores. Together, their sales represented 7.5 per cent of the total retail value of groceries sold in the Los Angeles area. Both stores had grown dramatically in the years prior to the case, but not by acquisition. From 1948 to 1958, the number of Von's stores almost doubled. Shopping Bag's sales increased sevenfold, and its share of the market tripled.

The district court allowed the merger because it did not think that there was a reasonable possibility that the merger substantially lessened competition. The Supreme Court reversed the decision. The Court was particularly impressed with the fact that the number of single grocery stores had dropped from 5,365 in 1950 to 3,818 in 1962, while the number of chain stores increased from 96 to 150. Given the declining number of small grocers in Los Angeles and the fact that Von's and Shopping Bag were "two of the most successful and largest companies in the area" the Court said, "the facts in this case present exactly the threatening trend toward concentration which Congress wanted to halt."[17] The Court decided that a merger violates Section 7 when "it takes place in a market characterized by a long and continuous trend toward fewer and fewer owner-competitors which is exactly the sort of trend which Congress with power to do so, declared must be arrested."[18] The fact that the merged company was competitive after the merger did not impress the Court. "Section VII requires not merely an appraisal of the immediate impact of the merger upon competition, but a prediction of its impact upon competitive conditions in the future."[19] Given this decision, it appears that if precedent is followed, any merger between leading firms will be declared illegal if the industry is becoming concentrated. This is true even when the industry is far from reaching a concentrated state.

Justice Stewart wrote a detailed dissenting opinion. His attack questioned the Court's following of precedent, its disallowing a merger which did not create monopoly power, its protection of small business, and its facts on concentration in the Los Angeles grocery market. Stewart observed that the test used in *Von's* differed significantly from the one used in *Philadelphia National Bank*. In fact, "The sole consistency that I can find is that in litigation under Section VII, the Government always wins."[20] Even though both decisions were based somewhat on a share-of-the-market test, he thought that Von's merger which increased the market share of the two largest firms by 1.1 per cent and the market share of the six largest firms by 6.6 per cent was not an "undue percentage" of the market, while Philadelphia National Bank's share could be construed as "inherently suspect." Stewart denied the Court's logic that the degree of competition is invariably proportional to the number of competitors in an industry, and claimed that the Court's decision was a "startling *per se* rule."[21] And he contended that "the Court's opinion is hardly more than a requiem for the so-called 'Mom and Pop' grocery stores . . . that are now economically and technologically obsolete in many parts of this country."[22]

Even assuming that the Court's test of concentration was appropriate, Stewart did not find an increase in concentration in the industry. While it is true that between 1948 and 1958, the combined shares of the top 20 firms increased from 44 per cent to 57 per cent, seven of the top twenty were not even in business in 1948. Given this rapid turnover, concentration was in different hands. And replying to the Court's contention that the small businessman was dying in the industry, he agreed that their numbers were decreasing, but not one of the firms was lost through merger activity. Replying to the market share held by the two firms, he observed that Von's stores were predominantly located in the southern and western portions of Los Angeles, and the Shopping Bag stores were located in the northern and eastern portions. Therefore, in many segments of town, they did not even compete. Summing up his argument, Stewart stated:

> The irony of this case is that the Court invokes its sweeping new construction of Section VII to the detriment of a merger between two relatively successful, local, largely family-owned concerns each of which had less than 5 percent of the local market and neither of which had any prior history of growth by acquisition. In a sense, the defendants are being punished for the sin of aggressive competition.[23]

Whether or not the Court meant to declare horizontal mergers illegal *per se* is unknown. However, if this decision is read literally and the precedent established is followed, merging companies charged under Section 7 of the Clayton Act will be hard put to defend their activity. Through the three cases we have seen, the Courts have gradually tightened the noose around merging firms' necks. In *Brown*, the Court largely relied on a share-of-the-market test, but observed that it should also consider other economic considerations. In *Philadelphia National Bank*, the Court relied almost solely on a share-of-the-market test. However, this was understandable because Philadelphia National Bank's market share would have been large after the merger. In *Von's*, it relied on the trend of concentration in the industry and even that was not analyzed in any detail. The Court said, in effect, that a merger might not substantially reduce competition, but it could still be found to be in violation of the Clayton Act. Instead of finding the "fertile ground" between the *Brown* decision and the *Columbia Steel* decision, the Court applied an even more stringent test than it used in deciding *Brown*.

CONGLOMERATE MERGERS

Technically speaking, a conglomerate merger brings together two or more firms which previously were neither horizontally nor vertically related. Conglomerates have been divided into three subcategories by the Federal Trade Commission.

1. Market Extension Conglomerates: the merging of two or more firms which produce the same products but which have sold them in different geographical areas.
2. Product Extension Conglomerates: the merging of two or

more firms which, although they do not produce identical products, produce products which are somehow related to existing distribution channels or production processes. The merging of a razor blade company and a shaving cream producer is a good example because similar marketing channels are used for the two products.

3. Pure Conglomerates: the merging of two or more firms which produce and sell completely unrelated products.

Given the first two categories, the reader will realize that the distinction between conglomerate, horizontal, and vertical mergers is not clear-cut. These three types of mergers can be thought of as a continuum with blurred points of distinction. Does the merger of a men's shoe company with a women's shoe company constitute a horizontal or conglomerate merger? How about the merger between a meatpacking house and a motel chain? Obviously the answer to the first question depends on the degree to which production and marketing channels can be used by the two shoe companies. The answer to the second question depends on the degree to which meat is an input into the operation of restaurants in the motel chain. The analysis of any merger case might have to begin with a determination of what types of mergers are involved, and this determination may not be an easy matter.

THE PREVALENCE OF CONGLOMERATE MERGERS

Measured in terms of percentage of total assets acquired through merger activity as well as sheer numbers, conglomerate merger activity has been significant over the past twenty years. This is demonstrated in *Table I*. Of all assets acquired through merger activity in the period from 1967 to 1968, 85 per cent were acquired through conglomerate mergers. Additionally, both the absolute number of mergers and the percentage of merger assets acquired through conglomerate mergers have steadily risen. Given this phenomenal growth pattern, it is important to ask why conglomerate mergers have been so prevalent. The following reasons explain their popularity.

(1) Firms may acquire nonrelated companies to seek higher profits. One of the basic tenets of microeconomic theory is that firms enter markets which promise high profits. In considering investment opportunities many firms will consider not only alternatives in their own company and industry but also alternatives in other industries. Where other industries promise higher-than-normal profits, the firms may acquire an existing firm in the high-profit industry.

TABLE I

CONGLOMERATE MERGERS 1951–1968

	1951–54	1955–58	1959–62	1963–66	1967–68
Number of Conglomerate Mergers	41	120	172	257	301
% of Merger Assets Acquired Through Conglomerate Mergers	52	46	57	72	85

Sources: U.S. House of Representatives, Committee on the Judiciary, Antitrust Subcommittee, Staff Report, *The Celler-Kefauver Act: Sixteen Years of Enforcement* (Washington: U.S. Government Printing Office, 1967), and U.S. Federal Trade Commission, Statistical Report, *Current Trends in Merger Activity* (Washington: U.S. Government Printing Office, March 1969), reported in F.M. Scherer, *Industrial Market Structure and Economic Performance* (Chicago: Rand McNally & Company, 1970), p. 110.

(2) The mergers may be explained by the rather severe antitrust treatment of horizontal and vertical mergers under the revised Section 7 of the Clayton Act. Decisions such as *Brown*, *Philadelphia National Bank*, and *Von's Grocery* brought fear that almost any horizontal or vertical merger would be disallowed by the courts and the Federal Trade Commission. Many firms desiring growth through acquisition concluded that conglomerate mergers were safer under the law.

(3) Two financial aspects of conglomerate mergers have prompted the merger movement. First, conglomerate mergers receive some special tax concessions which make them more desirable than some horizontal and vertical mergers. The tax advantages are received by the sellers, but this undoubtedly affects the price sellers are willing to accept for their company as well as their willingness to sell. Joel Dean, Emeritus Professor of Business Economics at Columbia University, explained this point.

> Tax laws supplied incentives to merger. By making possible "tax-free" mergers, by causing difficult estate-tax liquidity problems for the owners of hard-to-market stock, by creating an impelling superior estate-tax situation should one sell out to a conglomerate when his estate was mostly in the form of closely-held nonmarketable stock—the tax laws created willing sellers.[24]

Since Professor Dean wrote, the tax laws have been amended to reduce many exemptions but some still exist. Second, various means of financial reporting and accounting practices have distorted the profit picture of companies and prompted mergers which otherwise might not have taken place. Donald F. Turner explained this point in hearing before the Senate Subcommittee on Antitrust and Monopoly.

> Inadequate financial reporting by multiproduct corporations, . . . has made it extremely difficult for investors to evaluate accurately the economic performance of companies before and after merger, and to evaluate the financial terms of proposed merger bargains, and in these ways has contributed to stock market distortions that may well have facilitated a good many mergers that might not otherwise have taken place.[25]

Just recently, line of business reporting requirements have begun to make inroads into this "advantage."

(4) There are a number of reasons to suspect that conglomerate mergers create economies. These can reduce the cost of operating the divisions in the conglomerate and possibly reduce product prices. While most of the economies are not the same as the economies of scale encountered in horizontal and vertical mergers, they do result from a firm's being large.

(a) Conglomerates of large size may be able to acquire capital at a lower cost than smaller firms. It may be acquired internally or at a low rate of interest from outside the company.

(b) Personnel may be better allocated within a conglomerate. Staff personnel may be able to service all divisions in a more efficient manner than could separate staff personnel for each division. Additionally, employees can be shifted to a wide number of alternative uses and because of this, can be better utilized as compared to a situation where they have fewer alternative uses.

(c) Capital, like personnel, can be utilized in a wide number of alternative uses.

(d) Where market extension or product extension conglomerates are involved, economies of scale may result. Common production facilities and common distribution channels can be utilized just as they would be through a horizontal or vertical merger.

(e) Given the fact that truly creative entrepreneurs are limited in number, the placing of several divisions under such an entrepreneur may better utilize his talents, provided that the development of the conglomerate does not overextend the entrepreneur's ability.

Have conglomerate mergers brought about additional efficiency? A Federal Trade Commission staff report concluded that while not all conglomerate mergers increased efficiency, 60 per cent of those studied did bring about additional efficiency.[26] In his study of sixty multi-industry firms, Professor J. Fred Weston found that the earnings performance of the conglomerates was "not significantly different from all manufacturing firms. [But] Given the unfavorable earnings potentials in the industries from which many of the 'conglomerates' started as a base, their performance suggests that economies have been achieved."[27]

Certainly not everyone believes the conglomerates induce significant economies. Some even contend that diseconomies result from the mergers. John M. Blair, former Chief Economist for the Senate Subcommittee on Antitrust and Monopoly observed that "the mere fact that the product mix is disparate means that it tends to be noneconomic."[28] Nor did he think that the argument that conglomerates use management more efficiently was a viable one.

> Plausible but unproved is the new doctrine of "free-form
> management," which holds that managerial ability, having
> achieved the status of a profession, is readily transferable
> across industry lines. The analogy ignores the high degree
> of specialization that has developed within most profes-
> sions and the difficulty of applying to other fields ability
> and knowledge which are the products of years of experi-
> ence in a particular speciality. The unimpressive profit
> showings of conglomerates constitute persuasive evidence
> that except for certain specialized services, managerial
> skills are in fact not transferable.[29]

Blair concluded that to the extent that management skills could not be transferred and to the extent that products were unrelated, the opportunities for diseconomies would be enhanced.

Ronald H. Coase, writing for the Stigler Task Force on Productivity and Competition, probably best summarized the whole efficiency argument. He rightly pointed to the fact that economies will result from some conglomerate mergers and not from others. Moreover, it is impossible to determine through court proceedings which mergers will be efficient and which will not.[30] But unless the conglomerate merger is one which decreases competition, the issue is a moot one. We should not disallow mergers simply because they do not increase efficiency.

(5) Another reason firms may wish to form conglomerate companies is to reduce risk. By removing some of its eggs from one basket and placing them in another, the firm will no longer be as

susceptible to market fluctuations, and its profitability becomes more stable. It is easy to hypothesize, for example, that Philip Morris purchased a razor blade company at the time of the government's large scale attack on the consumption of cigarettes to reduce its risk. Although time has proven that the cigarette attack was not successful, diversification of the company toward razor blades and other nonrelated products provided it with a buffer against such attacks.

There are numerous other reasons which could prompt conglomerate mergers. Most of those not mentioned center around rather intricate financial advantages which are outside of the discipline discussed here. However, we have seen some compelling reasons for the large number of conglomerate mergers consummated in the past few years.

ALLEGED ANTICOMPETITIVE EFFECTS

It is not obvious why conglomerates come under the provisions of the antitrust laws. The anticompetitive effects of horizontal and vertical mergers that were studied earlier do not apply to conglomerate mergers. And while it is true that conglomerates make the overall economy more concentrated, they do not, by themselves, increase the concentration in any one industry. Despite these observations, critics of conglomerate mergers have offered a number of arguments to support their contention that such mergers can be anticompetitive. Most of the arguments are against bigness rather than conglomerates. Hence they apply to all large firms. These arguments should be analyzed carefully to formulate proper antitrust policy. Specifically, the following arguments against conglomerate mergers will be considered:

A. Conglomerate mergers increase economic concentration;
B. Conglomerate mergers promote business reciprocity;
C. Conglomerate mergers reduce potential competition;
D. Conglomerate mergers promote the use of predatory pricing;
E. Conglomerate mergers may promote limit pricing;
F. Conglomerate mergers promote oligopolistic behavior.

Concentration

One very interesting argument is that economic concentration on a national level threatens both economic and noneconomic national objectives. To see this in simple terms, realize that some of the conglomerates we have in this country have assets and employees in greater number than the assets and citizens of some countries in the world. Now assume that over the next fifty years we let them develop through conglomerate mergers so that by the year 2020 there are only ten businesses in the country. A conclusive picture of the implications of this business structure would be impossible to paint. The analysis takes us into the troublesome world of *1984* and whether that world comes, or what it would be like if it does come, cannot be described. But some interesting questions can be raised which should be considered in the development of governmental policy. Certainly a country composed of few companies would not be a democracy. Business lobbies are powerful today. What would they be like then? Would citizens really choose their president, their senators, their local mayor? It is doubtful. Anyone who has lived in a mill town knows the propensity of the mill to make decisions concerning the operation of the town, the social conduct of its citizens, etc.

What of the military-industrial complex? Would businesses be so powerful that they would, as Thorstein Veblen suggested, dictate not only production but war? Suppose the government could make independent decisions concerning monetary and fiscal policy. Would the policy be effective when applied to a highly concentrated economy? The answer to this question is "probably not." In fact, many economists believe that even today the standard Keynesian remedies are ineffective simply because they are applied in a highly concentrated economy which is insensitive to outside influences. If a worker wanted to start his own business, would he have a chance of competing against the ten conglomerates? Should he have the chance?

These questions are subjects for entire books, but they are crucially important questions which are applicable to the formulation of all types of merger policy. They are also the stuff which economists must consider. As we shall shortly see, there is no compelling reason for disallowing conglomerate mergers based on anticompetitive criteria. When analyzed on a case by case basis, only rarely will such merger activity forestall competition. But if each instance of conglomerate merger is allowed, the day may come when we have to evaluate the sum total of the activity, and on that day democracy may have disappeared. To be sure it will not disappear because business intended to control the government through merger activity, and it will not disappear with the permission of economists or lawyers. But such a world could develop if cases are analyzed on a piecemeal basis with no view toward the socio-economic implications.

Even assuming that the prophecy is valid, the antitrust laws are probably not the best vehicle to stop economic concentration. As Professor Bork suggested:

... the point to be emphasized here is that the supercon-
centration issue, whether genuine or synthetic in other
aspects, is a *bogus antitrust issue.* It has no proper place
whatever in enforcement decisions under the present statutes, because it is irrelevant to competition in particular
markets and to the allocation of resources by the market
mechanism. Consistent with the consumer-welfare standard, it is market concentration, not economy-wide concentration that is the subject of the Clayton Act's provisions concerning "competition" and "monopoly."[31]

Reciprocity

A second attack levied against conglomerate mergers is that they
increase the likelihood of reciprocity. Reciprocity is a practice where
one division of a conglomerate persuades its suppliers that they
should buy their requirements from another division of the conglomerate. The division of the conglomerate is, in effect, saying, "You
buy from another division of my conglomerate, and I'll buy from
you." For example, suppose that a conglomerate owns a grocery
chain and a pickle factory. The grocery segment of the conglomerate
may convince independent food processors that they should purchase its pickles if they want their food bought by the grocery chain.
Of course, this is really an old practice with a new wrinkle. By virtue
of the monopoly power the conglomerate has in the grocery segment, it is attempting to use economic leverage on the food processors.

The Federal Trade Commission has reasoned that although this
practice can occur as a result of a horizontal or vertical merger, the
likelihood of its occurrence increases when a company becomes
diversified. The commission has also concluded that the practice can
result in serious anticompetitive consequences. Supposedly, the anticompetitive consequence is that the practice forecloses markets (in
our example, food processors) to other competitors (pickle producers).

Most businessmen would naturally deny the use of reciprocity,
but Harold S. Geneen, President of International Telephone and
Telegraph, presented a logical reason for denying its use. According
to Geneen, each division of his company is treated as an individual
company, and each manager is responsible for the profitability of his
division. "The business of that center is to make money. The manager of that center has absolutely no incentive to seek anything but
the best price, the most reliable delivery, the best service and the best
quality in the goods and services he purchases. He couldn't care less
about trying to help the sale activities of some *other* profit cen-

ter. . . . Reciprocity, therefore, is impractical and impossible within an ITT complex."[32]

Of course the defense is only applicable to conglomerates that have truly independent divisions, but Geneen suggests a very important point about reciprocity. When in order to sell its own product, a firm has to purchase a product which costs more than it formerly paid, it is, in effect, lowering the price of its own product. Within the context of our earlier example, suppose that the grocery chain normally bought a certain product from the food processor at $5.00 a unit. Now, suppose that the chain requires the food processor to buy pickles at a noncompetitive price. This is an additional part of the bargain—one to the detriment of the processor. If the processor accepts it, it is getting less for its product even though the chain still pays $5.00. The processor is, in effect, reducing the price of its product. It might be willing to do this in times of excess supply or possibly where the firm it is bargaining with has monopoly power. Even then, however, if the grocery chain was buying from the food processing company at the lowest possible price, it could not impose an additional cost on the processor by requiring him to buy pickles at higher-than-competitive prices. To the extent that the price of pickles is higher than competitive, the grocery chain would have to pay a higher-than-normal price for the processed food.

Is it likely that the grocery division will pay higher prices for processed foods so that the pickle division can get a higher-than-normal price for its product? The logical answer is "no" and consequently many economists believe that the reciprocity argument is fallacious. However, there is evidence that despite the fact that the arrangement appears to be illogical, it is sometimes practiced.[33] There are two reasons which explain this. First, not all business decisions are logical. Second, the practice is not necessarily illogical when used in an oligopolistic market structure where price competition is minimized. And although the antitrust laws are not designed to protect businessmen against their own stupidity, they are designed to prohibit anticompetitive practices whether they result from stupidity or oligopolistic behavior.

The problem in formulating proper antitrust merger policy for conglomerate mergers is that not enough is known about the extent and effect of reciprocity to derive appropriate policies. While the great majority of recent studies have reached conclusions similar to the Stigler Report that "the economic threat to competition from reciprocity is either small or nonexistent,"[34] most of these studies also suggest that a more detailed analysis of the practice is needed. Yet, as we will presently see, the Federal Trade Commission has generally considered reciprocity to be a major threat to competition and has treated it accordingly.

Potential Competition

A major argument levied against conglomerate mergers is that they thwart potential competition. This argument has two distinct subdivisions. One approach suggests that when a large conglomerate enters an industry, other potential entrants will be less likely to enter. This conclusion is made by virtue of the power that the large conglomerate has to wage competitive warfare. As we will see shortly, the potential entrant might fear predatory pricing. Alternatively, the entrant might fear that the conglomerate would be able to build strong consumer attachment through nonprice competition. In short, the little fellow is simply afraid to wage a competitive war against the big conglomerate so he will not enter the industry.

Another subdivision of the potential competition argument suggests that if the conglomerate (or any firm) is not allowed to enter an industry by purchasing an existing firm, he might build his own firm in the industry. This would be more advantageous than the merger because it would increase the number of firms in the industry by one. And even if the conglomerate did not build his own firm, the mere fact that he wants to enter the industry might signal existing firms to keep their prices at competitive levels so that they do not offer additional incentive for the outsider to enter.

Predatory Pricing

Another argument levied against conglomerate mergers is that such mergers give the firm the potential to engage in predatory practices. It was discussed briefly within the context of "profit squeezing" in Chapter XIII. The argument is applicable to any large firm; it is not limited to conglomerates. The contention is based on the idea that because the conglomerate is large, it has a large "war chest" which can be used to subsidize some divisions in their war against competitors. Thus subsidization is often called "Cross-Subsidization" or the "Deep Pocket Theory." A simple example will make the argument clear. Suppose that a conglomerate has a division which operates refineries and retail gasoline stations. Its stations compete against companies which are not part of a conglomerate. If the conglomerate wants to put competing stations out of business, retard their expansion, induce them to merge, or induce them to adopt parallel pricing policies, it can sell gasoline at or below cost by using profits from the other divisions. Proponents of the argument would contend that competing oil companies which do not have a large war chest could not survive the battle and so they would be forced to acquiesce. Thus, the conglomerate could create additional monopoly power in the oil industry. Of course even the proponents of the argument would agree that monopoly power would only be created if entry into the industry were blocked.

In considering the validity of the subsidization argument, the *Prob* relevant issue is not "can firms do this?" but "will firms do this?" To answer the question one has to ask whether such warfare is rational. Several economists have studied the question, and their conclusions are pertinent to our inquiry. John S. McGee analyzed predatory price cutting within the context of the 1911 *Standard Oil* case which will be analyzed in Chapter XV. Price cutting designed to drive competitors out of business was not rational when compared with the alternative way of gaining monopoly power, acquisition of competing companies. A firm could probably be purchased for its competitive asset value. The purchaser would be willing, at most, to pay an amount equal to the discounted value of the expected monopoly profits which would be received by eliminating competition. For the predatory pricing scheme to be logical, the cost of waging the war must be less than the purchase price of the company. *1 firEle was sure now H merger illegal.*

What is the cost of the war? It is the sum of the loss incurred by the firm waging the war and the loss in monopoly profits during the war which could have been earned by buying out the company. According to McGee, the loss incurred by the firm waging the war could be extremely high.[35] While engaged in the struggle, the firm must supply customers raided from its competitors. This implies that it will be losing more money than its competitor because it is supplying more customers. It also implies that the company might have to build additional capacity to supply these customers, a job which would be unnecessary if the competitor had been bought out. Although it cannot be proven in absolute terms, it is quite conceivable that an outright purchase would be cheaper than war.

There are other reasons presented by McGee which suggest that the outright purchase is more rational. Competitors might shut down during the price war and start up again when it is over. This evasive action sentences the attacking firm to a continuing attempt to develop monopoly power which has no end. Also, even if the competitors are driven out of business, their assets will be available to any firm which later wishes to enter the market. Given his analysis, McGee concluded that "All in all, then, purchases would not be more expensive than war without quarter, and should be both cheaper and more permanent."[36]

Because McGee suggested that predatory pricing is not logical, this does not mean that it has not existed. He studied the *Standard Oil* case and concluded that it did not exist in that instance. However, Samuel M. Loescher studied the same case and concluded that although Standard did not use predatory practices to drive its competitors out of business, it used them to contain competitors' expansion.[37] Studies of *U.S. v. New York Great Atlantic and Pacific Tea Co.* have also brought conflicting reports on whether A&P used excess profits from some of its divisions to drive competitors out of business. Morris A. Adelman concluded that predatory prices were not used by A&P.[38] Dirlam and Kahn concluded that they were.[39] The most thorough study of the prevalence of predatory pricing was recently performed by Roland H. Koller in his doctoral dissertation at the University of Wisconsin. He studied twenty-six antitrust cases where the courts or the F.T.C. had determined that the firms involved engaged in predatory pricing. He included in his definition of predatory pricing, attempts to drive competitors out of business, attempts to get competitors to merge, and attempts to induce competitors to cooperate in monopolizing the market. He found that in sixteen of the twenty-six cases, predation did not take place. In three cases there was insufficient data to perform an analysis and in the remaining seven cases, predation was attempted but only four of the seven attempts were successful.[40] If future projections can be based on past results, predatory pricing will not be prevalent.

About the only thing that is clear is that predatory pricing can exist, and it can harm competition. The probability of its appearance is unknown. It is doubtful that it will occur in an industry which has free entry. It is also doubtful that it would occur in an industry composed of many large competitors, or an industry where the products are not standardized. Both of these conditions either decrease the probability of a conglomerate's being able to harm competitors or diminish the monopoly profits that can be received at the end of the war. It is important to note that even if predatory pricing is never used by a conglomerate, competitors may be mindful of the conglomerate's potential to engage in such warfare. This may make them disciplined competitors which follow the oligopolistic pricing behavior of the conglomerate division to escape its wrath.

Even though a conglomerate may use predatory pricing, is this a reason to outlaw conglomerate mergers? Donald F. Turner has suggested that predatory pricing, not the conglomerate merger, should be treated under Section 5 of the Clayton Act as well as Sections 1 and 2 of the Sherman Act if it appears after the merger.[41] This is an enticing argument. The Justice Department does not disallow horizontal mergers because they *may* result in the use of tying contracts.

So why should it disallow conglomerate mergers because they *may* result in the use of predatory pricing? Instead, allow the merger but disallow the pricing if it appears. Before the reader decides whether Turner's suggestion is appropriate, ask the question, "What really makes tying contracts anticompetitive?" Information used previously in this book can be used to answer the question. The answer is "horizontal monopoly power." And when that power is created through a merger, the merger should be disallowed if the origin of the power is to be cut off. The correct way to treat tying contracts is to stop the development of power, not outlaw the contract. Does the same logic apply to the potential for predatory pricing? The answer is "no" because the pricing would rarely be effective if one of the merging firms did not already have horizontal monopoly power. Firms with an insignificant share of a market rarely drive competitors out of business. The merger simply gives the new firm more assets, but the courts should not consider the holding of large assets to be anticompetitive. Therefore, Turner's suggestion is appropriate. Certainly it is better than trying to guess whether firms forming a conglomerate through merger may, someday, adopt predatory pricing.

Limit Pricing

A concept closely related to but distinct from predatory pricing is that of "limit pricing." This is the practice of setting a price at a level less than the profit-maximizing price to reduce the incentive for new firms to enter the market and for the growth of competitors. The effect of the practice on consumers is mixed. In the short run it allows the consumer to purchase a product at a lower price than would otherwise be charged. However in the long run it deters competition in an industry and results in higher-than-competitive prices.

A firm would engage in this practice if it estimated that its short run losses resulting from charging a less than profit-maximizing price were less than any losses it would incur from allowing firms to enter the market and competitors to expand. Presumably if the firm engaged in limit pricing this would imply that the consumer would be harmed over the long run.

Like predatory pricing, limit pricing is not unique to conglomerates. However, it has been asserted that conglomerates might have a greater tendency than other firms to discount future earnings. This could be true either because they experience lower capital costs or because they are more content with existing profits and hence have little motivation to increase their existing profits.[42]

Conglomerates and Oligopolistic Behavior

A final argument against conglomerates is that their existence may prompt noncompetitive oligopolistic behavior. This argument appears to be logical, although there is no empirical economic data to support it. Suppose that conglomerate A competes in markets 1 and 2, and conglomerate B competes in the same markets. Additionally, assume that A is less efficient than B in market 2, and B is less efficient than A in market 1. Although the natural tendency would be for A to win the competition in market 1, it might be "soft" on its rival, B. It does this because it fears that B might engage in fierce competition in market 2. This is really a modified form of conscious parallelism where the two conglomerates adopt a "live and let live" strategy. There are two essential requirements for the practice to work. First, the two markets must have roughly equal importance. Otherwise there would still be a tendency for the conglomerate in the important market to try to capture it through hard competition. Second, the same conglomerates must sell in both markets. Obviously, if B had not sold in market 1 there would have been no problem.[43] If this argument is valid, it suggests that conglomerate mergers involving firms without a dominant position in a market should be looked upon more favorably than those involving dominant firms.

POLICY RECOMMENDATIONS

Numerous studies of conglomerates have conclusions concerning the proper antitrust policy to deal with them. The most lenient policy was suggested by the Stigler Committee which concluded:

> We seriously doubt that the antitrust division should embark upon an active program of challenging conglomerate enterprise on the basis of nebulous fears about size and economic power. These fears should be either confirmed or dissipated, and an important contribution would be made in this resolution by an early conference on the subject. If there is a genuine securities market problem, probably new legislation is necessary. If there is a real political threat in giant mergers, then the critical dimension should be estimated. If there is no threat, the fears entertained by critics of the conglomerate enterprises should be allayed. Vigorous action on the basis of our present knowledge is not defensible.[44]

A slightly more stringent recommendation was made by the *White House Task Force Report on Antitrust Policy for President Johnson.*

The Report concluded that mergers between "very large firms and other firms that are already leading firms in concentrated markets significant in the national economy should be outlawed."[45] There is fairly universal agreement that conglomerates should not be attacked under the antitrust laws on the basis of their size. When Donald Turner was Chief of the Antitrust Division of the Justice Department, he concluded that:

> Not unless we can find some plausible theory, we will not attack a merger simply on the ground that the companies are large. It is our position that this is not reasonable under existing antitrust law, if for no other reason, although there are others, than that the issues raised by superconcentration should not be mixed up with the traditional issues of antitrust law, namely issues revolving around competition.[46]

When cases are studied on conglomerate mergers, we will see that the Federal Trade Commission and the Justice Department have a far more stringent policy.

Not all economists agree on the effects of reciprocity and cross-subsidization on competition and not all agree on the effect of national concentration on our economic, political, and social structure. Therefore there is no one policy recommendation representing all or even most economists. What can be said is that in judging conglomerate merger cases it is important to consider the logical basis for the alleged anticompetitive practices which could result from the mergers. It is certainly not obvious that these practices will be used by the conglomerates, or even if used, that the practices will be anticompetitive. And even where it is probable that they will occur and will be anticompetitive, it is important to ask whether they should be outlawed by forbidding the mergers or by forbidding the practices themselves. Finally, it is important to remember that the antitrust laws were not designed by Congress to attack large size when size has no anticompetitive effects. If size is to be outlawed, it should be done under new legislation. Before such legislation is deemed appropriate, more studies will have to be made on the concentration issue.

CONGLOMERATE MERGERS UNDER THE LAW

Reynolds Metals - Arrow

Reynolds Metals Company v. *F.T.C.* involved a vertical merger.[47] However, because the Court of Appeals for the District of Columbia chose to treat it as a conglomerate, the case is relevant to the formulation of conglomerate antitrust policy under Section 7 of the Clayton Act. Reynolds, a manufacturer of aluminum foil, was one of the aluminum companies formed in the aftermath of the *Alcoa* decision. It purchased Arrow Brands, Incorporated, a company which converted aluminum foil to the uses of florist shops. Arrow competed with seven other florist foil converters and supplied 33 per cent of that market. One might naturally think that the court would attack the merger on the basis of foreclosure since Arrow might have been foreclosed to other aluminum foil producers. Instead, the merger was attacked on the basis of cross-subsidization under the provisions of Section 7 of the Clayton Act. The court of appeals observed that prior to the merger the eight processors were independent and had relatively equal resources. However, after the merger, the court thought that

> Arrow's assimilation into Reynolds' enormous capital structure and resources gave Arrow an immediate advantage over its competitors who were contending for a share of the market for florist foil. The power of the "deep pocket" or "rich parent" for one of the florist foil suppliers in a competitive group where previously no company was very large and all were relatively small opened the *possibility* [emphasis added] and power to sell at prices approximating cost or below and thus to undercut and ravage the less affluent competition.[48]

The court made its decision on the basis of a possible effect of the merger, not a definite showing or even a probable effect. And even though the court was careful to state that the merger was not a *per se* violation, it established the precedent to disallow any merger of a large company with another company situated in an industry devoid of large firms.

Consolidated Foods

The Supreme Court considered the reciprocity issue in *F.T.C.* v. *Consolidated Foods Corporation.*[49] Consolidated owned food processing plants and a network of wholesale and retail food stores. It acquired Gentry, a manufacturer of dehydrated onion and garlic products. Although the acquisition could be viewed as both a vertical and conglomerate merger, the Court chose to treat it as a conglomerate merger. The major fear of the government was that through reciprocity, food processors would purchase Gentry's products to the exclusion of others. In return, Consolidated Food would purchase the food processor's products for resale in Consolidated's wholesale and retail outlets. Gentry had about 32 per cent of the dehydrated garlic and onion market and it, together with the largest firm in the industry, Basic Vegetable Products, held about 90 per cent of the industry market share.

After the merger there was some evidence that Consolidated tried to promote reciprocal buying. An official of the company wrote to the distribution divisions saying: "Oftentimes, it is a great advantage to know when you are calling on a prospect, whether or not that prospect is a supplier of someone within your own organization. Everyone believes in reciprocity providing all things are equal."[50] Consolidated actually mailed letters to its major suppliers asking them to purchase Gentry's products. Additionally, there was evidence that some food processing plants gave reciprocal orders. However, in the F.T.C.'s decision, it did not just rely on this evidence. It thought that the mere existence of the relationship between Gentry and Consolidated would give Gentry an unfair advantage over its competitors which would tend to make the industry oligopolistic.

When the court of appeals heard the case, it overturned the F.T.C. decision. The court of appeals relied heavily on the events in the ten years after the merger. While it found that Gentry's share of the dehydrated onion market did increase by seven per cent, its share of the garlic market decreased by twelve per cent. Based on this evidence it did not think that the reciprocal arrangements had been successful. The Supreme Court addressed itself to this argument in an interesting manner. It thought that the information covering the ten years after the merger should not be relied upon heavily. The Court presented two reasons to justify this attitude. First, it reasoned that a merged company should not get a free "trial period." Instead, the acquisition should be evaluated on the evidence at the time of the merger. This argument was largely based on the contention that firms would bide their time immediately after their merger. Then, when they were certain that the antitrust authorities would not attack them, they would engage in reciprocity.[51] Second, the Court observed that even though part of Gentry's market share decreased after the merger, it was impossible to tell what would have happened in the absence of the merger. Possibly the shares in both markets would have decreased. This is especially true given the fact that the Court thought that Gentry sold a product which was inferior to Basic Vegetables' products.

The Supreme Court considered the merger in violation of Section 7 of the Clayton Act. Although it did not set down a firm rule to follow in making the decision, it appears that it declared reciprocity illegal when a large firm is involved and when the acquired and acquiring firms are so structured to make reciprocity a strong possibility.

Procter & Gamble - Clorox

The first major conglomerate merger case was heard in 1967 by the Supreme Court.[52] Procter & Gamble is a leading producer of soaps, detergents, and cleansers with total sales in 1967 exceeding a billion dollars. Clorox, a manufacturer of liquid bleach, supplied 48.8 per cent of the bleach market. It, together with one other firm, Purex, supplied 65 per cent of the market. The merger was challenged under Section 7 of the Clayton Act.

The Court found that both industries were highly concentrated, and both firms had large market shares in their respective industries. Furthermore, these large market shares were largely a result of massive advertising campaigns. Although P&G did not sell liquid bleach, it had been diversifying into product lines related to its basic line, and diversification into liquid bleach was considered a "distinct" possibility by the Court. P&G preferred acquisition rather than building a liquid bleach company because it thought it would be a quick way of achieving a dominant position in the bleach market. It also thought that economies could result from the merger.

The Court disallowed the merger for three reasons. First, it believed that P&G's entry into the bleach market might dissuade the smaller bleach producers from aggressively competing. Within the context of the dominant-firm model, this simply means that with a more dominant firm in the industry, small firms may give up their competitive struggle and simply parrot the prices and trade activities of the large firm. Second, the Court believed that the merger might raise barriers to the entry of new competitors. It thought that the major competitive weapon in the bleach industry was advertising. This is probably true since the chemical composition of bleach is the same for all companies. The Court, using the cross-subsidization argument, thought that P&G might divert a large portion of advertising to Clorox to "meet the short-term threat of a new entrant."[53]

Additionally, it thought that due to P&G's mass advertising it could receive volume discounts for advertising and advertise many different products in one ad. This would give P&G a competitive advantage in advertising. Of course, most economists would consider this to be an economy and endorse it. Even those economists who do not look too favorably upon advertising used to create brand attachment rarely believe it should be disallowed under the antitrust laws. However, the Court, even though it recognized the advertising as an economy, said that "possible economies cannot be used as a defense to illegality. Congress was aware that some mergers which lessen competition may also result in economies but it struck the balance in favor of protecting competition."[54] Third, the Court used the potential entry argument to reason that if it disallowed the merger, P&G might develop its own bleach company which could provide additional competition in the market.

In summary, the prime argument in the case was that the merger intimidated potential as well as existing competitors. Although one argument to support this was the supposition that competing firms would be more fearful of P&G than of Clorox, the major basis for the conclusion was that economies would result from the merger. This was best expounded by the F.T.C. It said:

> Procter, by increasing the Clorox advertising budget, by engaging in sales promotions far beyond the capacity of Clorox's rivals, and by obtaining for Clorox the advertising savings to which Procter, as a large national advertiser, is entitled, is in a position to entrench still further the already settled consumer preference for the Clorox brand, and thereby make entry even more forbidding than it was prior to the merger. In addition, because a multiproduct firm of large size enjoys . . . very substantial competitive advantages in an industry marked by product differentiation through mass advertising, sales promotion, shelf display and related merchandising methods, the prospects become increasingly remote, given the substitution of Procter for Clorox . . . that small or medium-sized firms will be minded to enter the industry.[55]

The Supreme Court's agreement with this view can be interpreted two ways. Either the Court really believes that the antitrust laws are designed to protect competitors, not competition, or the Court is afraid that if allowed to compete strongly, the merged firm will win the competitive game. Everyone likes competition, but almost no one likes a firm to win the game. And if a firm is winning through "fair" means, one way to lessen its score is to take some of its competitive equipment away.[56] Although the point is arguable, such a policy might be better than living with a virtual monopolist. Of course, the problem is that the F.T.C. or the Court did not perform a thorough enough analysis to know whether it was probable that Procter and Gamble would win. As Robert Bork put it:

> The Court's reasoning teaches that competition in the quarterback market would be improved, and the public

thereby benefited, if Joe Namath's knees were twisted before every game and Fran Tarkenton was required to wear snowshoes.

The ITT Mergers

In 1969, the Antitrust Division of the Justice Department initiated divestiture proceedings against ITT for its acquisitions of Grinnell, Hartford Life Insurance, and Canteen. Under the leadership of Richard McLaren, the department hoped to stop ITT's drive to become a leading conglomerate and also to establish within the courts, a strong precedent against conglomerate mergers. Each of the three ITT cases is important because the district courts that heard them were more lenient in establishing rules against conglomerate mergers than was the Supreme Court in its *Procter & Gamble* decision.

(ITT-Grinnell)

In *U.S.* v. *International Telephone and Telegraph Corporation*,[57] the District Court for Connecticut closely followed the tests established in the *Procter & Gamble* decision. Compared to the Supreme Court's P&G decision, the district court performed a detailed analysis of the markets involved and the resulting effect of the merger on competition. ITT, a conglomerate, was the ninth largest corporation in the United States, with sales revenues exceeding five billion dollars and with 353,000 employees. Grinnell, the acquired firm, produced automatic sprinkler devices and total sprinkler systems, piping for power generating plants, and devices from which piping is suspended.

Most of the court's analysis centered around the sprinkler operation. It accepted the definition of the relevant market as the entire United States and the line of commerce to include all of Grinnell's products. It then contended that a conglomerate merger which acquired a firm having a dominant position in a market had been declared illegal in *Procter & Gamble.* Therefore it set out to determine whether Grinnell had a dominant position in any of its markets. Even though Grinnell's market shares ranged from four per cent to 44.4 per cent, the court concluded that the company was not dominant in any market. The court then said that the merger would have to be declared illegal if economies resulted which gave Grinnell a competitive advantage. This test also came from the precedent established in *Procter & Gamble*. The criterion proves an interesting contrast with Sherman Act litigation, where economies were a defense, not a liability. The court found no economies in marketing. In reaching this conclusion, it considered the relationship between Grinnell and the Hartford Insurance Company, another ITT acquisition. The government had argued that agents of Hartford would promote Grinnell sprinkler systems. The court disagreed, arguing that the practice did not make good business sense. If Hartford agents promoted Grinnell systems, agents of other insurance companies would not recommend them. With regard to economies of advertising and subsidization, the court found that Grinnell already had adequate resources for product promotion so there was no need for ITT to subsidize the company. Moreover, advertising did not appear to be important in the promotion of sprinkler systems.

The government also argued that the merger would foreclose sprinkler markets to Grinnell's competitors. This was based on the contention that ITT, itself, was a major purchaser of the systems. The court concluded that ITT's market represented no more than one-tenth of one per cent, and that was insignificant. Moreover, because each division of ITT operated as a separate "profit center" these centers purchased solely on the basis of price, quality, and delivery. The government also argued that the merger would result in reciprocal dealing. That is, ITT may say to its suppliers, "We will buy from you if you buy our sprinkler system."

The court rejected the reciprocity argument for a number of reasons. It heard numerous witnesses who contended that reciprocity was not substantial in the sprinkler business. Additionally, many sprinkler contracts came from nonindustrial users who bought on the basis of competitive bids. This, according to the court, minimized the probability of reciprocity. Nor did the court think the merger with ITT increased the likelihood of reciprocity. It observed that a number of features of ITT's operation prevented the practice. The existence of the separate profit centers was one of them. If each division of ITT was operated independently of the others, there would be no incentive for reciprocity. Also, ITT did not collect purchasing and sales data necessary to identify reciprocal purchasing opportunities. Finally, the court was impressed with the fact that ITT had a written policy against the practice of reciprocity. In reviewing this argument, the court established a set of criteria to determine guilt or innocence. A conglomerate merger would be disallowed on the reciprocity issue only if the merger significantly increased the opportunities for reciprocity, there was a reasonable possibility that the conglomerate would take advantage of the opportunity, and the resulting reciprocity had a tendency to reduce competition. Mere potential to engage in reciprocity was not enough to declare a conglomerate merger illegal.

The court performed a similar analysis of the other divisions of

Grinnell and found no anticompetitive effects. To the government's contention that although the merger did not increase concentration in a particular market but did increase overall concentration, the court replied that the Clayton Act did not outlaw overall concentration. "The decisional law uniformly has emphasized the importance of defining the specific product market or line of commerce in which alleged anticompetitive effects of a merger are to be measured."[58]

Based on its analysis, the court allowed the merger. In so doing, it established some rules to follow in judging conglomerate mergers. If a dominant firm is purchased, or if the merger creates economies which place competitors at a disadvantage, it will be disallowed. Firm rules were established to judge the reciprocity issue, and the court definitely used the rule of reason.

(ITT-Hartford)

At about the same time that ITT acquired Grinnell, it also acquired the Hartford Insurance Company. The Justice Department requested an injunction to stop the merger, and the request was heard by the U.S. District Court of Connecticut.[59]

Hartford ranked sixth in the nation among property and liability insurance companies. Among companies writing property and liability insurance through independent agents, it ranked fourth with assets of $1,891,700,000. There are many similarities between the *Grinnell* and *Hartford* cases because both were decided by the same court and argued in much the same manner.

The government argued that the Hartford merger would increase the likelihood of ITT's engaging in reciprocal dealing. That is, customers of ITT would buy Hartford Insurance. The court decided that insurance policies were not easily interchanged between customers, and therefore reciprocity was unlikely. Customer relationships with insurance companies tend to be long term for a number of reasons. There are substantial start-up costs involved in initiating a new large scale insurance program. Additionally, long-term customers can build up a surplus on their account during periods of few claims. Finally, in terms of cost, service, and coverage, insurance companies do not sell a homogeneous product. Therefore, customers are not indifferent toward their choice of an insurance company. The court also denied the government's argument against reciprocity on the basis of economic logic. "If the market within which a supplier operates is competitively structured, a buyer cannot readily exert pressure on the supplier to engage in reciprocal practices, since the supplier can replace the buyer by selling to other buyers at the same or a slightly lower price."[60] Finally, as in *Grinnell*, the court found that ITT was not structured to engage in reciprocal dealing. While it did agree that the evidence on reciprocal dealing was conflicting, the court did not think that the government had established a case against it.

The government's second contention was that ITT could use Hartford's financial resources to finance the ITT home-building subsidiary, Levitt & Sons, Inc. According to the government this would give Levitt a competitive advantage. The court thought that the subsidization argument would have to be accepted if Levitt & Sons had a dominant position in their market and if the resources would give Levitt a competitive advantage. But it contended that the government did not prove that Levitt had a dominant position in the market. Even assuming that it was dominant, the court thought that ITT did not intend to subsidize Levitt, that ITT was fully capable of raising all the capital it needed without acquiring Hartford, and that it was more economical to raise capital outside of the company than to purchase Hartford.

Third, the government contended that the merger had some vertical aspects because ITT might insure itself with Hartford policies. Supposedly this foreclosed markets to competing insurance companies. To support its argument the government relied on the modified quantitative substantiality test by presenting the total dollar value of insurance premiums which ITT and its subsidiaries paid to domestic insurers. ITT, however, showed that its purchases of insurance involved approximately 1/25 of one per cent of the total property and liability insurance premiums of domestic insurers during the period. The court thought that this was an insignificant share of the market.

Fourth, the government contended that the merger was partially a horizontal one since Hartford competed with several ITT subsidiaries in writing life insurance. ITT, on the other hand, demonstrated that the combined market position of ITT and Hartford in the insurance business was less than 3/10 of one per cent. The court thought that this was an insignificant market share.

Finally, as in the *Grinnell* case, the government contended that the merger brought about an increase in economic concentration in the country. Consistent with its *Grinnell* opinion, the court did not think that Section 7 of the Clayton Act made overall economic concentration illegal. Based on all of its conclusions, the court refused to enjoin ITT's purchase of Hartford.

(Canteen)

The third ITT merger attacked by the government involved ITT's purchase of Canteen.[61] The acquired company was primarily engaged in the sale of vending and manual food service to industrial, commercial, educational, and medical accounts. Additionally, it owned a division engaged in the vending of cigarettes and cigars and a small commercial finance business. It had sales of approximately $322 million in 1968, of which $307 million was derived from merchandise and equipment sales. It ranked second among companies operating in the on-site food service market, but ranked only eighth among food service companies which had diversified.

Reciprocity was the major attack used by the government against the merger. To evaluate this charge, the court used the three step test which originated in *Grinnell.* However, it amplified the first part of this test by noting that whether or not a conglomerate merger increased the opportunities for reciprocity depended on: "the extent to which ITT suppliers are actual or potential purchasers of food service; the scope of the market represented by ITT for products sold by ITT suppliers; the size and diversification of other companies to which ITT suppliers sell their products; the degree to which the market, within which ITT's suppliers operated, is competitively structured; and whether food service is the type of business which lends itself to reciprocal dealing."[62] The government was not prepared to argue its case within the context of most of the criteria. Moreover, the court thought that food service products were sufficiently different in price, quality, and service that customers would not readily shift from other companies to Canteen in return for reciprocal buying. In fact, even government evidence showed that customers tended to stick with their food service supplier for long periods of time.

The Court also did not think that the government demonstrated that the merger would result in significant reciprocity, even if the opportunities existed. It reviewed the 101 acquisitions of ITT over the past decade and found no substantial evidence of reciprocity resulting from them. Even the government had to agree that after studying the past acquisitions, "there was no instance where the government contended that ITT had practiced reciprocity."[63] Moreover, the court agreed with ITT that reciprocity did not make good business sense within the context of its business, and the existence of ITT's profit centers negated its use. Lastly, the court found no likelihood of an adverse effect on competition even if ITT did engage in reciprocity.

The government also argued that the merger would foreclose markets to other food suppliers if Canteen supplied all of ITT's plants. The court decided that even if Canteen did supply all of them, it would foreclose only 0.48 per cent of the market, and that share was insubstantial. The final argument used by the government was that the merger would harm small food service competitors. The court agreed with the defense that the more localized a firm is, the more effective and profitable it will be. Moreover, it found no evidence that Canteen needed financial resources from ITT, thus negating the subsidization argument. Based on its findings, the district court allowed the merger.

(ITT: The Aftermath)

Based on these three decisions, the Justice Department's attack on conglomerates could be termed a failure. Of course the department did have the right to appeal the cases and ITT was most aware of that fact. Moreover, ITT probably thought it would not get as favorable a reception from the Supreme Court as it did from the district courts of Connecticut and Illinois. Therefore, on September 24, 1971, the company entered into a consent decree in each of the three cases. It, in effect, made a package deal with the Justice Department.[64] It had to divest itself of the fire protection division of Grinnell and all of the assets of Canteen. Finally, it had to sell Levitt, Avis Rental Car, and Hamilton Life Insurance or, alternatively, Hartford. It chose to keep Hartford. It is unfortunate for the determination of the law on conglomerate mergers that one or more of the cases was not heard by the Supreme Court. Its interpretation of the lower courts' approach to the cases might be the same or might differ. But at the moment the law on conglomerates is unsettled.

LING-TEMCO-VOUGHT, INC.

In 1970, Ling-Temco-Vought, Inc. entered into a consent decree with the Department of Justice.[65] Because of the nature of the decree, the District Court for the Western District of Pennsylvania did not have to determine the legality of LTV's conglomerate merger. It only had to approve the decree. LTV was a large conglomerate which owned, among other things, Braniff Airlines, National Car Rental Systems, and companies engaged in the production of electronic equipment, carpeting products, copper wire, and meat products. LTV had revenues of approximately $4 billion in 1969. Jones & Laughlin Steel Company supplied approximately 6 per cent of the steel in the United States. The acquisition of 83 per cent of J&L stock was the issue in the case.

Both the government and LTV jointly filed a Stipulated Statement of Facts to the court. Included in the document were findings that the iron and steel industry was highly concentrated, entry was very difficult in the industry, the potential existed for reciprocity between the steel company and LTV's customers, and the merger made the U.S. economy more concentrated. The government thought that the provisions of the consent decree would prevent undue concentration of economic power. The decree specified that LTV was either to divest itself of J&L's assets or divest itself of Braniff Airlines and Okonite (a producer of copper wire products) within a period of three years. Additionally, for a period of ten years, it was not to engage in reciprocal buying, and both LTV and J&L were prohibited from buying any interest in a company with assets of $100 million or with a market share exceeding one per cent without first obtaining the consent of the government or of the court.

SUMMARY

While the analytical framework used by the courts to evaluate Section 7 merger cases is not fully established, several preliminary remarks can be made about the treatment of horizontal, vertical, and conglomerate mergers. The primary objective of Section 7 has been the prevention of oligopoly. Given this objective, the courts have largely relied on structure tests to evaluate merger cases. For example, acquisitions of dominant firms or of firms with a large market share have been looked upon unfavorably. Furthermore, the courts have relied heavily on industry trends, and if an industry is moving toward an oligopolistic market structure, the courts have not looked favorably upon mergers within the industry.

Still within the context of preventing oligopoly, the courts have brought a new objective into the antitrust laws; the protection of small business. This objective has caused the courts to consider merger economies as a negative consideration in evaluating merger cases. This can be contrasted with the Sherman Act merger cases where economies were looked upon as a reason for allowing mergers.

While the courts have applied the rule of reason to merger evaluation, the application has utilized less economic analysis than Sherman Act applications. If a merging firm is dominant, or if the industry trend is towards concentration, or if the merging firms have a large market share, the courts generally have concluded that the merger will have anticompetitive tendencies. Given these tests, there is little need for wide-scale economic studies. In fact, the only part of most Section 7 cases which have acquired any detailed economic analysis is the determination of the product and geographical markets.

The two major attacks against conglomerates, cross-subsidization and reciprocity, were practically accepted at face value as significant and harmful in the Supreme Court's *Clorox* decision. However, in the *ITT* decisions, the district courts established a detailed test to determine whether conglomerate mergers increased the opportunity for reciprocal dealing and whether, if they did, it was harmful. If the Supreme Court utilizes these tests it will be extremely difficult for the government to attack future conglomerate mergers on this issue. Although no formal test was established to evaluate cross-subsidization, the district courts were not willing to accept it as an anticompetitive factor at face vlaue. They applied a rule of reason to determine, in each specific case, whether cross-subsidization could create monopoly power. Hopefully, in the future, the Supreme Court will decide whether it believes such considerations are important. Judging from the *Clorox* decision, the Court will accept the government's argument at face value.

Although the district courts which decided the *ITT* cases were not willing to consider the economic concentration argument under Section 7, this argument will, no doubt, reach the Supreme Court in some future conglomerate merger case. At that time the Court will have to decide two far reaching questions. First, what should be the government's policy toward economic concentration? Second, should that policy be applied under Section 7 of the Clayton Act? The economic concentration argument is probably the most important consideration in evaluating conglomerate mergers, and it is an area ripe for study by economists as well as sociologists and political scientists.

NOTES TO CHAPTER XIV

[1]*Brown Shoe Co.* v. *U.S.*, 37 U.S. 303, 311-323 (1961).
[2]353 U.S. 586 (1957).
[3]353 U.S. 586, 606 (1957).
[4]*Brown Shoe Co.* v. *U.S.*, 370 U.S. 294 (1961).
[5]370 U.S. 294, 337 (1961).
[6]370 U.S. 294, 333 (1961).
[7]370 U.S. 294, 344 (1961).
[8]370 U.S. 294, 344 (1961).
[9]See for example, Robert H. Bork and Ward S. Bowman, Jr., "The Goals of Antitrust: A Dialogue on Policy," *Columbia Law Review*, 65 (March 1965), 370-373.
[10]*Ibid.*
[11]374 U.S. 321 (1963).

[12]374 U.S. 321, 355 (1963).
[13]374 U.S. 321, 364 (1963).
[14]374 U.S. 321, 362 (1963).
[15]374 U.S. 321, 363 (1963).
[16]384 U.S. 270 (1966).
[17]384 U.S. 270, 277 (1966).
[18]384 U.S. 270, 277 (1966).
[19]384 U.S. 270, 278 (1966).
[20]384 U.S. 270, 301 (1966).
[21]384 U.S. 270, 283 (1966).
[22]384 U.S. 270, 288 (1966).
[23]384 U.S. 270, 296-297 (1966).
[24]*Economic Concentration.* Hearings before the Subcommittee on Antitrust and Monopoly Pursuant to S. Res. 40, 91st Cong., 2nd Sess., November 4, 5, 6, 1969 and January 28, February 5, 18, and 19, 1970 (Washington: U.S. Government Printing Office, 1970), p. 5254.
[25]*Ibid.*, p. 4754.
[26]*Economic Report on Conglomerate Mergers*, Staff Report to the Federal Trade Commission (Washington, D.C.: U.S. Government Printing Office, 1969).
[27]*Economic Concentration*, p. 4740.
[28]John M. Blair, *Economic Concentration Structure, Behavior and Public Policy* (New York: Harcourt Brace Jovanovich, Inc., 1972), p. 174.
[29]*Ibid.*, p. 175.
[30]Ronald H. Coase, "Working Paper II: The Conglomerate Merger; Report of the Task Force on Productivity and Competition," *Antitrust Law and Economics Review*, II, No. 3 (Spring, 1969), 45.
[31]*Economic Concentration*, p. 4925.
[32]Harold S. Geneen, "Concepts of a Conglomerate or a Multi-Market Company: A Businessman's View," *Antitrust Law Journal*, XXXIX, No. I (1969-70), 13.
[33]See Willard F. Mueller, "The Rising Economic Concentration in America: Reciprocity, Conglomeration and the New American 'Zaibatsu' System, II," *Antitrust Law and Economics Review*, IV, No. 4 (Summer, 1971), 101.
[34]*Economic Concentration*, p. 5042.
[35]John S. McGee, "Predatory Price Cutting: The Standard Oil (N.J.) Case," *Journal of Law and Economics*, I (1958), 137-169.
[36]*Ibid.*, p. 141.
[37]Samuel M. Loescher, "A Sherman Act Precedent for Conglomerate Mergers," in *Industrial Organization and Economic Development*, Edited by Jesse W. Markham, and Gustav F. Papanek (Boston: Houghton Mifflin Co., 1970), p. 172.
[38]Morris A. Adelman, "The A&P Case: A Study in Applied Economic Theory," *Quarterly Journal of Economics*, LXIII (1949), 238.
[39]Joel B. Dirlam and Alfred E. Kahn, *Fair Competition: The Law and Economics of Antitrust Policy* (Ithaca, New York: Cornell University Press, 1954), pp. 211-241.
[40]Roland H. Koller II, "The Myth of Predatory Pricing: An Empirical Study," *Antitrust Law and Economics Review*, IV, No. 4 (Summer, 1971), 105-123.
[41]*Economic Concentration*, p. 5030.
[42]Scherer, p. 276.
[43]*Economic Concentration*, p. 4759.
[44]"Report of Stigler Task Force to President Nixon," Reported in U.S. Congress, Committee on the Judiciary, Subcommittee on Antitrust and Monopoly, U.S. Senate, 91st Cong., 2d Sess., *Economic Concentration* (Washington: Government Printing Office, 1969-70), 5043.
[45]"White House Task Force Report on Antitrust Policy for President Johnson," *Antitrust and Trade Regulation Report* No. 411 (May 27, 1969), 8.

[46]"An Interview with the Honorable Donald F. Turner," *ABA Antitrust Section*, XXX (1966), 104.

[47]309 F. 2d 223 (1963).

[48]309 F. 2d 223, 229 (1963).

[49]380 U.S. 592 (1965).

[50]380 U.S. 592, 596 (1965).

[51]In *U.S.* v. *General Dynamics*, 94 S. Ct. 1186 (1974), the Supreme Court finally clearly upheld the use of post-acquisition evidence in evaluating mergers although the competitive effect is still to be assessed at the time of the acquisition.

[52]*F.T.C.* v. *Procter & Gamble Co.*, 386 U.S. 586 (1967).

[53]386 U.S. 568, 579 (1967).

[54]386 U.S. 568, 580 (1967).

[55]"Final Order to Cease and Desist," *C.C.H. Trade Regulation Reporter*, paragraph 16, 673 (December 15, 1963).

[56]Robert H. Bork, "The Supreme Court Versus Corporate Efficiency," *Fortune*, LXXVI (August 1967), 92.

[57]324 F. Supp. 19 (1970).

[58]324 F. Supp. 19 (1970).

[59]*U.S.* v. *International Telephone and Telegraph Corporation and Grinnell Corporation, Defendants; U.S.* v. *International Telephone and Telegraph Corporation and the Hartford Fire Insurance Co., Defendants.* 306 F. Supp. 766 (October 30, 1969).

[60]306 F. Supp. 766, 789 (1969).

[61]*U.S.* v. *International Telephone and Telegraph Corp.*, U.S. District Court, Northern District of Illinois. *1971 Trade Cases*, 90530 (July 2, 1971).

[62]*Ibid.*, 90546.

[63]*Ibid.*, 90551.

[64]In December of 1971, Lawrence O'Brien, Chairman of the Democratic Party, accused the Justice Department of making a deal with ITT in return for the consent decree. Then in March of 1972, with the disclosure of a $400,000 Sheraton Corporation (an ITT holding) contribution to help finance the San Diego Republican Convention, the Justice Department, Deputy Attorney General Kleindienst and President Richard Nixon came under Congressional attack. It later became known through the White House tapes that President Nixon told the Justice Department that the ITT cases were not to be prosecuted further.

[65]*U.S.* v. *Ling-Temco-Vought, Inc., Jones and Laughlin Steel Corp. and Jones and Laughlin Industries, Inc., 1970 Trade Cases*, par. 73,105 (W.D. Pa. 1970).

MONOPOLIZATION AND SHARED MONOPOLY

CHAPTER XV

In most of the text we have studied the means by which firms acquire monopoly power. In this chapter we will analyze the manner in which they should be treated after they gain that power.

INTRODUCTION

Merger activity is certainly not the only means to attain monopoly power. It is conceivable that a firm can gain a dominant position in an industry by virtue of its superior efficiency in production and product promotion. In short, it may play the competitive game effectively and, as a result, win. It is also possible for a firm to gain dominance in an industry through the use of some unfair practices which give it an advantage over its competitors. Finally, we have already seen in the *American Tobacco* case that in a highly concentrated industry firms may engage in tacit collusion, thereby gaining monopoly power. This activity is frequently called "shared monopoly" and is characterized by a lack of meaningful competition between the firms in an industry. In this chapter we will explore the law on monopolization. Additionally, we will briefly study the manner in which shared monopoly has been treated by the F.T.C. and make some predictions about its future treatment.

MONOPOLIZATION

Section 2 of the Sherman Act is the antitrust provision most frequently applied to firms which monopolize. In theory the provision is only applicable to firms which acquire monopoly power through the use of unfair practices. However, after reviewing some monopolization cases, the reader will probably conclude that the provision is sometimes applied to firms which gain monopoly power through the use of fair practices. In an economic sense, it is correct to treat both fair and unfair methods of achieving monopoly power under the same antitrust provisions. While the manner of achieving the power is different, the result is the same; no matter how a firm achieves the power, it can exercise it to the detriment of the consumer.

However, if the courts prosecute the "good monopoly" they place the antitrust laws in direct opposition to the basic tenets of competition. Firms have to engage actively in economic warfare for viable competition to exist. In so doing, they further the interests of the consumer. Yet, if one of the firms wins by virtue of its superior efficiency, it gains monopoly power and may be subject to the provisions of the Sherman Act. This dilemma suggests that we like competitors, but we are opposed to winners. This is a common complaint of businessmen who perceive that they can be penalized if they do not compete and penalized if they compete too much. The problem, of course, is not caused by the laws themselves but is the result of the philosophical dilemma of the free enterprise system.

In evaluating antitrust cases involving monopolization, the use of the economic analysis presented in the chapters on mergers can aid in determining whether monopoly power exists. By analyzing a few monopolization cases, the reader will see that the courts struggle with the legal issue of whether monopoly can be determined by simply looking at industry structure or whether a firm has to "abuse" its power to be declared a monopoly. We will also see that the courts attempt to determine whether firms intend to gain monopoly power or whether it is "thrust upon" them. As we have said before, intent plays a much larger role in law than economics.

STANDARD OIL

The Standard Oil Company, created by John D. Rockefeller, was probably the most infamous of all the monopolies in the United States. From 1870 to 1911 the company gained monopoly power through the use of trusts, holding companies, price fixing, and the exercise of numerous forms of restraint on its competitors. In 1910, the company was charged with monopolization under Section 2 of the Sherman Act because it purchased or otherwise obtained interest in firms which purchased, shipped, refined and sold petroleum.[1] The government claimed that the combination established by Rockefeller was designed to fix the prices of crude and refined oil, limit its production, and control the transportation facilities for oil products.

The Supreme Court found that by 1872 the firm had acquired all but three or four of the forty oil refineries in Cleveland, Ohio. Additionally, it had obtained complete control over the pipe lines running from oil fields to refineries in Cleveland, Pittsburgh, Philadelphia, New York, and New Jersey. By virtue of this control and the preferential rates it received from the railroads, the company offered its competitors a choice: they could either conspire with Standard to fix prices or go out of business. The firms acquiesced, and through its collusive activity, Standard gained control of 90 per cent of the business of producing, shipping, refining, and selling oil in the United States.

Beginning in 1882 Rockefeller placed the various independent firms under a trust agreement. All of the companies, including Standard, transferred their stock to nine trustees in return for Standard Oil trust certificates. Since the trustees managed all of the companies, competition between the firms was eliminated. However, in 1892 the supreme court of Ohio found Standard Oil of Ohio, a member of the trust, guilty of unlawfully controlling the stock and ownership of corporations. Largely as a result of the threat of further prosecution, Rockefeller modified the trust agreement. The trustees transferred their stock to a holding company, Standard Oil of New Jersey. In return, Standard Oil issued common stock to the member companies. The arrangement successfully circumvented the law against trusts, but in terms of its effect on competition, the holding company was no different from the trust. Both organizations had absolute control of the oil industry.

Two defenses were presented to the Supreme Court by Standard Oil of New Jersey. It is interesting to note that neither defense denied the existence of monopoly power. First, it argued that the Sherman Act could not be applied to this case because the application would extend the power of Congress to include the control of production. Second, Standard argued that if the Sherman Act was applied in this case, it would impair property rights and destroy the freedom of contract. The Court was unsympathetic to both arguments. It believed that the Sherman Act was applicable to contracts between firms when the agreements resulted in monopolization. This decision was an important one, for had the Supreme Court agreed with Standard, the Sherman Act would have been completely nullified.

Justice White, who wrote the majority decision of the Supreme Court, centered his analysis on the intent and the effect of Standard's arrangement. The effect was found to be the creation of monopoly power. White noted that Standard's practices were "marked with constant proofs of wrong inflicted upon the public, and is strewn with the wrecks resulting from crushing out, without regard to law, the individual rights of others."[2] Since Standard clearly formed a monopoly and offered no redeeming arguments to justify it, the Court did not have to use any test to decide the degree of monopolization or to weigh the benefits against the harm. White found that the manner in which the company had combined independent firms was prima facie evidence of the intent of the company to monopolize the oil industry.

While most economists do not consider intent important in an antitrust case (since the result is the same no matter what the intent of a company might be), they cannot find fault with White's conclusion that the actions of Standard Oil of New Jersey were designed to create monopoly power. By emphasizing intent, Justice White implied that a company which acquired monopoly power without attempting to do so might not be in violation of the Sherman Act. His decision was important because it suggested that firms could compete in legitimate ways and even win the competitive game without fearing an antitrust suit.

The most significant part of White's decision was his support of the "rule of reason" approach in judging cases under Section 2 of the Sherman Act. The rule of reason requires that judges determine whether or not the monopolization involved in each case is reasonable, based on the facts in that case. Obviously, the approach is more difficult to apply than the *per se* illegal approach, but it increases the chances of reaching a correct antitrust decision. As we said, if a *per se* illegal approach was used, all forms of monopolization would be outlawed without regard to the facts of the specific case. We saw this approach applied to cases of overt price fixing in Chapter VI.

The Supreme Court found Standard Oil guilty and required it to divest itself of the stock of the independent companies. This explains why even today there are numerous independent Standard Oil companies throughout the United States. At least as important as the decision was the determination that the Sherman Act was constitutional and that a rule of reason should be applied to antitrust cases involving Section 2 of the Sherman Act.

U.S. STEEL

In *United States* v. *United States Steel Corporation*, the Supreme Court took a lenient view of the holding company established in 1901 by U.S. Steel.[3] The company was composed of twelve iron and steel producers which were horizontally related. Antitrust proceedings were started against the company in 1911. When it was formed, the holding company controlled 66 per cent of steel production. By 1911, its share of the market had dropped to 54 per cent. U.S. Steel contended that the major reason the holding company was developed was to take advantage of economies of scale. However, at least one of its actions betrays its contention. In 1907, U.S. Steel began holding "Gary dinners" which were attended by the members of the holding company as well as independent steel producers. The primary purpose of the meetings was to fix the price of steel. However, because the meetings ceased prior to the antitrust suit, the price-fixing scheme was not challenged by the Court.

A district court decided that U.S. Steel neither monopolized nor intended to monopolize the steel industry. The court also found that there was no evidence of the use of predatory practices by U.S. Steel against its competitors. In contrast to the district court's decision, the government argued that the holding company was powerful and that it had used its power to become dominant in the industry. This dominance was expressed by the fact that it had become the industry price leader, thus suppressing price competition in the industry.

The Supreme Court decided that U.S. Steel acted legally in the formation and operation of its holding company. The logic of the Court is worth following. Its reasoning centers around two major issues: (1) power and (2) size.

The Court did not believe that U.S. Steel had acquired sufficient monopoly power in the industry to restrain trade. In support of its conclusion, it observed that the holding company had to resort to the Gary dinners in order to control the activities of its competitors. The mere fact that the dinners were held indicated to the Court that the company did not have monopoly power. This reasoning is based on the fallacious assumption that monopoly power is an "all or nothing" concept. A firm can have monopoly power even if it has competitors in its industry which do not charge the same price. To be sure, its monopoly power is not absolute; it is less than that which a pure monopolist would have. The evidence presented in the case even suggests that U.S. Steel had such power. The government argued that U.S. Steel had become a price leader in the industry and that this suppressed competition. An economist testified that "when prices are constant through a definite period, an artificial influence is indicated." The economist was telling the Court that where monopoly power exists, firms might engage in tacit collusion to eliminate price competition. However, the Court was not impressed with the economist's testimony, reasoning that "there was a danger of deception in generalities, and in a case of this importance we should have something surer for judgment than speculation, something more than a deduction. . . ."[4] The Court also reasoned that since U.S. Steel did not use any predatory practices against its competitors, its monopoly power was not exercised.

This conclusion is based on the fallacious assumption that unfair practices are the only indicators of the existence of monopoly power. It should be fairly obvious that predatory practices do not necessarily result from monopoly power. In fact, where competitors are willing to follow the pricing policies of an industry leader, there is little incentive for the leader to attempt to drive them out of business. Yet, the Court decided that overt acts are necessary in order to find the firm guilty; " . . . we must adhere to the law, and the law does not make the existence of unexerted power an offense. It, we repeat, requires overt acts."[5] This analysis implies that it is perfectly legal for a firm to charge high prices and restrict output by virtue of its monopoly power, because charging high prices and restricting output are not predatory practices. Of course, they do represent the exercise of monopoly power.

After concluding that U.S. Steel did not exercise monopoly power, the Court considered whether mere size was an offense under the Sherman Act. In its view, the law required that size be obtained in a lawful manner and be developed by natural growth. If that is the case, then a firm " . . . is entitled to maintain its size and power that legitimately goes with it, provided no law has been transgressed in obtaining it."[6]

Since there is no evidence of the magnitude of the economies resulting from the holding company and no precise indicator of the monopoly power U.S. Steel acquired, it is difficult to second-guess the Court's decision. But it is highly probable that a firm acquiring control of 50 per cent of the market in an industry has monopoly power. Moreover, the Court record suggests that the monopoly power was utilized, not to drive competitors out of business, but to promote parallel pricing policies in the industry. In some instances, the Court's reasoning is somewhat less than brilliant concerning the issue of monopoly power. However, its decision is understandable. Economists did not have a clear notion of the nature of oligopolistic pricing until the 1930s. Moreover, the government lawyers did not offer a strong attack against U.S. Steel.

ALCOA

The Court also used a lenient application of the Sherman Act in the *International Harvester* case of 1927.[7] Because the two decisions were lenient, they severely limited the applicability of the Sherman Act. It was not until 1945 that a major antitrust case involving monopolization again appeared. The case, *United States* v. *Aluminum Company of America*,[8] was extremely important because a court of appeals decision rejected many of the legal attitudes developed in *U.S. Steel.*

Alcoa began producing aluminum in 1888. It had secured a patent on the production process, and by virtue of its patent rights it was the sole producer of the product from 1888 to 1906. Then a more economical production process was developed by an independent party, and Alcoa acquired the sole right to use this method. This extended Alcoa's monopoly until 1909. The question before the court was whether or not Alcoa had maintained its monopoly after 1909 through the use of unfair practices.

Judge Hand gave the majority decision of the court of appeals.[9] He first set out to determine whether Alcoa had monopoly power in the production of aluminum. The company was the sole producer of "virgin ingot" in the United States. However, it faced competition from foreign producers as well as from the secondary (used) ingot market. Judge Hand wanted to determine the percentage of the market which Alcoa controlled. This required a determination of what products to include in the overall aluminum market and what products to attribute to Alcoa. In an earlier decision, the district court had found that Alcoa's market share would be 33 per cent if you attribute to Alcoa the virgin ingot they sell, the secondary ingot which they indirectly control,[10] and dismiss from the overall aluminum market the virgin ingot which Alcoa itself used for fabrication. This is computed from the following formula:

$$\frac{\text{virgin ingot sold by Alcoa} + \text{secondary ingot}}{\text{virgin ingot sold by Alcoa} + \text{secondary ingot} + \text{imported virgin ingot}} = 33\%$$

If, on the other hand, you attribute to Alcoa the ingot that Alcoa itself uses for fabrication, as well as the virgin ingot it sells, and include in the overall market the virgin ingot sold by Alcoa, the virgin ingot used by Aloca, the imported virgin ingot, and the secondary ingot, Alcoa's market share is 64 per cent. This is computed in the following manner:

$$\frac{\text{virgin ingot sold by Alcoa} + \text{virgin ingot used by Alcoa}}{\text{virgin ingot sold by Alcoa} + \text{virgin ingot used by Alcoa} + \text{secondary ingot} + \text{imported virgin ingot}} = 64\%$$

Finally, if you attribute to Alcoa the virgin ingot it sells, and the virgin ingot it uses itself, and include in the over-all market everything except the secondary ingot, you will find that Alcoa has 90 per cent of the market. This is computed in the following way:

$$\frac{\begin{array}{c}\text{virgin ingot sold} \\ \text{by Alcoa}\end{array} + \begin{array}{c}\text{virgin ingot used} \\ \text{by Alcoa}\end{array}}{\begin{array}{c}\text{virgin ingot sold} \\ \text{by Alcoa}\end{array} + \begin{array}{c}\text{virgin ingot used} \\ \text{by Alcoa}\end{array} + \begin{array}{c}\text{imported} \\ \text{virgin ingot}\end{array}} = 90\%$$

By adopting the first approach, the district court attributed 33 per cent of the market to Alcoa. But Judge Hand adopted the last approach because he contended that the ingot Alcoa used for its own fabrication affected the overall market for ingot. He reasoned that the more fabrication Alcoa performed, the greater would be the supply of fabricated items. Hence, the independent fabricators would be able to sell less and produce less, which, in turn, affected their demand for ingot. Hand excluded secondary ingot from the market, reasoning that Alcoa neither sold it nor competed against that source of aluminum. Rather, by affecting the supply of virgin ingot, Alcoa had control over the supply of secondary ingot.

There is some reasonable doubt as to whether Alcoa had the ability to control the secondary market. Whether it could do so seems to hinge on its ability to project the future supply and demand of secondary ingot and take that into account in determining the optimum quantity of virgin ingot to produce. Additionally, other variables such as efficiency in reclaiming the secondary ingot as well as the competitive ability of secondary ingot producers would affect Alcoa's control over the market. In any event, Hand concluded that Alcoa supplied 90 per cent of the market for ingot and foreign producers supplied 10 per cent.

Alcoa had argued in the district court that it did not have monopoly power and claimed that evidence of this was the fact that it never earned profits in excess of 10 per cent. Judge Hand dismissed profit as an indicator of competition. He first argued that the profits on ingot were not necessarily the same as the overall profit of the company. Alcoa could have been earning exorbitant profits in the production of ingot and below average profits elsewhere. Second, Judge Hand said that "the mere fact that a producer having control of the domestic market has not been able to make more than a 'fair' profit, is no evidence that a 'fair' profit could not have been made at a lower price."[11]

Hand considered the issue of whether Alcoa intended to achieve a monopolistic position in the industry. He concluded that the mere fact that Alcoa "meant to keep and did keep that complete and exclusive hold upon the ingot market with which it started" was evidence of its intent to monopolize.[12] The reader will remember that in the *U.S. Steel* case, the Court required evidence of predatory practices in order to find the steel company guilty. Judge Hand did not require evidence of these practices. Instead, he emphasized the market share of the company as evidence of monopoly power. By so doing, he shifted the court's emphasis to a market-structure test.

Judge Hand was quick to say that not all forms of monopolization were illegal. If monopoly power had been thrust upon Alcoa it would have been allowed. Hand said that "persons may unwittingly find themselves in possession of a monopoly, automatically so to say: that is, without having intended either to put an end to existing competition or prevent competition from arising when none had existed; they may become monopolies by force of accident."[13]

Another statement by Hand tends to suggest that the law leaves room for the competitor who wins the game: "A single producer may be the survivor of a group of active competitors, merely by virtue of his superior skill, foresight and industry. In such cases a strong argument can be made that although the result may expose the public to the evils of monopoly, the Act does not mean to condemn the resultant of those very forces which it is its prime object to foster: the successful competitor having been urged to compete, must not be turned upon when he wins."[14] However, Judge Hand decided that Alcoa's actions went past those required just to be a successful competitor and in presenting his logic for this decision, he suggested that he did not really mean that a firm which gains monopoly power by virtue of being efficient can escape antitrust prosecution.

> Alcoa avows it as evidence of the skill, energy and initiative with which it has always conducted its business; as a reason why, having won its way by fair means, it should be commended, and not dismembered. . . . The only question is whether it falls within the exception established in favor of those who do not seek, but cannot avoid the control of a market. It seems to us that that question scarcely survives its statement. It was not inevitable that it should always anticipate increases in the demand for ingot and be prepared to supply them. Nothing compelled it to keep doubling and redoubling its capacity before others entered the field. It insists that it never excluded competitors; but

> we can think of no more effective exclusion than progres-
> sively to embrace each new opportunity as it opened, and
> to face every newcomer with new capacity already geared
> into a great organization, having the advantage of experi-
> ence, trade connections and the elite of personnel.[15]

Does Judge Hand's statement really leave room for a successful competitor? The items he cited as practices which suggest to him that Alcoa sought monopoly power are usually considered to be competitive practices. Is it anticompetitive to be prepared for future demand? Is it wrong to have trade connections and the elite of personnel? Contrary to some of his earlier observations, Hand's statement leaves very little room under the law for the firm that wins the competitive game. This statement should not imply that Alcoa's practices were always competitive ones. No doubt it had monopoly power, no matter which share-of-the-market test is used. Further-more, there is evidence that Alcoa went further in its actions than just meeting competition. But the point is that the wording of Hand's decision left little room for the successful competitor to pass by the prohibitions of Section 2 of the Sherman Act.

In summary, Hand found that Alcoa had 90 per cent of the ingot market. He further concluded that that monopoly position was gained by actions which went further than those required to be a normal competitor. Therefore, Alcoa was found guilty. Great empha-sis was put on the use of the structure test to determine whether monopoly power existed. Hand said that the court would not chal-lenge a monopoly position developed by a firm that is simply the best in the industry and wins the competitive game. However, the wording of his attack on Alcoa leaves reasonable doubt as to whether that is true.

The government produced aluminum itself during World War II. At the end of the war, the sale of its facilities initiated the formation of Reynolds Metal Co. and Kaiser Aluminum and Chemical Corp. The court thought that these new competitors would reduce Alcoa's monopoly power, and therefore Alcoa was not required to divest itself of any of its production facilities. The addition of Reynolds Metal and Kaiser no doubt increased competition because Alcoa's market share was reduced to 50 per cent. However, our study of oligopolistic behavior in Chapter II suggested that the existence of only three firms will not afford the public much competition. Nor is there much reason to expect additional competition through the entry of new firms. John V. Krutilla has said of competition in the aluminum industry:

It is not realistic to assume that the new market structure created by the Government's disposal program would have promoted anything approaching competitive behavior on the part of the Big Three. Moreover, a limitation on entrance of new firms resulted from the Government's policy of creating huge integrated operations. Except in time of war, or preparation for war, the normal growth in demand for aluminum is gradual and can be met easily by the addition of new potlines to existing reduction capacity—provided excess alumina capacity exists. This contrasts with the difficulty of entering the market with a completely integrated operation of economical scale. Thus the opportunity for the Big Three to expand by relatively small increments as postwar demand increased made it virtually impossible for new firms to enter the industry.[16]

E. I. DU PONT DE NEMOURS & CO.

Nowhere was the determination of the relevant market more important than in *United States* v. *E. I. du Pont De Nemours & Co.*, decided in 1956 by the Supreme Court.[17] In that case, the government argued that du Pont had obtained a monopoly in the production of cellophane. Since the government did not contend that the firm attempted to monopolize the market, intent was not a significant issue in this case. The district court had concluded that the relevant market included not just the production of cellophane but the production of all flexible wrapping materials. Viewed in this broad manner, the district court decided that du Pont did not have a monopoly. Moreover, it thought that even if the company did have monopoly power, "the acquisition of power was protected by patents and was acquired solely through du Pont's business expertise. It was thus thrust upon du Pont."[18]

The Supreme Court observed that the company had monopoly power in the market (about 75 per cent of the market) if cellophane was the relevant market in which du Pont competed. On the other hand, if all flexible wrapping materials were included in the definition of the market, then the Court thought the company did not have monopoly power (less than 20 per cent of the market). Therefore, the first problem was to determine the relevant market. To reach its determination, the Court relied on the cross elasticity of demand between cellophane and other flexible wrapping materials. Cross elasticity of demand can be used to determine whether goods are complements, substitutes, or are unrelated. Assume the existence of two goods A and B, for which we determine the cross elasticity of demand. The formula to compute the cross elasticity coefficient between the two goods is:

$$C_{E_D} = \frac{\text{relative change in the quantity demanded of product A}}{\text{relative change in the price of product B}}$$

The sign of the coefficient is the most important issue in the determination of cross elasticity. If it is positive, it means that the price and quantity variables move in the same direction: that is, an increase in the price of B increases the demand for A; a decrease in the price of B decreases the demand for A. This relationship implies that the goods are substitutes and therefore competitive. The greater the positive value of the cross elasticity of demand, the greater the substitutability of the two products.

If the sign of the coefficient is negative, the variables move in opposite directions: an increase in the price of B decreases the demand for A; a decrease in the price of B increases the demand for A. This implies that the goods are complements, meaning that they are products which are consumed together such as bread and butter. The Court was trying to see if cellophane was a substitute for other flexible wrapping materials, or, in other words, if the cross elasticity of demand between cellophane and other flexible wrapping materials was significantly positive. The only problem with the elasticity concept is that most companies will not allow experimentation with their prices to determine the cross elasticity coefficient. Therefore, in lieu of the actual computation of the cross elasticity of demand, analysts frequently have to logically deduce the degree to which products can be substituted for one another. When it is used in the courtroom, this judgment has been called the *Reasonable Interchangeability Test.*

Applying this test in the *Du Pont* case, the Court used the following facts to substantiate its findings that cellophane was in strong competition with other flexible wrapping materials.

1. Except with regard to permeability to gasses, cellophane has no qualities which are not possessed by a number of other wrapping materials.
2. "An element for consideration as to cross elasticity of demand between products is the responsiveness of the sales of one product to price changes of the other. . . . [The] 'great sensitivity of customers in the flexible packaging markets to price or quality changes' prevented du Pont from possessing monopoly control over price."[19]

In addition to finding that du Pont did not have a monopolistic position in the flexible wrapping material market, the Court said that du Pont did not attempt to exclude competitors from the market.

Not everyone has agreed with the Court's definition of the market. Chief Justice Warren wrote the dissenting opinion of the Court in which he argued that the relevant market was cellophane, not all flexible wrapping materials. He thought that the characteristics of cellophane differed significantly from the characteristics of other wrapping materials and cited as evidence the fact that from 1923 to 1947 cellophane enjoyed phenomenal growth. Yet during this period the price of the product was far greater than the price of other wrapping materials. Warren said: "We cannot believe that buyers, practical businessmen, would have bought cellophane in increasing amounts over a quarter of a century if close substitutes were available at from one-seventh to one-half cellophane's price."[20] Other evidence was given to show that du Pont had monopoly power. Sylvania, the only other cellophane producer in the United States, always followed du Pont's price changes. Additionally, from 1924 to 1932, du Pont dropped the price of its cellophane 84 per cent, while producers of other wrapping materials held their price constant. Warren concluded that "If 'shifts of business' due to 'price sensitivity' had been substantial, glassine and waxed paper producers who wanted to stay in business would have been compelled by market forces to meet du Pont's price challenge just as Sylvania was."[21] On the basis of its findings, the minority of the Supreme Court would have found du Pont guilty of monopolization.

After studying the cellophane case, George Stocking and Willard Mueller came to similar conclusions.[22] They observed that du Pont's actions implied that the company thought it had a monopoly in the production of cellophane.

> Du Pont's moves and countermoves to protect its domestic market were the strategy of a producer operating in a monopolistic, not a competitive, market. Its agreements with foreign producers to license patents and exchange technical data, its domestic patent program, its effort to get higher tariffs, its restrictive market agreement with Sylvania, all reflect du Pont's effort to preserve what it apparently regarded as a monopoly market.[23]

Stocking and Mueller concluded that du Pont was correct in assuming that it had monopoly power. They found that "cellophane is so differentiated from other flexible wrapping materials that its cross elasticity of demand gives du Pont significant and continuing monopoly power" and cited as evidence of the monopoly power the fact that du Pont followed a pricing policy independent of the producers of other flexible wrapping materials.[24] Finally, Stocking and Mueller found that du Pont earned monopoly profits on the production of cellophane.

The fact that the Supreme Court used economic analysis is admirable. It will be a long time before the reader again sees it applied to the degree that it was used in this case. However, the minority view of the Court appears to be correct. There is a strong possibility that the relevant market was limited to cellophane, and there is little question that du Pont had monopoly power in the production of cellophane.

SUMMARY

The courts have followed a general pattern in deciding monopolization cases. First, without exception, they use a rule of reason. In applying the rule of reason they first determine whether the firm involved has the intent to monopolize a market. Even if a firm does not gain monopoly power, it is sometimes guilty if it intends to do so. If a firm does gain monopoly power, the courts frequently consider this to be sufficient evidence of intent to monopolize. Next, the courts determine whether the firm has acquired monopoly power. To do this, they first attempt to determine the relevant market in which the alleged monopoly competes.

After defining this market, they find the market share controlled by the firm. According to the courts, just because a firm has a large share of the market does not imply that it is guilty of monopolization. Whether or not a large share constitutes a monopoly depends on how the firm got that share and how it used it. If, for example, monopoly power is acquired through fair competition, the courts say they will allow the monopoly, although some passages in the *Alcoa* decision leave reasonable doubt as to whether that is true. If the firm uses monopoly power to initiate predatory practices to harm its competitors, the courts have found the firm guilty of monopolization. Certainly the courts have relied much more heavily on a performance test than a structure test.

Since *du Pont*, there have been few cases on monopolization. This is true for three reasons. First, while there are fifteen or twenty extremely large companies in the U.S., few firms are able to achieve the size required for a monopolization charge under the provisions of the Sherman Act. Second, the courts' unwillingness to break up large firms has thwarted the government's desire to prosecute them. Finally, until recently the F.T.C. and the Justice Department have lacked the financial resources necessary to prosecute and restructure large companies. Certainly in the past twenty-five years antitrust has operated under a double standard. We have seen that the laws on mergers are strict. They are designed to prevent a firm from acquiring monopoly power. However, the firms which have already acquired it appear to be immune from prosecution.

SHARED MONOPOLY: THE PRESENT
AND THE FUTURE

Since the *American Tobacco* decision, both the F.T.C. and the Justice Department have been reluctant to prosecute oligopolies when their only sin is a concentrated market structure. It is evident in the U.S. economy that concentration itself is not illegal. Approximately one-third of the total dollar value of goods produced is manufactured in industries where four or fewer firms account for more than fifty per cent of production. Moreover, in some industries the concentration ratio is rising, although the overall level of concentration in the U.S. economy has remained relatively stable over the past twenty-five years.

Critics of industrial concentration claim that a concentrated market structure causes many evils.[25] Among those cited most frequently are restricted output, higher-than-normal prices, reduced employment of workers, lack of meaningful invention and innovation, retardation of the effectiveness of monetary and fiscal policy and undue control of government. Another adverse claim has been evident throughout this text; most of the cases we have studied result from firms' use of practices symptomatic of the monopoly power caused by economic concentration. Therefore, failure to declare concentrated industries illegal forces the courts and the F.T.C. to hear a never ending series of cases which are simply symptoms of the fundamental problem of monopoly power. Eradication of the power itself would, in the long run, reduce the antitrust workload.

While the case against concentrated industries is supported by the majority of economists, some argue that the case is not sufficiently strong to warrant an attack on the industries. According to Professor J. Fred Weston, concentration itself is not an evil and, as evidence of that fact, he found that price increases have been smaller in concentrated industries. According to Weston, "Concentration reflects and creates economic efficiency, which moderates the inflationary pressures rather than causing them."[26] The concentrated industries themselves express their innocence and their inability to understand why mere structure should be attacked when there is no evidence of abusive practices against competitors. Many legislators support the claim of these industries.

At the time of this writing, neither the F.T.C. nor the Department of Justice has officially censored economic concentration. However, at no time in history has it been more likely that concentrated industries will eventually be prosecuted. Enough economic studies have already been performed to warrant cases against some of them. Moreover, the political climate seems ripe for such an attack. The public has experienced shortages which have caused them to distrust big business. Adding to their distrust is the suspicion that business controls government. The courts themselves have clearly recognized that economic concentration can be harmful. In the *Philadelphia National Bank* and *Von's Shopping Bag* cases, the courts prohibited mergers in order to retard economic concentration. While the decisions in these cases do not establish the precedent to attack concentrated industries, they make it clear that the courts feared concentration. In fact, the whole thrust of Section 7 of the Clayton Act is to prevent the U.S. economy from becoming more concentrated.

Treatment of already-existing concentration would seem to be the next logical step. To do otherwise would be to perpetuate the double standard. Recently, the breakfast cereal industry and the oil industry have come under judicial attack. While it is too early to make any solid conclusions, it appears that the F.T.C. and the Justice Department have developed a new interest in attacking concentrated industry. While the thrust of their attack is based on the practices of the industries rather than their structure, the practices are so indicative of structure that perhaps antitrust will take the next logical step.

It probably would not be necessary to pass new legislation in order to permit the courts and the F.T.C. to attack oligopolies. Section 7 of the Clayton Act could be coupled with the "backward-sweep doctrine" to attack the great majority of industries. Additionally Section 2 of the Sherman Act could probably be broadened to include oligopolies. Nevertheless, new legislation has been proposed by two members of Congress. Senator Fred Harris introduced a bill in Congress in 1971. His *Concentrated Industries Act* is based on the 1968 recommendations of the *White House Task Force on Antitrust Policy*. Harris' bill would require that the F.T.C. and the Department of Justice prosecute industries which have sales of $500 million or more and which have a four-firm concentration ratio of 70 per cent or more. It also would provide for a special antitrust court to hear cases, and the court would be allowed to accept economies of scale as a defense. The proposal was unsuccessful in Congress.

Senator Philip Hart's *Industrial Reorganization Act* is more extensive than the Harris proposal. Like the Harris bill, it treats concentration itself as illegal. According to the bill, concentration is undue when:

A. The average rate of return for an industry is in excess of fifteen per cent over a period of five consecutive years out of the most recent seven years;

B. There has been no appreciable price competition among two or more firms in an industry for a period of three consecutive years out of the most recent five years;

C. Four or fewer firms have fifty per cent of the sales in the industry.

A concentrated industry may continue to exist only if its monopoly power results from the existence of valid patent rights or if breaking up the industry causes production and distribution costs to increase.

The act would be implemented by an Industrial Reorganization Commission, the chairman of which would be appointed by the president. Senator Hart believes that the commission could perform its work within fifteen years. Actual cases would be heard by an Industrial Reorganization Court, and cases could be appealed from that court directly to the Supreme Court. The bill requires that special attention be given to a study of the following industries: chemical products and drugs, electronic computing and communication equipment, electrical machinery and equipment, energy, iron and steel, motor vehicles, and nonferrous metals. The bill is an extremely far reaching one; one hundred and forty of the largest two hundred corporations are in these industries. The bill is still in Congress, but it is doubtful that it will be passed in the next two or three years.

Should economic concentration be attacked? The answer is an extensive one which would require a summary of hundreds of present and future studies. The scope of this text is not broad enough to perform that analysis. Perhaps it is enough to conclude that the avenue for prosecution should exist and that the decision to prosecute should be made on a case-by-case analysis. Certainly everyone can agree that some oligopolistic industries operate in a manner which is harmful to consumer welfare. We concluded in Chapter VI that it would be irrational to expect some of them to operate in any other way given their market structure. Of course prosecution of concentrated industries is not without problems even if economies of scale are allowed as a defense. Such prosecution might break up firms which simply played the competitive game fairly and won. Big business argues that this solution is unfair and moreover that it might lessen their incentive to compete. Deciding whether it is unfair involves a value judgment which each reader can make on his own. He must decide whether he wants to be fair to the consumer or to the producer. But the incentive argument is a fallacious one. Placed in a truly competitive industry, the firm will have to compete and compete strongly or else go out of business. That should be incentive enough!

NOTES TO CHAPTER XV

[1]*Standard Oil Company* v. *United States,* 31 S. Ct. 504 (1911).
[2]31 S. Ct. 508, 511 (1911).
[3]40 S. Ct. 293 (1920).
[4]40 S. Ct. 293, 298 (1920).
[5]40 S. Ct. 293, 299 (1920).
[6]40 S. Ct. 293, 302 (1920).
[7]274 U.S. 693 (1927).
[8]148 F. 2d 416 (1945).
[9]The court of appeals heard the case because the Supreme Court was unable to obtain a quorum.
[10]Since Alcoa had almost a virtual monopoly in the production of virgin ingot, the court reasoned that it could affect the supply of secondary ingot. That is, the quantity of virgin ingot placed on the market today affects the quantity of secondary ingot available in the future.
[11]148 F. 2d 416, 427 (1945).
[12]148 F. 2d 416, 432 (1945).
[13]148 F. 2d 416, 429-30 (1945). This viewpoint has never been formally sanctioned by the Supreme Court.
[14]148 F. 2d 416, 430 (1945).
[15]148 F. 2d 416, 430-431 (1945).
[16]John V. Krutilla, "Aluminum—A Dilemma for Antitrust Aims?" *Southern Economic Journal,* XXII (October, 1955), 166-67.
[17]70 S. Ct. 994 (1956).
[18]70 S. Ct. 994, 999 (1956).
[19]70 S. Ct. 998, 1010 (1956).
[20]70 S. Ct. 994, 1018 (1956).
[21]70 S. Ct. 994, 1019 (1956).
[22]George W. Stocking and Willard F. Mueller, "The Cellophane Case and the New Competition," *American Economic Review,* XLV (March, 1955), 29-63.
[23]*Ibid.,* p. 44.
[24]*Ibid.,* p. 63.
[25]For a thorough presentation of the case against concentrated industries see John M. Blair, *Economic Concentration: Structure, Behavior and Public Policy* (New York: Harcourt Brace Jovanovich, Inc., 1972).
[26]J. Fred Weston, "Implications of Recent Research for the Structual Approach to Oligopoly," *Antitrust Law Journal,* 41 (September, 1972), 634.

PRICE DISCRIMINATION AND THE ROBINSON-PATMAN ACT

CHAPTER XVI

When a producer charges different prices to different customers, he may harm some of the customers by making them uncompetitive. Yet the practice of price discrimination might evidence the fact that the producer is engaged in active competition. In this chapter we explore the economic nature of price discrimination as well as its legal status. We will see that the practice poses a special dilemma for antitrust enforcers.

INTRODUCTION

Price discrimination occurs when a seller charges different prices to different customers for the same product.[1] We can see examples of this practice every day in the United States. Doctors often charge lower prices to their poor clients than to rich ones. Magazines offer subscriptions at a lower rate for new subscribers than for their established customers, and phone companies vary their rates according to what time of day a customer uses the telephone. A firm's profit-maximizing price for one customer is not necessarily the same for all customers. Therefore the use of price discrimination simply indicates that customers have different elasticities of demand for a given product.

The presence of price discrimination also indicates that the seller has some degree of monopoly power. The practice would be irrational in a purely competitive market because the pure competitor faces a horizontal demand curve indicating only one profit-maximizing price. However, the firm with some degree of monopoly power faces a host of customers with differing degrees of product attachment, and the firm may find it advantageous to charge different prices. It will be able to discriminate as long as its submarkets can be separated—that is, as long as customers with a relatively inelastic demand are not free to buy in the lowest-price market.

TYPES OF PRICE DISCRIMINATION

A. C. Pigou divided price discrimination into three general categories: first-degree, second-degree, and third-degree price discrimination. A knowledge of each of these is important for an understanding of the reasons for the practice as well as its operation. First-degree price discrimination occurs whenever a seller is able to extract from each customer the very most he is willing to pay for the product. It is often attempted by automobile dealerships which, through various means, try to discover the highest price that customers are willing to pay for a car. Naturally the attempt is not perfectly successful, and the dealership usually receives only an amount approximating this price. First-degree price discrimination may be successful when a customer buys only one unit of a product. However, it is almost impossible to implement when the customer buys more than one unit. The customer would have to be charged lower and lower prices because as additional units are bought, the product's utility diminishes for him.

In graphical terms, the seller engaged in first-degree price discrimination moves down the demand curve as he sells additional units. For each unit sold, he receives the price shown on the demand curve for that unit. This is the one instance in economic theory in which, under conditions of imperfect competition, marginal revenue and average revenue are equal. If successful, first-degree price discrimination extinguishes all consumer's surplus.

Second-degree price discrimination occurs when a seller charges lower and lower prices for incremental units of a product sold. However, the increments exceed one unit. For example, an electric utility might charge a certain price for the first thousand kilowatt hours, and then lower and lower prices for each additional thousand kilowatt hours purchased. Under this degree of price discrimination each customer is treated equally in that all customers buying a certain quantity pay the same price. Yet those who buy larger quantities receive the additional units at a lower price. The implementation of second-degree price discrimination is depicted in *Figure I*. DD' is one consumer's demand curve. The seller charges P_1 for the first 1,000 units. For the next 1,000 units he charges P_2 and for the next 1,000 units, P_3. The consumer is left with some consumer's surplus under second-degree price discrimination. If the consumer buys 3,000 units, his consumer's surplus is equal to the sum of the striped triangles in *Figure I*.

Third-degree price discrimination describes a situation where a seller divides his customers into two or more groups according to their elasticities of demand, and then charges each group a different price. For example, industrial users of a product may have a higher elasticity of demand than other consumers and, as a result, may be charged a lower price. A store may have two branches—one in a wealthy section of town and one in a poor section. It might charge

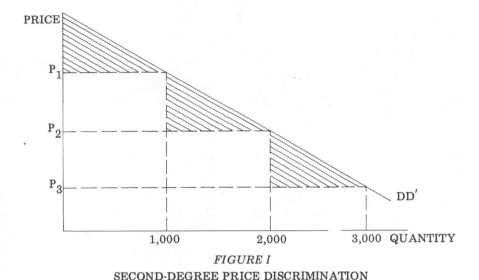

FIGURE I
SECOND-DEGREE PRICE DISCRIMINATION

higher prices in the wealthy section provided its wealthy customers do not shop in the poor section. On the other hand it might charge higher prices in the poor section if it is found that the poor, due to their immobility, have a lower elasticity of demand.

The model for third-degree price discrimination is shown in *Figure II*. In that figure there are two demand curves, DD'_1 and DD'_2, and their corresponding marginal revenue curves, MR_1 and MR_2. Each demand curve represents the demand of a different group of consumers. The DD'_2 curve shows both a greater product demand and a more inelastic product demand that DD'_1. In order to find his profit-maximizing quantity, the seller will first derive an aggregate marginal revenue curve for his firm. He can do this by horizontally summing the two marginal revenue curves, MR_1 and MR_2. This will give him the combined marginal revenue curve, ΣMR. He will then equate his marginal cost (MC in *Figure II*) with the combined marginal revenue (ΣMR), and where they intersect he will find his profit-maximizing quantity, Q_T.

To determine the quantity sold in each market, he will equate the marginal revenue in each market with the marginal cost of the last unit produced. By bringing a guideline horizontally over from the point where ΣMR equaled MC to show the level of the marginal cost of the last unit produced and finding this line's intersection with the marginal revenue curves for each market (MR_1 and MR_2), he can find the profit-maximizing quantity to sell in each market. In *Figure II*, Q_1 is sold in market one, and Q_2 is sold in market two. Price is

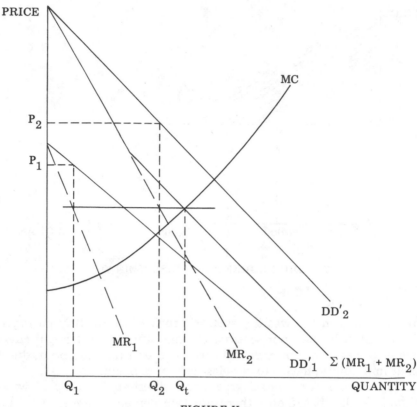

FIGURE II
THIRD-DEGREE PRICE DISCRIMINATION

found in the normal manner. It is on the individual market demand curves directly above the quantities sold. In this case, P_1 is charged in market one, and P_2 is charged in market two.

THE EFFECTS OF PRICE
DISCRIMINATION ON CONSUMER WELFARE

Price discrimination could conceivably alter consumer welfare in one or more of the following instances.

1. If a product is sold directly to the final consumer without affecting competitors unfavorably, it might alter consumer welfare.
2. If a product is sold directly to final consumers but at a price in some markets which is so low that competitors cannot meet it,

it might affect competitors unfavorably. While consumers might gain while the product is being sold at the low price, they may ultimately lose if competitors are driven out of business.

3. If a product is sold to some firms at a lower level of distribution at a price less expensive than that charged other firms at the same level of distribution, the competitive ability of the firms paying the higher price might be impaired. If these firms are ultimately driven out of business, consumers might be harmed.

Each of these instances will be discussed individually.

PRODUCT SOLD DIRECTLY TO FINAL CONSUMERS, COMPETITORS NOT HARMED

Suppose that a seller's product is bought by final consumers only, not by businessmen who would use it as an intermediate good. Can price discrimination be judged socially harmful in this instance? If the alternative to price discrimination is a single price monopoly and if the price discrimination does not seriously harm competitors, then the answer is "no". To be sure, consumers paying higher than an "average " price (the price which would be charged if price discrimination did not exist) are harmed by discrimination, but consumers paying less than the "average" price are helped. We saw in Chapter VII that when one is unable to measure and compare the relative harms and benefits of the two groups, it is impossible to say that the net effect of the practice is detrimental to society. Even if the framers of the Robinson-Patman Act failed to recognize this point, they did not outlaw price discrimination when it simply results in some consumers paying higher prices than others. To do so would be equivalent to outlawing profit-maximizing prices. Only when price discrimination harms competitors which, in turn, may eventually harm consumers, does it violate the provisions of the act.

Kaldor crit. ?

✱

PRODUCT SOLD DIRECTLY TO FINAL CONSUMERS, COMPETITORS HARMED

Suppose that a firm engaged in price discrimination sells its products to consumers at lower prices in one of its markets than in the other market. When it affects competition at the level of distribution where the price discrimination is exercised, it is called primary-line price discrimination. If the practice affects competitors adversely

retailers

it could conceivably be harmful to consumers in the long run. If, for example, a grocery chain charges lower prices in one market than in another, it might drive competitors out of business and acquire monopoly power. Of course, the practice is not always rational, to be successful it requires specific market conditions such as restricted entry, and it is difficult to separate this instance of price discrimination from hard price competition. Prices might be lower in one market because of intense competition, not because of an intent to drive competitors out of business.

PRODUCT SOLD TO FIRMS AT A LOWER LEVEL OF DISTRIBUTION, COMPETITORS HARMED

Suppose that a firm engaged in price discrimination sells its products to businesses which, in turn, sell to final consumers. If one businessman is able to obtain the product at a cheaper price than that charged his competitors, won't he have a competitive advantage? The answer is "yes". Therefore, price discrimination might decrease competition between the customers of the price-discriminating firm. Because the competition affected is at a lower level of distribution than the price discrimination, it is called secondary-line price discrimination. To visualize its competitive effects, suppose that there is one large tire producer and several small ones. When the various tire producers purchase their rubber requirements, they will bargain with their suppliers. By virtue of its buying power and its skillful bargaining, the large tire producer may be able to procure rubber at a discount and if he is able to do this, he will have a competitive advantage. Assuming the worst, suppose he charges a lower price than competitors, and eventually all of them are forced out of business. The market will be left with one tire producer who can extract monopolistic profits from all customers. The great majority of economists would say that there is nothing "unfair" about the tire producer's buying rubber at a lower price than competitors. After all, isn't driving a hard bargain in buying just as much a part of competition as driving a hard bargain in selling? But most economists would denounce the worst possible consequences of the bargain: monopoly power.

THE APPROPRIATE ANTITRUST POLICY

Assuming a reasonable likelihood that firms acquire monopoly power through the use of any form of price discrimination, there are a number of alternative policies which could remedy the problem. The government could require that each firm charge all of its customers the same price. This would eradicate the harmful effects of primary-line and secondary-line price discrimination. We will shortly see that this approximates the approach taken under the provisions of the Robinson-Patman Act. Alternatively, the government could eliminate the source of the problem. Firms which engage in price discrimination which harms their competitors probably have more power than competitors. Otherwise, they could not drive their adversaries out of business. The same is true for the monopsonistic firm which is able to buy at lower prices than can its competitors. This power could be eliminated through divestiture proceedings.

The whole problem of how to treat price discrimination is one of the greatest dilemmas in antitrust. To develop an analogy begun in the last chapter, if a football team is invincible, we could let it win every game it plays, break it up and scatter its players to all the competing teams, or outlaw some of the team's best plays. All alternatives seem equally unpalatable. And the issue of how the team gained the power to win every game is a moot one. The effect is the same no matter how the power is acquired. The government has chosen to outlaw some business plays by way of the Robinson-Patman amendment to Section 2 of the Clayton Act. Shortly we will see the application of the act to actual instances of price discrimination. Before doing this, a word of warning is appropriate. In our examples of both primary-line and secondary-line price discrimination we have assumed the most disasterous consequence imaginable; price discrimination resulted in the creation of monopoly power. But such an occurrence is not definite or even probable. Therefore, any antitrust agency or economist analyzing the competitive aspects of price discrimination must be mindful of the tendency of small firms to complain that they have been hurt when what they define as harm is really competition. Authorities have to discern the very narrow line between protecting competition and protecting competitors. The former objective protects consumers while the latter protects competitors, possibly at the expense of consumers. The situation is almost identical to that encountered in evaluating mergers under Section 7 of the Clayton Act.

APPLICATION OF THE ROBINSON-PATMAN ACT

The major provisions of the Robinson-Patman amendment to Section 2 of the Clayton Act have already been discussed in Chapter

X. However, before analyzing its application to specific cases, we should remind ourselves of a few of the amendment's features. Congress was primarily concerned with stopping the use of price discrimination when it lessened competition between a price discriminator and his competitors or between the customers of a supplier. Therefore, the framers of the Robinson-Patman Act did not intend to disallow all price discrimination, but only that which "may be to substantially lessen competition or tend to create a monopoly in any line of commerce." Moreover, even if the practice is found to be harmful to competition, the act permitted price discrimination in three instances. First, if a price differential results from actual cost savings, it would be allowed. Second, price discrimination would be allowed if selling to some customers at a lower price is necessary to meet competitors' prices. Finally, the act would not disallow the practice if the products sold to various consumers are different.

The following analysis of antitrust cases is designed to clarify the meaning of the law. The Robinson-Patman Act has been difficult for the F.T.C. and the courts to interpret. Consequently, both of these agencies have been somewhat inconsistent in their decisions. Although the following cases will give a general idea of the law, they will not leave us with a definitive statement concerning its interpretation.

LESSENING OF COMPETITION, PRIMARY-LINE DISCRIMINATION

The courts have considered primary-line price discrimination injurious to competition when it results in a reduction of a competitor's market share or profit level. Also, the practice is frequently considered injurious when profits from one geographical market are used to subsidize another market. An analysis of several cases will substantiate these observations.

Humble Oil

The practice of using profits in one market to subsidize outlets in other markets was important to the decision in *Shore Gas and Oil Company* v. *Humble Oil and Refinery Co.*[2] Shore was a distributor of Cities Service petroleum products in New Jersey, and Humble distributed Esso products in the same geographical area. One of Shore's most important customers had been the Asbury Park Radio Cab Company which bought about 50,000 gallons of gasoline yearly. Shore had charged the cab company 13.7 cents per gallon of gasoline until Humble signed a contract to supply the company at 12.9 cents a gallon. Because Shore lost the account and because Humble charged higher prices to other customers, Shore sued Humble under the provisions of the Robinson-Patman Act.

The District Court for New Jersey thought that subsidization is a prerequisite for injurious price discrimination. "When a seller underbids a competitor, thereby injuring him, the injury is an 'effect' of discrimination only if the low price is supported by other prices and their profits, wherever charged."[3] The court adopted this rule to help distinguish injurious price discrimination from competitive situations. It also noted that whenever a firm charged a price which was below cost, a reasonable assumption was that the market was being subsidized from profits made in other markets. On the other hand, if "the price is completely self-sufficient, it may be inferred that no relationship between high and low prices exists, and therefore the discrimination had not the proscribed 'effect.' "[4] Although it wanted to end injurious price discrimination, the court chose this rule because it realized that in the interest of competitive price rivalry, firms would often find it necessary to charge different prices in different markets. It stated that " . . . the Act must be read to encourage price competition and advocate price discrimination in the cause of competition wherever it is possible to do so within the bounds of the statute."[5] The court found that Humble's price was self-sufficient, and its discriminatory pricing was allowed.

Dean Milk

Although the *Humble Oil* decision permitted price discrimination even though it resulted in a loss of a competitor's market share, not all decisions have been so lenient. In *Dean Milk Company*, the Federal Trade Commission asserted:

> It is the Commission's opinion that a finding of possible substantial competitive injury on the seller level is warranted in the absence of predation where the evidence shows significant diversion of business from the discriminator's competitors to the discriminator or diminishing profits to competitors resulting either from the diversion of business or from the necessity of meeting the discriminator's lower prices, provided that these immediate actual effects portend either a financial crippling of those competitors, a possibility of an anticompetitive concentration of business in large sellers, or a significant reduction in the number of sellers in the market.[6]

This rule appears to make no distinction between price discrimination which is designed to drive competitors out of business and that which is really price competition.

Utah Pie

A more recent case, *Utah Pie Co.* v. *Continental Baking Co.,*[7] largely substantiates the *Dean Milk* decision. Utah Pie manufactured frozen dessert pies and had a plant located in Salt Lake City, Utah. Pet Milk, Continental Baking Company, and Carnation Company were its major competitors. All three companies were large but because none had a plant in Utah, Utah Pie benefited from a locational advantage. It had done extremely well, as evidenced by the fact that in 1958 its market share in Salt Lake City had grown to 66.5 per cent. Although its competitors were established in the Salt Lake City market before Utah Pie, the company had obviously made significant inroads into their business. Each of the three major companies soon cut its price below marginal cost plus its allocated share of the fixed cost. The prices were even lower than those charged near the plants of the large companies, and the effect of the price reduction was dramatic. Utah Pie's market share decreased to 34.3 per cent in 1959, 45.5 per cent in 1960, and 45.3 per cent in 1961. But despite this, the price discrimination did not cause Utah Pie to sell below cost. It continued to earn profits, and its sale volume increased throughout the four year period, 1958 to 1961.

The Court thought that the price reductions of the major companies were predatory and while predation was not necessary to find guilt, it played a significant part in the decision. The Court said, for example, that "Pet's own management, as early as 1959, identified Utah Pie as an 'unfavorable factor,' one which 'd[u]g holes in our operation' and posed a constant 'check' on Pet's performance in the Salt Lake City market."[8] The fact that Pet placed an industrial spy in Utah Pie's plant to find flaws in its inspection techniques did not help its case. Considering the competitive injury question, the Supreme Court overturned a court of appeals decision. The lower court had decided that competition was not hurt because Utah had not been deprived of pie business that it otherwise might have received by lowering prices. The Supreme Court thought it was enough to show that Utah Pie had to reduce its price to $2.75 (it entered the market at a price of $4.15). "A competitor who is forced to reduce his price to a new all-time low in a market of declining prices will in time feel the financial pinch and will be a less effective competitive force."[9]

Based on its finding of predatory intent and its feeling that there was a "reasonable possibility" that Utah could be hurt even though it continued to make a profit, the Court ruled in favor of Utah. This case demonstrates the impossibility of distinguishing between price discrimination which injures competition and that which is merely competitive. Facing Utah's inroads, isn't it natural to expect the large firms to reduce prices to regain their market shares? Although the major companies sold below average cost, is it irrational to sell at marginal cost? Was the consumer better off when Utah Pie had 66.5 per cent of the market and pie prices were high? On the other hand, was the price discrimination aimed at conditioning Utah Pie so it would join the large oligopolistic pie producers in parallel pricing? The truth of the matter is that no one outside of the pie industry really knows the answer to these questions, and if the pie industry knows, it is not talking.

Summary: Primary-Line Discrimination

We have seen that intent is an important factor in evaluating primary-line price discrimination cases, but not a necessary factor for courts to render a decision of illegality. To show harm to competition, the government does not have to demonstrate that if the discrimination continues, competitors will be forced out of business. In the *Utah Pie* case, all it had to show was that prices were reduced substantially, not even that they were reduced to the point where profits were zero. Although it was not explicit in the *Utah Pie* case, the issue of subsidization was important. Obviously, proof of harm to competition does not require harm to consumers. It only requires that there may be a possibility of harm to consumers in the future. Moreover, harm to competitors is usually taken as evidence of harm to competition even though the ideas certainly are not synonymous. This had led many critics to claim that the Robinson-Patman Act is not really designed to protect competition but only inefficient businessmen.

Even though the courts and the F.T.C. haven't considered the issue, it is important to distinguish instances in which primary-line price discrimination can hurt competition from those in which it cannot. Suppose A lowers his price and his competitor, B, meets it. Yet neither firm is selling at a loss. In this instance there is no harm of the type which drives firms out of business. However, if A lowers his price below his cost and B meets it, then potentially one or both of the firms may go out of business if they do not have the sense to rectify the problem before it drives them to that point. In what instance can one get an advantage over the other? If they are virtually identical firms, neither one can get an advantage. If A is more efficient than B, it can get an advantage but should this type of advantage be outlawed? If A can get funds from other markets to subsidize its operations, and B has no such source of funds and is not able to borrow money to withstand the price war, then he may have to drop out of the market. This instance seems to be the only one in which competition could unfairly be harmed and even then, harm is not certain.

If there are a large number of other competitors which A has to deal with, or if market entry is relatively easy, chances are that competition will not be affected. The fact of the matter is that rarely can injury to competitors be automatically equated to injury to competition. And to find instances in which the two correlate strongly, fairly detailed studies must be made. Certainly the question necessitates more study than the courts or the F.T.C. have been willing to undertake.

LESSENING OF COMPETITION, SECONDARY-LINE DISCRIMINATION

Morton Salt

The question of what constitutes a substantial lessening of competition in secondary-line price discrimination cases was partially answered by the Supreme Court in _F.T.C._ v. _Morton Salt Co._[10] At issue was Morton's policy of granting price discounts to large purchasers. Less-than-carload purchasers bought Morton table salt at $1.60 per case while purchasers of full carloads paid $1.50 per case. Finally, those customers who bought 5,000 cases in any consecutive 12 month period paid $1.35. Only five companies had bought enough to qualify for the $1.35 price, and less than 1 per cent of the customers had to pay the $1.60 price. Whether the differential pricing scheme could be justified by different supply costs was an important issue in the case, but it will be discussed later in the chapter. The consideration here is whether the scheme resulted in competitive injury.

The Supreme Court began its analysis by interpreting the Robinson-Patman Act to mean that competitive harm existed if the Court found a "reasonable _possibility_" that the use of price discrimination "_may_ have such an effect."[11] (Emphasis added.) Obviously this is a more stringent test than the requiring of a reasonable probability. Moreover, the Court emphasized that specific competitive harm did not have to be proven by the F.T.C. The only requirement of proof was that it be possible that the use of price discrimination may reduce competition in the future. Morton's quantity discounts allowed its customers to sell salt at differing retail prices, and the Court thought that this, itself, was evidence that competition was substantially lessened.

In its behalf, Morton argued that because table salt was only one of many items sold in retail stores, the fact that some stores were at a competitive disadvantage in the sale of salt did not mean that overall competition had been harmed. The Court argued that if goods were analyzed on an item by item basis, there probably would be no evidence of competitive harm, but when discrimination in a large number of goods exists, competitive harm can result. "Since a grocery store consists of many comparatively small articles, there is no possible way effectively to protect a grocer from discriminatory prices except by applying the prohibitions of the act to each individual article in the store."[12]   The Court also thought that the act was designed to protect small businesses, and it equated this objective to that of maintaining competition.

> Furthermore, in enacting the Robinson-Patman Act Congress was especially concerned with protecting small businesses which were unable to buy in quantities, such as the merchants here who purchased in less-than-carload. . . .
> The new provision, here controlling, was intended to justify a finding of injury to competition by a showing of 'injury to the competitor victimized by the discrimination.'[13]

In deciding against Morton Salt the Court thought that price discrimination tended to lessen competition when it enabled customers to charge different prices for their products. The fact that the product line in which the customer was at a disadvantage was a small part of his total business was unimportant. The Court also ruled that competition should be evaluated on a product-by-product basis. Finally, it implied that any price discrimination which harms a competitor is *ipso facto* harmful to competition.

Minneapolis-Honeywell
Regulator Co.

Although the Supreme Court came dangerously close to outlawing all price differentials in *Morton Salt*, some decisions have demonstrated that the F.T.C. and the courts have been willing to delve into the "cause-effect" relationship between price discrimination and harm to competition. One such instance of the use of this analysis was a court of appeals decision in *Minneapolis-Honeywell Regulator Co. v. F.T.C.*[14] The practice at issue was Honeywell's use of quantity discounts in selling automatic temperature controls to oil burner manufacturers. Its pricing scale ranged from $17.35 per unit for customers who bought less than 350 units yearly to $14.25 for customers who bought more than 10,000 units yearly. In an earlier decision, the F.T.C. decided that the arrangement caused customers buying small quantities of the thermostats to lose business. The F.T.C. thought that the fact that the thermostats were the most expensive component of a burner was particularly relevant as was the fact that several burner manufacturers complained of competitive harm.

The Seventh Circuit Court of Appeals decided that there was no substantial evidence that Honeywell's use of price discrimination injured competition. It found little relationship between the price Honeywell charged for thermostats and the final price of burners. Some customers who paid more for the thermostats were selling their burners at lower prices than those customers who paid less for the thermostats. Additionally, several customers who paid higher prices testified that many other variables played an important part in the pricing of their products. The court concluded:

> But where the controls were used in the manufacture of burners, the cost of which was determined by many other factors—cost of other materials and parts, service, advertising, to mention only a few—it cannot be said that discriminatory price differentials substantially injure competition or that there is any reasonable probability or even possibility that they will do so.[15]

Contrary to the *Morton* decision, the court added that it thought a mere possibility of injury was insufficient to sustain illegality under the Act.

Summary: Secondary-Line Discrimination

Secondary-line price discrimination cases, like primary-line cases, do not accept the mere existence of price discrimination as evidence of injury to competition. However, the courts and the F.T.C. do not require an actual demonstration of harm to competition either. Where secondary-line discrimination harms competitors, this is enough to demonstrate harm to competition. This approach leaves little room for the firm which lowers its price to be competitive and, consequently, it is conceivable that the court's approach to the determination of competitive injury can actually injure competition. The F.T.C. staff seems to be aware of this problem. As a result, the Robinson-Patman Act is regularly violated without resulting prosecution in industries where the common methods of pricing are inconsistent with the act. Ralph Nader's antitrust report terms this selective enforcement of the act "Robinson-Patman Roulette."

When can harm to competitors be equated to harm to competition in cases of secondary-line price discrimination? If A gets raw materials cheaper from his supplier than his competitor, B, because there is a cost advantage in supplying A, efficiencies explain the discrimination. If A gets his raw materials cheaper because he is a stronger bargainer by virtue of having a monopsonistic position, then he is exercising monopsony power to the detriment of B. A has an advantage in the competitive game which may result in his winning even though he has no special skill. Does this mean that in this instance protection of competitors and protection of competition are the same? The answer is still "no". If A competes with many other firms which get the same price advantage or if entry of firms which can get the same price advantage is relatively easy, competition probably will not be reduced. As with primary-line price discrimination, one cannot answer the question of whether competition is hurt in the affirmative by pointing to some bedraggled competitor.

COST JUSTIFICATION

Even if the courts or the F.T.C. find that price discrimination injures competition, they will allow low prices if there is a cost justification for them. In other words, if it is cheaper to supply customer A than customer B, A may receive a price reflecting the cost savings.

Morton Salt

We have already considered the *Morton Salt* case within the context of injury to competition, but the case is also important to the cost justification issue. The reader will remember that Morton offered quantity discounts to customers who bought large quantities. Morton argued that the discounts were justifiable because they were available to all, but the Supreme Court did not agree. It thought that while Morton was theoretically correct, in practice the low prices were not available to all customers. While small customers had the right to purchase 50,000 cases a year, their finances limited their purchases to a much smaller quantity. Of course, that fact alone did not make the discounts illegal because when it is cheaper to sell large quantities, lower prices are justified. Addressing itself to this issue, the Court said that the Robinson-Patman Act placed the burden of proof on the defendant. There is a practical reason for this decision because companies have more cost information available to them than does the government. Morton did not prove there were cost reductions justifying the low prices and given the nature of its pricing scale, a justification was probably impossible. To be sure, less-than-carload purchases could not be delivered as cheaply as carload purchases. However, it would be difficult to justify the fact that 5,000 case purchases in any consecutive 12 month period were cheaper to deliver than carload purchases. During a twelve month period there could be numerous deliveries, some of which could conceivably involve partial carloads. And even if the deliveries were in full carloads, it would be difficult to show that it is cheaper to deliver two carloads than one carload. Morton's pricing scheme did not pass the Robinson-Patman cost-justification test.

Borden

Does a firm have to justify each specific price reduction, or is it enough to prove that on the average it is cheaper to supply one customer than another? That question was answered in *U.S.* v. *Borden Co.*[16] The Borden and Bowman Dairies, suppliers of milk, gave independent grocery stores price discounts according to the quantity of milk purchased. However, all grocery chains were given a flat discount without regard to volume. This discount exceeded the maximum discount available to the independent stores.

Upon request, Borden submitted a cost study to justify its actions. It compared its average cost per $100 of sales to the chain stores with its average cost per $100 of sales to the independents. Bowman's defense was based on additional service given to the independent stores. Its servicemen often took the product into the store, placed it in a refrigerator, and rearranged milk containers. These services required Bowman's men to remain longer in a store, resulting in higher costs. Both companies worked with average estimates. They proved that on the average it was cheaper to supply chain stores, not that it was cheaper to supply each chain store. The problem with this analysis was that some independents could be supplied as cheaply as the chain stores; yet they did not receive as large a discount. The Court recognized this problem and consequently, it disallowed the justification.

> In sum, the record here shows that price discriminations have been permitted on the basis of cost differences between broad customer groupings, apparently based on the nature of ownership but in any event not shown to be so homogeneous as to permit the joining together of these purchases for cost allocations purposes. If this is the only justification for appellees' pricing schemes, they are illegal.[17]

Because of this decision, if a firm intends to justify price discrimination on the basis of cost justification it should be prepared to justify lower prices for *each* customer. While this rule is equitable, it causes firms to perform rather detailed economic studies.

THE GOOD FAITH DEFENSES

Suppose that one firm faces strong competition in market A and little competition in market B. It has been charging $2.00 a unit for its product in both markets, but now, in market A, its competitors charge $1.50. May it lower its price to $1.50 in market A? The Robinson-Patman Act provides a defense for discrimination when a seller charges low prices in "good faith" to meet the price of a competitor.

Standard Oil of Indiana

The Supreme Court's interpretation of the good faith provision was established in two Standard Oil decisions, one heard in 1951 and the other in 1958.[18] In the first case, Standard was charged with selling gasoline to four jobbers at a lower price per gallon than that charged many service stations in the same area. Although Standard used several defenses, its good faith defense was the major issue in the case. It argued that the low prices were necessary to retain the jobber customers and that the same price had already been offered by competitors.

In an earlier hearing, the F.T.C. had decided that the low prices injured competition, and concluded that the good faith justification was not valid when price discrimination injured competition. The Supreme Court thought differently. It reasoned that the Robinson-Patman Act was not designed to abolish competition or curtail it such that a seller had no right of self defense.

> For example, if a large customer requests his seller to meet a temptingly lower price offered to him by one of his seller's competitors, the seller may well find it essential, as a matter of business survival, to meet that price rather than to lose the customer. ... There is nothing to show a congressional purpose in such a situation, to compel the seller to choose only between ruinously cutting its prices to all its customers to match the price offered to one, or refusing to meet the competition and then ruinously raising its prices to its remaining customers to cover increased unit costs.[19]

Although the F.T.C. clearly intended to weaken the good faith defense, the Court sustained the defense and judged it acceptable even if competition is injured. But when the Court sent the case back to the F.T.C. to determine whether Standard really cut its prices to meet its competitors' prices, the F.T.C. tried once again to weaken the good faith rule. While it did find that Standard lowered its prices to meet competition, the F.T.C. contended that the prices were not lowered in good faith. It further argued that the low prices were in accordance with a general discriminatory pricing scheme, not as simple deviations from a nondiscriminatory price scale. The Supreme Court admitted that it thought the F.T.C.'s decision unclear, and it sustained Standard's right to reduce prices to protect its market.

Sunshine Biscuit

The *Standard Oil* decision was substantially altered in the *Sunshine Biscuit* case.[20] In selling its potato chips, Sunshine offered a seven per cent discount to four customers and a five per cent discount to fifteen customers. Other customers in the same geographical area received no discount. Sunshine argued that the low prices were necessary to meet the prices of its competitors and therefore were made in good faith. The Federal Trade Commission decided that Sunshine's practice did not fall within the good faith exception because, in meeting the prices of its competitors, Sunshine was able to attract some customers from them. This interpretation of the good faith clause seems to suggest that you can lower prices to keep your customers but not to get customers from your competitors. In his dissent, Commissioner Elman enumerated the problems that can arise from this interpretation.

> Does an "old" customer retain that status forever, regardless of the infrequency or irregularity of his purchases? Suppose an "old" customer transfers his business to another seller offering a lower price; how long a period of grace does the first seller have in which to meet the lower competitive price? If he waits too long, will the "old" customer be regarded as a "new" one, and hence unapproachable . . . ? If so, how long is too long? And if not, does it suffice that the buyer has at *any* time in the past, no matter how remote, been a customer of the respondent?[21]

Tri-Valley

The good faith defense was further weakened in the *Tri-Valley Packing Association* case.[22] Tri-Valley was a canner which sold to large grocery chains at discounts of from two to ten per cent. Tri-Valley argued that it gave discounts to meet competitors' prices. That point was not contested by the Federal Trade Commission, but the commission contended that Tri-Valley's prices could not be reduced unless its competitors' prices were not discriminatory. Commissioner Elman discussed the problems accompanying this interpretation. "A businessman who must operate in the pressures of the marketplace cannot be expected to conduct a survey into his competitor's costs or to prophesy whether the competitor's lower price will later be held unlawful."[23]

Whether or not the F.T.C.'s interpretation of the good faith defense would be accepted by the Supreme Court is unknown. The great majority of cases are settled at the commission level because most firms would rather change their pricing policies than submit to further litigation. One thing is fairly certain. The rules leave little room for the good faith clause as a defense. Many would argue that they also leave little room for active price competition.

THE ROBINSON-PATMAN ACT:
A CRITIQUE

No single piece of antitrust legislation has prompted more criticism than the Robinson-Patman Act. The heart of the critics' complaints can be expressed very succinctly; the act impedes rather than promotes competition. In an earlier part of this chapter we said that if the F.T.C. and the courts were to properly administer the act, they would have to walk a very thin line between distinguishing price discrimination which is anticompetitive and that which is competitive. The critics contend that that line has been overstepped by interpreting "protection of competitors" to mean "protection of competition." The critics also believe that this interpretation has placed the act in direct conflict with the Sherman Act, in that the Sherman Act is designed to promote intense price competition while the Robinson-Patman Act stifles it.

This contradiction was presented by two individuals who argued that firms walk a very thin line between being charged under the Sherman Act with not competing and being charged under the Robinson-Patman Act with competing. According to H. Thomas Austern a firm "might get out of the Robinson-Patman Act frying pan only to find himself in the fire of a Sherman Act price conspiracy charge."[24]   Lowell Mason, a former commissioner of the F.T.C., told the story of a man who said that the government challenged the same pricing scheme for both price fixing and price discrimination. Mason replied, "Then in that event, how can you win? We shall probably find you guilty of one or the other!" The man retorted that they had found him guilty of both.[25]

Another criticism is that the act, like some applications of the

Sherman Act, tends to treat symptoms of monopoly power instead of irradicating that power itself. When price discrimination is outlawed, firms will probably find another way to exercise their power. Massive advertising, for example, may be an alternative route for a company intent upon harming its competitors, and this method is virtually free from an antitrust attack unless the advertising is false or deceptive. Yet another attack—one tied closely to the protection of small business—is that the act attempts to bring fairness into the marketplace where fairness is defined as a situation in which all customers pay the same price. Yet fairness, as it is defined in this manner, has rarely been a requirement or a consequence of competition and when it does exist, price rigidities might develop among sellers. The rigidities represent a pricing scheme identical to that which develops under conscious parallelism; a practice the courts deplored in *American Tobacco*.

Such arguments have led two major committees studying the antitrust laws to conclude that the Robinson-Patman Act should be significantly changed. The Stigler Task Force concluded that:

> On the agenda for long-term legislative reform must be the Robinson-Patman Act. The act leads to rigidity in distribution patterns and to uniform, inflexible pricing. . . . Thus a prohibition against price discrimination may preclude the kind of competition that is most likely to lead to lower prices in oligopolistic industries.[26]

The White House Task Force on Antitrust Policy for President Nixon concluded that:

> Over the years, the Robinson-Patman Act has come to have unintended anticompetitive effects. The price-discrimination prohibition has discouraged types of price differentials which might have improved competition by lessening the rigidity of oligopoly pricing or by encouraging new entry.[27]

Not all critics agree that the act needs substantial modifications either in its philosophy or its structure. Speaking on the objective of protecting small business, Congressman John Dingell, Chairman of the Special Subcommittee on Small Business and the Robinson-Patman Act stated:

> Both the legislative and executive branches of Government have continually voiced their approval and support for the small business sector of our economy, and it is the belief of the subcommittee that the small businessman constitutes the foundation upon which a truly competitive econ-

omy must be based. It has been recognized historically that large economic concerns can exert pressure and power having tremedous economic and anticompetitive effects on small business. . . . It is the belief held by this subcommittee that the larger the number of efficient participants in a particular competing industry the greater the protection is for the consumer.[28]

In answer to the criticism that the act creates price rigidities, most defenders would agree but hasten to add that it stops large firms from getting yet a greater market share by harming small businesses. Nor do the defenders accept the argument that the Sherman Act and the Robinson-Patman Act are contradictory. With some justification they would argue that both acts were designed to protect the small businessman so that such firms could freely compete. Many defenders would also say that if there is a major difference between the two acts it is simply that the Sherman Act is designed to eliminate monopoly power when it exists, while the Robinson-Patman Act is designed to eliminate it before it exists.

The arguments, pro and con, have persisted for the past twenty-five years, and no doubt they will continue. And despite the fact that many argue for a change in the act, it is unlikely that change will come. Small businessmen are powerful people in both political strength and sentimental argument.

NOTES TO CHAPTER XVI

[1] This is the legal definition. The economic definition is that price discrimination exists whenever consumers are charged different prices for a product that costs the same or the same price for a product that has different costs.

[2] 224 F. Supp. 922 (1963).

[3] 224 F. Supp. 922, 926 (1963).

[4] 224 F. Supp. 922, 926 (1963).

[5] 224 F. Supp. 922, 928 (1963).

[6] CCH Trade Reg. Rp., ¶ 17, 357 (1965).

[7] 386 U.S. 685 (1967).

[8] 386 U.S. 685, 697 (1967).

[9] 386 U.S. 685, 700 (1967).

[10] 334 U.S. 37 (1948).

[11] 334 U.S. 37, 50 (1948).

[12] 334 U.S. 37, 49 (1948).

[13] 334 U.S. 37, 49 (1948).

[14] 191 F. 2d 786 (1951).

[15] 191 F. 2d 786, 792 (1951).

[16] 370 U.S. 460 (1962).

[17] 370 U.S. 460, 471 (1962).

[18] *Standard Oil Company (Of Indiana)* v. *F.T.C.*, 340 U.S. 231 (1951); *F.T.C.* v. *Standard Oil Company (Of Indiana)*, 355 U.S. 396 (1958).

[19]340 U.S. 231, 249-250 (1951).

[20]*Sunshine Biscuits, Inc.*, CCH Trade Reg. Rep., ¶ 15, 469 (1965).

[21]*Ibid.*, p. 20,346.

[22]*Tri-Valley Packing Association*, CCH Trade Reg. Rp., ¶ 15, 893 (1962).

[23]*Ibid.*, p. 20,706.

[24]H. Thomas Austern, "Problems and Prospects in Antitrust Policy—I," in Almarin Phillips, *Perspectives on Antitrust Policy* (Princeton: Princeton University Press, 1965), p. 29.

[25]Lowell Mason, *The Language of Dissent* (New Canaan, Conn.: The Long House, Inc., 1959), p. 27.

[26]*Economic Concentration.* Hearings before the Subcommittee on Antitrust and Monopoly Pursuant to S. Res. 40, 91st Cong., 2nd Sess., November 4, 5, 6, 1969 and January 28, February 5, 18, and 19, 1970 (Washington: U.S. Government Printing Office, 1970), p. 5045.

[27]*Ibid.*, p. 5063.

[28]Dingell Report on F.T.C.'s Enforcement of the Robinson-Patman Act: "Findings" and Recommendations. Reprinted in *Antitrust Law and Economics Review*, III (Summer, 1970), p. 65-66.

CONCLUDING
OBSERVATIONS

SECTION VI

Most of the important antitrust laws and cases have already been discussed. In the process our study has suggested some policies for future antitrust litigation and some issues which need further study. However, before completing our study some concluding remarks will be made about the successes and failures of antitrust. These are presented in Chapter XVII.

ANTITRUST
IN RETROSPECT

CHAPTER XVII

Here we explore the successes and failures of antitrust and chart a course for its future.

INTRODUCTION

In concluding our study of antitrust it is appropriate to ask whether its influence has been effective in promoting a competitive economy. Yet the question is impossible to answer in absolute terms. If by "effective" one means whether the economy is more competitive today than it would be in the absence of antitrust, the answer is "yes." Events in the latter part of the 19th century clearly indicated the noncompetitive consequences of a truly laissez-faire economy. But if the issue is whether antitrust has been as effective as practicably possible, many students of antitrust would answer negatively. They believe that economics has not sufficiently integrated the litigation process to allow the courts, the Justice Department, and the Federal Trade Commission to discern what is competitive and what is monopolistic. As a result, many people contend that these agencies have sometimes dealt at length with inconsequential issues, have allowed some anticompetitive industries to prosper, and have disallowed some business practices which are not harmful to the consuming public.

While part of the criticism can be mitigated with an understanding of the noneconomic constraints on antitrust discussed in Chapter IV, there are instances in which the courts and the F.T.C. have avoided economic issues for reasons which are not apparent. In these instances criticism is justified. This chapter is designed to identify some of the leading criticisms of antitrust presented in the past few years.

THE DOUBLE STANDARD

Using the phrase of the district court judge in *Colgate*, the courts and the F.T.C. have sometimes made a "distinction without a difference" which has created several double standards under the law. Two leading examples will be cited here.

One instance of the double standard can be seen in the dual treatment of vertically integrated firms and firms which use vertical arrangements. Resale price maintenance, vertical territorial arrangements, and refusals to deal constitute only a few of the vertical arrangements we have discussed. All firms which are vertically integrated to the retail level set resale prices with impunity from the antitrust laws. Conversely, some nonintegrated firms using resale price maintenance face the threat of antitrust prosecution. Presumably, vertically integrated companies could assign territories to their retail outlets. Yet when firms which are not vertically integrated use closed-territory distribution, the practice is *per se* illegal. The double standard would not really exist if the courts and the Federal Trade Commission used the same criteria to evaluate vertical arrangements that are used to evaluate vertical mergers. The use of the foreclosure test in exclusive dealing arrangements is almost identical to the foreclosure test in evaluating mergers. But the courts and the Federal Trade Commission rarely use the same criteria. For example, vertical mergers have never been disallowed because they give the integrated firm the power to set its final retail prices or assign territories to its retail dealers.

Not only is the double standard inequitable, it has created an incentive for vertical integration which increases economic concentration and even threatens the small businessman. Reference to patent rights (in *Dr. Miles Medical Company*) or the "ancient rule against restraints on alienation" (in *Schwinn*) does not sufficiently explain the double standard to the individual who is more concerned with the effects of a practice on competition than legal technicalities. Whether vertical arrangements are used by vertically integrated companies or by independent companies, the effect on consumer welfare is the same.

Recently, many individuals have criticized another double standard. The F.T.C., in particular, has been severely critical of all mergers because it fears market concentration. Yet, until recently, almost nothing has been done about the large number of industries which are already concentrated. Is it consistent to outlaw the Brown Shoe merger which would have given the merged firm five per cent of the market while leaving the automobile, cereal, photographic equipment and cigarette industries undisturbed? William Fellner's answer to this question typifies the attitude of economists. "There is not much logic in the position that socially unjustified mergers should be prevented but that the results of past mergers should be regarded as untouchable."[1]

While the F.T.C. as well as the courts probably would have

defended their past position by claiming that most firms in concentrated industries are doing nothing anticompetitive such as engaging in mergers or using predatory practices, many economists believe that a highly-concentrated market structure is, by itself, sufficiently anticompetitive to justify antitrust action. This philosophy has been expressed in numerous attempts to secure passage of a concentrated industries act which would specifically outlaw large market shares. The passage of such an act was one of the recommendations of the Neal Report to President Nixon. Until such legislation is passed or until the "backward-sweep doctrine" of *du Pont-General Motors* is intensively applied, no significant inroads will be made toward making the U.S. economy more competitive. As we noted in Chapter XV, there is substantial evidence that the F.T.C. and the Justice Department are developing an interest in making this inroad. Most lawyers and economists predict that this development will eventually eliminate the double standard. Certainly if steps are taken to eradicate concentration, antitrust will have a new and exciting frontier.

MONOPOLY
POWER AND ITS SYMPTOMS

Closely associated with the failure to prosecute highly concentrated industries is the courts' and the F.T.C.'s inability to distinguish between practices representing the exercise of monopoly power and those which create additional monopoly power. Professor Robert Bork is the leading exponent of this criticism, which has been a theme running throughout this book. By definition, monopoly power involves horizontal relationships. The internal expansion of business which increases industry concentration, horizontal mergers, horizontal division of territories, and price fixing can create monopoly power. Resale price maintenance, conscious parallelism, and vertical territorial arrangements merely represent the exercise of existing monopoly power. Even exclusive dealing, tying arrangements, refusals to deal and price discrimination can create more power only if the firm using them already has monopoly power. Declaring these practices unlawful attacks symptoms of the power, not the power itself. Sometimes it is impractical to eliminate monopoly power through divestiture and dissolutionment proceedings, and these instances justify the treatment of symptoms. But in a large number of instances it is more impractical to treat symptoms because firms can always find another way to exercise their unchallenged power.

THE PROTECTION OF THE SMALL BUSINESSMAN

The Celler-Kefauver and Robinson-Patman Acts focus on promoting the interests of the small businessman. While some students of antitrust argue that this is not a valid objective of antitrust, almost all complain that even if it is valid, antitrust is not the best vehicle of implementation. Antitrust policy is applied on a case-by-case piecemeal basis which only protects small businesses in the industries involved in antitrust cases.[2] Moreover, the cost of the objective is largely borne by consumers who make large purchases in these industries. Wouldn't it be better to offer protection to all small business and, if there is a cost, to have all citizens share it? A special tax concession, for example, would appear to be a better solution to the problem. Besides, with the protection of small business eliminated from the host of issues which must be considered by the F.T.C. and the courts, the complexity of antitrust cases would be reduced.

Hale and Hale offered one major reason explaining why the government would never adopt an across-the-board subsidy for small business.

> Psychologically and politically, . . . such a subsidy would be unacceptable. The sheltered businessman does not wish to admit that he needs a subsidy. The notion is that he is "independent": a citizen standing on his own feet and needing the aid of no one. A direct subsidy from the public treasury would destroy that illusion.[3]

Since 1958 when they expressed their opinion, there have been numerous judicial proceedings decided in favor of the small businessman, and some of the decisions have been at the consumer's expense. Economists, lawyers, and the members of Congress need to reconsider the objective, and if it is affirmed they need to develop a workable standard which clearly identifies the weight appropriated to the interests of the small businessman and the interests of the consumer. If the scales tilt in favor of the small businessman, antitrust will largely be a noneconomic issue.

LEGAL SHORTCUTS TO ECONOMIC ISSUES

The courts and the Federal Trade Commission have recognized that at times proper antitrust litigation requires economic inquiry as evidenced in cases such as *Alcoa, Times-Picayune Publishing Company*, and *International Telephone and Telegraph*. Yet in many cases economic analysis has been minimized. The use of the "ancient rule on restraints of alienation" in *Schwinn*, the quantitative substantiality test in *Standard Oil of California*, the emphasis on intent in Sherman Act cases, and the insistence that conglomerate mergers result in reciprocity and subsidization in spite of evidence to the contrary are but a few examples of short cuts taken in lieu of economic analysis. Most critics are understanding of both the heavy workload heaped upon the courts and the F.T.C. as well as the fact that judges and F.T.C. commissioners are largely untrained in economics. But critics see these as obstacles which can be overcome. Couldn't judges retain a staff to help them with economic issues? Is it unreasonable for the F.T.C. commissioners to use their economic staff extensively? Is it even unreasonable to require that the president appoint one or more commissioners trained in economics since much of the workload of the commission involves economic issues? The lawyer who suspects that these questions hint of an attempt to invade his domain is correct. But since antitrust involves economic as well as legal issues, there must be a place for the economist as well as the lawyer.

THE ESTABLISHMENT OF
PRIORITIES

Even before a case is heard, the Justice Department and the Federal Trade Commission encounter an economic problem of massive proportions. Every student of economics learns that the economy has scarce resources, the use of which is measured in terms of opportunity cost. Applying this concept to antitrust, a major problem is to determine what alleged anticompetitive practices and what companies using them should be prosecuted. As Samuel A. Smith, a Washington attorney, put it, "To select the wrong ones is to fail the 'opportunity cost' test; bringing a case that returns $2 (in terms of lower consumer prices and the like) for every $1 spent when there is available another case on which the return is not $2 but $10 is, by definition, to misallocate resources and to give the consuming public less for its total number of enforcement dollars than it could have been given."[4]

Many critics of antitrust have argued that neither the F.T.C. nor the Justice Department has a schedule of priorities, and they have not really considered the issue of maximum utilization of resources.

The Hoover Committee Task Force *Report on Regulatory Commissions* concluded in 1949 that:

> As the years have progressed, the Commission has become immersed in a multitude of petty problems; it has not probed into new areas of anticompetitive practices; it has become increasingly bogged down with cumbersome procedures and inordinate delays in disposition of cases. . . .
> The Commission has largely become a passive judicial agency, waiting for cases to come up on the docket, under routinized procedures, without active responsibility for achieving the statutory objectives.[5]

The American Bar Association Report on the Federal Trade Commission, submitted to President Nixon in 1969, concluded that the F.T.C. had failed to establish goals and priorities. The 1969 Stigler Task Force on Productivity and Competition urged that both the F.T.C. and the Department of Justice establish priorities, and even suggested that as a result of not doing so, the F.T.C. had done little in antitrust which promoted a competitive economy.

While it would be desirable to prosecute all anticompetitive practices in a costless society, such an approach is impractical in the real world. Much homework has to be done prior to selecting those cases which merit prosecution. The selection should not be based, as some have suggested, on the mere size of the firms involved or the dollar volume of business transacted by the firms, but on the consumer benefits which could result from successful prosecution.

THE CHOICE OF REMEDIES

We noted in Chapter IV that for several reasons the courts and the Federal Trade Commission have been reluctant to break up companies found guilty of monopolization. The reasons are understandable, but at the same time we must recognize that without such remedies the success of antitrust litigation is limited. Even though American Tobacco was found guilty, what remedy of significance evolved? Shortly after the case the members of the tobacco industry returned to conscious parallelism. Even though Alcoa was found guilty of monopolization, was the aluminum industry altered to make it more competitive? The addition of Reynolds Metals and Kaiser has not had much effect on the actions of Alcoa. Only in the old *Standard Oil of New Jersey* case did the Supreme Court take a bold approach in selecting a remedy.

This is not to say that both the courts and the Federal Trade Commission should indiscriminately divide up all of the large firms in the country. But if the firms are guilty of monopolization or shared monopolization and if the only remedy to end the instance monopolization is to alter market structure through divestiture or dissolutionment, that remedy should be applied. Otherwise, why prosecute the firms at all?

SUMMARY

This chapter has identified some of the leading criticisms of antitrust. By no means has it surveyed all criticism nor does it speak for all critics. What it has done is to suggest issues which should be evaluated in appraising antitrust as well as to suggest topics which need objective study. The preceding chapters have also suggested numerous areas of study for the student of antitrust. Foremost among them is the whole issue of the effect of conglomerate mergers not only on economic efficiency but also on individual freedom. In addition, the effects of economic concentration on the level of employment and inflation is ripe for study. The thesis that concentration retards the operation of fiscal and monetary policy has been presented but not proven. More studies need to be performed on the effects of increased business efficiency on prices, the importance of the almost extinct performance test in evaluating mergers, the cost of monopoly in the United States, the distinction between price discrimination which is competitive from that which is anticompetitive, and the nature of all vertical arrangements. Finally, perhaps the student of antitrust could help the courts and the Federal Trade Commission in deciding the correct policy for a firm that plays the competitive game fairly but, as a result, wins a large market share and charges higher-than-competitive prices. There are certainly enough unanswered questions in antitrust to satisfy those students looking for an interesting dissertation topic as well as the many economists and lawyers interested in exploring the subject. The answers to the questions are crucial in directing future application of the antitrust laws.

Despite the importance of these questions, there is another antitrust issue which is even more important. In the beginning of this book we observed that antitrust is an interdisciplinary subject and therefore requires a fusion of the knowledge of law and economics. Yet, by and large, the two disciplines have worked independent of one another despite the imperative to merge. Unless lawyers begin to communicate with economists on a grand scale, all of the economists' work will be purely academic; it will have no practical application. And unless the economist begins to understand the constraints placed upon the lawyer and presents the economics of antitrust issues to the lawyer in practical and manageable terms, the judicial tools will always be incomplete. To make antitrust truly interdisciplinary is the single greatest challenge to those who wish to make antitrust law and economics their life's work.

In a sense it is disappointing to both the reader and the writer of a book to end by raising questions because it suggests that the job of providing sound antitrust policy is unfinished. Yet, in another sense, it is optimistic to end in this way for, in the spirit of the popular quote, "today is the first day of the rest of your life," the important consideration is how effective will be antitrust's future, not how imperfect was its past.

NOTES TO CHAPTER XVII

[1]Senate Subcommittee on Antitrust and Monopoly, Senate Committee on the Judiciary, *Administered Prices: A Compendium on Public Policy* (Washington: U.S. Government Printing Office, 1963), p. 136.

[2]It also might affect decisions of firms which are contemplating an act injurious to small business but which do not engage in the act because of potential antitrust prosecution.

[3]G. E. Hale and Rosemary D. Hale, *Market Power, Size and Shape Under the Sherman Act* (Boston: Little, Brown and Company, 1958), p. 401.

[4]Samuel A. Smith, "Antitrust and the Monopoly Problem: Toward a More Relevant Legal Analysis," *Antitrust Law and Economics Review*, II (Summer, 1969), 23.

[5]Committee on Independent Regulatory Commissions, U.S. Commission on Organization of the Executive Branch, Report 125 (Hoover Commission. Task Force Rept. App. N., 1949), quoted in John M. Blair, *Economic Concentration: Structure Behavior and Public Policy* (New York: Harcourt Brace Jovanovich, Inc., 1972), p. 618.

SELECTED BIBLIOGRAPHY

Books

Bain, Joe S. *Barriers to New Competition: Their Character and Consequences in Manufacturing Industries*. Cambridge: Harvard University Press, 1956.

_____. *Industrial Organization*. New York: John Wiley and Sons, Inc., 1968.

Blair, John M. *Economic Concentration: Structure, Behavior and Public Policy*. New York: Harcourt Brace Jovanovich Inc., 1972.

Bock, Betty, and Jack Farkas. *Concentration and Productivity: Some Preliminary Problems and Findings*. Washington: National Industrial Conference Board, Inc., 1969.

Carver, Thomas Nixon. *Essays in Social Justice*. Cambridge: Harvard University Press, 1915.

Chamberlain, Edward. *The Theory of Monopolistic Competition*. Cambridge: Harvard University Press, 1962.

Clark, J. B., and J. M. Clark. *The Control of Trusts*. New York: The Macmillan Company, 1912.

Clark, J. M. *Competition as a Dynamic Process*. Washington: The Brookings Institute, 1961.

Dirlam, Joel B., and Alfred E. Kahn. *Fair Competition: The Law and Economics of Antitrust Policy*. Ithaca, New York: Cornell University Press, 1954.

Edwards, Charles E. *Dynamics of the United States Automobile Industry*. Columbia: University of South Carolina Press, 1965.

Edwards, Corwin. *Maintaining Competition*. New York: McGraw-Hill, 1949.

Einhorn, Henry A., and William P. Smith. *Economic Aspects of Antitrust*. New York: Random House, 1968.

Galbraith, John K. *American Capitalism: The Concept of Countervailing Power*. Cambridge: Houghton Mifflin Co., 1956.

Hale, G. E., and Rosemary D. Hale. *Market Power, Size and Shape Under the Sherman Act*. Boston: Little, Brown and Company, 1958.

Handler, Milton. *Antitrust in Perspective, The Complementary Roles of Rule and Discretion*. New York: Columbia University Press, 1957.

Heflebower, Richard B., and George W. Stocking. *Readings in Industrial Organization and Public Policy*. Homewood, Ill.: Richard D. Irwin, Inc., 1958.

Henderson, James M., and Richard W. Quandt. *Microeconomic Theory, a Mathematical Approach*. New York: McGraw-Hill Book Company, 1971.

Jewkes, John, David Sawyers, and Richard Stillerman. *The Sources of Invention*. London: Macmillan and Co., 1958.

Jones, Eliot. *The Trust Problems in the United States*. New York: The Macmillan Company, 1927.

Kaysen, Carl, and Donald F. Turner. *Antitrust Policy: An Economic and Legal Analysis*. Cambridge: Harvard University Press, 1959.

Kintner, Earl W. *An Antitrust Primer*. New York: The Macmillan Company, 1964.

Knauth, Oswald W. *The Policy of the United States Towards Industrial Monopoly*. New York: Longmans, Green, 1914.

Leonard, William N. *Business Size, Market Power and Public Policy*. New York: Thomas Y. Crowell Company, 1969.

Low, Richard E. *Modern Economic Organization*. Homewood, Ill.: Richard D. Irwin, Inc., 1970.

Machlup, Fritz. *The Political Economy of Monopoly: Business, Labor and Government Policies*. Baltimore: The Johns Hopkins Press, 1952.

Mansfield, Edwin. *Monopoly Power and Economic Performance*. New York: W. W. Norton & Co., Inc., 1968.

Mason, Lowell. *The Language of Dissent*. New Canaan, Conn.: The Long House, Inc., 1959.

Markham, Jessie W., and Gustav F. Papanek, ed. *Industrial Organization and Economic Development*. Boston: Houghton Mifflin Co., 1970.

Massel, Mark S. *Competition and Monopoly: Legal and Economic Issues*. Washington: The Brookings Institution, 1962.

Neale, A. D. *The Antitrust Laws of the United States of America*. Cambridge: Cambridge University Press, 1970.

Nelson, Ralph L. *Merger Movements in American Industry, 1895-1956*. Princeton: Princeton University Press, 1959.

Nelson, Richard, Merton Peck, and Edward Kalachek. *Technology, Economic Growth and Public Policy*. Washington: Brookings Institute, 1967.

Phillips, Almarin. *Market Structure, Organization and Performance*. Cambridge: Harvard University Press, 1962.

Robinson, Joan. *The Economics of Imperfect Competition*. London: Macmillan and Co., 1933.

Samuelson, Paul A. *Economics.* New York: McGraw Hill Book Company, 1970.

Scherer, Frederic M. *Industrial Market Structure and Economic Welfare.* New York: Random House, 1970.

Schumpeter, Joseph A. *Capitalism, Socialism, and Democracy.* New York: Harper and Brothers, 1947.

Sichel, Werner. *Industrial Organization and Public Policy.* Boston: Houghton Mifflin Co., 1967.

Stocking, George W. *Workable Competition and Antitrust Policy.* Nashville: Vanderbilt University Press, 1961.

Tarbell, Ida M. *The History of the Standard Oil Company,* Vol. II. New York: The Macmillan Company, 1952.

Thorelli, Hans. *The Federal Antitrust Policy.* Baltimore: The Johns Hopkins Press, 1955.

Articles and Periodicals

Adams, Walter. "Competition, Monopoly, and Countervailing Power," *Quarterly Journal of Economics,* LXVII (1953), 469-493.

_____. "Is Bigness a Crime?" *Land Economics,* XXVII (November, 1951), 287-296.

Adelman, Morris A. "The A&P Case: A Study in Applied Economic Theory," *Quarterly Journal of Economics,* LXIII (1949), 238-257.

"An Interview with the Honorable Donald F. Turner," *ABA Antitrust Section,* XXX (1966), 113-137.

Bailey, Martin J. "Price and Output Decisions by a Firm Selling Related Products," *American Economic Review,* XLIV (1954), 82-93.

Bain, Joe S. "A Note on Pricing in Monopoly and Oligopoly," *American Economic Review,* XXXIX (1949), 448-464.

_____. "The Profit Rate as a Measure of Monopoly Power," *Quarterly Journal of Economics,* LV (1941), 271-293.

Baldwin, W. L., and David McFarland. "Some Observations on 'Per Se' and Tying Arrangements," *Antitrust Bulletin,* VI (July-December, 1963), 433-439.

Bork, Robert H. "The Supreme Court Versus Corporate Efficiency," *Fortune,* LXXVI (August, 1967), 92ff.

_____, and Ward S. Bowman, Jr. "The Goals of Antitrust: A Dialogue on Policy," *Columbia Law Review,* 65 (1965), 363-466.

Bowman, Ward S., Jr. "The Prerequisites and Effects of Resale Price Maintenance," *University of Chicago Law Review,* XXII (1955), 825-873.

_____. "Tying Arrangements and the Leverage Problem," *Yale Law Journal*, LXVII (1957-58), 19-36.

Burstein, M. L. "A Theory of Full Line Forcing," *Northwestern University Law Review*, LV (February, 1960), 62-95.

Brewster, Kingman, Jr. "Enforceable Competition: Unruly Reason or Reasonable Rules?" *American Economic Review, Papers and Proceedings*, XLVI (May, 1956), 482-495.

Carlston, Kenneth S. "Antitrust Policy: A Problem in Statecraft," *Yale Law Journal*, LX (1951), 1073-1090.

Coase, Ronald H. "Working Paper II: The Conglomerate Merger; Report of the Task Force on Productivity and Competition," *Antitrust Law and Economics Review*, II, No. 3 (Spring, 1969), 45-46.

Comment. "Refusals to Sell and Public Control of Competition," *Yale Law Journal*, LVIII (1949), 1121-1141.

Frazier, Howard. "Consumers and the FTC: It Makes a Difference Who Sits on It," *Antitrust Law and Economics Review*, III, No. 3 (Spring, 1970), 41-48.

Fulda, Carl H. "Resale Price Maintenance," *The University of Chicago Law Review*, XXI (1954), 175-211.

Harberger, Arnold C. "Monopoly and Resource Allocation," *American Economic Review*, XLIII (May, 1954), 77-87.

Hicks, J. R. "The Foundations of Welfare Economics," *Economic Journal*, XLIX (December, 1939), 696-712.

Hotelling, Harold. "The General Welfare in Relation to Problems of Taxation and of Railway and Utility Rates," *Economica*, VI (July, 1938), 242-269.

Kaldor, Nicholas. "Welfare Propositions in Economics," *Economic Journal*, XLIX (September, 1939), 549-552.

Kaysen, Carl. "Basing Point Pricing and Public Policy," *The Quarterly Journal of Economics*, XLIII (1949), 289-314.

Koller, Roland H. II. "The Myth of Predatory Pricing: An Empirical Study," *Antitrust Law and Economics Review*, IV (Summer, 1971), 105-123.

Krutilla, John V. "Aluminum—A Dilemma for Antitrust Aims?" *Southern Economic Journal*, XXII (October, 1955), 164-177.

Lancaster, Kelvin, and Lipsey, R. "The General Theory of Second Best," *Review of Economic Studies*, XXIV (1956-1957), 11-32.

Lerner, A. P. "The Concept of Monopoly and the Measurement of Monopoly Power," *Review of Economic Studies*, I (1934), 157-175.

Lockhart, William B., and Howard R. Sacks. "The Relevance of

Economic Factors in Determining Whether Exclusive Arrangements Violate Section 3 of the Clayton Act," *Harvard Law Review*, LXV (April, 1952), 913-954.

Mansfield, Edwin. "Size of Firm, Market Structure and Innovation," *Journal of Political Economy*, LXXI (1963), 556-576.

Markham, Jessie W. "The Nature and Significance of Price Leadership," *American Economic Review*, XII (1951), 891-905.

_____. "An Alternative Approach to the Concept of Workable Competition," *American Economic Review*, XL (June, 1950), 349-361.

Mason, Edward S. "Monopoly in Law and Economics," *Yale Law Journal* XLVII (1937-38), 34-49.

McGee, John S. "Predatory Price Cutting: The Standard Oil (N.J.) Case," *Journal of Law and Economics*, I (1958), 137-169.

McKie, James W. "The Decline of Monopoly in the Metal Container Industry," *American Economic Review Proceedings*, XLV, No. 2 (May, 1955), 499-508.

Morgan, Theodore. "A Measure of Monopoly in Selling," *Quarterly Journal of Economics*, LX (May, 1946), 461-463.

Mueller, Charles E. "Rapping the 'System': Reform or Revolution?", *Antitrust Law and Economics Review*, III (Summer, 1970), 15-46.

Mueller, Willard F. "The Rising Economic Concentration in America: Reciprocity, Conglomeration and the New American 'Zaibatsu' System. II." *Antitrust Law and Economic Review*, IV (Summer, 1971), 91-104.

_____, and George W. Stocking. "The Cellophane Case and the New Competition," *American Economic Review*, XLV (March, 1955), 29-63.

Nicholls, William H. "The Tobacco Case of 1946," *American Economic Review*, XXXIX (1949), 284-296.

Papandreou, Andreas G. "Market Structure and Monopoly Power," *American Economic Review*, XXXIX (1949), 883-897.

Phillips, Almarin, "A Critique of the U.S. Experience with Price Fixing Agreements and the Per Se Rule," *Journal of Industrial Economics*, VII (1959), 13-32.

Rothschild, K. W. "The Degree of Monopoly," *Economica*, IX (1942), 24-39.

Scalon, Thomas M. "First Negative," *Antitrust Law Journal Section of Antitrust Law Proceedings of the National Institute on Prices and Pricing*, XLI (October, 1971), 22-27.

Schwartz, Louis B. "Potential Impairment of Competition—The Impact of Standard Oil Co. of California v. United States on the Standard of Legality Under the Clayton Act," *University of Pennsylvania Law Review*, XCVIII (November, 1949), 10-40.

Scitovsky, Tibor. "A Note on Welfare Propositions in Economics," *Review of Economic Studies*, IX (November, 1941), 71-88.

Smith, Samuel A. "Antitrust and the Monopoly Problem: Toward a More Relevant Legal Analysis," *Antitrust Law and Economics Review*, II (Summer, 1969), 19-58.

Stigler, George J. "Mergers and Preventive Antitrust Policy," *University of Pennsylvania Law Review*, CIV (November, 1955), 176-184.

Stigler, George J. "The Kinky Oligopoly Demand Curve and Rigid Prices," *Journal of Political Economy*, LV (October, 1947), 432-449.

Sweezy, Paul M. "Demand under Conditions of Oligopoly," *Journal of Political Economy*, XLVII (August, 1939), 568-573.

Telser, Lester G. "Why Should Manufacturers Want Fair Trade?" *Journal of Law and Economics*, III (1960), 86-105.

Turner, Donald F. "The Validity of Tying Arrangements Under the Antitrust Laws," *Harvard Law Review*, LXXII (1958-59), 50-75.

Warren, Russell G. "Economics of Closed-Territory Distribution," *Antitrust Law and Economics Review*, II (Winter, 1968-69), 111-124.

Weston, J. Fred. "Implications of Recent Research for the Structual Approach to Oligopoly," *Antitrust Law Journal*, XLI (September, 1972), 634.

"White House Task Force Report on Antitrust Policy for President Johnson," *Antitrust and Trade Regulation Report* No. 411 (May 27, 1969).

Williamson, Oliver E. "Economies as an Antitrust Defense: The Welfare Trade-offs," *American Economic Review*, LVII (March, 1968), 18-35.

Public Documents

Attorney General's National Committee Antitrust Report. Washington: U.S. Government Printing Office, 1955.

Federal Trade Commission Staff Report. *Economic Report on Conglomerate Mergers*. Washington: U.S. Government Printing Office, 1969.

Hart, Phillip. "Distribution Problems Affecting Small Business," *Hearings Before the Subcommittee on Antitrust and Monopoly of the Committee on the Judiciary, United States Senate,* Washington: U.S. Government Printing Office, 1966.

Press Release Accompanying U.S. Department of Justice. *Merger Guidelines.* (May 30, 1968), Washington: U.S. Government Printing Office, 1968.

U.S. Attorney General's National Committee to Study the Antitrust Laws. *Report.* Washington: Government Printing Office, 1955.

U.S. Senate, Subcommittee on Antitrust and Monopoly of the Committee on the Judiciary. *Concentration in American Industry.* Washington: U.S. Government Printing Office, 1957.

U.S. Senate, Subcommittee on Antitrust and Monopoly of the Committee on the Judiciary. *Economic Concentration,* 91st Cong., 2nd Sess., 1969-70.

INDEX OF CASES

INDEX